ESSAYS IN HONOUR OF LORD ROBBINS

Essays in Honour of Lord Robbins

Edited by
Maurice Peston and Bernard Corry

WEIDENFELD AND NICOLSON
5 Winsley Street London W1

ISBN O 297 00353 4

Printed in Great Britain by KP Litho Ltd., Brighton, Sussex.

Contents

vi

PREFACE

The essays in this volume were presented to Lord Robbins to honour him on his seventieth birthday. Even from the standpoint of professional economists one volume is far too little to house all those who wish to be associated with this venture. The editors therefore wish to apologise yet again to all those friends of Lionel Robbins who were excluded from this volume. The papers here presented are by professional economists; many more volumes could be filled by those who would wish to acknowledge his contribution to many other fields. He has been a dominant figure in the intellectual and cultural life of this country since the early 1930s, and has served his country more than generously as a professional economist and adviser, as a university teacher and administrator, as a defender of the arts and cultural heritage of our society and as a humanitarian.

From 1931 until 1965 Lionel Robbins was Professor of Economics in the University of London at the London School of Economics and Political Science. His career as an academic economist and university teacher has been and still is inextricably bound up with LSE. The history of that institution and hence the history of the development of social science in the post − 1914 period cannot be written without considering Lionel Robbins' key position and influence.

His contributions to economics are widespread; his key articles and books have taken their place in the seminal literature of our subject. Of course many of his contributions were (and still are!) controversial; bitter intellectual debates raged over them and sometimes in the heat of battle friendships came temporarily adrift. But naturally the matters upon which he has dwelt in his long career are questions of fundamentals; these are the areas where intellectual battle must take place, and there is no place in them for the faint-hearted or uncommitted. To believe passionately is what generations were taught by Lionel Robbins − and they still do. Passions however are no substitute for scientific enquiry and patient scholarship, they are rather a complement to it. His first book (already a reprinted classic) − *The Nature and Significance of Economic Science* − was an attempt to set economics clearly upon the path of scientific enquiry and to isolate those areas where this was possible from areas where other criteria had to appear. So often, even today, the purpose of that book is misunderstood as an 'attack' on economists indulging in political economy. Far from this being the case, as Lionel Robbins' own contributions demonstrate, it is a clarification of the conditions under which economic science relates to political economy.

vii

Throughout his career one of his special loves has been the history of economic thought. He has been one of the few who has kept the torch of scholarship alight in a period when recently it has been at a discount. Luckily there are signs of a revival of interest in intellectual history generally for which he is in no small measure responsible. This interest was shared by one of his own great teachers — Edwin Cannan. They are parallel in another respect: both always put their teaching role to the forefront of their daily work. Hundreds of us — thousands of us — as undergraduates or graduates, from different countries, different social, religious and economic groups, were taught economics and learnt how to be economists under the wing of Lionel Robbins. We learnt much more than this: the appreciation of liberal values and true friendship. This is what he has given to generations. Long may he continue to do so.

MAURICE PESTON
BERNARD CORRY

1. ECONOMIC THEORY AND METHODOLOGY

The Foundations of the Theory
of National Income:
An Analysis of Some Fundamental Errors [1]

R.G. Lipsey

In this paper I wish to argue that current teaching of macroeconomic theory, as evidenced by the great majority of elementary and intermediate macro textbooks published in the English language, contain a series of basic errors, all traceable to fundamental confusions over the nature of behavioural relations and identities. Not only do we continue to introduce macro theory with a series of identities which we ourselves generally accept to be uninformative statements which add '.... nothing ... to our understanding of the working of the economic system',[2] but we are led by this practice to make specific errors of analysis. The main errors that will be treated in this article are listed below.

I. The Static Model in Equilibrium

1) The equilibrium of a Keynesian model is given by the intersection of the aggregate demand function and the 45° line which expresses the accounting identity $E \equiv Y$.

1.   I am greatly indebted to Mr. John Stilwell for very valuable research assistance and for his comments at every stage of this study. I have also benefited greatly from the detailed and painstaking criticisms of earlier drafts by G.C. Archibald, F.P.R. Brechling, A. Budd, R. Cassen, B.A. Corry, R.L. Crouch, R. Gould, K. Klappholz, E.J. Mishan, P.O. Steiner and B.S. Yamey.

2.   L.R. Klein, [9], p. 112, cited by Klappholz and Mishan, [8] p. 117. The Klappholz-Mishan article is devoted to a criticism of the practice prevalent in economics today of attempting to deduce empiral implications from definitional statements. The criticism of this invalid procedure is fully developed but all of their analysis is confined to the static equilibrium properties of models. Since most of the erroneous deductions only arise when empirical propositions concerning *dynamic* behaviour are deduced from definitional statements, Klappholz and Mishan were led (incorrectly) to exonerate existing practices from the charge of causing serious error.

II. The Static Model in Disequilibrium

2) Although people may try to save different amounts from what people try to invest, this is impossible; thus actual realised savings must always equal actual realised investment.

3) Out of equilibrium, planned savings do not equal planned investment, and it follows from (2) that someone's plans must be being frustrated; thus there must be some *unintended* savings or dissavings, and investment or disinvestment.

4) The simultaneous fulfilment of the plans of savers and investors can occur only when income is at its equilibrium level in just the same way as the plans of buyers and sellers can only be simultaneously fulfilled at the equilibrium price.

III. The Dynamic Behaviour of the Model

5) Whenever savers plan to save a different amount than investors plan to invest, a mechanism works to ensure that actual savings remain equal to actual investment, in spite of people's attempts to make it otherwise. Indeed, this mechanism is the source of dynamic change in the circular flow of income.

6) Since the real world, unlike the simple textbook model, contains a very complex set of inter-relations, it is not an easy matter to see how it is that savings stay equal to investment even in situations of the worst disequilibrium and the most rapid change.

7) The dynamic behaviour of a Keynesian circular flow model in which disequilibrium implies unintended investment or disinvestment can be analysed by moving upwards or downwards along a diagonal cross diagram in the 'step-fashion' illustrated in figure 1.

Each of these statements can be found in the majority of standard treatments of national income theory and there are few books that do not make some of them. The statements would appear to be regarded as part of established knowledge in the subject.[3] Yet everyone of them is wrong.

3.   To assure ourselves that these statements were so regarded we made a

In Parts I, II and III of this paper, the seven errors mentioned above are analysed in some detail. Their general nature is discussed, and a simple model is developed and used to provide counter examples to those of the statements that are amenable to refutation by this means. In Part IV, we attempt a brief outline of an approach to national income theory that avoids the above errors by avoiding all reference to national income accounting identities.[4]

I. THE STATIC MODEL EQUILIBRIUM

The first error that must be cleared away is the one made in Statement (1). Errors of this type have been analysed in great detail by Klappholz and Mishan [8] and so our treatment can be brief. The

check of thirty-six English language textbooks published on both sides of the Atlantic. We found that virtually all of the books contained at least one of the statements and that the minimum number of examples of any of the statements was eight occurrences of statement (4), while the maximum was twenty-four occurrances of statement (1). In the face of this evidence, and since there were many books not included in our sample of thirty-six, it seemed unnecessary to give a detailed list of references to the occurrences of each statement. Only where readers of earlier versions of this paper have doubted that the error was prevalent have we given examples.

4.   Aside from my desire to try to clear up the muddle, there is one more immediate reason for writing this article. I first stumbled over these problems in May 1961 when I began to write Chapter 29, The Structure of the Circular Flow of Income for my text book, *An Introduction to Positive Economics.* [10] (References throughout this article are to the first edition.) I tried to treat income theory in the correct way in Chapter 29, and to meet head-on the problems created by the traditional approach in an Appendix that I somewhat misleadingly entitled National Income Accounting (pp. 356-60). Evidently I failed to convince many teachers. My mail since publication date has contained many complaints from teachers that my analysis was defective and complaints from students that having mastered my own treatment (so that, for example, they were no longer frightened to talk about *actual* savings not equalling *actual* investment) they have been told by their teachers that they were in error or were not properly understanding national-income theory. Clearly, it is necessary either to abandon my approach or else to defend it publicly and fully. Since it is my experience that it is vastly easier to teach income theory correctly than in the traditional fashion, I have chosen the latter course. This was the decisive reason in my deciding to write this article after several years of procrastination. In the American textbook, *Economics,* by P.O. Steiner and myself, we tried to introduce income theory in the correct way but we did not try to compare our approach to the traditional one. (We were nonetheless criticised in a review in the *A.E.R.* for 'ignoring the fundamental distinction between *ex ante* and *ex post* magnitudes'. The reader who perseveres with this article will understand why we did so on purpose.)

elementary comparative-static treatment of income theory is usually based on two relations. The first is the behavioural relation between aggregate expenditure *(E)* and national income *(Y)*,

$$E = E(Y) + A,$$

which divides E into an endogenous and an exogenous component. The second relation is expressed graphically by the 45° line and it is usually developed from an accounting identity.[5]

The equilibrium level of income is determined, as in figure 1, by the intersection of the aggregate expenditure function and the 45° line. If we write this system out algebraically, we should see immediately that it is not a theory:

$$E = E(Y) + A, \tag{1}$$
and
$$E \equiv Y. \tag{2}$$

That these two relations cannot constitute a theory of income determination should have been shown by one of the basic points agreed on at the end of the great Savings and Investment Debate of the 1930s: that definitional identities added nothing to our knowledge of the world. If we believe this, we must be able to remove equation (2) and lose nothing. If we do so, then either we are left with a 'theory' of one equation in two unknowns:

Theory A: $\qquad E = E(Y) + A,$ \hfill (3)

or, if we stick to saying that we mean the same thing by E as we do by

5.   'The line in figure 1 that passes through the origin and bisects the right angle formed by the axes represents equation (1), the accounting identity between income and product.' Bailey [4], pp. 9-10. According to Schneider [16], who also defines it as an identity, pp. 100-1, the 45° line was first introduced by Ivor Jantzen in 1935. G.L. Bach [3] solves for equilibrium income on p. 132 by substituting $C = .75Y$ and $I = 100$ into the definitional identity $Y \equiv C + I$. More surprisingly perhaps, Carl Christ [6] uses this two-'equation' model of a behaviour equation plus a definitional identity to introduce macro models in Chapter III, see pp. 55-6, 62 and 65; but see also footnote 17 on p. 67 where the statement 'If we were to examine (31) [the income definition] carefully, we would find that it is not simply a definition but a mixture of that with an institutional restraint and an equilibrium condition . . .' shows that Christ is not unaware of the problems involved in his unsatisfactory treatment in this chapter.

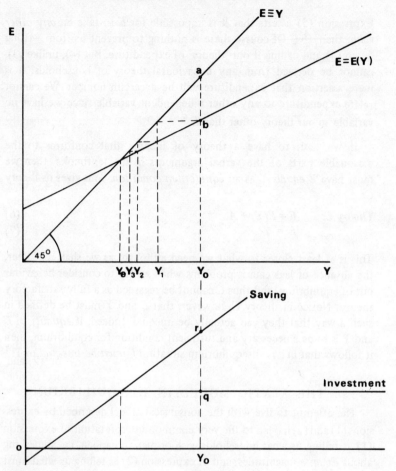

Figure 1

Y, we are left with a theory which says:

Theory B: $E = E(E) + A.$ (4)

In the case of a linear E function, the theory becomes $E = bE + A$, which solves for

$$E = \frac{A}{1-b}$$ (5)

7

Expression (5) asserts that it is impossible for E to take on *any other value* than $\frac{A}{1-b}$. Of course there is nothing to prevent us from writing down (4) and calling it our 'theory' of expenditure. But (4), unlike (3), cannot be derived from any behavioural theory of households, it is mere assertion that expenditure will be a certain number. We cannot relate expenditure to any other independent variable since we have no variable in our theory other than E.[6]

If we wish to have a theory of income that conforms to the reasonable parts of the verbal arguments in the textbooks, then we must have *E equals Y* as an *equilibrium condition*. This gives us theory C:

Theory C:
$$E = E(Y) + A \tag{6}$$
$$E = Y. \tag{7}$$

This is at least closer to what we need although, as we shall see later, the absence of lags causes problems when we try to consider behaviour out of equilibrium, and thus C cannot be regarded as a fully satisfactory theory. Notice in theory C, however, that E and Y must be defined in such a way that they can actually be unequal. Indeed, if *equality* of E and Y is to be a necessary and sufficient condition for equilibrium, then it follows that in *any* disequilibrium situation E *must be unequal* to Y.[7]

II. THE STATIC MODEL IN DISEQUILIBRIUM

The attempt to live with the nonsensical model described by expressions (1) and (2) has led to the very common interpretation of expression (1) as telling us what households wish or plan to happen, i.e. something about *ex ante* magnitudes, and of expression (2) as telling us what must

6. We can see that (5) is nothing more than assertion by reversing the process. We start by asserting that E will take on same value X and thus write $E = X$. We then divide X up into two constants: $X \equiv 1\text{-}a$. We now have $E = \frac{\beta}{1\text{-}a}$ and simple algebra produces $E = \beta + aE$ which is the form of (4) in the text. This tells us nothing more than that the assertion E will always take on a specific value X.

7. Since the mathematical manipulations of comparative static analysis produce the same answers with $E \equiv Y$ or $E = Y$, comparative static analysis does not produce error when the identity is used. Nonsense usually results, however, when attempts are made to explain *why* the system moves from one equilibrium to the other — i.e. when dynamics is considered. All of the erroneous statements analysed subsequently in this paper, not surprisingly, refer to the disequilibrium behaviour of the model.

happen, i.e., something about *ex post* magnitudes.

The error in this interpretation lies in the belief that the identity $E \equiv Y$ can tell us what can and cannot happen in the world. If it were possible that a definitional identity could rule out certain imaginable events, then such a definitional identity would be an informative statement having empirical content! If it is a genuine definitional identity (which follows from our use of words and is compatible with all states of the universe) then it is only telling us that we are using E and Y to refer to the same thing, and this statement no more allows us to place restrictions on what happens in the world than does the statement that we are *not* using E and Y to refer to the same thing $(E \not\equiv Y)$.[8]

This faulty interpretation of an identity as putting restrictions on what can happen in the world has led to a series of characteristic errors found almost universally in the literature. Consider figure 1, which shows the system in the two forms in which it is normally presented. Assume that the system is at a disequilibrium level of income, Y_O. It now follows from the interpretation given above that, since *ex post* E must equal *ex post* Y, national income must be at point a, but since *ex ante* E is at b there must be unintended expenditure of ba. This is usually equated with unintended investment in inventory accumulation equal to qr in the bottom of figure 1. In this figure, planned I is $Y_O q$, planned S is $Y_O r$ and qr represents unplanned actual I. This gives rise to the statements quoted under 2, 3 and 4 in the introduction. In general it should be apparent that there must be something wrong with these inferences, since they are all dependent on the interpretation that $E \equiv Y$ puts restrictions on what can happen in the world. They thus presume that from definitional statements we can draw empirical inferences (such as the one that inventories must be accumulating when actual Y exceeds equilibrium Y). Conclusive refutation of each of these statements is most simply established by counter example and we shall attempt such refutations once we have constructed an appropriate dynamic model. It is to the construction of such a model that we must now turn our attention.

We first consider a discrete period multiplier of the Robertsonian

8.   The reader will have no trouble in providing examples where $E \equiv Y$ is referred to as one of the *fundamental* identities on which national income theory is erected.

sort. In this model, consumption lags one period behind income. Output, however, adjusts instantaneously to changes in expenditure so that there is no unintended investment or disinvestment in inventories. Also, all planned consumption and investment expenditures are assumed to be realised. Unless savings are explicitly stated to be for another purpose, the difference between income received and spent $(Y_{t-1} - C_t)$ is assumed to be used to purchase bonds. Savers first purchase the bonds offered for sale by private firms (in order to finance current investment) and any additional demand for bonds is met by the central authorities who sell bonds (or buy them if necessary) in unlimited quantities at a fixed price. Changes in the level of employment take the form of changes in hours worked per week by all households, rather than of changes in the number of households fully employed and the number wholly unemployed.

The model can now be laid out as follows:

$$C_t = a\, Y_t^h, \tag{8}$$
$$I_t = \bar{I}, \tag{9}$$
$$Y_t^f \equiv C_t + I_t, \tag{10}$$
$$Y_t^h = Y_{t-1}^f, \tag{11}$$

C is desired and actual consumption, Y^h is household disposable income, Y^f is the income received by firms, and I is desired and actual autonomous investment.[9] Equation (8) says that, in period t, households spend a fraction, a, of the disposable income available to them in that period. Equation (9) says that desired and actual investment is constant, which implies that inventories do not change during the course of any adjustment. Equation (10) is an *identity* telling us that we have defined 'firms' in such a way that all money spent on the purchase of consumption and investment goods is immediately received by firms. Equation (11) says that there are no leakages (such as taxes and business savings) between the receipts of firms and payments to households. But there is a one period lag. If firms receive extra money this period they produce more *this period* (since inventories do not change), but they pay out extra money to households only at the very end of the period so that it is not available for expenditure by house-

9.   For simplicity, we assume that desired inventory changes are always zero so that inventories remain constant through any adjustment process that occurs.

holds until the *next period*. To get this model in the form usually presented, we substitute (11) into (8) and drop the superscript *f*, but must not forget that *Y* now means the receipts of firms, which, by virtue of our behavioural assumption about inventories, is the same as the output of firms. This gives us

$$C_t = a\,Y_{t-1} \tag{12}$$

$$I_t = \bar{I} \tag{13}$$

$$Y = C_t + I_t. \tag{14}$$

Equilibrium occurs when the level of income is unchanged from period to period. This equilibrium condition is written

$$Y_t = Y_{t-1} = \bar{Y} \tag{15}$$

where $\bar{Y}$ is the equilibrium value of *Y*.

Assume that the economy is in equilibrium, and that in period 0 there occurs an autonomous downward shift in the consumption function. In period zero, expenditure falls by some amount *X*. In period 1 expenditure falls a further fraction *a* of the original reduction. Our assumption that output adjusts without lag to changes in expenditure implies *that all cuts in consumption expenditure are exactly foreseen and that production is cut accordingly so that inventories do not change.*

We now consider a numerical example in which $\bar{I} = 100$, and *a* shifts from 0·9 to 0·8 at period zero. We follow the course of the downward adjustment in Table 1.

TABLE 1

Period	Y_{t-1}	$C_t = aY_{t-1}$	I_t	Y_t
-2	1000	900	100	1000
-1	1000	900	100	1000
0	1000	800	100	900
+ 1	900	720	100	820
+ 2	820	656	100	756
+ 3	756	605·8	100	705·8
......	......	......	......	......
∞	500	400	100	500

11

This is a familiar numerical example, and we can use it to analyse statement (3), that disequilibrium involves the frustration of someone's plans. A typical statement of this view is found in Allen [2, p. 18] '...the existence of a Robertsonian lag implies that there is unintended saving (or unintended dis-saving) at any time that income is changing'. The analysis of this statement provides much of the material necessary to clear up the whole muddle and we must consider it at length. We shall find that there is a meaning of the term 'unintended' for which this statement is correct. If the economist is careful, as Allen is, never to deviate from this meaning, no error need occur. The meaning, however, differs from the usual meaning of the word 'unintended' and the danger is that the economist will think he has proven something about 'unintended savings' in the normal meaning of the term. Indeed, it is this confusion that has caused much of the trouble. Evidently the problem is a subtle one, and we must approach it with some real care.

Let us first consider planned and unplanned behaviour in the *schedule sense.* The plans of investors to spend $\bar{I}$ on fixed investment are fulfilled each period; the plans of households, (i) to spend aY_{t-1}, and to consume goods to this value during period t and (ii) to consume in period t an amount equal to $(1-a)\ Y_{t-1}$ are always fulfilled, and the plans of producers to keep inventories unchanged are also fulfilled. *In each period no one's plans are unfulfilled in the sense that no one is off his schedule relating his income to his desired expenditures on consumption goods, investment goods, and purchases of bonds.* Income, however, is clearly not in equilibrium, and, according to statement (3), someone's plans must be being frustrated.

To restore the statement, we must interpret plans not in the schedule sense, as is common in English language writings, but in the point sense, as is common in Scandinavian writings. We say that, in period t, households plan to save the quantity $Y_{t-1} - C_t$, but they actually succeed in saving the quantity $Y_t - C_t$, so that, unless $Y_{t-1} = Y_t$, planned saving does not equal actual saving. Thus, in the example of Table 1, households planned to increase their saving from 100 to 200 in period zero but only succeeded in saving 100. Thus, their plans were frustrated by 100, and actual savings of 100 equal actual investment of 100. In period 1 household plans to save 180 are frustrated by 80, and so on, period by period, with households only succeeding in saving 100 each period. Finally, when income has fallen to 500, planned saving will be back to 100, and equal to actual saving and actual investment, so that equilibrium will be restored.

Now there can be no quarrel with the following:

$$S^1 \equiv Y_{t-1} - C_t \qquad (16)$$

$$S^2 \equiv Y_t - C_t \qquad (17)$$

$$S^1 = S^2 \text{ if, and only if, } Y_{t-1} = Y_t. \qquad (18)$$

If we *call* S^1 'planned savings' and S^2 'actual savings', then a nominalist cannot quarrel merely over the use of words, but he can legitimately ask if expressions (16) and (17) conform to the normal uses of the words planned and actual, and, if they do not, he must ensure that error does not creep in as a result of thinking that propositions such as (18) say something about what we normally understand by plans and realisations.

We have already seen that, in this example, households succeed in adding to their bond holdings by 200 in period zero and by $. 2Y_{t-1}$ in each subsequent period, and we must be led to wonder in what sense their savings plans are frustrated.

In order to see what is happening we must add a few more needed details to the Robertsonian model. We assume that households work throughout the month (period) and are paid in arrears for such work at the end of the last day of the month. The money earned from producing in month t is, thus, available for spending in period $t+1$: hence the one period time lag in Table 1. We assume that, on the first day of each month, households purchase bonds with the money they are intending to save, and hold the remainder of their receipts as a transactions balance, spending it in equal daily increments, so that on the last day of the month their balances reach zero; only to rise at the end of that day as the month's pay cheque is received. Thus, in Table 1, in each period up to period zero households would have bought £100 of bonds on the first day of the month and gradually run down the £900 balance over the month but would have ended the month with total assets equal to (i) bonds bought in all previous months, (ii) £100 of bonds bought this month, (iii) £1000 cash received today as pay for the month's work.

Now, in period zero when the consumption function shifts down wards, households change their bond acquisition plans. On the first day of the month they try (successfully) to purchase £200 in new bonds. They then reduce their current expenditures to a daily rate that will just consume their remaining £800 over the month. This reduction of 11·1 per cent in the rate of expenditure causes production and employment to fall immediately. Income currently being earned by households falls by 11·1 per cent, but because of the lag between production and factor payments, households' disposable income and expenditures do not fall this month. On the last day of the month, households' transactions balances will be reduced to zero, *as planned,* but, when their pay cheques are received, the amount will total only £900 instead of the £1000 received in all previous months. Households' total assets are now (i) all bonds purchased in previous months, (ii) £200 of bonds purchased this month, (iii) £900 cash received as pay for work rendered this month.

If we now assume that, when they raised their bond purchases, households planned to have a £200 increase in total assets by the end of the month then, indeed, their plans have been frustrated by £100. But note the following:

(i) The plans to acquire more bonds have been fulfilled.

(ii) The whole of the change is in transactions balances, and, indeed, fewer balances will be required to fulfil spending plans for period *t+*1

(iii) The fall cannot be said to be unexpected. Employment fell on the first day of the month so that households *knew* that their transactions balances would be reduced by £100 at the end of the month, and that they would require £100 fewer transactions balances in order to finance their expenditures in the following month.

But this is not the only assumption we can make about the plans of households. Indeed, it would be more in keeping with standard monetary theory to assume the following: (i) households plan to add a certain increment to their bond holdings, (ii) households intend to start the next period with a certain level of transactions balances, the desired level necessarily being defined in the schedule sense – in the simplest case it would be aY_t.[10] In this case nothing unplanned happens to

10.   In the case in which there are only transactions balances which are run down to zero at the end of the period then average monthly $a = \frac{1}{2}$, but, if there are

households at any period. In each period they add bonds to their holdings equal to $.2Y_{t-1}$ and at the end of each period they have a level of transaction balances adequate to finance the purchases of the following period. Indeed, as we have already seen, even the change in disposable income is not a surprise; it is clearly foreseeable from the first day of the month when current output and employment falls.

It is now clear that, whether or not the actual real plans laid by households are frustrated, depends on what plans households lay, i.e., it depends on our behaviour assumption, not on our definitions. If we assume that households make point plans about their bonds, and schedules plans about their transactions and precautionary balances,[11] then no frustration of plans occurs.

There is one way in which the defender of the traditional view might try to avoid the conclusion we have reached, but it only needs to be stated to be dismissed. This is to argue that when households planned to save £200 in year zero, they planned to add this to their bond holdings indefinitely, and, since their new bond purchases fall continually, their plans are continually frustrated. It only needs to be observed that this plan would be frustrated even in equilibrium, and that this, as well as the less drastic 'plan' to do the same next period as this period, amounts to defining plan-frustration to be *identical with* income change. There is nothing wrong with this but the 'conclusion' that income change *necessarily* causes plan frustration is no longer informative for we are now only discovering our own definitions.

When the savings function shifted upwards at period zero it is possible that this reflected a determination on the part of households to increase the rate at which they were adding to their bond holdings. If this was the plan then, qualitatively at least, the plan is fulfilled through the whole of the disequilibrium but it is unfulfilled once equilibrium is reached!

precautionary balances as well, we would expect $a > \frac{1}{2}$ so that there would be positive (precautionary) balances remaining on the last day of the month. If, however, $Y_{t+1} < Y_t$ these balances would then be excessive and would be available for the purchase of bonds or goods, (i.e., in the schedule sense, savings plans are overfulfilled at the end of the month!)

11.   Indeed, there is little in modern monetary theory to suggest that households would, or should, make point plans about their transactions balances.

The Foundations of the Theory of National Income

The conclusion to be drawn from this lengthy discussion is that, if the statement quoted in (3) above is meant to have empirical content, it depends on a very specific hypothesis about households' savings plans. These plans must be made in the point and not in the schedule sense, and the plans must include not only additions to the stock of income-earning assets, but also point-plans concerning transactions balances even though the household does not now know what level of transactions the balances will be required to facilitate. The only other sense in which statement (3) can be interpreted is that laid out in equations $(16) - (18)$ where S^1 is called 'planned savings' but does not necessarily relate to the plans actually made by households. This establishing of the statement by definition will not cause any harm so long as we do *not* relate any subsequent deductions about *'planned'*, S^1, *savings* to households' real intentions, or to alterations of real household behaviour in response to non-fulfilment of their *real* plans.

After this lengthy analysis we are now in a position to see what is wrong with statement (2), that actual savings must always equal actual investment, and statement (5), which draws the analogy with demand and supply analysis. Consider statement (2) first.

In the *General Theory* Keynes stressed the fact that savings and investment decisions are made by different groups and that there is, thus, no reason why planned investment should equal planned saving. The attempts to live with the 'theory' described by equations (1) and (2) have led writers to argue that, although plans can differ, actual realised savings *must* always be equal to actual realised investment, and, therefore, when planned S does not equal planned investment, either the plans of savers, or of investors, must be frustrated. Of course, it is quite possible to define savings and investment so that they are the same thing, but it is a basic error to equate the magnitude so defined with the magnitude about which savers actually lay plans. Since *ex post* S and I as defined bear no relation to the magnitudes about which savers actually made plans, we can deduce nothing about what happens when *ex ante* S is not equal to *ex ante* I from the fact that we chose to use the terms *ex post* S and *ex post* I to refer to a single, and different, magnitude. *The basic error arises from the assumption that households and firms make plans about the same magnitude when they are planning their savings and investment.* The traditional theory defines investment as goods produced and not sold to households (= capital goods plus changes in inventories). According to our theory of the behaviour of firms, this is what firms *do* lay plans about: they plan to add so many capital goods and so many inventories to their existing holdings. The theory then says $I \equiv S$, and, thus, builds in the implicit assumption that households lay plans about the same magnitude. But according to the standard theory of household behaviour, they do not do so![12] Households, not subject to money illusion, are assumed to cash or used to purchase bonds. There is nothing in the standard theory of household behaviour that leads us to hypothesise that households care whether or not there exists — produced but unconsumed — a physical stock of goods which is the counterpart of the money they have laid aside. Indeed, why should they? All they are assumed to care about is the potential real purchasing power of their savings, and this depends only on the amount of money saved, the present price level, and the expected future price level.

This is one of the keys to the whole present confusion: *households lay plans about a magnitude that is different from the one that firms lay plans about.* Firms plan to have produced and unconsumed a certain quantity of goods, while households plan to leave unspent a certain quantity of purchasing power. This means that it is quite possible for planned investment to differ from planned savings and *to have both sets of plans fulfilled so that actual, realised investment differs from actual, realised savings.*[13]

To illustrate this discussion let us return to Table 1 and assume that in period zero the propensity to consume had remained at .9 but investment had fallen. To make the change as dramatic as possible, let I fall to zero. The sequence will, of course, begin as shown in Table 2. Since the period-by-period reductions in demand are by assumption exactly anticipated, there is no unintended inventory accumulation. Thus,

12. Neither do they do so according to any empirical study of which I am aware. For a very casual 'test', ask yourself if you ever encountered a household the members of which cared whether or not there existed a real unconsumed counterpart to their money saving — or a household that altered its behaviour according to whether or not there was such a counterpart.

13. Now, of course, we mean by realised S and I the realised magnitudes about which firms and households are actually laying plans. This, of course, does not interfere with the statistician saying that realised savings is identical with realised investment since he refers to a different magnitude when he speaks of realised savings.

there is no investment whatsoever and, if we use the national income identities, we must also say that there is no saving. The savings 'plans' of households are said to be frustrated in spite of the fact that, in each period, households succeed in buying bonds equal to 10 per cent of income received at the beginning of the period. (In this case the bonds will all be sold by the central authorities.)

TABLE 2

Period	Y_{t-1}	$C_t = .9Y_{t-1}$	I_t	Y_t
-1	1000	900	100	1000
0	1000	900	0	900
+1	900	810	0	810
+2	810	729	0	729

Of course, we are not trying to refute any identities and, of course, any definitions are possible if consistently used, but this use of the word 'unintended' has nothing to do with intended and unintended *behaviour*. To preserve the identity we must say that the plans of households were frustrated because a *real* counterpart of the savings they *successfully* made was not produced. We may say this if we wish, but the danger is that we will think we have said something about the world, and about the actual experiences of households. Indeed, a perusal of established textbooks shows that this confusion has occurred over and over again.

Thus we conclude that, when we define investment as production not consumed, and savings as income (valued in money or real terms) as long as by 'real' we understand

$$\frac{money\ saved}{an\ index\ or\ prices}$$

there is no reason why actual savings should not differ from actual investment.[14]

14.   Palander [13] has argued that savings and investment plans are equal to purchase and sales plans and therefore since we know purchases must equal sales it follows that savings must equal investment. This argument depends crucially on $E \equiv O \equiv Y$ which is a national income accounting identity, but, as soon as this is departed from, as we do in Section IV, we can no longer get $S \equiv I$ in this way we can get *purchases* $\equiv$ *sales*.

18

The Foundations of the Theory of National Income

We may now consider the erroneous but nearly ubiquitous analogy between savings-and-investment macro analysis, and demand-and-supply competitive price theory given in statement (4) above.

In the simplest theory of price we can write

$$D = D(p), \tag{19}$$

$$S = S(p), \tag{20}$$

$$D = S, \tag{21}$$

where D is desired purchases and S is desired sales. We now say that actual purchases are the same thing as actual sales:

$$purchases \equiv sales \tag{22}$$

and it is apparent that (19) and (20) describes two sets of plans about the same magnitude.[15] Thus we can say that the plans of purchasers

15. Some quite subtle points are involved in relation (22). These need not concern us here but a fully satisfactory interpretation of the demand and supply model requires that they be handled correctly. The equation is probably better interpreted as an empirical statement that, in the world in which we live, the goods that buyers get are the same as the goods that sellers give up and the money that buyers give up is equal to the money that sellers get. This is analogous to a conservation hypothesis (mass-energy) in physical science. In a world of spontaneous creation and destruction of goods and money, this relation need not hold. Since the relation does hold in our world, it does not matter too much if we think it is true by definition (and that this definition is a *useful* part of our theory), but in a world in which it did not hold, it would be obvious that it was the empirical

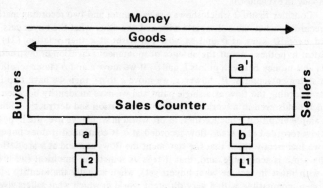

Figure 2

and the plans of sellers cannot be simultaneously fulfilled unless we are in equilibrium (i.e. unless (21) is satisfied). The difference between this model and the national income one is that, in the present price-theory case, both sets of real plans (buyers and sellers) *are laid about the same magnitude* (the amount of goods to be transferred in ownership), while in the national income case the two sets of real plans (savers' and investors') are laid about *two different magnitudes*. Thus the analogy often drawn between the two theories in respect of plans and realised quantities is an incorrect one.

III. THE DYNAMIC BEHAVIOUR OF THE MODEL

The three characteristic errors analysed in Section II give rise to a fourth (see (4) above) which is the most patently absurd of all. This is the error of describing the dynamic *mechanism* producing a change in income in the real world as the mechanism needed to produce the *ex post* equality between S and I even when planned S and planned I are unequal. Consider the following examples which are chosen hap-

relation, not the definitional one, that mattered. Consider, for example, how to incorporate into standard theory the (imagined) observation that sellers were often unobservant so that, on average, 1/20 of buyers' plans were always fulfilled by theft but there was a seasonal component in sellers' inattentiveness. Now, it is always possible to define things so that 'actual sales' ≡ 'actual purchases', but the theory would only work when we used an operational definition in which value of goods obtained by households did not equal the value of receipts of suppliers. (If you doubt this ask yourself how you would develop a theory of the seasonal variation of prices if you insisted in maintaining that every time a 'buyer' fulfilled his plans to obtain a good a seller fulfilled his plans to sell the good and get money in exchange.)

Consider figure 2 which shows a sales counter and two recording machines, one recording what the seller parts with and the other what the buyer gets. If we record *ex post* sales at b and *ex post* purchases at a then relation (21) is an empirical hypothesis about the absence of spontaneous creation or destruction of goods and money between points L and b. If we move a and b closer together the same statement applies. If, however, we move a to a' then we have two instruments recording the flow at a single point and we have an identity between a and b which holds even in a world of spontaneous creation and destruction. Since we have ample empirical evidence that, in the world in which we live, the hypothesis, the flow recorded at a = the flow recorded at b, is confirmed it does not matter that we incorrectly think that the statement the flows at a and at b are defined to be the same is acceptable, and, that it tells us something empirical (what sellers part with must in fact be what buyers get), when actually the identity is, as we have seen, compatible with a very different world in which what sellers give up is not equal to what buyers get.

hazardly since many macro textbooks contains equally absurd remarks.

> *...measured S* and *measured I* stay identical even during the worst disequilibrium − *by virtue* of some people's experiencing unintended losses or gains and/or experiencing unintended investment or disinvestment.[16]

> The important point about all this, of course, is not so much the equality between saving and investment as the fluctuation in the national income which must occur *as a result of* this equality, assuming that variations occur in the rate of investment.[17]

> Saving is income less expenditure on consumers' goods; investment is output less output of consumers' goods; and national income is the same thing as national output. Hence *saving and investment are merely two different names of the same thing,* namely the increase in the physical assets of the community . . . How, then, is equality *brought about* between total saving and total investment? . . . Equality between saving and investment is maintained not by changes in the rate of interest, but by changes in the size of the national income . . . The consequent expansion of the national income results in an increase in saving, simultaneous with and equal to the increase in investment that is responsible for the expansion.[18]

> Although we now know that investment and saving are equal, it is still necessary to find out *what determines the actual size of both of them: is it investment, or is it saving?* The answer to this question is the key to the whole of employment theory, and it is worthwhile to consider it in some detail before we go on to review the whole theory systematically.[19]

Every one of these passages is saying that there exists a *real world mechanism* that works (sometimes very hard for the task is clearly a difficult one) to ensure the realisation of a definitional identity!

Since the identity $E \equiv Y$ follows from our use of words and is compatible with any state of the universe, we clearly do not need any real world mechanism to establish it. The source of dynamic change in income cannot be the 'frustration' caused by the identity of S and I whenever people try to plan $S = I$. If it were think of what dramatic changes would occur in the economy if economists suddenly decided to define E so that it could never equal Y!

16.   Samuelson [14] p. 261, footnote, italics added.
17.   Nevin [11], p. 363, italics added. The context makes it clear that equality means identity.
18.   Benham [5], pp. 329-330. Italics added.
19.   Shackle [15]. It is clear from the context that the 'equality' referred to is the definitional identity, not some equality in equilibrium.

Our decision to use E and Y to mean the same magnitude has *no operational significance in any way.* There is no mechanism in the world which operates to establish a definitional identity. Neither does there need to be one. The standard statements of how equilibrium is reached, such as those quoted above, can only be described as utter nonsense.

The correct statement of why the level of income changes is that the amount of actual current withdrawals from the flow does not equal the amount of actual current injections, everything suitably defined. In a one-withdrawal, one-injection model, this means that the actual flow of current savings does not equal the actual flow of current investment.

Consider the example of Table 1. Investment at period zero is 100 per month or 3 1/3 per day while savings are at the rate of 200 per month, or (assuming now that bonds are purchased in a steady flow over the month) 6 2/3 per day. During month zero, 3 1/3 per day is actually injected in terms of investment expenditure, and 6 2/3 per day is actually withdrawn in terms of income received by households and spent purchasing bonds rather than goods.

We now come to statement (6). So far we have seen that the static model given in most textbooks and laid out in (1) and (2) above is faulty and that attempts to make some sense of it have led to the nonsensical idea that a mechanism is needed to ensure the realisation of an identity. The belief that the identity in (2) told us something about the world has inevitably led to the very curious view that there is some mystery involved in how savings do manage to remain identically equal to investment. A classic example is provided by Ackley.

In this simplest of all possible formulations, one may perhaps be able to grasp, *in words,* the equality of saving and investment. When we complicate even to the extent of recognising that 'net investment' is not a kind of spending but only an abstraction, verbalisation of the equality begins to escape us; and when we get to the complicated relationship which exists in a more nearly 'real' world, no one can possibly explain in words why saving equals investment. But, as we shall see, it is just as unmistakably so in the real world as in this very simple world with which we have been dealing.[20]

20. H.G. Ackley [1], p.63.

There should, of course, be no mystery whatsoever about how a definitional identity is established. It may be hard to measure I in the real world but, if we use the term S to mean the same thing as I, it is exactly as difficult or as easy to measure S as it is to measure I. There is no difficulty in seeing why or how they are the same thing. They are just two terms both referring to the same occurrence.

In the traditional income theory, investment is defined as the value of what is produced and not sold to households during the period,[21] and savings is defined as the value of what is produced during the period and not sold to households. Can there be any mystery whatsoever that, through thick and thin, '... even through the worst disequilibrium, ... *measured S* and *measured I* stay identical'?[22]

An exact parallel to the S and I identity is the statement that three feet equals one yard. Given this definition, there is no mystery in the statement that the square footage of an African Republic with very irregular boundaries is nine times its square yardage, even though there may be great uncertainty about how we managed to estimate the area of an irregular land mass in whatever units we chose. But we need to know nothing about the Republic and nothing about measurement procedures to assert (with 100 per cent confidence) that whatever is its area in square feet, this will be nine times its area in square yards.

Finally we come to statement (7). *In order to get unintended inventory changes at all* (we did not have them in the adjustment process outlined in Table 1), we need a Lundbergian lag between expenditure and output. We will assume that producers always expect sales to remain unchanged, so that output this period is the same as sales last period. When income is falling, producers' expenditures will exceed their receipts, and we need to know where the excess comes from. We assume here that the extra expenditure is obtained by borrowing from banks which have excess cash reserves and are, therefore, able to create all the credit needed by the firm. We maintain all the other assumptions given for the derivation of Table 1 and add only this supply lag to them.

---

21.   For a fuller statement of this point, which I assume needs no further elaboration by now, see R.G. Lipsey [10], p. 256-8.

22.   P.A. Samuelson [14], p. 226, n.l. (See also p. 230, n.l.)

We can now repeat the example of Table 1. In period zero, consumption expenditure falls *unexpectedly* to £800, but since the reduction is now unexpected an extra £100 is produced and is added to inventories. To find disposable income we now need an assumption about factor costs, and we assume that there are only two factor payments: wages, which are 80 per cent of the sale price of goods, and profits, which are 20 per cent. We now say that in period zero there was unintended inventory investment to the value of £80.[23] Thus at the end of period zero, payments of £980 have been made to households and these are available for expenditure in period 1. In period 1, expenditure on consumption goods only falls slightly over period zero, but production is now reduced by £100 (in the light of sales in period zero). The value of unintended inventory accumulation is, thus, only £12·8, and 80 per cent of this amount goes to households in the form of wage payments in return for the production of these unsold inventories. Income available to spend in period 2 falls, therefore, by a large amount and consumption falls correspondingly, but now production (based on sales in period 1) only falls a bit and there is a large unintended rise in inventories. The whole adjustment process is displayed in Table 3.

TABLE 3

Period	y_{t-1}^d	$C_t = aY_{t-1}^d$	I_t^i	I_t^u	Y_t^d
-2	1000	900	100	0	1000
-1	1000	900	100	0	1000
0	1000	800	100	80	980
$+1$	980	784	100	12·8	896·8
$+2$	896·8	717·44	100	52·248	870·688
$+3$	870·688	696·55	100	16·712	813·262
$+4$	813·262	650·6096	100	37·24	787·240
∞	500	400	100	0	500

Note that the process of adjustment is no longer a smooth one: disposable income falls by a large amount every other period and by a small amount every other period. This is because disposable income is kept up by the mistaken expectation that sales will not fall below what they were in the previous period. When the mistake is observed, the

23.   In other words we are valuing inventories at cost and when they are sold we will say that there is dissaving of 80 and new production of 20 (the profit component of the inventories).

downward adjustment is made in the following period.

It should be evident that a different dynamic path will be observed *for each assumption we make about how well, or how poorly, firms anticipate the reduction in sales.*

Standard dynamic treatments almost invariably show the smooth adjustment of Table 1 or its geometrical equivalent shown in figure 1. This is precisely the case that arises when all changes in sales are exactly anticipated so that *no* unintended investment occurs. If we wish to have a model in which sales plans *are unfulfilled* so that unintended investment does occur, then the dynamic course of income is *not* the one usually shown, and *in no case* can it be read from figure 1, because the change in income depends on the change in output and the change in output is a function of factors other than current income (e.g. expectations about future sales).[24]

IV. THE OUTLINES OF A SATISFACTORY TREATMENT

We may now briefly address ourselves to the question of how to introduce income theory satisfactorily to beginning students.

The first thing to agree on is that no 'true' set of definitions, nor one 'fundamental' set of identities, better describes the world than does any other 'less fundamental' set.[25] We have certain flows in the world, and certain flows in a water-flow model, which we think is a useful analogue of real-world flows, and the questions are: 'Which of these flows are we interested in?' and 'Can we describe them with sufficient precision so that we can *measure* each of them satisfactorily?' The

24.   I am not saying here, as many readers of my earlier drafts seemed to think, that the step diagram in figure 1 is not 'good dynamics'. I am saying that the path shown in figure 1 is necessarily inconsistent with the assumption that unintended inventory accumulation occurs during the downward adjustment process because production of goods for inventories, whether intended or unintended, necessarily creates disposable income.

25.   I have, for example, heard it said that the main contribution of the Keynesian revolution was to change our way of looking at things (with which I agree) and in particular *to show us which are the key, fundamental identities in the economy.* It is not important whether you use one or *n* symbols to refer to one real-world magnitude but the belief that doing so can tell us something is encouraged by current treatments of macrotheory.

belief that we are discovering truth when we define things[26] has led us to think that there is only one true set of definitions. The correct reply to this true-definition idea is 'you tell me how you think the income flow behaves *and* what part of it you are interested in studying and *then* I shall provide a set of definitions that will allow a statistician, ignorant of economics, to go out and measure the numbers we require.'

Actually, there are as many relations and equilibrium conditions as there are imaginable economies. Let us consider one set. First we define the following flows in which we are interested.

(1)   The total of output produced during time t, valued at *current* market prices (thus inventories are valued at market price which includes profits rather than at cost which does not), $= O_t$.

(2)   The total payments made by firms to factors on account of wages, interest, rents and distributed profits + profits earned and not paid out during the period, $\equiv$ Income.

(3)   The total value of expenditure on goods and services by households and by firms on those goods that they have purchased and not re-sold by the end of the period, $\equiv$ Total Expenditure $\equiv E \equiv$ Total Sales $\equiv S$.[27]

All of these three magnitudes are defined in such a way that they can differ from each other, and also in such a way that the difference between any two is itself a clearly identifiable magnitude. Let us consider each of the possible differences.[28]

26.   Arguments about the 'true' or 'correct' definition of national income abound. The common examination question 'should the services of households be included in national income' can only invite an essentialist answer, while the question 'should the services of households be included in Y for purposes of testing the hypothesis that employment is a function of income' invites the nominalist, and non-essentialist, reasoned answer of *'NO'*.

27.   Note that expenditure may be divided between purchasers of consumption goods by households C, purchase of capital goods by firms $I^f (T \geqslant 0)$ and the increase in inventories $I^i (\geqslant 0) : E = C + I^f + I^i$ (if inventories are decumulating I^i must take on a value of zero in the expenditure equation). This is easily seen by noticing that consumer expenditure is the same whether the goods are produced out of inventories or out of current production. It makes a difference to current output but not to current household expenditure if the goods purchased come from current productions or out of inventories.

28.   Some of these points are considered in more detail in *Lipsey* [10], pp. 343-360.

Income, as defined in (2) above, is the total of payments actually made to factors plus undistributed profits. This does not need to equal O_t as defined in (1) above because there may be payments to factors in return for no current output,[29] because unsold inventories do *not* give rise to an accrual of profits so that the market value of inventories exceeds the factor incomes earned during the period by the value of profits on unsold inventories (which will be earned when the inventories are sold), because goods may be produced and factors not paid for the services rendered,[30] and, finally, because the possibility of a lag between production and the payments to factors allows O_t to differ from Y_t.[31]

Total expenditure as defined in (3) above is expenditure by households and firms on goods sold by other firms.[32] Expenditure can differ from the value of current output, O_t, because sales can be made from inventories. In this case expenditure will be the total value of sales, but current household income will equal only the profit component on the inventory sales. If inventories remain unchanged, and if we ignore second-hand goods, then the only further assumption that we need to get current expenditure equal to the value of current output is that

29.   Many recent studies have shown that employment reacts to changes in output with a distributed time lag so that a change in output at time t need not be reflected in a change in payments to factors at time t.

30.   Such default is normally ignored but it can, of course, occur since normally there is a lag of anything from one to several weeks between the rendering of a factor service and the payment for it. During times of sudden financial crisis such defaults could be a major reason why the value of output could exceed the value of income payments.

31.   If t is one year and a rise in O occurs during the last week of the year then this will not be reflected in a rise in Y during period t. Clearly, on this account at least, O_t can differ from Y_t.

32.   This is usually defined to be expenditure on currently produced goods and services but this requires that we distinguish between expenditure on goods currently produced and on goods sold from inventories. If money spent on goods goes up during period t and all the new sales are met from inventories, we would have to say, using the traditional definitions, that expenditure did not go up. In our system we say that it did go up but that output did not, so clearly we do *not* have $E \searrow O$.

33.   This is just to emphasise that $E \equiv O$ is a convention that says nothing about the world. If we define E and O independently then the statement $O = E$ is an empirical hypothesis about the absence of significant quantities of fraud (and other things as well) for clearly, if there were fraud, expenditure of households could exist where there was no counterpart in actual goods produced.

neither fraud nor bankruptcies occur between payment for goods and
delivery of goods.[33] Current expenditure can also differ from current
income because households can borrow or use up past savings in order
to spend (of course this will raise future income but we are talking
about the relation between household expenditure this period and
income received by them in the same period) and because of lags in the
adjustment of expenditure to changes in income.[34]

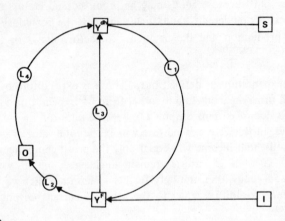

Figure 3

We can now lay out the flows of income and expenditure on the
assumption that there is no foreign trade and no government and, for
the moment, no savings and no investment. These are shown in figure 3.
Household disposable income becomes household expenditure with a
possible time lag, l_1. Household expenditure becomes the income of
firms without lag. Sales influence output, with a possible lag l_2 and
output produces wage payments[35] with a possible lag l_4. Profits accrue
when goods are sold not when they are made; thus a link joins sales to
household income through the distribution of profits with the possible
lag l_3.

34.   In the case of wages the lag may be short but in the case of profits it is long
because of the lag between the accrual of profits to firms and the payment of
extra dividends to the owners of the firm. Of course we can say that the lag
indicates short-term savings on the part of households but we must be very careful
to remember that we have now made savings a function of the change in income
as well as the level.
35.   Wage payments here stand for all factor services actually used and paid for
in the course of production.

If there were no lags, we could never observe a disequilibrium situation. If we wish to discuss disequilibrium behaviour at least some of these lags must be non-zero. If they are non-zero, and if the level of income is changing, then income received by households this month will not equal income received by firms this month and this in turn will not equal the value of output this month. Only if the flow around the circuit is constant will the flow measured at Y^{dh}, Y^f and O be the same.

Now let us add household savings and firms' investment as the only leakage from, and the only injection into, this system. We define household saving as income received by households and not spent on consumption goods. Since in a lagged system this may not be easy to identify, we can clarify matters by assuming that all current savings are used to buy bonds, and then define savings as the net addition to households' stock of bonds over the period. Investment is defined as expenditure on capital goods and inventories.

The circular flow now has a withdrawal and an injection. The equilibrium of the flow is not ensured by the condition $S = I$. If we start from equilibrium then increase, say, S so that income begins to fall the flow within the circuit will react to the various lags I_1 to I_4, some of which can be quite complex distributed lags. If we now restore S to its original level equal to unchanged I we can get fluctuations within the flow for a long time and indeed, for some lag structures, permanent oscillations can be set up. What then can we say at an elementary level without assuming any mathematics? First we can give sufficient conditions for disequilibrium. Assume the flow is in equilibrium and then disturb it by changing S or I. Say, as in Table 1, we raise the propensity

36.   The introductory chapter of many textbooks describes a water flow analogue to the circular flow of the type actually built at the London School of Economics by Professor A.W. Phillips (described in [12]). At this stage savings are shown as a flow of water out of the system and investment as a flow into it. It is apparent to students that these two actual flows need not be equal. Our definitions relate to quantities analogous to these two observable flows. The standard text books, however, seldom mention the analogue after the introduction, but immediately switch over to a set of definitions in which actual savings are identical with actual investment without trying to show the water flow analogue of these new definitions. Not only does this bother thoughtful students, it throws away the intuitively appealing concepts of savings and investment as implicitly defined by a water flow machine.

to save. Now the actual realised flow of savings withdrawn from the system will exceed the actual realised flow of investment expenditure injected into the system.[36] Clearly, we can say that when actual withdrawals differ from actual injections, the system, *ceteris paribus,* will be subject to forces of change. Next, we can argue that with $S = I$ and with any internal, lag-generated fluctuations removed, the system will be in equilibrium. Equilibrium requires as a necessary condition that actual withdrawals be equal to actual injections, which, in the simplest one-withdrawal, one-injection model only, requires that actual savings equal actual investment.

This treatment allows the student to relate his theory to a flow analogue he can see, read about, or at least readily imagine. It relates savings and investment to flows easily identified and measured in the analogue machine. It never makes mention of the national-income accountants' definitions during the development of the theory. This is similar to our treatment of price theory where we do not discuss the problems of measuring demand (either in the schedule or in the point sense) until we have developed sufficient theory to know exactly what we want to measure, and why we want to measure it. Similarly, once the theory outlined above has been presented and developed, the problems of measurement can then be raised, and the statisticians' measures can be related to the model. At this stage we can show what the statistician is measuring, but at no time will we be suggesting that the statisticians' decision to measure the flow at one point rather than another has any operational significance in terms of how people actually behave.

The first thing we need to point out to students at the measurement stage is that, if the flow of income is changing, and if we put meters at three different points on the circuit, they will give different readings. Indeed, a condition for change is just this, and a condition for equilibrium in the flow is that the three meters give the same reading. Thus, when the flow is changing, we expect income of firms this month to differ from output of firms this month which in turn differs from incomes paid out to households this month. (Of course by pure accident of specific lag structures they may be equal.) We then point out that the statistician defines expenditure, income and output to be the same magnitude. This means that he has made a series of adjustments to the terms as we have defined them which have the effect of

30

moving three measuring devices around the circuit until they are all measuring the flow at a single point on the circuit. If in figure 3 we start with measuring devices at Y^{dh}, E^h and O, we know that they will give us different readings unless the circuit is in equilibrium. The only way to ensure that they give identical readings at all times is to move them to some coincident point. It is now a minor diseconomy in the use of symbols to use Y, E, and O to refer to the flow measured at this one point but nothing worse follows provided we know what we are doing. But the identity of $Y \equiv E \equiv O$ tells us absolutely nothing about the nature of the flow around the circuit. It could behave in any imaginable way including spontaneous creation and destruction of goods and money, systematic fraud and robbery equal in value to half that of production at numerous points or anything else and, except for errors in the meters, the flow at any one point will be the same when measured by each of the three meters. The adjustments that are made are too complex to detail here but they are largely designed, of course, to get the measure of the market value of current output. This value must belong to someone so it is possible to account for all of it in terms of claims on it by individuals or organisations. When the accountant speaks of income he means the value of output broken up in terms of claims on it; these claims may or may not have been met, indeed, if inventories are valued at market price, some of the value (the gross profit component) will not even have been received by the firms.

Next we need to point out to our students that the statistician uses savings and investment to refer to the same thing: goods produced but not consumed in the period. This differs from our flow-model definition of savings, and some quite difficult problems are involved in relating the two. Let us consider only one situation: that described by Table 1. The current flow of actual savings defined in our flow model is $Y_{t-1} - C_t$, and this is the value of funds available to households in period t but *not* spent on goods (e.g. £200 in period zero). The statistician defines actual savings as $Y_t - C_t$. We have seen on page 22 what he does. In terms of Table 1 in period zero, £200 was not spent by households but instead of accumulating transactions balances of £900 over the month as sales proceeded, firms only accumulated £800. If we call these transactions balances past savings, then firms have dissaved £100 so total saving is only £100. Thus, in the one period lag model any difference between S and I *must* show up in changes in the transactions balances accumulated by firms during the course of the month's trading. Thus, if we define savings to be the withdrawals out of the system *plus* the change in the flow measured where the appropriate lag occurs (in this case it is firm's receipts), it must equal I (i.e., the statistician's measured saving = our measured savings + [our measured I – our measured S]). Then, of course, the statistician's measured $S \equiv$ our measured I. But note that the statistician's measured S *cannot* now be equated with the flow of withdrawals from the circuit because it also includes the difference between funds accumulated by firms during the course of last month and the funds accumulated by firms during the course of this month.[37] There is nothing to stop us using this measure when we need it, while at the same time conducting our theoretical analysis in terms of actual withdrawals from, and injections into, the circular flow and defining savings as a withdrawal and then talking about actual savings being unequal to actual investment.

V. CONCLUSION

The standard practice of introducing income theory by means of a series of accounting identities has led to a number of specific errors and to a misunderstanding over the dynamic adjustment mechanism in a circular flow model. It has also contributed to a general 'essentialist' flavour to much of macroeconomics. Judging from the written evidence many of us still seem to believe that we can learn something about the world from the way we define our terms, and that there are key and important definitions (identities) which somehow exist in the world waiting to be discovered by a genius such as Keynes. This was the method of Plato which, under the modern name of essentialism has been discarded by most working scientists in favour of a nominalist view of definitions.

The acceptance that definitions are necessarily true, combined with the idea that we learn something from them, represents a hangover from an older methodology that argued it was possible to establish empirically relevant propositions that had the force of logical necessity.[38] This methodology is no longer generally accepted and today most scientists agree that an empirically relevant statement must

37. If the lag is placed elsewhere the funds will be accumulated elsewhere. The basic point is that the statistician's definition of savings includes not only what can be measured as withdrawn from a real flow model but also a change in the flow within the circuit.

say that some potentially observable things cannot happen and that such statements can thus be shown to be in conflict with the facts. Such statements cannot, therefore, be established with certainty. It is a shame that in this one area so many traces of a generally discarded methodology still linger on to confuse students and to cloud the many issues of real substance that exist in macroeconomics.

38. This methodology has been clearly stated and cogently criticised from a nominalist point of view by Klappholz and Agassi [7].

REFERENCES

1   Ackley, H.G. *Macroeconomic Theory*, 1961
2   Allen, R.D.G. *Macro-Economics*, 1964
3   Bach, G.L. *Economics*, 1963
4   Bailey, M.J. *National Income and the Price Level*, 1962
5   Benham, F. *Economics*, 6th ed., 1960
6   Christ, C. *Econometric Models and Methods*, 1966
7   Klappholz, K. and Agassi, J. 'Methodological Prescriptions in Economics', *Economica*, 1960
8   Klappholz, K. and Mishan, E. 'Identities in Economic Models', *Economica*, 1962
9   Klein, L.R. *The Keynesian Revolution*, 1961
10 Lipsey, R.G. *An Introduction to Positive Economics*, 1st ed., 1963
11 Nevin, E. *A Textbook of Economic Analysis*, 1963
12 Phillips, A.W. 'Mechanical Models in Economic Dynamics', *Economica*, 1950
13 Palander, T. 'On the Concepts and Methods of the Stockholm School', trans in *International Economic Papers*, 1953
14 Samuelson, P.A. *Economics – An Introductory Analysis*, 6th ed., 1964
15 Shackle, G.L.S. *et al. A New Prospect of Economics*, 1958
16 Schneider, E. *Money, Income and Employment*, 1962

Appendix
A Short History of the Muddle

J.A. Stilwell and R.G. Lipsey

Before the General Theory little attention was paid in the U.K. to savings and investment as factors which might influence the general level of employment. Mill ([1871] Chapter XIV, Book III) had described depressions; he saw them as temporary crises of confidence which in no way affected the long run validity of Say's law. This was also Marshall's ([1922] p. 710) position, and was further developed by Pigou [1932]. The attention paid to the relation between savings and investment by Continental economists since the beginning of the century, and the work being done by the Swedish economists (especially the development of the ideas of Wicksell by Lindahl) seemed to have little influence here. D.H. Robertson, however, did not follow the main English stream; he considered it desirable to incorporate precisely defined variables corresponding to the various aspects of saving and investment in his analyses [1933]. Perhaps because of the ignorance of the work being done in Sweden[1] textbooks prepared in England during the thirties were immune to errors stemming from the treatment of tautologies as equilibrium conditions. The first edition of Benham [1938] treats saving and investment completely operationally: 'Investible funds which are used to pay for the labour . . . come from any or all of four sources; amortisation quotas, new savings, new money, and balances previously idle'.

---

1.   Lindahl [1939], Myrdal [1939] and Ohlin [1937] all defined *ex post* saving and investment as necessarily equal although others of the Swedes did not. They were not immune to error on this score. G. Myrdal [1939] makes mistake number 1 — and this book introduced to the English speaking economists the concepts *'ex ante'* and *'ex post'*. Palander [1941] says (p. 40), when describing the ways by which divergences between investment and saving occur, 'Such a lack of agreement assumes a *lack of congruence* in a certain situation *between the expectations of different parties concerning the same amount'* (His italics. It is the last phrase which is crucial). Whether the errors sprang from the influence of Keynes and Kahn in Sweden, or arose on their own, we cannot say

As soon as the General Theory was published, Keynes' treatment of saving and investment, differing so much from his earlier treatment in the Treatise, received much attention, and was naturally compared with Robertson.[2] Robertson's definitions were thought by many (e.g. Lutz [1938]) to be equivalent to the Swedish definition of *ex ante* saving and *ex post* investment. The work of the Swedes became known through Myrdal's *Monetary Equilibrium*, Lindahl's book *Studies in the Theory of Money and Capital,* and an article by Bertil Ohlin [1937] which appeared shortly after the General Theory, although, as Ohlin points out ([1937] p.57), they were by no means representative. They were not in fact equivalent, since Robertsonian saving is an *ex post* quantity. Robertsonian investment[3] was perhaps equivalent to the *ex post* investment of Ohlin, Lindahl and Myrdal, but his assumptions were so much more rigid (the exclusion, for example, of inventory accumulation) that to force the equivalence is pointless.

Commentaries on Keynes always aver that his personality split is the treatment of saving and investment,[4] and that his excursion into the world of 'significant tautologies' could not conceal his real intention of stating '... the savings-investment relation in terms of intersecting schedules of economic behaviour, which determine an equilibrium position'.

Yet Hansen[5] admits that Keynes himself did not make the distinction between $I = S$ as an equilibrium condition and $I = S$ as a tautology. 'He was realistic enough to see this, as is revealed again and again in different sections of his book. But he never explicitly stated it,

2.   Keynes [1931] and Kahn [1931] had long since defined saving as necessarily equal to investment, and Robertson had referred to this in [1933]. These articles did not have the impact of the General Theory.

3.   Robertsonian investment was the product of desired 'instrumental goods'. According to the rigid assumption which he made (he was after all, analysing changes in the price level, not in the level of output) this was equivalent to received income minus consumption expenditure. Yet as soon as we make the realistic assumption that expenditure upon their product is not the only source of income for factors of production the equivalence disappears. The assumption of bank borrowing to pay an under-utilized labour force would not have offended Robertson. In that case, if Robertsonian investment is still to be defined as 'the amount of investment *which an entrepreneur would call investment* that actually gets done', when used in output analysis it must not be held to equal received income minus consumption – as Ackley does [1961] (p. 322).

4.   Klein [1952], p. 91.

5.   Alvin Hansen [1953], pp. 58 ff.

doubtless because the matter had not been clearly thought through' (p.59).

Indeed, several reviews (see below) ignored Keynes' definition of investment as saving, concentrating on the description of disequilibria caused by an excess of one over the other. They largely discussed the assertion that since saving was not undertaken solely in order to invest, as in the classics, but in order also to satisfy desires for liquidity, there might occur the situation where the rate of interest could not restore equality at the level of full employment.

Klein, in order to protect Keynes from the charge of logical error, does not see the distinction as one between tautologies and behaviour equation, but as one between schedules and observables. Since observable savings (he says) undoubtedly equal observable investment at any time, each level must represent an intersection point of the saving and investment schedules. 'The economic process is viewed as made up of a series of intersections of equilibrium points of saving and investment schedules' (Klein [1952] p.111). The conclusion of this reasoning is that the economy is always in equilibrium; and since the equality of 'observed' savings and investment stems from the fact that they are two names for the same thing, the 'intersections' to which Klein refers must be very odd things indeed.[6]

At any rate, the publication of the General Theory, and the reviews and articles which immediately followed, were the start of what is referred to as the great saving investment controversy of the thirties.[7]

Perhaps the central articles were those appearing in the *Economic Journal*, 1937, written by Keynes, Robertson and Hawtrey. The definitional controversy appears here, and has two aspects; first, did Keynes so define saving and investment that they were two names for the same thing, or did he merely define them as equal, and if so is there an important difference; and secondly, whether such a definition (either of the above) was preferable to its competitors.

Keynes' article [1937] is mainly a comment upon Ohlin's previous

6.   But Klein seems no longer to hold the view that the controversy was not sterile − see his comments in the discussion which followed (Klein [1952]).
7.   H.G. Johnson [1961], p. 6 'a violent and prolonged controversy'.

article [1937]. He also replies, however, to Hawtrey [1937] , who asserts that savings and investment, according to Keynes, are merely different names for the same thing. Keynes riposte is that, just as buying and selling are not identical terms, neither are saving and investment — the quantities are *equal*, but not *identical*. Yet this confuses the act with the actor. A murdered person is not a murderer, but a murdering is a being murdered; it is useful to know something about murderers and their victims, but not useful to be told that if a murder took place then someone was murdered. Moreover (top p.249), Keynes maintains 'The novelty in my treatment of saving and investment consists, not in my maintaining their necessary aggregate equality, but in the proportion that it is, not the rate of interest, but the level of incomes which (in conjunction with certain other factors) ensures their equality'.

D.H. Robertson, in his reply [1937] makes the correct criticism:

(Mr. Keynes' critics) have merely maintained that he has so framed his definition that Amount Saved and Amount Invested are identical; that it therefore makes no sense even to inquire what the force is which 'ensures equality' between them; and that since the identity holds whether money income is constant or changing, and, if it is changing, whether real income is changing proportionately, or not at all, this way of putting things does not seem to be a very suitable instrument for the analysis of economic change.

Hawtrey [1937], makes similar points to Robertson; one of them however, is a little odd. He describes the identity of saving and investment as an arithmetic identity, not a purely verbal proposition. There is a sense in which an identity need not be a tautology — 'that man is the man whom I saw yesterday' — but reference is not being made to this type of identity. An arithmetic identity is as much a tautology as a verbal identity — the type of symbols employed is irrelevant.

Among the other articles which appeared after the General Theory there was a considerable amount of confusion; a number, however, were almost free of error and some completely so. Few concerned themselves solely with the definitional debate, and among those who criticised Keynes correctly on this score perhaps the best was G. Haberler [1937]. He points out the source of the confusion, taking as his starting point the exposition of the 'instantaneous' multiplier.

An increase in I cannot occur without an increase in aggregate Y as determined by the multiplier not, as Keynes says, because otherwise the public would not be prepared to provide the necessary savings, but because we have assumed that it cannot occur otherwise.[8]

Pigou [1936], Viner [1936] and A. Hansen [1936] either ignore the definition of investment as saving, describing Keynes as asserting that, since new saving will take the form of hoarding, and there will be no compensatory wage-price adjustments, or money creating, saving is likely to exceed investment, or mention it, admittedly with confusion and a certain amount of error (specifically error No. 2) in minor sections of their articles. Hicks [1936], refers to the definitional equality of saving and investment in the General Theory, regarding this as an indication of a considerable change in viewpoint since the Treatise. Hicks does not therefore discuss the possibility of utilising a tautology in a statement of equilibrium condition,[9] but seems to assume that, together with an anticipation equation, it rehabilitates equilibrium analysis as a technique of real use.

A. Lerner [1936] and W.B. Reddaway [1936] both make mistake No. 2; that is, they write that there is a real mechanism which brings about the necessary equality. F.A. Lutz [1938], draws all the correct conclusions including the suggestion that part of the error stemmed from a false analogy with the supply and demand for particular commodities 'always being equal'. He prefers a Robertsonian, lagged, analysis. Lerner [1938], disagrees with Lutz's presentation of the multiplier fallacy, but again refers to the fact that $I = S$ definitionally, and that no conclusion about anything except language can be drawn from this.

We have, therefore, the two facts that the majority of modern elementary and intermediate textbooks, together with parts of much more advanced literature, treat the Keynesian identity as an inexorably self-establishing equilibrium condition, and that the pre-war saving and investment debate, although giving rise to much confusion, contained a number of articles which correctly exposed the errors and changes — notably those of Robertson, Haberler and Lutz. How can these be

8. Compare Joan Robinson [1937] pp. 20 ff.
9. As Klein implies [1952], p. 100.

reconciled? The error did not enter the most influential textbooks, Benham and Samuelson, until relatively late. The fourth edition of Benham [1948] was free of the errors that first appeared in the fifth edition [1955]. Benham's book was, however, innocent of Keynesian economics until 1958 so that the errors are introduced the first time Benham attempts to expound Keynesian theory. The case of Samuelson's extremely influential textbook is more interesting. Samuelson's book was of course Keynesian in spirit from the outset but it is error free until the fourth edition. It is only in 1958 that the footnote already quoted on page 23 of this article is introduced into the fourth edition.

Perhaps the error in its modern form originated somewhat independently of Keynes. It might have stemmed from the combination in most textbooks of a chapter dealing with elementary national income accounting, and a chapter dealing with income flows where the simplest model, that of one injection, one withdrawal, system is considered, the quantities being labelled respectively investment and saving. The definitions used in the accounting chapter may have crept over into the latter parts of the other.

Alternatively it is possible, and perhaps more likely, that by the middle fifties the salutory effects of the debate which followed the publication of the General Theory had been forgotten, and the reputation of Keynes led to the inclusion in textbooks of the crudest expressions of the errors. This is only speculation; the fact which we have is that the customary exposition of simple macro-static models is worse that it was twenty years ago.

BIBLIOGRAPHY

Ackley, G.   (1961), *Macroeconomic Theory*, New York.
Benham, F.   (1938), *Economics*, 1st ed., London.
               (1948), *Economics*, 4th ed., London.
               (1955), *Economics*, 5th ed., London.
               (1958), *Economics*, 6th ed., London.
Haberler, G. (1937),   'Mr. Keynes' Theory of the "Multiplier": A Methodological Criticism', *Zeitschrift fur Nationalokonomie*, Vol. 7.
Hansen, A. (1936),   'Mr. Keynes on Unemployment Equilibrium', *Journal of Political Economy*, Vol. XLIV.
               (1953), *A Guide to Keynes*, New York.
Hawtrey, R. (1937),   'Alternative Theories of the Rate of Interest: Three Rejoinders III', *Economic Journal*, Vol. XLVII.
Hicks, J. (1936),   'Mr. Keynes' Theory of Employment', *Economic Journal*, Vol. XLVI.
Johnson, H.G. (1961), 'The General Theory After Twenty-Five Years', *American Economic Review*, Vol. LI.
Kahn, R. (1931),   'The Relation of Home Investment to Unemployment', *Economic Journal*, Vol. XLI.
Keynes, J. (1931),   'A Rejoinder', *Economic Journal*, Vol. XLI.
               (1937), 'Alternative Theories of the Rate of Interest', *Economic Journal*, Vol. XLVII.
Klein, L. (1952),   *The Keynesian Revolution*, 1st ed., New York.
Lerner, A. (1936),   'Mr. Keynes' General Theory of Employment, Interest and Money', *International Labour Review*, Vol. XXXLV.
               (1938), 'Alternative Formulations of the Theory of Interest', *Economic Journal*, Vol. XLVIII.
Lindahl, E. (1939),   *Studies in the Theory of Money and Capital*, London.
Lutz. F.A. (1938),   'The Outcome of the Saving-Investment Discussion', *Quarterly Journal of Economics*, Vol. 52.
Marshall, A. (1922),   *Principles of Economics*, 8th ed., London.
Mill, J.S. (1871),   *Principles of Political Economy*, 7th ed., London.
Myrdal, G. (1939),   *Monetary Equilibrium*, London.
Ohlin, B. (1937),   'Some Notes on the Stockholm Theory of Savings and Investment', *Economic Journal*, Vol. XLVII.

Palander, T. (1941),   'On the Concepts and Methods of the Stock-
                         holm School', *Economisk Tidstenft,* reprinted
                         in *International Economic Papers,* 1953.
Pigou, A. (1932),   *The Economics of Welfare,* 4th ed., London.
          (1936),   'Mr. J.M. Keynes' General Theory of
                         Employment, Interest and Money', *Economica*
                         Vol. III.
Reddaway, W.B. (1936),'The General Theory of Employment, Interest
                         and Money'. *Economic Record,* Vol. XII.

Robertson, D.H. (1933),'Saving and Hoarding', *Economic Journal,* Vol.
                         XLIII.
              (1937),   'Alternative Theories of the Rate of Interest:
                         Three Rejoinders II', *Economic Journal,* Vol.
                         XLVII.
Robinson, J. (1937),   *Introduction to the Theory of Employment,*
                         London.
Viner, J. (1936),   'Mr. Keynes on the Causes of Unemployment',
                         Quarterly Journal of Economics, Vol. LI.

Operationally Relevant Characteristics in the Theory of Consumer Behaviour [1]

Kelvin Lancaster

The associated ideas of a hierarchy of wants and of want satiation figured prominently in the writings of the early marginalists, then fell into disuse. In this essay, I shall develop related ideas for application in modern consumer theory. The emphasis here is on contemporary application, with only passing reference to the earlier literature.[2] Ironically, the earlier forms of these ideas were discarded because they were considered non-operational, but it is because they are useful for the *operational* development of recent models of the consumer, that they are discussed here.

The context of the present discussion is a model of the consumer, the general structure of which has been set out in some detail elsewhere.[3] The essential feature is that the consumer's relationship to goods is viewed as having two (at least) stages. Goods, singly or in combination, possess properties which I refer to as *characteristics*. These are typically viewed as joint outputs of a consumption activity, in which goods are the input. The consumer's preferences and choices are assumed to be concerned with the various collections of characteristics[4] that are available to him, these being derived in turn from the

---

1.   The work in this paper was partly supported by the National Science Foundation. The idea was the product of some comments by Nicholas Georgescu-Roegen on another paper of mine, and seemed an appropriate topic to develop as a tribute to Lionel Robbins.

2.   One of Lionel Robbins' great contributions as a teacher was, of course, his lectures in the history of economic thought. I failed to take advantage of these at the appropriate time, and that lacuna remains unfilled.

3.   See Lancaster [4], (1) and (2), also (3), pp. 113-18.

4.   The term 'characteristics' was an arbitrary choice. Given the emphasis on the quantitative aspect which is stressed in most uses of the idea, 'qualities' seemed inappropriate. Somewhat related concepts have been called 'commodities' (Becker) and 'abstract modes' (Baumol and Quandt).

available collections of goods. In the simplest case, the available goods are limited by a budget constraint. The goods collections give rise to characteristics collections, from which the consumer chooses his preferred collection, the choice being manifest by his choosing the *goods* collection which gives this particular collection of characteristics.

The version of the model which shows particular promise in operational and empirical approaches, at this early stage of its development, is that in which we confine our attention to cases in which we can work with characteristics which

(1) are objectively observable and measurable
(2) have linear properties, so that twice as much of the good has twice as much of the characteristic
(3) are additive, so that if one pound of Good A has one unit of a characteristic and one gallon of Good B has two units, the combination of one pound of A plus one gallon of B contains three units.

For the purposes of this essay, the essential features of the model can be illustrated by figure 1, which shows a case in which there are two characteristics and three goods. Quantities of the two characteristics are measured along the two axes. All three goods are assumed to possess both characteristics, but in different proportions. The points A, B, C, show the quantities of both characteristics contained in Goods *1, 2, 3,* respectively, taking a unit quantity of each good. Thus the ray OG_1 represents all the combinations of the two characteristics that can be obtained from various quantities of Good *1* only, with similar interpretations for OG_2 and OG_3. By consuming goods in combination, characteristics in proportions which lie inside the cone G_3OG_2 can be obtained.

Suppose the budget constraint and prices were such that the consumer could, by spending all his money on one good, purchase two units of G_3 or G_1, or one unit of G_2. Then the budget would confine the consumer to characteristics collections A', C' or B if he bought only one good. If the goods are divisible, the consumer could attain characteristics combinations from combinations of goods — combinations of characteristics along $A'C'$ —by spending the whole budget on combinations of G_1 and G_3, along $A'B$ by spending it on combinations of G_1 and G_2, and along BC' for combinations of G_2 and G_3.

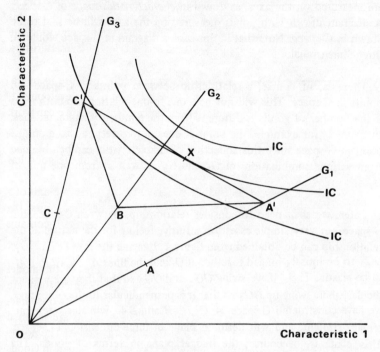

Figure 1

In the particular case shown in figure 1, more of both characteristics can be obtained by combinations of G_1 and G_3 than by any combination including G_2. At the current prices, it would be *inefficient* to purchase G_2, assuming that more of both characteristics is desired. The earlier discussions of the model were primarily concerned with the consequences of efficient and inefficient combinations of goods, a topic that does not concern us here.

Since the consumer's preferences are in terms of characteristics his preference map can be drawn directly on the diagram. Assuming regular preferences, the consumer whose indifference curves are drawn in the figure will choose characteristics collection X, a particular combination of G_1 and G_3 that can be determined from the characteristics content of the two goods.

45

We shall refer to a diagram, such as figure 1, in which characteristics are measured on the axes, as drawn in *characteristics-space* or *C-space*. A diagram drawn with goods measured on the axes will be said to be drawn in *G-space*. Note that in this case, a diagram in G-space would be three-dimensional.

There is, of course, a relationship between points in C-space and points in G-space. This will not be a one-to-one relationship both ways if the number of goods is different from the number of characteristics. In figure 1, for example, the point B does not correspond to a unique point in G-space since this collection of characteristics can be obtained from various combinations of G_1 and G_3, as well as from one unit of G_2.

Later, we shall need to consider relationships between C-space and G-space, for very simple cases. An intuitive feeling for the nature of the relationship can be obtained from figure 1. Imagine the rays OG_1, OG_2, OG_3 to be loosely hinged together at O, and the lines $A'C'$, $C'B$, BA' to be elastic. Then, if we swing OG_1 and OG_3 so that they are perpendicular, then swing up OG_2 so that it is perpendicular to the other rays, we have constructed G-space. $A'C'$, $C'B$ and BA' will all stretch, but remain straight, and will define a plane in three-dimensional G-space. This plane is, of course, the budget plane in terms of goods. The indifference curves will become indifference surfaces, but with curvature only in two dimensions — it will be possible to draw a straight line through every point on every indifference surface such that it lies everywhere on the surface.

In the linear version, with which we are concerned, the relationship between C-space and G-space is linear in the sense that a linear form (line or plane) in one space corresponds to a linear form in the other. Although (as in the example given) there may not be a unique point in G-space corresponding to a point in C-space, there will always be a unique point in C-space corresponding to a point (that is, a goods collection) in G-space. The relationship is given by

$$z = Bx$$

where z is the vector of characteristics, x the vector of goods. The matrix B consists of elements b_{ij}, giving the amount of the ith characteristic contained in unit quantity of the jth good. Since the relationships expressed by the b_{ij}'s are assumed both objective and universal, they depend on the *technical* properties of the goods and not on subjective considerations. We refer to the matrix *B*, therefore, as the *consumption technology*.[5] It depends on the available goods and their exact specifications.

RELEVANT CHARACTERISTICS

The characteristics model of the consumer has important superiority in explanatory power over the traditional[6] model in many cases, especially in the explanation of such 'intrinsic' substitutability as between butter and margarine and in the analysis of differentiated products. It also has great potentialities in empirically oriented studies.

The application of the model is most useful in situations (such as the market for differentiated goods) in which the number of effective characteristics is smaller than the number of goods. The earlier discussions of the model, to which reference has already been made, assumed that the number of characteristics was less than the number of goods.

Now it is clear that, if we count as a characteristic every property of a good that is objectively observable and measurable, the number of such 'characteristics' might be almost limitless. In the use of the analysis, we are interested only in *relevant* characteristics. The idea of relevance was implicit in the earlier discussion of the model, but was not explicitly dealt with. To face this problem and to investigate criteria for deciding whether a characteristic is or is not relevant, is the purpose of this essay.

We are interested in the problem of selecting the relevant characteristics for a given situation, where we mean, by *situation*, a relationship between some set of consumers (possibly containing only one member) and some set of goods. A characteristic possessed by one or more of the goods is *relevant* to the situation if ignoring its existence

---

5. The number of goods may bear any relation to the number of characteristics, so *B* may have more rows than columns, or less, or be square. In this model, it is easy to answer the question, when is a good the same as another good? The answer is, when the ratio b_{ij}/b_{ik} is the same for every *i*, the goods *j* and *k* are the 'same'.

6. I use the term 'traditional model' to refer to the Hicks-Samuelson analysis and its modern formal refinements, such as in Debreu [1].

would change our conclusions about choice or ordering of the goods by the consumers.

A brief discussion how *ex post* relevance might be established from market data was given in an earlier paper,[7] and this idea has been developed further in unpublished work on the automobile[8] market. This technique requires, however, that one commences from a set of characteristics reasonably close to the ultimate relevant set, and so needs a preliminary screening.

Here we shall be concerned with a general discussion of some of the criteria that are useful in deciding *ex ante* whether a characteristic is likely to be relevant or not, in a specific situation.

Some characteristics might be ruled out as *ex ante* irrelevant in all situations simply on broad general considerations. One characteristic of automobiles, for example, is their serial numbers. We would expect that ignoring this would leave our predictions of behaviour in the automobile market unchanged. We need not discuss such trivial cases further.

Characteristics bear a double relation to a given situation. On the one hand, characteristics have a *technical* relationship to the goods which possess them, and on the other hand characteristics have a *human* relationship to the consumers in question. Thus a characteristic may be ruled out as irrelevant for either technical or human reasons.

Technical irrelevance is not our prime concern here, but a brief discussion of some of the criteria is useful. Leaving aside such trivial bases as when a characteristic is simply not possessed by the goods under discussion, we can rule out some characteristics as *redundant* or *invariant* in the technical sense.

A characteristic is invariant over a situation if it is possessed to the

7.   Lancaster [4], (1),pp. 152-53.
8.   Automobiles represent a group of differentiated products with a large number of observable characteristics which have been measured by various testing organisations and which can also be assumed to be known to consumers. Unfortunately, an automobile is a 'one-shot' capital purchase, to which the simple budget constraint is not applicable in defining the choice situation.

same degree by all goods being considered. For a situation involving only choice between automobiles, the flying ability of cars is the same (zero) and thus not a relevant characteristic for choice. But if the choice situation involved both planes and cars, flying ability would be a relevant criterion — and it may one day be so between cars. On the other hand, 'startability', which once used to be a relevant criterion in the market for new cars, is no longer so, because it is possessed to the same degree (maximal[9]) by all. Thus technological change may alter the set of technically relevant characteristics.

We have technical redundance when a group of characteristics is related to each other in some fixed technical way. In such a group it may be, for example, that all goods have the same shape and same density so there is a mathematically fixed relationship between length, width and height, and between any of these and volume or weight. Thus 'size' can be represented by a single parameter which acts as a proxy for all other size parameters,[10] the other 'characteristics' of size being redundant. More complex cases arise, as when the 'performance' of equipment may be expressed in a very large number of characteristics, all but one subset of which may be redundant, although difficult to choose.

In operational applications of the model, we can usually try to reduce the number of characteristics as much as possible by extending the above idea to 'almost redundant' characteristics and to use broad 'proxy characteristics' which stand for many characteristics bearing *approximately* fixed relationship to each other.

CHARACTERISTICS AND PEOPLE

As pointed out above, characteristics may be relevant or irrelevant because of their relationships to goods, or their relationships to people. It is this latter set of relationships which now concerns us.

9.   We might also interpret this as a satiation effect, discussed later. The interpretation as technical invariance is simpler.
10.   If we are concerned with the simple linear model, the chosen parameter must be one having the requisite linear property. For a diet choice, the appropriate parameter would be weight or volume, since nutrients will vary linearly with these. In this case, we would probably aggregate almost identical foods by weight and use a weight unit of measure. That is, instead of regarding 2″ and 3″ diameter apples as different goods, we would presumably just consider pounds of apples.

In the earlier marginalists, goods were considered to be related to people because they satisfied 'wants'. I do not wish to enter into a discussion of what these writers really meant by 'wants'. It is sufficient that they were considered entirely human properties that were, in some way, matched with or 'satisfied' by certain goods, and that preferences depended on the relationship between wants and the properties of goods.

It was not supposed by these writers that there was a one-to-one correspondence between wants and goods. On the contrary, it was generally assumed that a particular good could satisfy a large number of wants, which were arranged in a hierarchy so that the first quantity of the goods satisfied the most urgent want, the next quantity the next most urgent, and so on. Thus Menger[11] describes the isolated farmer allocating corn first for his own, then his family's basic survival, then for above survival food, then for seed, then for beer (!), then for fattening livestock, and so on.

Characteristics, in our model, are observable properties of goods, but their relevance to *people* lies in their ability to generate some response (perhaps negative) in consumers. In this sense, we could refer to a characteristic as 'satisfying wants', in some fashion. Because of its conceptual redundance we shall avoid this way of stating the relationship, but there is an undoubted similarity to what the earlier writers had in mind. Since a characteristic is only a single property of a good, which may possess many, there is a closer matching of single characteristics with single psychological aims than there is of single goods.

A prominent feature of the 'wants' approach, which we wish to take up, is that of a *hierarchy*. One of Menger's examples has already been given and there are many others. Georgescu-Roegen[12] points to examples in Plato, Jevons, Wieser, Walras, Marshall, Pareto and Knight. At the behavioural level there are hierarchical implications in Engel's Law and other well-established relationships between income and the expenditure on a particular class of goods. Recently, Paroush[13] has found consistency in the order in which consumers acquire durables,

---

11.   Menger [5], p. 129. Note that these and similar hypotheses by other writers are eminently testable!
12.   See Georgescu-Roegen [2], p. 194.
13.   See Paroush [7].

again with hierarchical implications.

Hierarchy in goods does not necessarily represe
hierarchy of wants, since technical relationships may
especially in the case of durable goods. A person ma
driving, yet may buy a car before a boat because,
cannot transport the boat to water, but, without a boa
his car. Characteristics, like goods, may be subje
complementarities that give hierarchical properti
psychological implications. We can also have a hiera
teristics (for pyschological reasons) without any goods h
manifest, because the characteristics in question are not cc
easily identifiable group of goods.

Closely associated with the idea of a hierarchy of wants is sc
of *satiation* effect. In the original arguments of Menger and
writers in the same vein, the hierarchy was relevant becaus
consumer satisfied his wants in order of importance. Obviously, u
the most important want was satiable, the next most important wo
be irrelevant. Jevons, for example, wrote[14]
'the satisfaction of a lower want ... merely permits the higher want
to manifest itself'.[15]

In contemporary economic analysis, satiation appears only negatively
as the *nonsatiation* postulate built into formal versions of the traditional theory.[16] Nonsatiation is a convenient, rather than essential,
assumption in formal traditional theory.[17] It is an easy assumption to
live with in traditional consumer theory which is, in spirit, orientated to
the description of consumer behaviour with respect to 'goods' conceived in rather broad terms. A typical good would be an aggregate —
automobiles, rather than 1969 Plymouths — and Hicks, appropriately,
devoted considerable effort to his proof of the composite commodity

14.   Jevons [3], p. 54.
15.   The implied Victorian moral judgement, that wants satisfied at higher
income levels after more basic needs have been met are 'higher', is not essential to
the argument.
16.   See, for example, Debreu [1], p. 55. Nonsatiation in this context means
the consumer always prefers more of at least one of the goods.
17.   It is built in to the formal proofs of existence of equilibrium, but can be
relaxed to require only that there be no satiation in an attainable state of the
economy. See Lancaster [4], (1), pp. 155-56.

in *Value and Capital*.

:aditional consumer theory can be regarded as an adequate *coarse-*
cture theory, concerned primarily with the analysis of consumer
aviour with respect to broadly conceived goods such as 'food',
othing'. It is concerned with what I have elsewhere[18] described as
acro-microeconomics.

The characteristics model, on the other hand, is particularly adapted
to *fine-structure* theory, such as the choice between differentiated
products within a group. Inevitably, in moving from a broader
coarse-structure model to a more detailed fine-structure analysis, we
may expect to lose some smoothness and continuity. Thus we need to
pay more attention to such phenomena as satiation.

SATIATION

A satiation relationship between a consumer and a characteristic
implies that the consumer has no positive interest in further quantities
of the characteristic. This may mean either of two things, leading to a
classification of satiation into two types. The consumer may have had

(1) zero interest in further quantities of the characteristic

(2) a *negative* interest in further quantities.

We can illustrate the two types from a diet example. Consider a
sophisticated consumer whose choice is restricted to choice of food
only, who considers (among other things) the nutritive content of his
food, and who needs (and knows he needs) a daily intake of 2500
calories and 5000 units of vitamin A. Thus, among the various
characteristics of his food, he seeks to attain these particular levels of
the nutrients.

Once he has obtained 5000 units of vitamin A, he has no further
interest in this characteristic. Assuming that amounts of vitamin A
above 5000 units have no effects, good or bad, we can assume the
consumer has zero interest in further quantities. We shall refer to this
type of satiation, where the consumer simply ceases to note the
characteristic once the minimum level has been attained, as *open
satiation*.

18.   See Lancaster [4], (4).

But once the consumer has attained 2500 calories, he may well be anxious to avoid gaining weight and so may have a negative interest in further calories. This does not imply that he will not, under any circumstances, consume further calories, merely that he will only do so if the excess food contains other characteristics (flavour, for example) in which he retains a positive interest. We shall refer to this type of satiation, in which a characteristic changes from being desirable to being undesirable, as *closed satiation.*

More formally, for a consumer's world of two characteristics[19] z_1 and z_2, the consumer reaches

(1) *open satiation* at level z_2 for characteristic z_2 if, for any characteristics collections Z, Z' such that

$$z_1 = z_1'$$
$$z_2, z_2' \geq \bar{z}_2$$

we have $Z I Z'$, whatever the relationship of z_2, z_2'.

(2) *closed satiation* at level $\bar{z}_2$ for characteristic z_2 if,

(a) for any collections Z, Z' such that

$$z_1 = z_1'$$
$$z_2 > z_2' \geqslant \bar{z}_2$$

we have $Z' P Z$, and

(b) for any collections Z, Z' such that

$$z_1 = z_1'$$
$$z_2 \geqslant z_2' \geqslant \bar{z}_2$$

we have $Z' \bar{R} Z$ (that is, Z' preferred or indifferent to Z).[20]

Representative indifference maps illustrating the two types of satiation for the two-characteristic model are shown in figure 2. In the open satiation case (figure 2a), the indifference curves are vertical above the line $z_2 = \bar{z}_2$, while in the closed satiation case (figure 2b), they have a positive slope in this region.

19.   Easily extended to any number of characteristics.
20.   Use of the weak relationship $Z' R Z$, rather than the strong relationship $Z' P Z'$, provides for the possibility of a change from open satiation to closed satiation at z_2. If we had $z_1 = z_1'$ and $z_2' > \bar{z}_2 > z_2$, the preference ordering could not be predicated, of course, without an exact preference map.

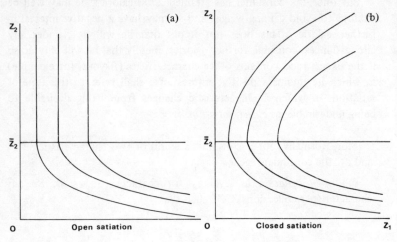

Figure 2

In some instances (including the calorie example already given) it may be more realistic to assume that open satiation is reached at one level, then closed satiation at a higher level. The consumer may, for example, decide he has approximately enough calories at 2000 and lose interest in them so long as he does not exceed 3000, at which level his negative reaction starts. This gives a region of open satiation or *neutral zone* with respect to the characteristic, as illustrated in figure 3.

Satiation is generally assumed to be open satiation in the economics literature. Stigler's diet problem[21] (a precursor of the characteristics approach as well as of linear programming) assumed open satiation, permitting a linear programming solution for minimum cost subject to *minimum* nutrient content, without worrying about excess nutrients.

The 'want satiation' of the early marginalists was, of course, *open* satiation. Any characteristic of a good concerned only with supplying a more urgent want was assumed to have zero effect on the satisfaction of less urgent wants.

Satiation with respect to a characteristic may or may not appear as a

21.   See Stigler [8].

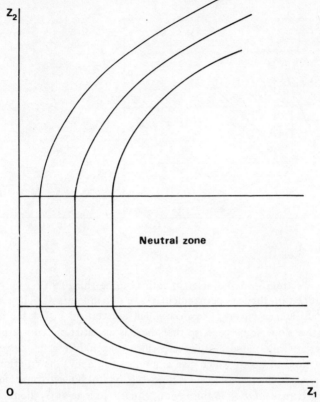

Figure 3

satiation effect with respect to a good. To investigate the relationship, consider the simple case of a two-characteristic model, in which one characteristic is subject to either open or closed satiation with respect to the consumer(s) in question. The other characteristic is assumed to be nonsatiable. We shall consider a world of two goods, both of which possess both characteristics.

Figure 4 shows an illustration of the open satiation case. Figure 4a is drawn in C-space, with characteristics z_1 and z_2 measured along the axes. Characteristic z_2 is subject to open satiation at level $\bar{z}_2$. Rays OG_1, OG_2 represent the proportions in which the two characteristics are contained in goods G_1, G_2.

55

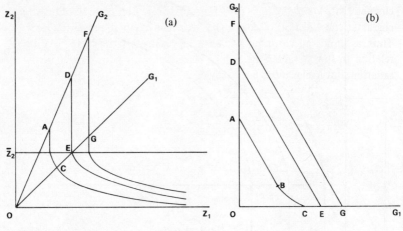

Figure 4

If we transform the diagram into G-space (hinging OG_1 and OG_2 about O until they are perpendicular), we obtain figure 4b. The sections of indifference curves (like FG) which are vertical in C-space have a negative slope in G-space, so that there is no satiation with respect to either of the goods. However, since the indifference curves for collections of goods which give amounts of z_2 above the satiation level are straight lines, choice subject to the typical budget constraint will give a *corner solution* in this region, either G_1 alone or G_2 alone, unless the budget line has exactly the same slope as FG.

In the satiation region, we could predict which of the goods G_1 or G_2 would be chosen *without reference to* z_2. In the G-space diagram, point F (G_2 only) would be chosen if the budget line passed through F and some point on the G_1 axis to the left of G, such as E. Reference back to figure 4a shows that F has more z_1 than does E. Similarly, if the budget line sloped from D to G in figure 4b, the consumer would choose point G, containing more z_1 than point D. Thus a characteristic becomes *irrelevant* in the region of open satiation with respect to it. In the example, all consumer behaviour in the region *beyond DE* in figure 4b could be predicted from a knowledge of the content of z_1 in each of the goods and the relative prices.

Open satiation, therefore, does not necessarily lead to any satiation

56

effects (even open satiation) on goods,[22] but it does make a characteristic *operationally irrelevant* in the region of satiation. The characteristic will not, of course, be irrelevant below the satiation level. Thus, assuming all consumers to have approximately the same satiation relation to the characteristic, it may be relevant in a poor society below satiation, but irrelevant in a rich society.

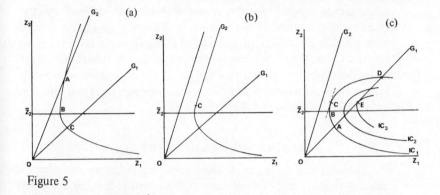

Figure 5

If there is closed satiation with respect to z_2, the situation with respect to goods is quite complex. Representative indifference curves showing three cases are given in figure 5. In figure 5a, the indifference curve slopes positively above satiation, but with a slope steeper than that of OG_2 inside the attainable cone (defined by OG_2 and OG_1). Transformed into G-space, the portion AB of the indifference curve will have a negative slope, even though the slope is positive in C-space. There will be no satiation effect with respect to goods.

In figure 5b, the indifference curve is shown straight and parallel to OG_2 from the point A. Transformed into G-space, this portion of the indifference curve will be vertical, giving *open satiation* on G_2, but no satiation effects on G_1.

In figure 5c, the indifference curves slope over enough to cut OG_1. Assuming both goods to have positive prices, any point to the northeast

22.   Open satiation may occur, however, if a good contains no characteristic other than the one which is satiable. In such a case, the vertical portion of the indifference curve in C-space is also vertical in G-space.

of C along IC_1 would be an inefficient choice, since a preferred position (on IC_2) could be obtained with less of both goods. C is the point on IC_1 at which the slope is the same as that of OG_2. In this case, there is a most preferred goods collection (corresponding to the point E) giving satiation of *both* goods in the sense that with no budget constraint of any kind, the consumer would choose only G_1 and that only up to the amount corresponding to the point E. With no budget constraint, the consumer is subject to the *technical* constraint defined by the characteristics content of the two goods. If a new good was introduced with a higher proportion of z_1 to z_2 than G_1 (giving a ray OG_3 lying below OG_1 in figure 5c), the consumer's attainable characteristics set would be expanded. Thus a new variant of a class of goods may result in expanded consumption of those goods, although there was satiation with respect to existing goods of that class.

DOMINANCE AND HIERARCHY

The simplest notion of a hierarchical kind that we can apply to characteristics is that of *dominance*. A characteristic is dominant within some group of characteristics, in some set of situations, if the consumer always prefers a collection with more of the dominant characteristic, whatever the amounts of the other characteristic.

Let us return to our diet example. For a starving man, all other characteristics of food may be dominated by calorie content, interest in other nutrients being subordinated to the need to obtain sufficient calories for survival in the short run. An alcoholic may rank wines by their alcohol content alone, irrespective of any other characteristics.

The alcoholic example is often used to illustrate lexicographical ordering.[23] Dominance is a weaker assumption than lexicographical ordering, requiring, in effect, only that all words beginning with A come before all words beginning with B and not worrying about the ordering of words within the A-group. Operationally, dominance is observable, lexicographic ordering only so in rare instances.

Dominance, as in the diet example, may occur only over some region of choice. Consider the nutrition model, for we can illustrate

23. See, for example, Newman, [6] pp. 23-25.

many effects in it. Suppose that food has only two characteristics, calories and flavour.[24] A consumer is assumed to be given all non-food items in fixed quantities so that his choice context is confined to food.

We shall assume the following to be true of the characteristics-consumer relationship in this case:

(1)   at very low calorie levels, calories are dominant

(2)   at medium calorie levels, flavour is relevant

(3)   there is a neutral zone with respect to calories — open satiation at one level, followed by closed satiation at a higher level

(4)   flavour is nonsatiable.

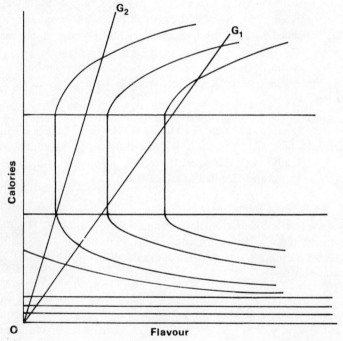

Figure 6

24.   Flavour is not easily measurable (although, in principle, it might be analysed into components and measured) and would not be suitable in a working model. We assume, for the sake of a simple two-characteristic example, that it has the desirable properties of a linear, measurable characteristic.

An indifference map expressing the above properties would look like that in figure 6. The lowest indifference curves would be horizontal (calories dominant), while higher ones would have a vertical segment (open satiation in the neutral zone) turning into a positive sloped segment (closed satiation).

If there were only two goods, G_2 having the higher ratio of calories to flavour, and the consumer faced a regular linear budget constraint, his choice would be determined in the following way:

(i) at very low income levels, he would be interested only in obtaining the most calories for his money. This would be determined from the calorie content of the two goods and their relative prices. Note that he would *not* necessarily consume G_2, with the highest calorie/flavour ratio. He would consume the more flavoursome G_1 if that happened to have the highest calorie/outlay ratio at the market prices.[25]

(ii) in the next income bracket, calories and flavour both count, and the content of both characteristics in both goods needs to be known.

(iii) the next income bracket covers the neutral zone, with calories subject to open satiation. In effect, flavour is a dominant characteristic[26] here and choice will be decided by the flavour/outlay ratio.

(iv) finally, both characteristics count once more at high income levels, with calories regarded negatively.

Thus, in a single simple example, we see how the set of operationally relevant characteristics is reduced from two to one (a different one each time) at different income levels, while both characteristics are relevant (although one is first desirable then undesirable) at other income levels.

CONCLUSION

This essay has given a brief glimpse of the kind of ways in which

25.   If the calorie/outlay ratio happened to be the same for both goods, he would presumably choose G_1 for more flavour. Thus we would establish lexicographic ordering. We shall, however, work with the simpler notion of dominance that suffices for all but this case.

26.   This is, of course, because there are only two characteristics. With n characteristics. open satiation of one of them does not lead to dominance because there are still $n-1$ characteristics, rather than just one, that must be considered.

the very large number of potentially relevant characteristics in some situation involving consumer choice can be reduced to a much smaller number of *operationally relevant* characteristics. Part of the reduction can be made by considering *technical* (goods-characteristics) relationships, such as invariance and redundancy. Further reduction is possible by using *human* (goods-people) relationships, such as dominance and satiation.

As far as technical relationships are concerned, the relevant set may change with the introduction of a new good, but does not depend on the group of consumers involved. Human criteria do, of course, depend on the consumer group. Thus the calorie content of food may be the dominant characteristic in a starving African society and, negatively, in a wealthy American society, while being irrelevant in a moderate-income European society.

The simple outline of ideas given here can be expanded very greatly. The idea of dominance can be extended to cover a *group* of characteristics which are the only relevant characteristics at low income levels. We could investigate social lag phenomena which occur as consumers move out of a region in which dominance by a group of 'basic' characteristics ceases, but when awareness of other characteristics is not yet developed.

Like any economic model, however, the characteristics model of consumer behaviour is designed to simplify reality. Fitting it to any given situation ultimately involves some art as well as science. The aim of the essay has been to provide some guide to the artist, as well as analysis for the scientist.

REFERENCES

1 Debreu, Gerard *Theory of Value: An Axiomatic Analysis of Economic Equilibrium,* 1959, Cowles Monograph 17
2 Georgescu-Roegen, N. *Analytical Economics, Issues and Problems,* 1966
3 Jevons, W.S. *The Theory of Political Economy,* 4th edn., 1924
4 Lancaster, Kelvin (1) 'A New Approach to Consumer Theory', *Journal of Political Economy,* 74, 132-57, 1966
      (2) 'Change and Innovation in the Technology of of Consumption', *American Economic Review, (Papers and Proceedings),* 14-23, May 1966
      (3) *Mathematical Economics,* 1968
      (4) *Introduction to Modern Microeconomics,* 1969.

5 Menger, Karl *Principles of Economics,* Eng. trans., 1950
6 Newman, P.K. *The Theory of Exchange,* 1965
7 Paroush, J. 'The Order of Acquisition of Consumer Durables', *Econometrica,* 33, 225-35, 1965
8 Stigler, G.J. 'The Cost of Subsistence', *Journal of Farm Economics,* 27, 1945.

Some Comments on the Theory of Monopoly [1]

Lucien Foldes

The familiar pair of equations (of perfect competition) is deduced by the present writer from the first principle: equilibrium is attained when the existing contracts can neither be varied without recontract with the consent of the existing parties, nor by recontract within the field of competition. The advantage of this general method is that it is applicable to the particular cases of imperfect competition, where the conceptions of *demand and supply at a price* are no longer appropriate.

.... the influence of monopoly is well traced by Cournot in a discussion masterly, but limited by a particular condition, which may be called *uniformity of price not (it is submitted) abstractedly necessary in cases of imperfect competition.* Going beyond Cournot, not without trembling, the present inquiry finds that, where the field of competition is sensibly imperfect, an indefinite number of final settlements are possible .... and in the absence of imposed conditions, the said final settlements are not *in the demand-curve,* but on the contract curve. (Edgeworth, F.Y., *Mathematical Psychics,* pp. 31 and 47-48.)

I

According to the main proposition of the theory of monopoly, a seller who cannot discriminate fixes a price which equates marginal revenue with marginal cost, and meets the demand at that price. Since the price exceeds marginal cost, there is (subject to certain conditions) a loss of welfare, which in the absence of entry can be corrected only by public intervention. The theory of discriminating monopoly, apart from the limiting case of perfect discrimination, is similar though more complicated: the equation of marginal revenue and cost must be applied to determine simultaneously the prices in each of several 'horizontal' or 'vertical' sub-markets.[2]

The present paper reconsiders this theory, paying attention in particular to two questions: (i) whether and in what circumstances the Cournot solution for simple monopoly is an equilibrium and whether it is the only equilibrium; (ii) whether even in the absence of entry there

1.   I am indebted, as always, to Kurt Klappholz for valuable discussions and unfailing encouragement. I am also indebted for their helpful comments to Miss C.R. Hewlett and Professors F. Hahn, J.D. Sargan and B.S. Yamey.

may not be market forces which 'automatically' eliminate or limit losses of welfare due to simple monopoly.

The traditional analysis does not deal adequately with these questions, largely because the treatment of monopoly has been dominated by the concepts and methods of competitive theory. This problem of method, which affects the theory of value as a whole, is considered briefly in the next Section. The discussion then turns to a critical review of basic definitions and assumptions in the theory of simple monopoly, pointing out various inadequacies in the usual treatment (Section III). Various mechanisms are then examined by which market forces may alter the situation of simple monopoly, and so perhaps realise additional gains from trade (Section IV). The essay concludes with some general remarks on the analysis of monopoly and the approach to problems of policy.

II

As the quotations at the head of this paper show Edgeworth pointed long ago to some of the main shortcomings of what may be called the classical procedure in the theory of value. The main feature of this procedure is its primary emphasis on the resolution of conflicting interests within a given framework of perfect competition, and on the correspondence between competitive equilibrium and optimality.

Other market forms are classified according to their relationship with the competitive model, and the methods and formulations of

2.   By horizontal discrimination is meant the usual system, called by Pigou discrimination of third degree, in which different prices are charged to each of several groups of customers. Vertical or second degree discrimination operates 'in such wise that all units with a demand price greater than x were sold at a price x, all with a demand price less than x and greater than y at a price y, and so on' (*Economics of Welfare*, p.279). This system has been studied mainly by German writers, whose contributions appear largely to have escaped notice in the English literature. The main paper is Stackelberg H.V., 'Preisdiskrimination bei willkürlicher Teilung des Marktes' *Archiv für mathematische Wirtschafts- und Sozialforschung*, Vol. 5, 1939. More recent contributions, which discuss the convergence of second degree to first degree or perfect discrimination as the number of vertical 'slices' tends to infinity, include Gutenberg E., *Grundlagen der Betriebswirtschaftslehre*, Vol. 2, p.280, 1955, and Ott A.E., 'Zum Problem der Preisdifferenzierung', *Schweizerische Zeitschrift für Volkswirtschaft und Statistik*, 1959. These models suffer from the fundamental limitation that they apply strictly only where each buyer takes no more than one unit.

competitive theory applied to them as far as possible. Whatever the objections to this approach, it must be admitted at the outset that there is for many purposes no practicable alternative, particularly in problems of general equilibrium. The fascinating possibility, suggested by Cournot and Edgeworth, of a general theory of markets in which perfect competition and monopoly appear as limiting cases is still far from realisation, despite recent work on games and the core of an economy.[3] Nevertheless Edgeworth's approach to contract and bargaining provides an important complement to classical methods, notably at the level of partial equilibrium. In an extended form it has recently been applied to the theory of social costs[4] and even to the economic analysis of political action.[5] But apart from bilateral monopoly and oligopoly, it has had relatively little influence on the theory of imperfect competition, and on occasion it has even been taken for granted that this approach is not applicable to ordinary monopoly.[6] This limitation is unjustified, as will be argued below.

Edgeworth's approach, in its modern version, can be summed up in three main rules of method, which are briefly discussed in the remainder of this Section; they are not distinct principles, but are rather to be regarded as increasingly general applications of the same point of view.

First, the central problem in the analysis of a given market form is not to be formulated initially as the determination of equilibrium price, but as the determination of the equilibrium patterns of contract. Apart from perfect competition, the assumption that a contract establishes a single price applying to alternative quantities generally needs special justification. This principle has gradually found acceptance in the theory of bilateral monopoly, though some writers assumed until quite recently that one party to the bargain would name a price and leave the other to select a quantity, even though this would normally lead to an

---

3.   See in particular Scarf H.E., 'The Core of an N Person Game', *Econometrica* Jan. 1967.
4.   See, for example, Coase R.H., 'The Problem of Social Cost', *Journal of Land Economics* 1960, and Buchanan J.M., and Stubblebine W.C., 'Externality', *Economica* 1962. A discussion of some limitations of this analysis is given by S. Wellisz, 'On External Economies and the Government-Assisted Invisible Hand', *Economica* 1964.
5.   Buchanan J.M., and Tullock G., *The Calculus of Consent*.
6.   See, for example, Wellisz, *op.cit.*, 'On External Economies . . . . ,p. 349.

inefficient contract.[7] In unilateral monopoly, the seller's problem is still generally formulated *a priori* as one of determining the price to be charged − or, if discrimination is possible, the prices in various sub-markets, or the prices at which successive units are to be sold. A more appropriate general formulation would be to consider the tariff, or schedule of alternative bargains, to be offered to each category of buyers. As will be shown below, the assumption that a 'straight' price is charged is not entirely satisfactory even in the traditional model of simple monopoly.[8]

Secondly, market forms, and perhaps some other institutions, should where possible not be postulated definitely in advance, but are to be regarded as responsive to the interests of individuals; the application of this principle is evidently a matter of degree, since some institutions must be assumed if others are to be explained. Now, it has always been realised that market forms are responsive to economic pressures. In particular, many authors have emphasised the tendency for traders to create monopolies, and some − notably Schumpeter and J.K. Galbraith − have stressed the incentives to counteract certain monopolistic influences. But this line of thought has not been thoroughly integrated with the formal micro-economic theory of markets. The analysis of imperfect competition and discriminating monopoly has tended, under the influence of the classical procedure, to be primarily a taxonomy of deviant species, in which emphasis is laid on the functioning and incidence of each variant rather than on the conditions for its emergence and survival.[9] The present paper does not deal with the emergence of monopoly, but the question whether simple monopoly creates incentives for its own destruction is considered in Section V below.

The third and most general principle is that the tendency of a system of free enterprise to realise gains from trade and thus perhaps to attain optimality, should be analysed in as general a framework as possible,

7.   For surveys, see Machlup F., and Taber M., 'Bilateral Monopoly, Successive Monopoly, and Vertical Integration', *Economica* 1960, and Schneider E., *Einführung in die Wirtschaftstheorie* Part II, 5th ed., 1958.
8.   A general mathematical treatment of certain monopoly tariffs will appear in a further publication.
9.   An extreme example of this tendency is Triffin R., *Monopolistic Competition and General Equilibrium Theory*.

not merely in the case of perfect competition. Indeed, perfect competition itself can be expected to survive only when those gains from trade which can be realised at all can be realised by a market system in which communication among traders relates only to prices.

This statement of the principle is not intended to be precise, and a detailed discussion of its content and scope would be out of place here: but a few remarks are necessary if misunderstanding is to be avoided. Emphasis on the possibility of optimal allocation even without competition is associated in recent writing with the political standpoint of extreme liberalism. This connection is not inevitable, and the principle as stated here represents only a methodological commitment; no factual or moral opinion is implied, apart from the general judgement of relevance without which no method of analysis can be adopted. In particular, it is not argued here that a system of private enterprise tends invariably to eliminate misallocations due to monopoly or other causes, or that its ability to deal with them may not be improved by intervention, or that some activities may not be more efficiently conducted in the public sector.

The confusion between questions of method and of substance is connected with careless interpretation in informal discussion of the usual concepts of equilibrium and optimality; a short review of alternative definitions will clarify this point. An equilibrium is defined as a state such that no individual, or group of individuals acting in agreement, could be made better off by changing his or their own action; an optimum is a state such that no individual could be made better off without another being made worse off. The relation between these states – in particular the question whether an equilibrium of a system of private enterprise is necessarily an optimum – depends entirely on the considerations taken into account in each case in defining what 'could' be done, and on the set of actors considered. In particular, three possibilities may be noted. (i) If exactly the same actors and the same actions are considered in the definitions of both equilibrium and optimality, the proposition that an equilibrium is an optimum is logically true whatever the market form; though the converse may still be false, for example, where an optimal situation leaves scope for a person to extort payments from others by threatening actions which would not directly benefit himself but would damage them. (ii) If optimality is defined as 'Pareto' or 'first best' optimality (in the usual sense which takes into account only the constraints represented by the production and consumption sets), while the definition of equilibrium takes into account all practical constraints and all actions available in practice to all parties except government, then the proposition that an equilibrium is necessarily optimal can be false empirically. Gains from trade measured relative to Pareto optimality are necessarily realised in full only if there are no costs of information, bargaining or administration, and if negotiations never end in deadlock until all possibilities of mutual benefit are exhausted. (iii) Finally, if both definitions are framed with reference to the same practical possibilities, except that certain actions of government are taken into account in defining optimality but not in defining equilibrium, it is again clear that an equilibrium need not be optimal. Government may be able to alter institutions so as to reduce the costs of information etc. or diminish the chances of deadlock in negotiations, or may provide generally beneficial public goods, or even improve the efficiency of a monopoly by nationalisation – quite apart from intervention on distributive grounds.

It is important to distinguish carefully among these definitions in informal discussion, if false impressions are to be avoided. Consider, for example, the following passage by Buchanan and Tullock:[10]

'We shall argue that, if the costs of organising decisions voluntarily should be zero, *all* externalities would be eliminated by voluntary private behaviour of individuals regardless of the initial structure of property rights.'

When read carefully in its context, this appears to be merely a version of definition (i), and as such is not a proposition from which practical conclusions can be drawn; but as it stands it could be misleading.

The preceding remarks are concerned primarily with definitions; but they suggest that the method under discussion can take into account a wide range of considerations relevant to issues of policy, and do not lead inevitably to tendentious formulations. Indeed, a systematic development of this method would do much to make theory more relevant to the problems of monopoly policy. Action by government tends at present to be narrowly pragmatic, fostering one monopoly and condemning another in a way which owes little to theory. One reason

10.   *The Calculus of Consent*, p. 47.

for this attitude is a suspicion of facile arguments for regulation based on comparisons of the Cournot solution or one of its generalisations with marginal cost pricing. More useful guidance can be given even by static theory if account is taken of the methods by which private enterprise can deal with inefficiencies in the absence of competition, of the help which public intervention can give in this process, and of the costs of communication, administration and bargaining which these processes involve.

III

Unilateral monopoly is defined by two conditions:

a) a single seller confronts numerous buyers acting independently and each taking a negligible proportion of output;[11]

b) buyers have no bargaining power.

The second condition is not easy to define precisely in general terms, but for present purposes it is enough to specify that a buyer may only accept one or other of the alternative options offered by the seller or refuse to deal, knowing that a refusal will not elicit further offers, and that the seller knows that this is the situation and knows that the buyer knows it.

Simple monopoly is unilateral monopoly in which two further conditions hold:

c) the seller quotes a 'straight' price common to all buyers, leaving them to choose the quantities which they will take at that price;

d) resale of goods among buyers is unrestrained and costless, and takes place in a perfectly competitive market.

For most purposes, it may be assumed as an alternative to (d) that direct buyers are intermediaries who resell in a common, perfectly competitive market; but for simplicity the case where goods are sold direct to final users is usually considered. Interdependence with markets in other goods is also ignored.

---

11.   To be rigorous, it should be assumed that the buyers form a set indexed by a continuum - say, the interval $[0,n]$. For a given set R of tariffs proposed to buyers by the monopolist, let $F(i,R)$ be the total purchases by buyers with indices $I \leqslant i$; the assumption that each buyer makes negligible purchases then means that F is absolutely continuous in i for given R.

Some Comments on the Theory of Monopoly

Even these elementary conditions call for some critical comment. It is usually taken that (b) is a consequence of (a), but in general this appears to be incorrect. First, it may be that each buyer spends only a negligible part of his income on the monopolised good, and therefore derives only a negligible part of his welfare from it.[12] Even assuming that this is not the case, (a) implies only that the monopolist derives a negligible *proportion* of his profit from each buyer, but in general this sum is of the same *absolute* order of magnitude as the consumer's surplus, and there is no reason in general to assume that bargaining power is related to the proportional gains from trade. In particular, even if assumption (d) applies and a straight price is normally quoted, one buyer among many might still try to bargain with the monopolist for discounts on intramarginal units of purchase, and might even obtain a special concession if he could convince the monopolist that he would not otherwise buy.

It is also generally assumed that condition (c) follows from (a), (b) and (d), at least if the monopolist has perfect knowledge of all costs and demands. In other words, a unilateral monopolist who is unable to restrict resale etc. cannot do better than charge a straight price — which is then fixed to equate marginal revenue and cost, so that the Cournot solution is the only possible equilibrium. This also is subject to certain exceptions, when account is taken of the possibility that the monopolist may deliberately create uncertainty about prices and quantities (in a world which is otherwise free from uncertainty and strategic considerations). Specifically, suppose that the monopolist maximises expected profit, while customers maximise expected utility and are risk averters; then the monopolist may be able to devise various schemes which raise his expected profit above the Cournot level. For example, he might conduct his dealings in two stages. At the first stage, each customer may take a consignment of fixed size in return for a lump-sum payment; at the second stage, a price is chosen at random from a suitable distribution, and the monopolist buys or sells in the free (resale) market until the chosen price prevails. It is possible to construct cases where the terms of sale at the first stage and the probability

12. More precisely, the buyer may choose from a continuum of goods, and the distribution function of expenditure may be absolutely continuous at the point corresponding to the monopolised good. Incidentally, this assumption does not exclude the possibility of a positive density of net benefit or consumers' surplus at that point.

70

distribution at the second can be so chosen that the expected profit exceeds the Cournot level. The essence of the procedure is that the monopolist takes advantage of the customers' risk aversion. Of course, the scope for practical application of such schemes is very limited — they work best when goods are produced instantaneously without cost and cannot be stored by customers, and even then the additional profit is unlikely to be large. Nevertheless, they illustrate some typical subtleties of monopoly charging.

Because of these difficulties, it is necessary for the usual theory of simple monopoly either to assume (b) and (c) directly, or to introduce some considerations of law, convention, administration or communication from which these conditions can be inferred when (a) and (d) hold. Of course, if (c) is postulated directly, the usual results can be obtained without (d); but the assumption that a price rather than a tariff is quoted can hardly be maintained in general without (d) or some equivalent condition.

IV

Attempts to realise gains from trade by modifying the simple monopoly solution can operate through various mechanisms. Three possibilities are briefly discussed here, namely:

(i) the replacement of straight pricing by two-part tariffs combined with the limitation of resale;

(ii) the formation of unions of customers to bargain about terms of sale;

(iii) vertical integration, in particular the acquisition of shareholdings in the monopoly by groups of buyers.

The discussion which follows applies with suitable changes to monopsony. Of course, in markets for personal services the mechanism of resale cannot operate in the manner usually assumed for goods markets; but its place in the analysis can often be taken by such devices as the replacement of direct labour by purchase or sub-contracting.

(i) *Two-part tariffs and limitation of resale*
The first device to be considered leaves the unilateral character of

the market in being — at least initially — but modifies conditions (c) and (d) of Section III. The change is connected with the assumption, which is basic to the theory of simple monopoly as usually stated, that people do not necessarily honour their contracts, or alternatively that enforcement of contracts is costly. This assumption, although sometimes realistic, has no essential connection with monopoly as such and is not made in competitive theory. If it is altered to conform with the competitive case, and appropriate changes are consequently made in conditions (c) and (d), Cournot's solution for simple monopoly in a world of certainty leaves scope for mutually profitable recontract and therefore is not an equilibrium in Edgeworth's sense.

For example, both the monopolist and any one buyer can be made better off by an agreement providing for (i) sale at a (marginal) price equal to marginal cost, (ii) an undertaking by the buyer not to resell, and (iii) a lump-sum payment sufficient to compensate the monopolist for any loss of profit due to the price reduction under (i), but not exceeding the buyer's gain in surplus. If a separate lump-sum can be fixed for each buyer, such contracts for two-part tariffs allow the realisation of an optimum (at the level of partial equilibrium). Of course, if the system of simple monopoly is superseded, and two-part charges are fixed unilaterally for all customers by the monopolist, it is not true to say that everyone will benefit by the change. On the contrary, the monopolist will be able to absorb practically the whole of the consumers' surplus through the fixed charges (at least to the extent that they can be varied among individuals). The buyers will generally be worse off unless they are somehow protected, for example by a law requiring the monopolist to offer, as an alternative to the two-part tariff, a straight price at the Cournot level. But the situation will be both an optimum and an equilibrium, at least so long as the market remains unilateral.[13]

13.   The use of two-part charging, both as a method of maximising profit by perfect discrimination and as a device for reconciling marginal cost pricing with solvency in public utilities with decreasing costs, has been known for some time. Both aspects are discussed in Paine C.L., 'Some Aspects of Discrimination in Public Utilities' *Economica 1937*; see also Lewis, W.A., *Overhead Costs*, Ch. 11, and Coase R.H., 'The Marginal Cost Controversy', *Economica 1946*. Paine realised (op. cit. p. 439) that the introduction of a two-part tariff might make all the monopoly's customers worse off, but wrongly inferred from this that the allocation of resources would then be worse than under simple monopoly. If

Some Comments on the Theory of Monopoly

This argument is evidently subject to reservations. The enforcement of contracts forbidding resale may be costly in practice and perhaps even impossible.[14] The determination of differential lump-sum charges entails costs of information and administration which a simple monopolist could avoid. The attempt to appropriate most of the consumers' surplus might stimulate the formation of unions and convert the situation into one of bilateral monopoly, which according to circumstances might lead either to efficient contract or to deadlock.

Nevertheless it is possible to state a simple but important conclusion, which does not appear to have been noticed: the famous losses of welfare due to simple monopoly cannot exceed the costs of operating a scheme for the control of resale combined with a system of two-part tariffs. This statement assumes that the losses are measured, on the usual partial basis, with reference to a system of marginal cost pricing, and that the market remains unilateral when the two-part tariffs are introduced. (If a bargaining situation emerges the analysis is complicated by the possibility of deadlock before an efficient solution is reached; this point is briefly discussed below). The other mechanisms modifying the simple monopoly solution which are considered below define upper bounds for the loss of welfare in a similar way; the argument will not be repeated.[15]

some uniformity of charging is essential - owing perhaps to administrative or legal constraints, or to ignorance of the circumstances of particular customers - it may be advantageous to use more complicated tariffs, because a uniform fixed charge generally leads to the loss of some customers who would be willing to pay the costs of serving them. This problem is not pursued here.

14.   The difficulties are particularly serious where goods are distributed through independent intermediaries with overlapping market areas, or where they are used as components or materials in goods which compete in final markets. In such cases, all sorts of arrangements for sharing markets, vertical integration and restriction of resale prices might be needed in order to achieve the desired results.

15.   Upper bounds for welfare losses due to monopoly are estimated by Harberger A., 'Monopoly and Resource Allocation', *American Economic Review, Proceedings* 1954, and Schwartzman D., 'The Burden of Monopoly', *Journal of Political Economy* 1960. These studies suggest that the losses in practice are small. The procedure adopted is to apply to supposedly monopolistic industries the relations between welfare losses and rates of profit, or profit margins on output, derived from the theory of simple monopoly. This theory points to an increasing relation; but the use in monopolistic industries of two-part tariffs and other discriminating schemes may diminish welfare losses while increasing profitability. There is therefore no clear-cut connection between the theoretical argument given here and these estimates, except to suggest further reasons why

73

(ii) *Buyers' unions*

The creation of unions to deal with a monopolist may have two main objects: to acquire bargaining power by threats of collective action and thus to redistribute the gains from trade; and to create additional gains from trade by introducing more efficient contracts.[16]

The main obstacle to unions is the problem of indiscriminate benefit. Members have to bear costs of organisation and possibly losses from disruption of trade, which they will do only if some benefits can be reserved to them or losses can be inflicted on outsiders and late entrants. Where union members enjoy special terms of contract, incentives may be created for arbitrage through the resale market, which tends to destroy the union. The monopolist may take advantage of this mechanism deliberately to damage the union; and this threat is the more potent, the greater the privileges which its members enjoy. Finally, unions like other organisations may disintegrate owing to disputes over the division of their gains.[17]

In general, the market form which results from the formation of unions in simple monopoly is a complicated N-person game, which cannot be analysed in detail here. But it is necessary to consider more specifically whether, and in what circumstances, there is scope in the usual model for customers to combine in order to overthrow the Cournot solution. This depends on the assumptions, which usually are not stated very explicitly.

One difficulty occurs in connection with conditions (b) and (c), which exclude bargaining power and non-price contracts. Clearly these assumptions must somehow be modified if the problem under discussion is to have content; but merely to drop them might introduce new possibilities which have nothing to do with unions as such. It has already been mentioned that even a single individual might obtain

the upper bounds estimated for welfare losses probably exceed the true values. I am indeed indebted to Basil Yamey for this point.

16.   Economies from joint negotiation and transport are ignored here. In principle they can be realised without the formation of a bargaining union, although it may be economical to use a single organisation for both purposes.

17.   An interesting hypothesis about organisations in general, which merits further investigation, is that moderate success is best for the long-run survival: marginal enterprises are destroyed by fluctuations of fortune, outstanding ones by internal dissension.

discounts on intra-marginal units if he could convince the monopolist that he would not otherwise be a buyer; and similar discounts might be obtained by a union even if it represented only a negligible proportion of buyers. Unfortunately, there seems in general to be no simple way either to measure bargaining power or to separate the influence of size of purchase from an analysis of market strategy as a whole; and the influence of unions can generally be isolated only by considering the effect on this analysis of a change in the rules of the market game which relate to coalitions.

A second and crucial problem concerns condition (d), which stipulates costless, unrestrained resale in a perfectly competitive market. The assumptions that resale is costless and the market perfect are accepted here as data. But the restraints on dealings may change with the formation of a union – indeed, the essence of a union is the mutual promise to engage in specified dealings only with collective approval. If condition (d) is retained as it stands, the only possible union is one which has the sole right to deal with the monopolist on behalf of its members, but which cannot restrain their dealings in the resale market. Such a union could have no effect on relative bargaining power if intermediaries could buy from the monopolist and supply members at second hand. With comprehensive membership and complete loyalty, a union could threaten to cut off trade and so secure discounts which a single buyer could not obtain; though cohesion could hardly be maintained without some legal or social sanctions.

The usual assumption behind (d) is presumably that unions, if they can exist at all, suffer from the same disability in relation to the resale market as does the monopolist – namely that they either cannot enforce on their members contractual obligations to refrain from certain dealings, or can do so only at prohibitive cost. Such an assumption may in certain cases be acceptable for limited purposes; but in general the balance between the incentives and obstacles to organisation should if possible be analysed as part of the theory, not postulated in advance.

It may well be that the state of simple monopoly is a local, but not a global, equilibrium with respect to the formation of unions. A small union may be unable economically to control the dealings of its members or to obtain for them any exclusive benefits which would repay the costs of organisation, and may therefore not be viable without special support from some extraneous source such as the government. But a large union, once it had come into existence and met the initial costs of organisation, might greatly reduce the cost of controlling the resale market; and it could, if it wished, impede the entry of new firms into the industry. On both counts, it would possess bargaining power; and its control of dealings at second hand would allow the use of contracts, such as two-part tariffs, which realise gains from trade not available under simple monopoly. Moreover, the monopolist might see a balance of advantage in the existence of a union if he thought he could appropriate a part of these gains; thus he might not merely refrain from attempts to destroy it, but even give support by allowing discounts to members or by refusing to supply outsiders. If such support were given even while the union was small, in anticipation of later benefits, the Cournot solution might not even be a local equilibrium. Of course, the move from simple monopoly to bargaining by unions is quite likely to be irreversible; a large union need not collapse if it loses the support of the monopolist and the government, because the initial costs of organisation have already been met, and because for most members it is usually an equilibrium strategy to conform to union policy as long as other members continue to do so.

These remarks envisage a single union bargaining with the monopolist. This is sufficient to allow the occurrence of cases where simple monopoly is not the only equilibrium; but in general the range of possibilities is very wide — including rivalry among unions, combinations between the monopolist and one group of buyers to exploit another group, 'closed shop' arrangements imposed jointly by a union and a monopolist in order to preserve gains from trade dependent on price discrimination, the same arrangement imposed on an unwilling monopolist by a union anxious to maintain its bargaining power, and various devices of inter-industry organisation.

Finally, a word about the limitations of unions as instruments of efficiency and redistribution. Even where a union manages to establish full bilateral monopoly, it must not be assumed too readily that contract is necessarily efficient. Apart from the costs of administration and negotiation, the possibility of obtaining favourable terms from the monopolist depends on threats to disrupt trade, which sometimes have to be carried out. Inefficient arrangements which damage the interests of all parties often survive for long periods because terms for their elimination cannot be agreed. Sometimes they are kept in being because they allow the extent of damage to trade to be varied continuously in changing conditions, so that contracting parties can apply pressure without having to choose between complete disruption and quiescence. It must also not be assumed that a change from simple to bilateral monopoly invariably redistributes welfare in favour of buyers. If the buyers' union takes the form of an indissoluble merger, the limits of contract are widened, and the seller may be able to push the buyers closer to their no-trade indifference curves than under simple monopoly. Even if the buyers can invoke the possibility of dissolving their union in support of a claim for terms at least as favourable as in simple monopoly, they can enforce the claim only by actual dissolution, which may sacrifice their power to bargain for a long time ahead. The hope of future improvement may therefore lead them to accept worse terms in the short run.

(iii) *Shareholding schemes and co-operatives*

The last possibility to be considered is that the Cournot solution would be modified, in the direction of 'ideal' output, if most of the monopoly's shares were held by its customers. It might even be that the customers would be led by self-interest to acquire shares in order to influence policy. Of course, this is only one of several methods of integration and arrangement of property rights which could modify simple monopoly; it is selected for discussion because it is of theoretical interest and has apparently not been analysed.

The possibility that share ownership by customers might eliminate monopolistic 'waste' is suggested by the theory of consumers' co-operatives. It has been argued that the interests of co-operative members, who are both proprietors and consumers, are best secured by a policy of marginal cost pricing, which maximises the sum of producers' and consumers' surpluses.[18] Unfortunately, it can be shown that further conditions are necessary for static equilibrium with marginal cost pricing, and that in general they are satisfied simul-

18. Enke S., 'Consumer Co-operatives and Economic Efficiency', *American Economic Review* March 1945. An analysis which takes account of various possible conflicts of interest among members of a co-operative is given by Yamey B.S., 'The Price Policy of Co-operative Societies', *Economica*, 1950.

taneously only by accident. It is assumed for the purpose of this analysis that members' purchases are influenced only by net prices, i.e. prices after deduction of prospective rebates (usually called 'dividends'). Profits also are computed after payment of these rebates; if the firm's business is neither growing nor declining, they are precisely equal to the sums (usually called 'interest') which are distributed to members in proportion to their shareholdings.

Suppose first that only a straight price can be charged. In general, there will be a conflict of interest among members as to its level whenever shareholdings are not proportional to purchases at the ruling price; and this may lead to the formation of a coalition strong enough to change the price, possibly after some changes in the society's membership. Further, if members can vary their shareholdings independently of purchases, it is a condition of equilibrium that the scale of the firm should be such that the return on shares equals the cost of capital; it should be recalled here that co-operative shares are issued and redeemed on request by the shareholder at nominal values, without capitalisation of anticipated profit. Leaving aside the possibility of induced shifts in the demand curve, this condition cannot in general be satisfied at the point where price equals marginal cost. Even if average costs (including the cost of capital) are increasing at that point, the society is not strictly in equilibrium unless it can limit the inflow of funds; and in general some members – possibly a majority – could be expected to resist such a limitation, in an effort to increase their share of the excess earnings. Presumably this difficulty would not arise if shares *just happened* to be distributed proportionally to purchases at marginal cost price at the time of the proposed limitation; in this sense equilibrium with marginal cost pricing is possible. But it cannot be secured by a rule which *formally ties* shareholding to purchases, since this leads effectively to average cost pricing. If average costs including the cost of capital are decreasing with output, the return on shares is below the cost of capital, and a policy of marginal cost pricing leads to an outflow of funds. In this case, the greatest feasible sum of surpluses is attained with average cost pricing. This is consistent with equilibrium if shareholding is proportional to purchases, and such a distribution can if necessary be maintained by a formal rule.

Suppose now that departures from straight pricing are possible, and consider for simplicity a system of two-part tariffs with a uniform variable charge equal to marginal cost. Then the two conditions of equilibrium stated above can be satisfied if the difference between average and marginal costs can be absorbed by standing charges (or discounts) fixed independently of customers' purchases and share-holdings. The rate of return on shares is then equated with the cost of capital, and a scheme which ties shareholding to purchases can be used to ensure that the condition of proportionality is satisfied. Of course, the two conditions mentioned may not be sufficient for equilibrium, because further problems of strategy among coalitions arise in determining the pattern of fixed charges; this question is not pursued here.

The conditions of the problem are changed in two main respects if the monopoly is a quoted joint-stock company. Voting is by shares not by heads, so that permanent control can be bought and sold. And, once the shares have been issued, their value is adjusted so that the yield equals the cost of capital, provided that this is possible with a positive value; if not, the value is zero.

Suppose again that only a straight price can be charged and that average costs are increasing. If the shares have already been issued and just happen to be distributed in proportion to purchases, a system of marginal cost pricing is an equilibrium in a limited sense : no one of a large number of shareholders acting independently could be made better off by small changes in purchases, shareholding or pricing policy. If costs are decreasing, a system of average cost pricing is an equilibrium in the same sense (if it is assumed that the firm's capital is just sufficient to sustain production at that level; otherwise a lower price might temporarily be maintained). But in neither case is there global equilibrium, because it would pay someone to buy a controlling interest at the low share values corresponding to marginal or average cost pricing, in order to revive profit-maximising simple monopoly.

If control of the resale market allows departures from straight pricing, the analysis is similar to that for a co-operative. The main difference is that a take-over is always possible as long as profits, and therefore share values, are below the level corresponding to unilateral monopoly. (This is not to say that the consumer-shareholders must necessarily maximise profit, since their special organisation may allow a degree of control of the resale market, and therefore a level of profit, not attainable by an ordinary monopolist.) Of course, to the extent that a new owner could control resale, a take-over need not mean a change to simple monopoly or a loss of gains from trade, though it may change the distribution of these gains.

At first sight this discussion suggests that shareholding by customers can do nothing to solve the problem of simple monopoly which could not be done by action in the product market alone. Such a conclusion would be incorrect. It is true that shareholding schemes alone can achieve little when customers are numerous, but they can contribute to the success of other methods. Fear of distributive consequences may lead a monopolist or a union of buyers to destroy schemes which could realise gains from trade not available under simple monopoly; for example, a monopolist might oppose a growing union, and a union might object to the gradual introduction of two-part tariffs. Shareholding by customers reduces the conflict of interests, and so diminishes the incentive to act in this way; and in general makes it less likely that gains from trade will be lost through deadlock in bargaining.

The preceding discussion considers only the conditions for an equilibrium with customer shareholding and marginal or average cost pricing, and does not ask how such a state might be attained. If the number of customers is large, there is in general no incentive for individuals to buy shares in the monopoly, so that this solution is unlikely to be adopted without some special organisation or legislative intervention. It is also clear, without going into details, that full attainment of the equilibrium conditions discussed above is not usually possible in practice. The situation is, of course, quite different for a monopoly selling only to a small number of large customers.

V

This paper has done no more than sketch a certain approach to the theory of monopoly; but a few general conclusions can be suggested. An examination of the model of simple monopoly shows that various assumptions are made which usually are not specified or are not stated precisely, and that the Cournot solution can be regarded as a full equilibrium only in special cases. In special circumstances the monopolist can, by unilateral action, raise his expected profit above the Cournot level even if no restriction of resale is possible. More generally, the self-interest of seller and buyers may bring into play a variety of mechanisms capable of exploiting some of the gains from trade which in the Cournot solution remain unrealised. The choice among them depends on several considerations, including the costs of information and organisation, the possibility of reaching agreement without wasteful conflict, and flexibility in changing conditions. These mechanisms tend to transform simple monopoly into a complicated N-person game, with many strategies and many possible coalitions and, perhaps, with many solutions. The analysis merges with that of bilateral monopoly and oligopoly. It cannot be claimed that an equilibrium of such a game is necessarily a Pareto optimum, or even that all gains which in some sense are obtainable in practice will automatically be realised without intervention by government.

The kind of analysis pursued here has relatively little direct bearing on the traditional methods of state regulation of monopolies. It directs attention rather to the search for legal and institutional reforms which would assist the working of 'automatic' corrective forces. Unfortunately, arrangements which allow the realisation of certain gains from trade often have features which are regarded as undesirable in other respects. For example, gains which are not available in simple monopoly may be obtainable with the aid of such 'restrictive' practices as the prohibition of resale, discriminatory charging and the closed shop. In general, there is a complicated interdependence involving restrictive contracts, bargaining power, the distribution of gains from trade and the attainment of optimality, which can be adequately evaluated only if detailed attention is paid to the circumstances of particular markets. Nothing could be less conclusive in its implications for policy than a diagram showing that price in simple monopoly exceeds marginal cost. It is a merit of the approach used in this paper that it relates the pure theory of monopoly in a natural way to various phenomena of charging, bargaining, organisation and shareholding which occur in monopolistic markets. The resulting complexity is also its most serious limitation − the range of possibilities is too vast for a useful predictive theory. For this reason the method of analysis recommended by Edgeworth as 'applicable to the particular cases of imperfect competition' must remain to some extent a theory *in posse* − an approach which organises study and suggests the possibilities to be considered in particular instances, but which does not supply an exhaustive analysis of all conceivable solutions or a definite prediction of events.

Fiscal Means and Political Ends[1]

A.T. Peacock

I.   INTRODUCTION

Lionel Robbins has constantly reminded economists that their intellectual influence for good cannot be based solely on their technical competence as applied mathematicians.[2] Taking this as a text, I should like in this contribution to investigate the pretensions of a branch of economic theory which is increasingly employed as the technical basis of economic planning and which at the same time offers a method of selection of instruments of economic policy designed to promote particular policy aims. I refer, of course, to the Dutch or Theil/Tinbergen theory of economic policy.[3] As an economist with a special interest in public finance, I am particularly concerned with the implications for the size and structure of budget of this ends/means approach.

The theory of economic policy *à l'hollandaise* has had some influence on the approach to the study of public finance, notably in the well known works of Bent Hansen and Leif Johansen.[4] Theil himself

1.   I am indebted to Professors John Williamson and Jack Wiseman for comments and criticism. The analysis in Part II of this contribution has been developed further in Peacock, Alan and Shaw, G.K., *The Economic Theory of Fiscal Policy*, 1971, chapter 9.
2.   See, for example, Robbins, Lionel, 'The Economist in the Twentieth Century', *Economica*, May 1949, reprinted in the volume of the same name, 1954. Also his address on the occasion of his Installation as Chancellor of the University of Stirling, 5 April, 1968, part II.

3.   Theil, H. *Economic Forecasts and Policy*, 2nd Edition, 1961 and Tinbergen, J. *On the Theory of Economic Policy*, 2nd Edition 1963.

4.   See Hansen, B., *The Economic Theory of Fiscal Policy*, 1958, Part I and Johansen, Leif, *Public Economics*, 1965, Chapter 2. Both authors employ a Tinbergen-type model in which policy ends are reflected in separate and independent target values. In this contribution, a Theil-type model is used in which a 'trade-off' between policies is specified. In an earlier contribution I investigated the former approach with reference to simultaneous pursuit of

has employed as an example of his linear decision rule model of
economic policy the use of the budget as an instrument to reconcile the
twin objectives of stabilisation of incomes and the choice between
public and private goods.[5] However, in the practical design of fiscal
systems, innocence of the sophistication of modern economic theory is
a well known phenomenon and the theory of economic policy is no
exception in this respect.

The primary purpose of this contribution is to show that, while the
theory of economic policy does much to clarify our thinking about
fiscal problems, there are formidable difficulties in its application, and
that these difficulties are not solely based upon irrational resistance to
improvements in economic analysis used in planning.

In Section II, I present a highly simplified version of a Theil-type
model designed to illustrate the task of fiscal policy in maximising a
given community welfare function and also the need for co-ordination
of fiscal policy with other instruments. I then examine the practical
problems of applying the model, using its constituent elements as
points of departure for the discussion in each section (see sections III,
IV and V). Section VI contains the usual peroration with the author
taking his leave sitting firmly astride the divisive fence between theory
and reality.

II. A HIGHLY SIMPLIFIED MODEL

Two policy objectives of the community are identified and are
associated with two economic variables. The first is the price level,
or rather its rate of change through time, i.e. $\dot{p} = \frac{dp}{dt} \cdot \frac{1}{p}$. The
objective is to minimise the value of $\dot{p}$, subject, however, to achieving
simultaneously a 'satisfactory' level of employment. The second
objective, therefore, is to minimise the amount of unemployment,
denoted by U. By definition, 'the best of all possible worlds' is reached
when the value of both $\dot{p}$ and U are zero, which would be represented
by the origin in a two dimensional diagram with $\dot{p}$ measured along one

stability and growth policies promoted by fiscal means. See my 'Stability, Growth
and Budgetary Planning', *The Budget Today*, College of Europe, 1968.

5.   See Theil, H. 'Linear Decision Rules for Macrodynamic Policies', in
Quantitative Planning of Economic Policy (ed. B.G. Hickman), Brookings
Institution, 1965.

axis and U along the other. However, it is assumed that the 'cost' of reducing the value of $\dot{p}$ is a rise in the value of U. Following the conventions of welfare theory, we can draw a series of community indifference curves which delineate the 'trade-off' between the rate of price change and unemployment. We assume that over a specified range of $\dot{p}$ and U the indifference curves are both concave to the origin and also continuous. Thus, the 'trade-off' between $\dot{p}$ and U denotes that successive equal decrements of $\dot{p}$ can only be 'bought' by successive decrements of U of diminishing value. More formally, we describe the community's objective function π as:

$$\pi = \pi (\dot{p} , U) \tag{1}$$
$$(f_{\dot{p}} , fu < O)$$

Although it is not fundamental to the analysis, we may introduce two constraints. It would not be too unrealistic to assume that there is a maximum value of $\dot{p}$ which the community will tolerate, whatever the value of U, and, equally, a maximum value of U, whatever the value of $\dot{p}$; e.g. $\dot{p}$ = 10 per cent per annum, and U = 6 per cent of working population.

The community could reach its chosen nirvana at the origin, but this is not vouchsafed by the operation of the market economy. The 'opportunity slope' of the community is represented by the relationship between the rate of change in the price level and the unemployment rate which results from market forces. In this contribution, we shall conveniently domesticate the Phillips curve for our use, which is based on the observed relationship, in a number of countries, between the two variables.[6] This relationship is represented by a downward sloping curve in a two dimensional system with $\dot{p}$ on the vertical and U on the horizontal axis as shown by L in figure 1. A common algebraic form of this relationship is:

$$\dot{p} = a + bU^{-1} \tag{2}$$
$$(a < O \text{ and } b > O)$$

6. The original Phillips curve described the relation between unemployment and the rate of change in money wages: see Phillips, A.W. 'The Relation between Unemployment and the Rate of Change of Money Wage Rates in the United Kingdom', *Economica*, Vol. XXV, 1958. I was unaware until after I had prepared section II that the 'trade-off' problem using the Phillips curve had been developed, at least in graphical form, in Lipsey, R.G., 'Structural and Deficient-Demand Unemployment', in *Employment Policy and the Labour Market*, (ed. A.M.

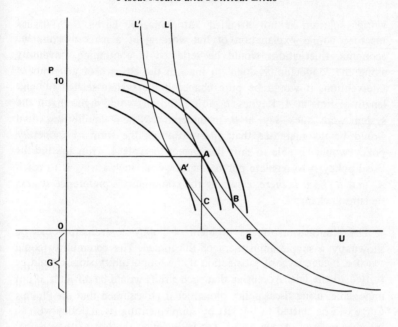

Figure 1

The problem of policy is to minimise $\dot{p}$ and U, subject to the constraint represented by the Phillips curve. The identification of the fulfilment of this condition is easy. It is simply the point of tangency between the Phillips curve and the highest (concave) community indifference curve, denoted by A.[7] However, this 'best-in-an-imperfect-

Rose) 1965, and latterly in Fromm G., and Taubmann, P., *Policy Simulations with an Econometric Model,* pp.101,110, Brookings Institution, 1968.

7.   This is a simple example of a constrained maximum problem which can be solved by the usual Lagrange undetermined multiplier technique.

Max. $\pi = \pi\,(\dot{p}\,,\,U)$ $(f\dot{p}\,,\,f_u < O)$ (1a)

Subject to $\dot{p} - a - bU^{\,1} = 0$ $(a < 0,\,b > 0)$ (2a)

Forming the Lagrange function

$$L = \pi\,(\dot{p}\,,\,U) + \lambda\,(\dot{p} - a - bU^{\,1})$$

and setting its partial derivatives equal to zero, the solution is

$$\lambda = \frac{fu}{f\dot{p}} = \frac{b}{u^2} \tag{3}$$

where λ is the Lagrange multiplier.

world' solution is not attained automatically. Given the familiar macroeconomic explanation of the working of a market economy, economic fluctuations would be reflected in continuing movement along the 'opportunity slope' so that, in the absence of government intervention, it would be pure chance if the system settled for any length of time at *A*. Keynesian purists, indeed, would argue that if the system were stuck, say, at *B*, in underemployment equilibrium there would be no guarantee that intervention in the form of monetary policy would be able to shift the system towards *A*. Thus the task of fiscal policy is to regulate purchasing power in such a way as to reach *A*, and *to keep it there*, assuming the community's preference system remains unchanged.

The illumination of the problem of policy co-ordination can be shown by a simple adjustment of the model. The community could reach a higher level of satisfaction if the 'opportunity slope' could be shifted to the left. Accepting that such a shift would be difficult, if not impossible, using fiscal policy alone, let it be assumed that the Phillips Curve can be shifted to the left by supplementing fiscal policy with an incomes policy.[8] A new curve, L', is drawn to the left of the original one, L, which denotes that, for a given fiscal policy, $\dot{p}$ can be held at a lower value for a given level of unemployment. If fiscal policy remains unchanged, the point *C* is attained which is preferred to *A*. The interesting point, however, is that this is not the optimal situation for the community would prefer to be at A' rather than *C* with a lower level of unemployment and a higher $\dot{p}$. The result of the (successful!) operation of an incomes policy, means that fiscal parameters must be changed to adjust the system to reach A' In short, this offers again a useful illustration of Bent Hansen's important point that attainment of given ends presupposes an optimal mix of policies and therefore co-ordination between the various authorities responsible for them.[9]

This highly simplified representation of the application of the theory to fiscal policy does less than justice to its versatility. The analysis

8.   See Lipsey, R.G., 'Structural and Deficient-Demand Unemployment', in *Policy and the Labour Market*, 1965.

9.   See, Hansen, B. *The Economic Theory of Fiscal Policy*, pp.12-25. For a useful exploration of the 'optimal mix' problem with reference to stability and economic growth, see Shaw, G.K. 'Monetary-Fiscal Policy for Growth and Balance-of-Payment Constraint', *Economica*, May 1967.

transcends the type of economic system under scrutiny. Those interested in policy choices in Eastern European-type economies, for example, may prefer to consider instead the trade-off between consumption and growth which embodies planners' preferences but in this model, of course, the 'community' indifference curves would be convex to the origin. The 'opportunity slope' would reflect whatever model of the accumulation process is thought appropriate. Clearly, more than two objectives can be embedded in the analysis at the cost of complicating the algebra. Nevertheless, the main problems of applying this approach in mixed economies can be illustrated by our highly simplified case, so that we need not be diverted into an elaboration of its more sophisticated variants.

III. THE OBJECTIVE FUNCTION IN PRACTICE

The presentation of the analysis of a 'given' community preference system reflecting some pre-conceived political decision avoids a great deal of unnecessary and tedious argument about the possibility of deriving policy prescriptions from economic analysis.[10] Nevertheless, while the economic analyst may argue that the specification of the community preference system is not his concern, the *process* by which policy aims are arrived at and translated into intelligible directives to the economic administration has an important bearing on the feasibility of using the theory of economic policy as a guide to budget provision. Further, there is a special sense in which economists as planners are likely to seek to influence the pattern of objectives. The reason for this lies not so much in the desire to impose their own value judgements on the rest of us but in the particular difficulties and therefore the inconveniences which confront them if the community preference curve obstinately refuses to stay in one place! The remaining discussion of the objective function in practice elaborates this point with particular reference to public finance.

Normally we think of the 'relevant' preferences as being those of some sovereign body. In Western-type political democracies, however, the sovereign body is not an immutable decision-maker with a

10.   For some strong words on this subject, see Robbins, L.'On the Relations between Politics and Economics', *Politics and Economics: Papers in Political Economy*, 1963. For example, 'any theory of economic policy must depend partly on conventions and valuations which are imported from outside', p. 19.

consistent and stable set of objectives which can be translated easily into a set of smooth, continuous preference curves. In an elected Parliament, even a political party which succeeds in remaining in power a relatively long time may do so precisely because it is prepared to adapt policy objectives to suit the continually changing views of a supporting electorate. 'Maximising the length of political life' of a dominant political group does not postulate a stable objective function and this clearly poses great problems for budget planners. If the desired magnitude and relative importance of the 'dependent variables' keep changing, it is difficult, even with full knowledge of the working of the economy, to achieve the technical adjustment in the 'independent variables', i.e. the tax, expenditure and debt instruments, which will pin the system to the elusive point of tangency.

Indeed, a principal reason for continuous alteration in the relative importance of policy objectives may be the reaction of the electorate to changes in the value of these independent variables themselves. An increase in the level of taxation designed, say, to control price rises is something more than a mere 'technical adjustment' to the individual taxpayer. His attitude to the increase, and therefore his preference system, will depend not simply on whether he accepts stabilisation policy in principle but on how he is personally affected by its operations and how he views his relative share of the burdens it imposes. Thus, put in terms of our model, it cannot be assumed throughout the process of 'technical adjustment' to achieve some point of tangency that the community preference system, insofar as it reflects taxpayers' views, will be independent of changes in the parameters which determine movements along and shifts in the opportunity slope. As things stand at present, the theory of economic policy does not allow for this kind of feedback.

The fact that policy instruments may themselves affect the objective function of the community is highly inconvenient to economic planners, who have devised various strategies in order to gain immunity from continuous political intervention. The most obvious one is to persuade the sovereign body that they must have 'peace to plan', that the price of a rational fiscal policy, for instance, is executive control over the budget. There is ample evidence of at least partial success in their attempts, particularly in the budgetary field, as is evidenced in recent budgetary reforms, in government support for long-term budgetary projections if not budgetary plans, and, particularly in Britain, the acceptance of changes in indirect tax rates outside the annual budget. Indeed, with the growing acquiescence by the electorate in the need for budgetary intervention in order to promote economic growth coupled with stabilisation, political opposition has crumbled remarkably quickly in major Western economies.

By concentrating on two competing objectives which are relatively new, if commonly accepted, one has avoided a much more sensitive area of debate between public, politicians and planners, viz. the perennial problem of deciding on the allocation of resources between public and private uses,[11] and thus the relative share of the G.N.P. devoted to government use. Political consensus being much more difficult to achieve in this area, planners' strategy in order to minimise intervention by the legislature might be expected to be more subtle. This, however, is not so. Whereas the argument for 'peace to plan' for stabilisation purposes has a firm technical basis, one is struck by the relative crudity of the arguments which even economists deploy when it comes to allocation problems. A 'pseudo-science' of optimal allocation has developed, the most notable example of which is to be found in attempts to define the percentage of G.N.P. which 'should' be devoted to a particular service, e.g. health or education. First of all, health or education 'needs' are derived from statements by medical or educational specialists. These are transmuted into a demand for resources and finally, depending on the extent of government provision of these needs, into a quantum of government expenditure for a period of, say, ten years ahead. Such specialists frequently draw the conclusion that expenditure programmes derived from these calculations must be 'taken out of politics' in the interest of the public weal. The exercise of projection is difficult enough[12] but this is not the gravamen of my charge. In leaving 'needs' to be defined by specialists, the politician would have to agree that the value judgements of 'experts' count for

11.   For a recent investigation of the properties of a community welfare function embodying a choice between public and private goods, but at the local government level in the USA, see Henderson, J.M. 'Local Government Expenditure: A Social Welfare Analysis', *Review of Economics and Statistics,* May 1968.
12.   For examination of the hazards with particular reference to the British National Health Service, see Peacock, A. and Shannon, R. 'The New Doctor's Dilemma, *Lloyds Bank Review,* January 1968.

more than his own or those of the electorate who will have to foot the bill. Furthermore, if one group of experts is allowed to define 'need', a demonstration effect will soon produce a clamour from other experts for consideration of their proposals for pre-empting a slice of the cake. If the theory of economic policy did nothing else, it would soon demonstrate that the ends implicit in these 'inviolable and essential' programmes based on 'technically-determined' needs would exhaust any likely available means, i.e. it would demonstrate the obvious inconsistency in the totality of plans.

A more subtle branch of this 'pseudo-science' is to be found in certain forms of cost-benefit analysis. In many cost-benefit exercises, the evaluation of benefits from public investments is markedly affected not simply by the calculable benefits and costs usually derived from market data, but by the 'intangible' benefits and the choice of a time preference discount rate of benefits. The valuation of intangibles and the choice of a time preference rate is not something which is automatically churned out by a computer. The computer must be fed with *someone's* estimates of community benefit (which could be negative) from intangibles and *someone's* view of the relative weights to be attached to the needs of future as against present generations of beneficiaries.[13] Bureaucrats concerned with public investment programmes will clearly have a much more peaceful life if they are allowed to exercise their judgement in these matters and are not faced with the prospect of having to argue incessantly with those charged with representing the community about their right to judge for others. But 'peace to plan' is bought at the cost of sensitivity to the choices of the electorate. In circumstances in which those responsible for budgetary policy are not going to have it their own way, and have to accept this, the objective function is neither within their control nor is it precise data, for the reasons given above. If the sovereign body is not prepared to abrogate responsibility for formulation of policy aims nor willing to commit itself for any length of time to the avoidance of changes in aims and their priorities, budget analysts have to forecast as best they may the strength and direction of the wind of change and maintain flexibility in planning, however inconvenient to them.

13. For further elaboration of this point, see my joint article with Wiseman, J. 'Measuring the Efficiency of Government Expenditure', in *Public Sector Economics* (ed. A.R. Prest), 1968.

IV. THE ECONOMIC MODEL

The usefulness of economics as a policy technique depends on rapid collection and collation of data, the specification of the correct model and of the right values of parameters. To mount a comprehensive review of each stage in model-building with reference to fiscal policy would practically require us to examine the pretensions of economics as a science. One may be forgiven, perhaps, for singling out only one or two matters for the present discussion.

The preparation of a policy model is hardly a costless process. It presupposes not only technical expertise in preparing relevant statistics, but, as economics, like other social sciences, has to use direct enquiry through questionnaire as a substitute for experiment, there is a considerable 'hidden' cost. This takes the familiar form of the time and effort which must be spent by businesses and private individuals in filling in questionnaires. In developing countries such enquiry methods may be even more expensive in resources because of the absence of literacy and therefore the need for skilled enumerators. The building of a policy model itself requires particular skills, and the interpretation and implementation of the model's 'solutions' require experience as well as intelligence. The days have gone when the economic information of relevance to policy was a by-product of the census of population and tax returns. Judging by results so far achieved, particularly in developing countries in which the opportunity cost of using skilled manpower in government is high, it is worth speculating on what the results of a cost-benefit analysis might reveal about the activities of fiscal planners.

In Britain, in which political obstacles to stabilisation measures through fiscal policy are less formidable than elsewhere, and there is clear evidence of the use of modern economic analysis in fixing the values of fiscal parameters, recent analyses have shown that the effect of fiscal policy has been the opposite of what was intended![14] One cannot necessarily conclude from this experience that the benefit/cost ratio would not justify fiscal planning. It is at least arguable that the

14.   For a review of the evidence, see Dow, J.C.R. *The Management of the British Economy*, 1945-60, 1964, Chapter VII and also R.A. and P. Musgrave,'Fiscal Policy', in *Britain's Economic Prospects* by Richard Caves and Associates, Brookings Institution, 1968.

results are unsatisfactory simply because of too little rather than too much input of economic skills. Furthermore, any results must be compared with those which might be achieved by the use of other tools of policy, always remembering that not all tools will be compatible with the constituent parts of the objective function. For example, it is conceivable that the balance of payments position would be improved by preventing the emigration of capital and skilled manpower and by strict import controls, but such draconian measures may simply not be acceptable to an electorate which regards these measures as being incompatible with their desire for personal choice, including freedom of movement. It has to be proved that fiscal policy is more vulnerable than other policies to the criticism of being an inefficient means of attaining a given objective in whole or in part.

Granted that we must guard against over-optimism in the employment of economic models embodying fiscal transactions, there is still a great deal to be said in favour of the ends-means approach as a method of formulating fiscal policies. The approach imposes a discipline on our thinking which demands the clear statement and quantification of policy aims as well as of their relative importance. In addition, the link between specific budgetary measures, e.g. adjustment of direct tax rates, debt provision etc., and the desired mixture of objectives, e.g. x per cent growth per annum, balance of payments 'equilibrium', can only be discerned if the economic analyst clearly reveals how the economy is supposed to adjust to forge it.

This disciplining procedure designed to impose consistency in budgetary planning has often been lacking, even in influential surveys of the fiscal systems of developing countries. As Mrs Andic and I have argued,[15] several of these are open to the criticism that it is not possible to trace the connection between so-called 'practical' reforms in the tax system and the ends they are designed to achieve. While the measures themselves may be 'feasible' and will therefore have an immediate appeal to policy-makers, this is no guarantee that they are appropriate. The economic or fiscal analyst cannot avoid building a model of some such logical construction in order to prove that the changes in the 'exogenous' variables, i.e. the fiscal instruments, will

15.   See, Andic, Suphan and Peacock, A.'Fiscal Surveys and Economic Development', *Kyklos*, No. 4, 1966.

produce the required changes in the values of the 'dependent' variables, i.e. the aims translated into suitable economic indicators. However sceptical one may be of elaborate model-building for developing countries, for which data are difficult to obtain and 'natural forces' such as weather and institutional peculiarities such as political instability make forecasting difficult, this offers no reason for assigning the highest cost-benefit ratio to particular tax measures solely because they are technically operable. This is tantamount to saying that in a cost-benefit analysis, we need neither define the nature of the benefit nor specify whose benefit we have in mind.

V. POLICY CO–ORDINATION

Our simplified model presupposes that policy instruments are co-ordinated. It may do no harm to give a further simplified example of the need for co-ordination. In the usual Keynesian fiscal policy model, control of expenditure fluctuations is achieved by balancing saving and investment through compensatory budgetary action which may require an *ex-ante* budget surplus or budget deficit. This budget imbalance may result in a change in the stock of government bonds or bills in the market or in the supply of cash in the economic system, so that unless there is further action by the monetary authorities, changes in the structure of interest rates caused by these disturbances in the credit or capital market may render fiscal policy partially or wholly ineffective.[16]

Co-ordination necessary to guarantee that one set of policy instruments will not produce results which conflict with those produced by another set may take a variety of administrative forms. It may vary from an attempt to 'unify the mandate',[17] which defines, possibly by legislation, the tasks assigned to various economic Ministries or government bodies controlling policy instruments, to attempts to subordinate the 'tradition-bound' Ministry of Finance to a powerful Ministry of Economic Affairs with surveillance of and even full control

16.   As demonstrated in many standard textbooks, e.g. Bailey, M.J. *National Income and the Price Level*, Chapter VI, 1962.
17.   The phrase used by *The Report of the Commission on Money and Credit*, Committee for Economic Development, 1961. Chapter X of the Report contains a penetrating discussion of problems of co-ordination in the USA.

over the 'exogenous variables' in the policy model operated by relevant branches of government.[18] However, even apparently monolithic organisations designed to co-ordinate economic policy may conceal wide divisions of view on appropriate policy measures, and *competition* in the use of policy instruments is not uncommon. In addition, as we have seen, the choice of policy instruments may be constrained by the choice and evaluation of interdependent objectives.

To take the latter point first, a clear case is instanced in the problem of 'vertical co-ordination' by layer of government. Decentralised government involving the conferment of considerable taxing powers to state (local) governments is often considered to be 'inefficient'. The reason given is that such decentralisation makes it more difficult to apply the full weight of the control of government taxing and spending to the task of promoting, say, economic growth and stabilisation, for local governments are not necessarily interested in or capable of promoting these objectives. The 'inefficiency' argument masks a confusion between political ends and fiscal means. De-centralisation of government and therefore of political power can clearly be an end in itself, so that it is perfectly logical policy-wise to place a constraint on the operation of a policy instrument which would require strict central control of the magnitude and composition of state (local) taxing and spending.[19]

The problem of 'horizontal co-ordination' is more relevent to the present discussion. The intellectual apparatus embodied in the theory of economic policy represents a challenge to public administrators trained in a previous tradition of public finance as an instrument of economic control and, to the extent that it becomes influential, it may render some of their traditional skills obsolescent.[20] Those adminis-

18.   For an interesting survey of the strains and stresses produced by economic planning, primarily in developing countries, on reorganisation of government, see Moodie, G.C. (Editor), *Government Organisation and Economic Development,* Development Centre, O.E.C.D. 1966.

19.   See Wiseman, J. *The Political Economy of Federalism* (mimeographed), prepared for the Canadian Royal Commission on Taxation (Carter Commission).

20.   For two examples of problems of adapting planning needs in the teeth of opposition from civil administration 'interest groups', see Arndt, Hans-Joachim, *West Germany: Politics of Non-Planning,* Chapters IV and V 1966 and Joseph La Palombara, *Italy: Politics of Planning,* Chapter VI, 1966.

trators placed in this position would be less than human if they preferred to acknowledge their need for extensive retraining rather than fight a rearguard action against the steady erosion of their position by *'soi-disant'* economic experts. Once a government has accepted the use of the budget as something more than a mechanism for financing the provision of collective services, the 'traditionalists' have to be very skilful if they are to keep open their route to advancement. At the same time, governments have often had to adopt rather clumsy devices in order to obtain the technical 'know-how' which will further the 'new' objectives of fiscal policy, such as the creation of a cluster of advisers attached to the President or Prime Minister, or of a new and separate Ministry or department. These devices may be the only realistic alternatives to early retirement, dismissal or demotion of public servants who, although they may not have permanent employment, may be strongly unionised. Yet it is a crass generalisation to maintain that governments, having accepted the need for fiscal reform for planning purposes, are necessarily prepared to invest heavily in economic experts as an alternative to 'specialists in non-specialism', if only because there is no guarantee that experts will always agree among themselves. Economists in public service need not expect that politicians will rush to offer them a large chisel in order to chip away at the 'lawyers' monopoly'.[21]

Even if all relevant government agencies are agreed on the interpretation of objectives (x per cent of unemployment and y per cent of price rise) and on the economic model in which the 'exogenous variables' are embedded, there may be competition between, for example, the monetary authorities and the fiscal authorities because, to some extent at least, they offer alternative ways of achieving the same objective. For instance, curbing investment can be carried out by tax policy, by cutting government investment, or by open market operations which affect the structure of interest rates. Regulation of the economy, as a fairly recent innovation, has often grown out of more traditional functions of government bodies, so that even today a central bank responsible for monetary policy may still have some residual banking functions just as Ministries of Finance have accounting and auditing functions. Hardly surprisingly, traditional

---

21.   A shorthand phrase for the dominant professional group in public service in many countries, but not, of course, in Britain.

separation of responsibility does not foster a desire by officials to be indifferent between the choice of policy instruments. Thus monetary authorities frequently differentiate their product from fiscal authorities in subtle ways such as the issue of quite separate bulletins on the prospects of the economy with more emphasis on monetary policy as compared with the equivalent publications of the fiscal authorities. In more extreme cases, this differentiation of their product may represent something more than informative advertising, and extend to a denial of the potency of the alternative policy instruments in private and even in public.[22]

However, it is clearly not true that policy instruments are inevitably perfect substitutes for one another, so that fiscal policy might be claimed to be a more efficient means of reducing employment than monetary policy, whereas monetary policy may be more successful in reducing the pace of inflation. It is understandable, although to be deplored, if in consequence an authority with specific responsibility for one set of policy instruments, e.g. monetary controls, seeks public support for its operations by actively canvassing for that political objective or combination of objectives which promotes *its* claims for pride of place in the regulation of the economy. Unfortunately, this is not an unknown situation.[23] More dangerous still for rational economic planning is the possibility that not only may the fiscal and monetary authorities not see eye to eye over objectives and may cast doubt on the efficacy of each other's policy instruments, but, because of their very preoccupation with one set of exogenous variables, may employ *different* models of the working of the economy. Fiscal authorities may tend to use a model in which monetary forces play little part, and the monetary authorities one in which only the monetary effects of budgets are considered as economically significant. In terms of figure 1 (p. 85) the difference of view may not be merely about the shape and the position of the Phillips curve but about its very existence. The position at the national level is not helped by the fact that these differences are reflected in the policy recommendations of influential international agencies. If we take a particular objective such as balance of payments equilibrium, there is certainly more emphasis in

22.   For a more general analysis of utility maximisation by public servants, see McKean, R.N. *Public Spending,* Chapter 2, 1968.

23.   Cf, for example, Tobin, J. *National Economic Policy,* Chapter 12, 1966.

O.E.C.D. reports on the use of fiscal and incomes policy as corrective measures than in, say, I.M.F. reports which emphasise control over money supply. There is sufficient evidence that these differences arise from differing views on the way particular economies operate.

VI. CONCLUDING REMARKS

Reviewing the pretensions of the theory of economic policy, there is clearly a lot that can be said in its favour. So far as public finance in concerned, it has both a pedagogic and a practical value.

First of all, it is reasonable to claim that, whereas many economic models seem designed more to exercise the intellect than to discover the truth, the theory of economic policy is exempt from this charge. The use of the system of public finance as an instrument of economic policy makes it essential for the student to know the place of that system in the economy, the tasks it is expected to perform in conjunction with other instruments and how the system may be adjusted to the tasks in view. The theory of economic policy performs the necessary act of integration of economic analysis and public finance which is often sadly lacking in our textbooks.

Yet the theory offers more than an agenda for textbooks. Suitably developed to take account of the multiplicity of objectives and garnished with appropriate econometric data, it is the framework for plans and projections actively used in economic policy in several countries. In any such planning process, the general tasks of the budget can be broadly defined and the co-ordination necessary with other policy instruments tested for consistency.

There are, nevertheless, clear limitations to placing reliance on the theory of economic policy as the *vade mecum* of fiscal economists. In the first place, even an elaborate model can never specify in sufficient detail how exactly fiscal institutions need be adapted to conform to policy objectives. The model may reach the stage of supporting, for example, the introduction of a value-added tax, but leave unstated what exact form the tax should take and what precisely its effects will be. (The economic planners' innocence of the intricacies of the analysis of incidence is well known to hardened public financiers!) When this point is taken together with the next, viz. that the economic models governing economic plans may be subject to a fairly rapid rate of obsolescence or at least to continual adaptation, it is understandable if fiscal economists may prefer rule-of-thumb methods in devising proposals for fiscal reform.

Lastly, as argued above, it is not difficult to engender support in principle for such objectives as stabilisation, growth and equity and for plans designed to achieve them. Once the budgetary details are worked out, however, it may be a different story. As we have seen, the budgetary changes which follow the dictates of constrained maximisation may be viewed by the individual taxpayer or bureaucrat as having unfavourable effects on their opportunity slope. One can hardly be surprised if their reactions in seeking to maximise their individual welfare frustrate the attainment of the community objectives, which they may still claim to accept in principle. It is no use for planners to fulminate against the irrationality or irresponsibility of such tactics of evasion. They must accept that it takes more than the solution of a set of equations to devise fiscal institutions, including changes in the structure of government, to 'minimise the feedback'.

To conclude, quantitative economics deserves to increase its influence on fiscal thinking, but political economy as the art of the possible in economic policy must not be killed off in the process.

The Universal Bogey

Fritz Machlup

The 'bogey' to whom this essay will be devoted is Economic Man. It was Lionel Robbins who suggested that *homo oeconomicus* would probably not have become 'such a universal bogey' if those who wrote so contemptuously about him had known him better.[1] He has been quite unpopular even among some good economic theorists, who contended that they could do better without him. Others who appreciated his services, were nevertheless intimidated by the irate accusations persistently reiterated by his detractors; so they decided to avoid his name. He was admitted into most respectable company under such aliases as 'behaviour equation' or 'objective function', names by which his enemies would not recognise him.[2]

Antitheoretical economists and anti-economists in general have raged and roared with fury about that wicked and despicable Economic Man. To deal with their accusations may appear 'foolish and exasperating ... to any competent economist' but, nevertheless, Robbins thought it was 'worth some further examination.'[3] I have found it entertaining to read the angry charges against the innocent creature and I propose, before engaging in still further examinations of the nature and significance of Economic Man, to share with the reader some of the juiciest denunciations.

1.   Robbins, Lionel, *An Essay on the Nature and Significance of Economic Science*, 1935, p. 97.
2.   I do not know who was the first to use the name objective function, but he certainly had no feeling for language or he would have sensed the possibility of misunderstandings. Objective as an adjective is the antonym of subjective; as a noun it is a synonym for goal or aim; what is it if it precedes and modifies a noun? French translators have had hard times; they were prone to mistranslate objective function as *fonction objective* instead of *fonction d'objectif.* Coiners of new terms and phrases ought to feel morally obliged to test them for non-ambiguity and intelligibility.
3.   Robbins, *An Essay on The Nature and Significance of Economic Science*, 1935, p. 94.

A SAMPLE OF DENUNCIATIONS

What irked the critics most was that the Man's 'desire of wealth' had frequently (and unwisely) been described as a desire to acquire or possess *material* goods satisfying *physical* wants, and sometimes as a desire for *pecuniary* gains; and the goal of getting the most out of what he has had been identified with *selfishness*. Thus we read in the work of John Barton, an early and almost forgotten critic of the Ricardians, that 'a reasoner who is incapable of measuring and appreciating the higher influences, confining his views to this one sordid and narrow motive, must infallibly arrive at conclusions as false as they are grovelling.'[4]

The members of the earlier Historical School in Germany were still quite civil in their rejection of Economic Man. Opposed chiefly to the use of abstraction and the emphasis on egoism, they wanted to have 'abstract' man replaced by 'real' man, and self-interest exorcised by strong appeals to ethical values. The British branch of the Historical School, led by Leslie, was not very original. Leslie mainly commended the 'realism' of the Germans in repudiating abstract and unhistorical concepts and in deprecating the 'Love of Money'.[5] He thought he was disposing of Economic Man by reminding us that money bought not only material things but also intangibles that satisfied the finest cultural aspirations – such as cleanliness and knowledge.

The American Henry C. Carey showed some originality in the venom he directed at the Classical School and especially at Mill. He quotes Mill first on economic motives – to acquire wealth, to avert labour, and to enjoy consumption – and then on population – pressing wages down to the subsistence level – and proceeds to make the following observation regarding these two assumptions:

That having been done, we have the political-economical man, on one hand influenced solely by the thirst for wealth and on the other so entirely

4.   Barton, John, *A Statement of the Consequences Likely to Ensue from Our Growing Excess of Population if not Remedied by Colonization*, 1830, p. 47. (Reprinted in John Barton, *Economic Writings*, Regina, Sask.: Lynn Publishing Co., 1962, p. 293.)
5.   Leslie, Thomas Edward Cliffe, 'The Love of Money', in *Essays in Political Economy*, 1888, pp. 1-8. (This essay was first published in 1862.)

under the control of the sexual passion as to be at all times ready to indulge it, however greatly such indulgence may tend to prevent the growth of wealth.[6]

Fascinated by Carey's angry exclamations, I cannot resist quoting him more extensively. He expects the reader of the classical writings to wonder:

He [the reader] might perhaps ask himself, has man no other qualities than those here attributed to him? Is he, like the beasts of the field, solely given to the search for food and shelter for his body? ... Has he no feelings of affections to be influenced by the care of wife and children? ... That he did possess these qualities he would find admitted, but the economist would assure him that his science was that of material wealth alone, to the entire exclusion of the wealth of affection and of intellect ... and thus would he ... discover that the subject of political economy was not really a man, but an imaginary being moved to action by the blindest passion...[7]

Again:

The British School of Economists recognizes, not the real man of society, but the artificial man of their own system. Their Theory, occupied with the lowest instincts of humanity, treats its noblest interests as mere interpolations of the System.[8]

And again:

Such is the error of modern political economy, its effects exhibiting themselves in the fact that it presents for our consideration a mere brute animal to find a name for which it desecrates the word 'man' ...[9]

To set him apart from this brute, Carey spells 'real MAN' with capital letters.

A disciple of Carey's, Robert Ellis Thompson, angry about the free-

6.   Carey, Henry C., *Principles of Social Science*, Vol I. 1858, p. 29. In a later book, *The Unity of Law*, 1872, p. 59, he repeats this statement almost literally, except for the insertion, after 'politico-economical man', of the words 'or monster'.

7.   Carey, *Principles*, p. 30; also *Unity*, p.61.

8.   Carey, *Principles*; p.xiii, in the table of contents describing § 5 of Ch. I.

9.   Carey, *Unity*, p. 61.

traders' interest in the 'consumer' (as distinct from 'producer') and their opposition to protective tariffs, managed to combine his antagonisms against the 'consumer', against the 'economic man', and against all abstract reasoning in one statement:

> Who this consumer is, that is neither a producer as well, nor directly dependent upon the prosperity of other people who are producers, is hard to say. ... But most likely he is an innocent *ens logicum,* manufactured by the same process of abstraction by which the economists devised their economical man – 'a covetous machine inspired to action only by avarice and the desire of progress'. That is, they cut away or stole away (abstracted) the better half of the real being, and persisted in treating the remaining human fragment (if we can call it human) as a living reality.[10]

One more sample of this group of writers may be offered, John Ruskin – in my opinion, one of the most overrated writers of nineteenth-century England. He too protested vigorously against the classical economists 'considering the human being merely as a covetous machine' – although he prided himself on never having read any book on political economy except Smith's *Wealth of Nations*. This is what he had to say about the economic principle operating in exchange and commerce:

> So far as I know, there is not in history record of anything so disgraceful to the human intellect as the modern idea that the commercial text, 'Buy in the cheapest market and sell in the dearest,' represents, or under any circumstances could represent, an available principle of national economy.[12]

THE GROUNDS OF THE OPPOSITION

Some of the strictures and denunciations included in this sample can probably be best explained as the result of misunderstandings – due to ignorance or incompetence. But not all opposition to Economic Man is of this sort. The ranks of the opposition are not filled entirely with

10. Thompson, Robert Ellis, *Social Sciences and National Economy,* 1875, p. 269.

11. Ruskin, John, *Unto This Last,* 1901, p. 2. The four essays collected in this book were first published in 1861. The phrase 'covetous machine' was widely quoted, for example, also by Thompson, in 1875, in the passage reproduced above.

12. Ruskin, *Unto This Last,* p. 59.

anti-analysts, anti-theorists, anti-classicists, anti-liberals, and anti-economists. Some eminent economic theorists, skilled in analysis and respectful of classical economics, have also condemned the use of the concept of Economic Man. What are the grounds of their opposition?

Several such grounds should be distinguished, since different critics have different quarrels with Economic Man's nature, character, and function. One issue relates to the breaking up of Whole Man into parts and the construction of a Partial or Fragmented Man, who has only a few specific traits or objectives; there are those who object vigorously to all analytical dissection of man (as if it were physical vivisection). Other controversial questions are whether the construction of an abstract Partial Man is sound either in the sense that all disregarded traits or objectives can reasonably be dispensed with without vitiating the conclusions deduced with the help of the construct, or in the sense that the traits or objectives which are singled out for emphasis are sufficiently realistic to yield useful conclusions. Several objectors deny both propositions, some only one. There is a group of economists who are greatly worried that we may obtain only 'hypothetical' rather than incontrovertible, categorical, or 'positive' conclusions. Some object to the use of heuristic fictions and counterfactual assumptions; they hold that no worthwhile inferences can come from untrue hypotheses. The largest number of critics merely take exception to poor formulations of the behaviour equation called Economic Man.

In order to avoid the impression that the parties to this controversy can be nicely tagged and boxed, we had better go back for a bit of doctrinal history; we shall confine it, however, to a few of the main protagonists: John Stuart Mill, Nassau Senior, Walter Bagehot, James E. Cairnes and Philip H. Wicksteed.

THE HYPOTHETICAL NATURE OF SCIENTIFIC DISCOURSE

Re-reading John Stuart Mill after reading the comments and observations of his critics, one cannot help finding a strong suspicion confirmed: that many authors, even highly respected ones, read with insufficient care or poor retention. Far too many of the methodological issues raised about Mill's procedure, and about his (unnamed) Economic Man, had been anticipated and largely resolved by Mill.

Mill insisted on the hypothetical nature of all science — reasoning from assumed premises — and on the especially hypothetical nature of economics (Political Economy) — presupposing 'an arbitrary definition of man'.[13] He stressed the 'uncertainty inherent in the nature of these complex phenomena [in the moral sciences in general] ... arising from the impossibility of being quite sure that all the circumstances of the particular case are known to us sufficiently in detail'.[14]

'Man..., the subject matter of all moral sciences' has to be dealt with 'under several distinct hypotheses'. The major division, in Mill's exposition, is between 'ethics' and 'social economy', and a branch of the latter was 'political economy'. 'The science of social economy embraces every part of man's nature, in so far as influencing the conduct and condition of man in society ...'. 'Political economy', in contradistinction, 'does not treat of the whole of man's nature as modified by the social state, nor of the whole conduct of man in society. It is concerned with him solely as a being who desires to possess wealth, and who is capable of judging of the comparative efficacy of means for obtaining that end.'[15] The fundamental assumption is that man will 'prefer a greater portion of wealth to a smaller...'[16] This is, I submit, a common-sense way of formulating the postulate of maximising.

Mill makes it perfectly clear that this basic hypothesis may be contrary to fact. 'Political Economy' he states, 'reasons from *assumed* premises — from premises which might be totally without foundation in fact, and which are not pretended to be universally in accordance with it...'[17] Several times Mill points to the fictitious character of the fundamental hypothesis of economic science, in particular to the 'entire abstraction of every other human passion or motive', except 'desire of wealth', 'aversion to labour', and 'desire of the present enjoyment of costly indulgences'.[18] He cautiously warns the reader against mistaking

13.   Mill, John Stuart, 'On the Definition of Political Economy; and the Method of Investigation Proper to It' *Essays on Some Unsettled Questions of Political Economy*, p. 144.

14.   Mill, *Political Economy*, p. 150.

15.   Mill, *Political Economy*, pp.134-137. [The same sentences appear in Mill's *System of Logic*.]

16.   Mill, *Political Economy*, pp.138-139.

17.   Mill, *Essays*, p. 137.

18.   Mill, *Essays*, pp. 137-138.

a heuristic counterfactual hypothesis for a statement of fact:

> Not that any political economist was ever so absurd as to suppose that mankind are really thus constituted ... [But] the manner in which it [Political Economy] necessarily proceeds is that of treating the main and acknowledged end as if it were the sole end; which, of all hypotheses equally simple, is the nearest to the truth... This approximation is then to be corrected by making proper allowance for the effects of any impulses of a different description, which can be shown to interfere with the result in any particular case.[19]

POSITIVE TRUTH AND MERE SUPPOSITION

Not all classical or post-classical writers were agreed on the hypothetical or postulational character of Economic Man, or of the Economic Principle. Several of them, before Mill as well as afterwards, wanted the basic assumption recognised as a factual premise, stating an unquestioned, positive truth. The most out-spoken critic of merely hypothetical economics was Senior.

Long before Mill, Senior had formulated the 'First Proposition' of Political Economy: 'That every person is desirous to obtain, with as little sacrifice as possible, as much as possible of the articles of wealth'.[20] In later reformulations he omitted the reference to 'articles' and was careful to point out that wealth included such intangibles as 'power', 'distinction', 'leisure', 'benefits for acquaintances and friends', and even contributions of 'advantage to the public'.[21] However, Senior was dissatisfied with Mill's reliance on a hypothesis which, in Mill's words, was not 'universally in accordance with fact' or was even 'totally without foundation in fact'. From mere suppositions only conclusions of uncertain truth or applicability could be inferred. Senior wanted economic science to state positive truths, not just hypotheses. 'It appears to me', he wrote in 1852, 'that if we substitute for Mr. Mill's hypothesis, that wealth and costly enjoyment are the *only* objects of human desire, the statement that they are universal and constant objects of desire, that they are desired by all men and at all times, we shall have laid an equally firm foundation for our subsequent

19. Mill, *Essays*, pp. 139-140.
20. Senior, Nassau W., *Introductory Lecture on Political Economy*, 1827, p.30. Quoted from Bowley, Marian, *Nassau Senior and Classical Economics*, 1937, p.46.
21. Senior, *An Outline of the Science of Political Economy*, 1836, 6th ed. 1872, p. 27.

reasonings, and have put a truth in the place of an arbitrary assumption'.[22]

USEFUL FICTIONS

Senior's ambition for economic science — to yield absolutely true, not merely hypothetical propositions — was criticised by Walter Bagehot, who also criticised earlier classical economists for confusing useful fictions with established facts. For example, Bagehot claimed that Ricardo 'thought that he was considering actual human nature in its actual circumstances, when he was really considering a fictitious nature in fictitious circumstances'.[23]

According to Bagehot, 'English political economists are not speaking of real men, but of imaginary ones; not of men as we see them, but of men as it is convenient to us to suppose they are'.[24] The convenience lies in the simplicity of disregarding elements of lesser relevance. For this reason, 'Political Economy deals not with the entire real man as we know him in fact, but with a simpler, imaginary man..., because it is found convenient to isolate the effects of this force from all others'.[25]

Bagehot thus sided completely with Mill and against Senior, who wanted positive 'truths' in place of mere 'hypotheses'.

PREMISES AND CONCLUSIONS

James E. Cairnes defended Senior on some points and criticised him on others. He took his side on the question of fact or fiction in the assumption regarding the economic motive. The fundamental assumption of economics is, for Cairnes, not a mere supposition, let alone a counterfactual hypothesis, but a proposition which rests on well established facts of experience: 'The economist starts with a knowledge of ultimate causes.'[26] For their discovery or confirmation 'no elaborate process of induction is needed', for we have 'direct knowledge of these

---

22. Senior, Nassau W., *Four Introductory Lectures on Political Economy*, 1852, p. 62. Quoted from Bowley, *Nassau Senior*, p.61.
23. Bagehot, Walter, *Economic Studies*, 1880, p. 157.
24. Bagehot, *Economic Studies*, p. 5.
25. Bagehot, *Economic Studies*, p. 74.
26. Cairnes, James E., *The Character and Logical Method of Political Economy*, 1st ed. 1858, 2nd ed. 1875, p. 87.

causes in our consciousness of what passes in our own minds...' After
all, 'every one who embarks on any industrial pursuit is conscious of
the motives which actuate him in doing so'.[27]

However — and here Cairnes dissents from Senior's position — that
the economist can start with 'facts' rather than a 'hypothesis' does not
guarantee that his conclusions are anything but hypothetical. For, in
Cairnes' view,

> an economist, arguing from the unquestionable facts of man's nature —
> the desire of wealth and the aversion to labour — and arguing with strict
> logical accuracy, may yet, if he omit to notice other principles also affecting
> the question, be landed in conclusions which have no resemblance to existing
> realities. But he can never be certain that he does not omit some essential
> circumstance, and, indeed, it is scarcely possible to include all: it is evident,
> therefore, that... his conclusions will correspond with facts *only in the absence
> of disturbing causes,* which is, in other words, to say that they represent
> not positive but hypothetic truth.[28]

Thus Cairnes accepts one half of Senior's and one half of Mill's
position: 'the premises are not arbitrary figments of the mind', but the
conclusions are hypothetical and 'may or may not correspond to the
realities'.[29] He attributed Senior's dilemma, regarding the question
whether economics was a positive or a hypothetical science, to 'an
ambiguity of language'. If the two adjectives are used 'with reference to
the character of [the] premises' of a science, they may point to a
genuine difference: the 'positive' premises of the physical sciences,
dictated by 'the existing facts of nature', can be contrasted with the
'hypothetical' premises of the science of mathematics, which are 'arbitrary conceptions framed by the mind'.[30] If, however, the two adjectives are used 'with reference to the conclusions of a science', the
advanced physical and other empirical sciences may be regarded as both
positive and hypothetical: positive in the sense that there is a probability that the conclusions deduced from the premises 'represent
positive realities', and hypothetical in the sense that these conclusions
can be true only 'on the hypothesis that the premises include all the

27. Cairnes, *Character and Logical Method,* p. 88.
28. Cairnes, *Character and Logical Method,* pp. 63-64. (Emphasis in the original.)
29. Cairnes, *Character and Logical Method,* p. 62.
30. Cairnes, *Character and Logical Method,* pp. 60-61.

causes affecting the result', of which we 'can never be sure'.[31]

Cairnes' view, in a nutshell, is that 'it is surely possible that the premises should be true and yet incomplete — true so far as the facts which they assert go, and yet not including all the conditions which affect the actual course of events'.[32]

EGOISM, TUISM, AND SIMPLIFIED PSYCHOLOGY

Cairnes' disquisitions were lost on Philip Wicksteed, who embraced Senior's position on several issues. Like Senior, Wicksteed (quite rightly) insisted on keeping maximising behaviour apart from egoism and from the desire to possess material goods; like Senior, Wicksteed rejected mere suppositions as the basis of economic deductions; and like Senior, Wicksteed was not satisfied with a merely 'hypothetical science'.

Wicksteed was well advised in restating the irrelevance of material possessions and of self-interest, simply because so many exponents of economic theory continued to advertise these false criteria of economic conduct. But the issues had been fully discussed and understood by many. If wealth was defined as material goods, this was partly a device to eschew problems of statistical estimation, which were especially difficult with regard to intangible values. This, at least, was Malthus' explanation, back in 1812. The issue as to whether the scope of egoism had to be narrowed to the fulfilment of bodily desires or could be extended to include 'higher' impulses had already been discussed by Hobbes,[33] back in 1651. Why then, in the opinion of so many eminent writers, the desire to attain with given means a maximum of ends (objectives, satisfaction, utility) had to be identified with egoism or self-interest is nowadays difficult to understand. Senior was one of the few who recognised that the economic motive could accomodate altruism along with any other preferences of the acting individuals. Yet we find reversions at much later, more enlightened times. Edgeworth, for example, in 1912 stuck to the old, unreconstructed view according to which 'the first principle of pure economics' was 'the prevalence of self-interest'.[34]

31. Cairnes, *Character and Logical Method*, p. 61.
32. Cairnes, *Character and Logical Method*, p. 68.
33. Hobbes, Thomas, *Leviathan*, 1651.

Wicksteed offered the most patient exposition of the egoism-altruism issue. He has no difficulty demonstrating that it is quite irrelevant whether a decision-maker acts on the basis of a preference system that includes only his personal interests or also those of his family, his friends, his clients, his compatriots, or any *alteri*.[35] In any case the principle of 'true economy', that is, of 'making the best of existing conditions',[36] yields the same results, regardless of whether the 'maximum advantage'[37] is desired only for the decision-maker himself or for other beneficiaries.

Wicksteed makes one exception to the possible inclusion of other persons' interests among the aims of a decision-maker: the interests of a trading partner must not actuate his behaviour. If I bargain with you, I, *ego*, may think of my own interests or of the interests of others, *alteri*, but I must not think of you, *tu*, and of your interests. Hence, egoism and altruism are both all right, but 'tuism' must be ruled out. 'It is only when tuism to some degree actuates my conduct that it ceases to be wholly economic'.[38] Thus, 'The specific characteristic of an economic relation is not its "egoism", but its "non-tuism" '.[39]

Wicksteed, although he could accommodate altruism along with egoism, thought that he had to exclude tuism, probably because otherwise the terms of an exchange between two transactors would be indeterminate. He evidently overlooked that an isolated exchange, outside a competitive market, would be indeterminate in any case, with or without tuism. On the other hand, if the market is competitive, a trader may wish to give his trading partner a 'break', and thus include the partner's interests in his own considerations, without any harm to the determinateness of the market price; the 'rebate' in the case of the 'tuistic' trader would be an understandable deviation.

Wicksteed rejected the construction of Economic Man, less because of the awkward traits of materialism and egoism with which some

34.   Edgeworth, Francis Y., 'Contributions to the Theory of Railway Rates, III', *Economic Journal*, Vol. XXII, 1912, p. 199. Reprinted in *Papers Relating to Political Economy*, Royal Economic Society, 1925, Vol. I, p. 173.

35.   Wicksteed, Philip H., *The Common Sense of Political Economy* 1910, pp. 170-183.

36.   Wicksteed, *Political Economy*, p. 94.

37.   Wicksteed, *Political Economy*, p. 70.

38.   Wicksteed, *Political Economy*, p. 181.

39.   Wicksteed, *Political Economy*, p. 180.

model-makers had endowed him than because of the other two limitations: the 'artificial simplification' through isolation of selected motives and abstraction from all others, and the restriction to 'hypothetical' conclusions which is involved in the reliance on unrealistic assumptions. In his arguments against these limitations Wicksteed engages in a great deal of verbal hair-splitting, particularly when he tries to do away with an 'economic motive' and replaces it by an 'economic relation'.

Wicksteed's stance in his opposition to an abstract construct of man resembles that of the anti-analytic, anti-vivisectionist holists: he rejects 'the hypothetically simplified psychology of the Economic Man' and the convention of 'imagining man to be actuated by only a few simple motives; and he proposes that we 'take him as we find him... under the stress of all his complicated impulses and desires'.[40] Many of Wicksteed's observations are perfectly sound, for example, when he states that

> a man may be just as strenuous in the pursuit of knowledge or of fame, or in his obedience to an artistic impulse, as in the pursuit of wealth... The demands of vanity may be as imperious as those of hunger, so that all the motives and passions that actuate the human breast may either stimulate or restrain the desire to possess wealth. How, then, can we isolate that desire as a 'motive'?[41]

And in a similar vein:

> There is no occasion to define the economic motive, or the psychology of the economic man, for economics study a type of relation, not a type of motive, and the psychological law that dominates economics dominates life. We may either ignore all motives or admit all to our consideration, as occasion demands, but there is no rhyme or reason in selecting certain motives that shall and certain others that shall not be recognised by the economist.[42]

We shall later justify how we can reasonably regard these observations as sound and yet irrelevant. The apparent contradiction has to do with the distinction between (spontaneous) action and (induced) reaction, and with the differences in complexity in explaining the two types of decision-making. Wicksteed was one of many who failed to

40.   Wicksteed, *Political Economy*, p. 4.
41.   Wicksteed, *Political Economy*, p. 164.
42.   Wicksteed, Philip H., 'The Scope and Method of Political Economy in the Light of the "Marginal" Theory of Value and Distribution', *Economic Journal*, Vol. XXIV, March 1914, p. 9.

recognise these differences. His opposition to the basic simplifying assumption was based on a methodological tenet:

> We have now to ask further, are these psychological data, whether facts or principles, to include all the psychological considerations that actually bear upon the production, distribution, etc. of wealth, or are we artificially to simplify our psychology and deal only with the motives supposed to actuate the hypothetical 'economic man'? In the latter case political economy will be a hypothetical science. In the former it will aim at positivity.[43]

Here we meet again the objection Senior had raised against Mill's 'hypothetical science'. The ambition for something 'more positive', which would assure *true* deductions from *true* assumptions rather than merely valid deductions from fundamental postulates, moved Wicksteed, as it had moved Senior, to oppose the construction of a simplified model in favor of a supposedly complete one. This ambition reached its extreme in Ludwig von Mises' praxeology, the all-embracing theory of human action, in which economic action, rational action, and action of any kind become one and the same.[44]

THE OBJECTIVES OF ECONOMIC MAN

From the sample of quotations offered here it should be clear that the exact content of the 'fundamental hypothesis' embodied in the construction of *homo oeconomicus* has changed from one economic treatise to another. Many critics have suffered from a tendency to interpret the descriptions of Economic Man too narrowly and too literally. The differences in the scope of Economic Man's aspirations can perhaps be visualised in the following schema: Economic Man is assumed to seek (A) more wealth with given sacrifices of other advantages, (B) the largest gains in exchange and trade, (C) greatest pleasure with given pain, (D) highest returns from given resources, (E) highest pecuniary and nonpecuniary benefits from business, or (F) maximum utility from given means.

In some of the constructions proposed, Economic Man was only a

43. Wicksteed, Philip H. 'Political Economy and Psychology', *Palgrave's Dictionary of Political Economy,* 1926, Vol. III, p. 142.
44. von Mises, Ludwig, *Nationalökonomie: Theorie des Handelns und Wirtschaftens,* 1940, also English edition, *Human Action: A Treatise on Economics,* 1949.

consumer, only a trader, only a producer, only an investor, only a businessman. Some writers insisted that the construct could never fit some of these roles, whereas others were convinced that it fitted them all, indeed, a few were even prepared to extend it to other roles, such as the politician, the government, or society as a collective decision-maker.

Within each of the constructs several further variations can be found. The wealth which the first Economic Man sought to maximise was thought of as a stock by some, as a flow by others; as consisting of material consumer goods, of material assets of any sort, of tangibles and also intangible goods and services, or of money or general purchasing power. The failure to distinguish between a stock and a flow of 'wealth' has trapped a good many, friends and foes of Economic Man. Smith said 'wealth' but explained that he meant 'the necessaries and conveniences of life', hence, a stream of income. Mill said 'necessaries, conveniences, and luxuries', but at the same time spoke of the desire to 'possess' wealth. No wonder that critics with literal minds found these descriptions wanting and thought the whole conception useless.

The idea of confining wealth to material goods was supposed to serve statistical convenience, to ease quantitative estimation. But, surely, where no statistical operations were intended or needed, it was supererogatory to subject the construct to an operational constraint. The distinction between physical wants 'of a low order' (Jevons) and gratification of higher values was entirely uncalled for. The substitution of money or general purchasing power for goods and services of any sort was all right, but of course not with the disparaging connotation of a miser's 'love of money', avarice and cupidity. The difference between selfish and nonegoistic desire of wealth is understandable in the light of the discussions of utilitarian philosophy, but proved irrelevant to the maximisation postulate. In the same context, emphasis on the 'calculus of pleasure and pain' and the conception of Economic Man as a 'pleasure machine' (Edgeworth) were instances of misplaced hedonism and made it harder for the student of economics to arrive at an understanding of 'utility maximisation'.

The Economic Man in business was also having serious problems of a schizophrenic nature: was he a pure maximiser of money profits or did he have also other objectives, was he subject to various pulls and pressures of conflicting obligations, responsibilities, loyalties, and preferences? The problems of the multi-goal firm in business have been much discussed in the last thirty years and perhaps we should only remind the reader that most of these problems are serious only as far as spontaneous business action is concerned, but quite innocuous with regard to reactions and responses to changes in the conditions confronting the firm.[45]

THE LOGICAL NATURE OF ECONOMIC MAN

Homo oeconomicus is the metaphoric or figurative expression for a proposition used as a premise in the hypothetico-deductive system of economic theory. This settles, however, only the question of the logical *status,* not of the logical *nature* of the proposition, especially regarding its derivation, evidence or truth value.

Alas, this question has remained as controversial as it ever was. We have sampled some of the methodological positions defended in the older literature and have seen that Mill, Senior, Cairnes, Bagehot and Wicksteed had rather different views on the subject. We have not quoted any of the pronouncements of Mises, Knight, Robbins, Samuelson or Friedman — to name only a few of the major living disputants on economic methodology — chiefly because their views are more widely known, and known to contradict one another. The fundamental assumptions of economic theory — the 'economic principle', 'the postulate of rationality', the 'assumption of maximisation', or whatever they have been called — have been characterised in so many different ways that an enumeration must suffice:

... they are regarded as "self-evident propositions", "axioms", "*a priori* truths", "truisms", "tautologies", "definitions", "rigid laws", "rules of procedure", "resolutions", "working hypotheses", "useful fictions", "ideal types", "heuristic mental constructs", "indisputable facts of experience", "facts of immediate experience", "data of introspective observation", "private empirical data", "typical behaviour patterns", and so forth.[46]

Going from *a priori* statements and axioms, via rules of procedure, useful fictions and ideal types all the way to empirical data, the spectrum of logical possibilities seems to be complete. Since there is no

45.   Machlup, Fritz, 'Theories of the Firm: Marginalist, Behavioral, Managerial', *American Economic Review,* Vol. LVII, March 1967, pp. 1-33; and 'Corporate Management, National Interest, and Behavioral Theory', *Journal of Political Economy,* Vol. 75, October 1967, pp. 772-774.

way to settle conflicts of methodological taste, we shall refrain from attempting arbitration.

One suggestion, however, may be permissible and, indeed, may stand a good chance of being acceptable to the representatives of the most divergent views. It is probably agreed that *homo oeconomicus* is not supposed to be a real man, but rather a man-made man, an artificial device for use in economic theorizing. Thus, he is not a *homo* but a *homunculus*. It is *homunculus oeconomicus* we have been talking about all along.

THE FUNCTION OF ECONOMIC MAN

Economic Man, I repeat, is a figurative expression for a proposition which serves as a premise in the theoretical system of economics. To ask for the function of the construct Economic Man is, in effect, to question the need for that premise. To put it bluntly: is the behaviour equation expressed by that construct really necessary — necessary, that is, for the theoretical system in which it is employed?

I shall try to answer this question in the form of an argument that focuses on the most important tasks of economic theory, namely, the explanation of changes in output and changes in price (exchange value). Illustrations will help illuminate the argument.

Changes in output. The output of any product never, or hardly ever, increases unless some producers allocate additional productive services to the particular activities or improve the techniques of production. The output of any product never, or hardly ever, decreases unless some producers reduce the quantities of productive services allocated to the particular activities. Hence, changes in output can be satisfactorily explained only by stating (a) the conditions under which producers are likely to take any of these actions, and (b) the general motive or objective that is likely to induce them to respond in the specified way to the stated changes in conditions.

Changes in price. Prices of anything sold, bought, or exchanged never rise unless some suppliers ask for higher prices and buyers are

46. Machlup, Fritz 'The Problem of Verification in Economics', *Southern Economic Journal*, Vol. XXII, July 1955, p. 16.

willing to pay them, or some buyers bid higher prices and suppliers are willing to accept them. Prices of anything sold, bought, or exchanged never fall unless some suppliers offer to sell for reduced prices and buyers are willing to pay less, or some buyers bid lower prices and suppliers are willing to accept less. Hence, changes in prices can be satisfactorily explained only by stating (a) the conditions under which suppliers and buyers are likely to take such decisions, and (b) the general motive or objective that is likely to induce them to respond in the specified way to the particular changes in conditions.

A universal principle. There are obviously many different changes in conditions that could have the results mentioned and, likewise, one could think of a variety of motives or objectives that would induce the stated responses. No theoretical system, however, can be built if *all* premises vary from case to case; at least *one* premise must be found that can serve to deduce applicable conclusions in a very large number of cases. If no such universal premise could be found, but all assumptions had to be chosen from a large variety of possibilities, it would be impossible ever to predict the outcome of any change in conditions with any degree of confidence. A fundamental postulate acceptable as universal premise of at least approximate universal relevance is needed, and it stands to reason that an assumption of a pervasive and invariant objective or behaviour equation can serve in this capacity. Three examples shall be given in order to clarify the meaning of uniformity or universality in the basic hypothesis.

First example: more research.. We do not doubt that many a person may, as Wicksteed reminded us, 'be just as strenuous in the pursuit of knowledge' as in the desire for more wealth. Would it then be wise if we tried to explain the large increase in the number of persons devoting their time to research and development, say, for space ships and moon shots, as a result of their thirst for knowledge? Or are we not better advised to point to the improved job opportunities and pay levels offered these persons in the research and development activities financed by government and industry — conditions of which they were glad to take advantage?

Second example: more music. Undoubtedly many persons 'may be just as strenuous in the obedience to an artistic impulse' as in the desire for more wealth. Should this lead us to attribute the increase in the number of professional musicians solely to heightened obedience to their artistic impulses? Or had we not better look for the cause in such pecuniary factors as the offer of more positions in more symphony orchestras thanks to larger appropriations of funds to musical organisations, out of increased tax revenues due to higher national incomes?

Third example: vanity and sloth. No one in his right mind has any doubt that 'vanity' and 'love of ease' are strong motives of human action. But are there many changes in quantities produced or in prices paid and received that would be most credibly explained by changes in the love of ease or by changes in the degree of vanity? To be sure, an increase in incomes or earnings opportunities may affect prices and production in ways that could be explained by reference to given degrees of desires of leisure or prestige, but the substantive change is then on the pecuniary side, not in the system of subjective valuations.

Action and reaction. The preceding three examples should have illuminated the clue for solving the issue: the economist's chief task is not to explain or predict human action of every sort, or even all human action related to business, finance, or production, but instead only certain kinds of people's reactions (responses) to specified changes in the conditions facing them. For this task a *homunculus oeconomicus,* that is, a postulated (constructed, ideal) universal type of human reactor to stated stimuli, is an indispensable device for a necessary purpose.

Example of an exception: We must not be dogmatic and exclude exceptions to the rule. For we cannot always find the explanations in economic reactions or adjustments to changes in opportunities that present themselves in changes of prices or incomes. Consider the following case: All during the 1950s and later, there was a substantial flow of Austrian maids and waitresses to England, where they could earn much better wages than at home. In the 1960s, however, there began a movement of English girls to Austria, where their wages were lower. Needless to say, wage differentials can explain why Austrian girls go to England, but not why English girls go to Austria to work in hotels and pensions. What hypotheses could be adduced? We may have two plausible explanations: one, the English girls' newly discovered love for learning — learning to speak German, to ski, to have fun —; the other, newly obtained information about these existing opportunities. The first explanation posits a change in *preferences,* perhaps a fashion, the second a change in the availability of *information,* perhaps furnished by employment agents or by travel agents. These hypotheses are, of course, not inconsistent with the economic principle (utility maximisation), but if the bulk of all cases were of this kind, the usefulness of our theoretical system would be much reduced. For most of our explanatory and predictive assignments we need to assume given preferences and given information.

No quantitative predictions.   The conclusions deduceable from the theoretical system with its objective function as fundamental assumption will, by and large, be only qualitative, that is, they will indicate only the direction of change to be expected from certain changes in conditions. No exact quantitative predictions can be derived from the system, although it may be possible to give plausible limits for the deduced changes. For example, the imposition of an excise tax on the product of an oligopolistic industry will be most unlikely to result in a price reduction, but similarly unlikely to result in a price increase by several times the amount of the tax. The increase will most probably be greater than zero and not much greater than the tax. If this appears 'plausible', it is so only from the conjunction of the maximisation assumption with several assumptions concerning cost and demand conditions, possibly also managerial ambitions, political considerations, and institutional constraints. There are other instances in which quantitative estimates may be possible, for example, in macroeconomic problems, but there the estimates are usually derived from correlational regularities (empirical laws), which themselves are not deduceable from any general hypotheses and for which no claims of universality can be made. On the other hand, these empirical laws will not have any great standing — apart from their place in economic history — if they are not at least understandable by reference to individual reactions consistent with the economic principle.

Conclusion.   I move the following resolution: The fundamental assumption — whether it be regarded as a conventional postulate, a useful fiction, or a well-known fact of experience — of maximising behaviour, that is, of utility-maximising reactions of households and firms, is recognised as a useful and probably indispensable part of the theoretical system of economics. This assumption has frequently been hypostasised into the symbolic figure or 'person ideal type', the Economic Man.

Economic Theories of Educational Planning

Richard Layard

OUTLINE

There are two main schools of thought on educational planning. One says that education should adjust to the demand for manpower in the labour market; the other that it should satisfy the private demand for education *per se*. Each school is again divided. Manpower specialists differ on whether to do rate-of-return analysis or manpower forecasting; while those who believe in satisfying the private demand for education disagree about criteria for financing, on which the private demand depends.

Much has been written on these issues.[2] The aim here is to help in developing an integrated framework for resolving them. Part I deals with the relation between cross-sectional social rate-of-return analysis and manpower forecasting, within the framework of a general cost-benefit approach. It first considers the case for using the rate of return on its own — as a signal variable in a control system where the student intake is the controlled variable; but this is rejected owing to the lead time between policy decisions and their effects in the labour market.

The next step is to examine what affects the relative importance of the cross-sectional rate of return and the manpower forecast, for policy purposes. The former shows how graduate numbers need changing due to current imbalances of supply and demand, while the latter deals with shifts in demand. The change indicated by the rate of return increases with the difference between the rate of return and the social discount rate and with the elasticity of demand for graduates; while the change

1.   I should like to thank M. Blaug, H.G. Johnson, G.R.J. Richardson and G.L. Williams for most useful comments on an earlier draft and L.P. Foldes for some very helpful suggestions.

2.   I have in mind particularly the writings of Mark Blaug which have provoked many of the ideas in this paper, see Blaug (1965), (1966) and, especially, (1967).

indicated by the manpower forecast increases with the growth rate of demand and with the lead time. The planner's research priorities should thus depend on the elasticity of demand and on the lead time, and on the costs of getting better estimates of rates of return and growth rates of demand. Psychic benefits and external effects may make it difficult to interpret the absolute level of the calculated rate of return, but trends in the rate can be valuable for avoiding echo effects and for. reducing the inadequacy of the coefficients used in manpower forecasts.

Finally, two practical arguments are considered in favour of forecasting. A high proportion of educated people are employed in public services, where rates of return are peculiarly difficult to interpret and where the government, as the future employer, may be able to make a more reliable estimate of the future demand than it can for the private sector. In addition, there may be substantial cost-savings when educational decisions are made not marginally from year to year, but as part of an integrated though flexible longer-term strategy.

However, most educational systems are not planned on cost-benefit grounds, but are regulated by the private demand for education. In Part II of the paper, therefore, we ask: What are the cost-benefit implications of meeting this private demand? We assume that individuals pursue education until the private rate of return to the marginal graduate equals the private discount rate. If so, the difference between the actual stock of graduates and that required on cost-benefit grounds depends on the proportion of the social cost of education that is subsidised and on the share of the social returns that goes in taxes and external effects, as well as on the private and social discount rates and the elasticity of demand for graduates.

However, if these are constant, the proportional divergence of the stock from its desirable level will not alter through time, if the educational system expands as directed by private demands. Thus if the stock is satisfactory now, it will remain so in future. But this assumes that we have got the subsidies right, which requires information on social rates of return, and it ignores the short-term problems of leads and lags, which are the main argument for forecasting.

We finally consider some alternative sociological explanations of how educational systems grow, and find them stimulating but somewhat lacking in explanatory power.

I. SOCIAL RATE OF RETURN ANALYSIS VERSUS MANPOWER FORECASTING

1 The cost-benefit objective

Assume a world in which education is publicly provided: not all worlds are like this but we are not discussing here the question of how education should be supplied. Assume too, for this part of the paper, that the government decides how many places to provide by setting its own targets rather than by responding to the private demand for education. The question is: How should it arrive at its decisions? What weight should it give to evidence on cross-sectional rates of return and how much to attempts at manpower forecasting?

Despite the general disarray on methods, most economists would agree on the *objective* of expanding the numbers who receive each type of education to the point where, taking into account all social costs and benefits, the present value of the education of the last man educated falls to zero. Since the net return stream to education has only one sign-reversal and different types of educational provision can in practice be varied independently, the same result is obtained by following the more convenient rate-of-return criterion: Expand the numbers educated until the marginal social rate of return of education (r_S) falls to equality with the social discount rate $(\bar{r}_S)$.[3]

The basic idea is that education, like most other things, yields diminishing returns and hence, assuming costs fall less steeply, a falling rate of return. If the number of graduates is not expanded enough (e.g. only to g_O in figure 1), there is a loss corresponding roughly to triangle

3. For an explanation of why it is more convenient to deal with rates of return than present values in educational planning see Blaug, Layard and Woodhall, 1969, p. 26. The most convenient formulation is to take as r_s the rate of social time preference, provided the costs of education are measured to allow for their social opportunity cost (Marglin, 1963B). It is somewhat arbitrary to take the rate of social time preference as independent of the investment decision, but this may not be serious, at least with reference to investment in one small sector (Feldstein, 1964). The whole cost-benefit approach is naturally subject to certain reservations about the income distribution effects of the way in which education is provided and financed.

A[4] Each extra unit of resources used in producing graduates would have yielded r_S, whereas society would have been indifferent between an investment yielding only $\bar{r}_S$ and no investment at all. There would thus be a surplus on each extra unit invested in education. Conversely if the number of graduates is too great (e.g. g_1) there is a loss corresponding roughly to triangle B.

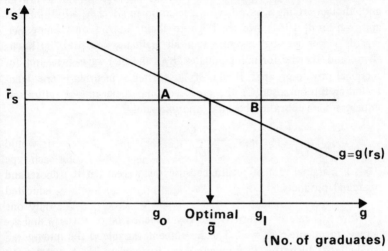

Figure 1

But what is the rate of return on education? Most people would agree on some broad listing of the social returns and costs of an individual's education, along the lines of the left-hand column of the following table. (The right-hand column becomes relevant in Part II.)

	To society	To the individual
Returns	Direct gains in production + Psychic benefits + External economies (net)	Gains in earnings (post-tax) + Psychic benefits

4.   For an investment yielding a permanent income stream the present value per £ invested is £$(r_S - \bar{r}_S)/\bar{r}_S$ and this measures the gain from spending one more £ on such an investment. For investments yielding other than permanent income streams or single-period returns, there is no strict relation between r_S, $\bar{r}_S$ and the **present value per £ invested.**

Costs	Loss of student's production + Cost of tuition	Loss of earnings (post-tax) + Fees − Grants to student

The rate of return is the discount rate which equates the return to the cost. It will help to use a simplified way of representing it. Psychic benefits and external economies are notoriously difficult to estimate, and, though attempts have been made to do so (Becker, 1964, p. 119 and Weisbrod, 1964), we shall ignore them for the time being. As regards wages we shall assume that all graduates are paid the same (W_G), and likewise for non-graduates (W_N) and that wages measure the marginal private product. If all costs are treated as incurred in one year, including tuition costs (C), the cross-sectional social rate of return on undergraduate education becomes approximately[5]

$$r_S = \frac{W_G - W_N}{C + W_N}$$

It is a marginal rate of return because the wages that it uses reflect marginal products.

Now this rate of return is the government's target variable and its aim is to maintain $r_S = \bar{r}_S$. The instrument variable is the number of graduates, which the government aims to regulate by its pattern of educational provision.[6] The relation between instrument and target comes through the demand for graduates. Suppose that this depends on the relative wages of graduates and on time. Then $g = g^1(W_G/W_N, t)$. But $r_S = (W_G - W_N)/(C + W_N)$, and therefore $g = g^2(r_S, W_N, C, t)$ or more simply, taking W_N and C as depending on time, $g = g^3(r_S, t)$. The

5.   The income stream generated by education is not of course perpetual but ends after about forty years. However, at a 10 per cent discount rate, 98 per cent of the present value of a perpetual income stream is accounted for by the income over the first forty years: the approximation is thus quite close. The assumption of a one-year course is simply to reduce the number of symbols, and the denominator can be multiplied by an appropriate number without significantly affecting the argument at any point. The relevant wage differential is between what the same man would be paid as a graduate and as a non-graduate: if we use the wages of actual graduates and non-graduates, it needs to be reduced to allow for the non-educational determinants of income.

6.   As Part II brings out, the government has also to ensure by subsidies or other means that the places are taken up.

desired equilibrium stock of graduates is $\bar{g} = g^3(\bar{r}_S, t)$. One can, if one likes, call this number the nation's manpower 'need', provided this is understood to mean the optimal from a set of possible numbers.

The optimal number changes over time in response to shifts in demand. In general it seems likely that the demand for graduates relative to non-graduates rises with time, capital being more complementary to graduates than to non-graduates, and technical progress likewise raising their relative marginal product. Provided the consequent rise in W_G/W_N (for given g) is not completely offset by simultaneous changes in W_N and C, the result will be a rise in the rate-of-return function $g = g^3(r_S, t)$ as time passes.[7] Thus, unless $\bar{r}_S$ varies significantly over time, the desired stock of graduates rises.

Granted this general framework for looking at the problem, the argument should be one about *methods* of achieving the desired stock and not about objectives. The issue is: How much can we learn for policy purposes from studying the cross-sectional rate of return and how important is the forecasting of shifts in demand?[8]

2   What does the social rate of return indicate for policy?

In principle there might be general agreement about the desirability of forecasting, if it were possible. In the ordinary cost-benefit analysis of a project, for example, it is standard practice to estimate the future demand for its product and thus to forecast the price which the public would be willing to pay for the proposed increase in supply. Applying this approach to education, one might for example be considering the admission of an extra 500 engineering students. The problem is then to estimate the future demand for engineers and thus the wage which the extra 500 graduates could command, taking uncertainty into account if possible. Since the future wages of those who graduate today depend also on the future output of graduates, we are in principle involved in a problem of the simultaneous optimisation of investment over all points of time.

7.   A sufficient condition for r_s to rise as W_G/W_N rises is that C does not rise relative to W_G since $r_s = 1 - \dfrac{W_N/W_G}{C/W_G + W_N/W_G}$

8.   Blaug (1967) pp. 285-6 proposes a different framework for considering the question, in which the role of the social discount rate as the target variable is less explicit. His model predicts what will happen and then evaluates it; our model is explicitly prescriptive.

However, daunted by the obvious perils of forecasting, a school of thought has developed which argues that educational planning should devote its main research effort to the study of the current cross-sectional rates of return. But the way in which policy conclusions should be drawn have not been very fully examined, and some rate-of-return practitioners seem to have been rather incautious in their approach to this. For example W. Lee Hansen (1963, p. 148) found that the rates of return on college graduation over each other level of education were greater than 10 per cent – college education over 'no education' yielded for example 12.1 per cent. In his view these facts, using a 10 per cent alternative rate of return, 'suggest the obvious advantages of seeing to it that everyone completes college'. If the rate of return had been under 10 per cent, would this have suggested the obvious advantage of giving no-one higher education? The approach seems to ignore the possibility of diminishing returns or, in the reverse example, of growth in the demand for graduates. It seems more appropriate to think of responding to rates of return by marginal variations in current flows than by such discontinuous changes.

This is the approach advocated by Mark Blaug: 'Rate of return analysis merely provides a signal of direction: invest more or less. But how much more or less? A little more or less is the answer and then recalculate the rate of return' (Blaug, 1967, p. 268). This argument may be couched in terms of a control system. Deviations of the signal variable (the rate of return) from its desired level should produce automatic variations in the controlled variable (the student intake) such that the signal variable never strays far from its optimum.

The problem, of course, as with all control systems, lies in the lag between the change in the controlled variable and its effect on the signal variable. In education a change in student intake has no effect on labour supply for at least two or three years (the length of course) and the relevant lead time may be even longer if we allow for the time needed for buildings to go up and institutions to adapt. Therefore, in general, it may or may not be appropriate to act on the signal of the rate of return, depending on what happens in the period between action and its effects in the labour market. However, since action is needed, it is of practical importance to ask: In what qualitative circumstances will acting on the basis of the rate of return lead to a policy change in the right direction?

124

We have to distinguish between the case where rate of return data are available for the current year only, as for example in Hansen's early study referred to above, and that where we have time series data, as would be the case with Blaug's control system. In most countries except the USA policy makers using rates of return have in fact as yet only one year's data to go on.[9]

The problems of using such data are illustrated in figure 2. This shows the rate of return function $g = g^3(r_s, t)$ for three years, the curve being labelled D to indicate that it reflects the demand side of the labour market. At the current (t_O) balance between demand and supply the rate of return is too low. Does this definitely suggest that we should reduce the rate of growth of supply?

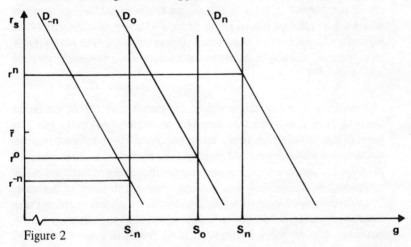

Figure 2

The problem is one of adjustment from a non-optimal capital stock to an optimal stock that is growing over time. In principle the adjustment path should of course be optimised over all points of time but this aspect is not considered in the preliminary thoughts put forward in the present paper. Instead we assume that for practical purposes policy should simply aim at reducing the gap $|r_s - \bar{r}_s|$ between now (t_O) and the first year (t_n) in which the number of graduates can be affected by this year's decisions.

9.   This is so, for example, in India where an attempt to draw policy conclusions from rates of return is made in Blaug, Layard and Woodhall, 1969.

As figure 2 shows, the policy of reducing growth rates $(S_n - S_O < S_O - S_{-n})$ will not necessarily lead to a smaller gap between r_s and $\bar{r}_s$ than if growth rates had been left unchanged $(S_n - S_O = S_O - S_{-n})$. The reason is that demand has been assumed to grow faster in future than in the past and that it was already growing faster than supply. We can however be sure of improving things by acting on the signal of a low rate of return when (a) demand is not expected to grow faster in future than in the past and (b) past demand did not grow faster than past supply.[10] The same is true of a high rate of return, with the inequality conditions reversed. If these conditions are not met the rate of return signal could lead to a policy step in the wrong direction.

If we have time series data we do not have to make assumptions about past trends in rates of return: we know them. We can then see whether low rates of return are in process of correcting themselves, as may often happen when poor social returns correspond to poor private incentives. In this way it should be relatively easy to dampen any major echo effect.[11]

But there remains the problem of guessing at future trends in demand. How likely is it that they will resemble trends in the past? In general this assumption seems more reasonable in developed than in underdeveloped countries and in large countries than in small ones. In developed countries there is of course the major discontinuity of technological change, but this is in any case very difficult to forecast. In underdeveloped countries this problem is much less acute, making forecasting easier, while discontinuous changes in the structure of the economy may be more common; making forecasting more necessary.

10. The demand functions referred to here are the demand-derived rate of return functions $g = g^3 (r_s,t)$. The argument is as follows. We can only be certain that a marginal reduction in the growth of supply will help if the neutral policy of setting $\dot{S}$ *(future)* = $\dot{S}$ *(past)* would reduce r_s still further. Sufficient conditions for this are that $\dot{S}$ *(past)* $> \dot{D}$ *(past)* $> \dot{D}$ *(future)*, since in this case $\dot{S}$ *(future* $> \dot{D}$ *(future)*. If $\dot{S}$ *(future)* $< \dot{S}$ *(past)*, r_s will fall less and may rise. If on the other hand $\dot{S}$ *(past)* $< \dot{D}$ *(past)* $< \dot{D}$ *(future)*, as in figure 2, the neutral policy will raise r_s and may raise it too far, in which case we need to increase the growth of supply. The whole argument here and in the text could of course be presented in terms of growth rates $(\dot{D}/D$ and $S/S)$ which for some purposes would be more useful.

11. Trends in earnings of new entrants to the labour market are particularly sensitive to changes in the balance of supply and demand and deserve special study.

Consider, for example, Indian engineering education in 1955, before the Second Five Year Plan. Rates of return were probably fairly near to the relevant discount rate. But a massive surge of demand was in sight. A conservative expansion policy based on rate of return calculations would have led for some years to an excessive rate of return. Happily, from that point of view and at that time, policy was in the hands of forecasters.

3 The relative role of rate of return analysis and manpower forecasting

But how serious is it if future trends in demand are not foreseen? This depends mainly on two variables: the lead time, already mentioned, and the elasticity of demand. If the elasticity of demand for graduates is high, their marginal product will rise little when demand rises. Equally, if the rate of return is inappropriate, it will take massive changes in the number of graduates to correct it; and these changes will dwarf in importance those required by changing demand conditions.

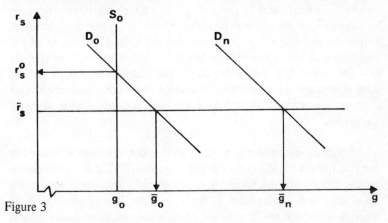

Figure 3

This point is crudely illustrated in figure 3. Here we assume that the social discount rate is the same at t_0 and t_n and that in t_n we wish to have the desired stock of graduates $\bar{g}_n$. At present we have a sub-optimal stock g_0. Thus the desired increase in supply between t_0 and t_n is $(\bar{g}_n - g_0)$, which can conveniently be broken down into $(\bar{g}_n - \bar{g}_0)$ and $(\bar{g}_0 - g_0)$.[12] The first is the increase due to growth of demand and the second is that due to the unsatisfactory balance of present demand

12.   Note that $(\bar{g}_0 - g_0)$ could be negative $\dot{r}_s < \bar{r}_s$

and supply, as revealed in the current rate-of-return calculation. In this sense, rate-of-return analysis is a method of evaluating the base from which a forecast is made and adjusting it to eliminate the effect of current imbalance. Once this important task is done — and so often it is not — forecasting is acceptable.

The magnitudes of the two adjustments are approximately $\bar{g}_O - g_O = \bar{g}_O \eta (r_S^O - \bar{r}_S)/\bar{r}_S$, where η is the elasticity of demand, and $\bar{g}_n - \bar{g}_O = \bar{g}_O(\dot{D}/D)\, t$, where $\dot{D}/D$ is the annual rate of growth in the optimal number and t is the number of years for which the forecast is needed (the lead time).

The relative size of the effects thus depends on $\eta(r_S^O - \bar{r}_S)/\bar{r}_S$ and $\dot{D}/D.t$. Thus research strategy should concentrate more on rate of return analysis (relative to forecasting) the higher y and the lower t, and the cheaper an improved estimate of r_S and the more expensive an improved estimate of $\dot{D}/D$. As for the magnitudes, lead times *(t)* vary between levels and specialities of education and between countries. On the elasticities (η) there is deplorably little information and research here has perhaps the highest priority in all the economics of education.[13] The lower the elasticity, the stronger the case for forecasting. Advocates of flexible planning urge steps such as later specialisation, which would shorten lead times and might also improve the substitutability of manpower and hence raise demand elasticities.

As regards accuracy, estimates of $\dot{D}/D$ and r_S are both difficult, but the real question is the cost of improving them. If $\dot{D}/D$ is quite likely to be the same as in the recent past and to make any better estimate is very expensive, then there is little case for manpower-forecasting research — though still a need for explicit guesses about future growth rates of demand. Equally it may be hard to ascertain the true social rate of return, which must include external effects and psychic benefits as well as allowing for divergencies between wages and marginal private product and for the effects on wages of determinants other than education. Thus in some cases one may not be able to improve on a

13.   Bowles (1969) argues that it is very high and uses this as an argument for assuming non-declining marginal productivity of educated people. For a fuller explanation of the relevance of elasticities of demand (or, more accurately, of substitution) in educational planning, see Dougherty (1971).

judgement, based perhaps on job analysis or international comparisons, as to whether the present stock is optimal. Since externalities and psychic benefits are likely to be positive, especially for general education as opposed to training, rate-of-return analysis may be more useful when the rate of return is suspected of being too high than too low. Neither rate-of-return analysis nor forecasting are free of the danger of substantial error, but both can hopefully, with proper attention and loving care, be improved.

This is not the place to pursue this point, except to remark that the best way to improve manpower forecasting seems to be to combine it ever more closely with rate-of-return analysis. The forms of manpower forecasting are many and varied,[14] but the simplest and most useful form is based on input/output coefficients indicating numbers of educated people per unit of output. The two standard problems with these coefficients are, first, that their present level may be non-optimal and, second, that their trends (which might be extrapolated) are also non-optimal. Both these points can be checked by rate-of-return analysis, and suitable adjustments made. For example in figure 4 the input coefficients have been falling and at the same time the rate of return has been rising to an unacceptably high level. The first step is to adjust up the level of the input coefficient to eliminate the current imbalance, using some assumption about elasticities of demand as suggested earlier. This is a standard use of rate-of-return analysis. But the next step is to adjust upwards the trend in the coefficient, which was evidently too steeply downward, since it led to a rising rate of return. This adjustment could again be done using standard elasticity assumptions. The suggestion is made, however, largely to illustrate the point that rate-of-return analysis may be as valuable in what it tells us about trends in the manpower balance as in what it says about the optimality of the current position. The snags are a good deal less in the former than the latter.

4   Two cheers for manpower forecasting

The preceding discussion has been less than concrete about the practical problems of planning, and it is time to make two points which justify a great deal of the forecasting work which is actually done. First, a very high proportion of the more educated people in most countries

14.   For a fair sample of methods of manpower forecasting see Blaug (ed.), 1968, pp. 263-348.

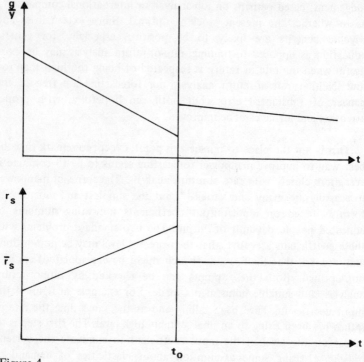

Figure 4

are, for better or worse, employed in the public sector. In Britain and India for example the proportions are about two-thirds of graduates and a similar proportion of those with completed secondary education.

This has two implications. Public sector wages are administered and it is therefore particularly difficult to interpret the calculated rates of return. Even if the public sector has no monopsony power but operates in the labour market on the same footing as the private sector, this only tells us that public sector wages correspond to the marginal product of labour in the private sector. We have no way of knowing whether the public sector is operating on its own 'true' demand curve — corresponding to its curve of marginal social productivity. There is certainly no market discipline which could ensure that it did. Thus it seems impossible to avoid the need for some elements of judgement in settling such questions as: What is the right number of teachers, given the school population and the costs of training teachers and of diverting their services from other employments? There is also the second point that over time the government should be better placed to foresee changes in its own demands than in those of the private sector. In any case it seems only natural that the government, which we have assumed plans education under one hat, should also put on its other hat and count up its demands as a future employer. When governments fail to foresee future demands for, say, teachers and doctors, they are not always forgiven by their electorates.

Making such forecasts need not imply that their results get mechanically translated into plans for educational provision. With some forecasts, such as the British forecasts of demand for school teachers, this is made quite explicit and the forecasts merely aim to show what the number of teachers would be, given various pupil/teacher ratios, so that the resulting numbers can be compared with supply forecasts on various policy assumptions. The forecasts are made, not to commit the future, but simply to add another dimension to thinking about it. The fact that forecasts of this, and any other, kind are bound to be wrong to some extent, provides no logical reason for supposing that things would have been better without them. Decisions are bound to be taken on some implicit or explicit assumption about the future and a wrong forecast may well be more realistic than the assumption that would otherwise prevail.

The second argument for forecasting concerns the length of the planning period. Our earlier discussion assumed that this need only be as long as the lead time between educational policy decisions, say to expand the student intake, and their impact on the labour market. But this implies that efficient educational decisions can always be marginal. This is not so. Many educational investments are lumpy, and a new university, for example, can be built much more cheaply if its early development is based on some general idea of its subsequent growth.

If foresight of this kind can save costs, what is there against it? There is the danger that long-term plans once made cannot be changed. But long-term plans can quite well be rolling plans, so that what ultimately happens is the short-term parts of a series of long-term plans. The aim of including the long-term part of the plan is to reduce the ultimate cost of the sequence of short-term plans — by allowing for the cost reductions made possible when decisions about interdependent projects are taken jointly.[15] Efficient spending requires that spenders have definite ideas about how much they are likely to be spending over a period of time. This applies not only to education but to health, defence and the rest; and the resources they get depend in part on how much goes to education.

There are two remaining criticisms of forecasting (in Blaug, 1967) that call for comment. The first is that it encourages excessive specialisation. In Britain this is causally not so – our deplorable specialisation began long before forecasting was dreamed of. And if one looks at other countries, one finds that some countries that are more planned than Britain have less specialisation (e.g. France) and others (e.g. in higher education, Russia) have more. The correlation between specialisation and planning appears to be low.

The second criticism of manpower demand forecasts is that there may be no way of telling whether they turn out right or not. According to Blaug the only case in which a forecast can be falsified is if the G.D.P. target from which it comes is hit but manpower falls short of the forecast demand. This implies that the forecasters believe that manpower, say graduates, and all other factors of production are so complementary that a certain G.D.P. can only be produced with the specified number of graduates. Perhaps some forecasters have implied this, but it is not the point of view put forward in this paper. A forecast of the demand for, say, graduates should be an estimate of the optimal number of graduates over a series of future years: that is, the number for which the rate of return would be right. It should thus take into account the facts both of substitutability, ignored by rigid manpower forecasters, and of diminishing returns, ignored by pure rate-of-return advocates. And the test of the forecast is this: Would the rate of return have been suitable if the projected number of graduates had been educated? The answer can be got from the actual number and the actual rate of return in the target year, together with an estimated elasticity of demand.

15. The rate-of-return approach, despite the boldness of many of its supporters, thus implies a series risk of overcaution. It has another conservative aspect in that it can only be used to evaluate courses already in existence and long-enough established to yield data on earnings by age. But this does not imply that all manpower forecasters are paragons of innovatory thinking.

II. COST-BENEFIT IMPLICATIONS OF MEETING THE PRIVATE DEMAND FOR EDUCATION

1 *Educational planning as it actually happens*

Partly because of the difficulties of evaluating manpower demand, no country outside the centrally planned economies uses this as its main criterion for educational planning. For particular forms of specialised manpower — doctors, teachers, engineers and trained craftsmen — manpower assessment is certainly used. But in nearly all countries the broad structure of the educational system is determined quite otherwise. In general, the minimum level of compulsory schooling is based on a mixture of general reasoning about human rights (enabling the poor to protect themselves against money-lenders, politicians and the like) and about income distribution (giving to each individual the capital source of a minimum income stream), as well as unquantified reasoning about rates of return to universal literacy, externalities being often invoked. Needless to say at compulsory levels of education it often proves necessary to force the people to come in.

At post-compulsory levels, there is a different story. Most governments simply respond to the private demand for places. This is often described as bowing to political or social pressure, but this pressure after all transmits the demands of individuals. In Britain the most obvious examples of provision adjusted to private demand are in post-compulsory schooling and in 'further education'. In universities we do not, as on the continent, have an open door policy, even for arts and science places. But the Robbins Committee put forward the principle that 'courses of higher education should be available for all those who are qualified by ability and attainment to pursue them and who wish to do so'. This is not of course the same as providing higher education to all who want it, since places are to be rationed to those 'qualified'. But it does mean that the number of places in higher education should grow as fast as the numbers who get the qualifications. For higher education as a whole, but not for the university sector, the government have acted on this policy. And the result has been a steady rise in student numbers.[16]

16. For a more discriminating analysis of the degree to which British higher education responds to the private demand for places see Layard, King and Moser, 1969, pp. 21-25. In teacher training of course the plans have been based on forecasts of demand for school teachers.

Some might question whether an approach like this can be dignified with the title of educational planning. But there seems to be no real problem. The government simply sets the terms on which education is available, and then plans to provide for the number of students who, using their own foresight, demand it on these terms. The remarks which follow are addressed mainly to this case but would be equally relevant where education is privately supplied at constant cost but the state provides subsidies and maintenance grants.

These kinds of arrangement, where education responds to the private demand, are often contrasted with a system that expands in relation to manpower 'need'. But how sharp in fact is the contrast? How does the pattern of manpower thrown up by a system of this kind compare with the pattern that is optimal on cost-benefit grounds?

2   What determines the private demand for education?

To answer this we need a theory of what determines the private demand for education. The proposed theory is that individuals weigh up the benefits and the costs, and decide whether to seek education by comparing its internal rate of return with their own private discount rate $(\bar{r}_p)$.[17] If we imagine the individual to form his picture of his own expected rate of return by looking at current wage differentials and costs, and if we ignore psychic benefits until later, we can construct a simplified theory of the demand for undergraduate education.[18]

As before, we use a model of the labour market, so that the demand for undergraduate education is not shown directly but corresponds to changes in the supply of graduates (plus replacement of those who retire). On the vertical axis we again have the rate of return, but this time it is the private rate (r_p), where (from the table on pp. 121-2)

17.   Strictly the rate-of-return criterion is inappropriate for private choices in education, since different types of education may be mutually exclusive while differing in cost. When there is no capital rationing, the rate-of-return rule can thus lead to the wrong decision, but it is still true that in general equilibrium, given diminishing returns and ignoring psychic benefits and risk, the rate of return on each type of education will become equal to the interest rate. The assumption in the text may thus be adequate for describing the general equilibrium position. Under capital rationing, the market outcome depends on the pattern of access to capital.

18.   A number of objections to the theory will be raised and discussed at the end of the paper.

$$r_p = \frac{(W_G - W_N)(1 - T)}{W_N(1 - T) + F - M}$$

and T is the average tax rate, assumed the same for graduates and others, F is the fee and M is the maintenance grant per student. As before the rate of return is related to the number of graduates. The demand function is $g=g^1(W_G/W_N,t)$, and thus $g=g^4(r_p,W_N,t,T,F-M)$. If all the independent variables except r_p vary with time, we have a series of simple rate-of-return functions $g = g^5(r_p, t)$, of which two are illustrated in figure 5. They are again labelled D to show that they reflect the demand side of the labour market. We assume that the demand curve rises over time, and hence likewise the rate-of-return curve, provided the effect is not offset by changes in fees, maintenance grants or tax rates.[19]

What of the supply of graduates? We could of course draw the normal upward-sloping curve. However we have not so far introduced any source of individual differences which would account for the upward sloping character of the supply curve, and it seems helpful to start with the simplest possible model. Accordingly we assume a capital market so perfect that the private discount rate of all individuals

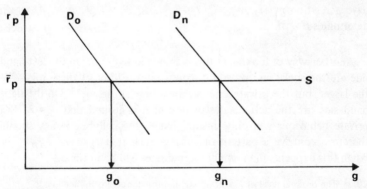

Figure 5

becomes equal, and we also assume that it remains constant over time at $\bar{r}_p$. Thus any rise of r_p above this level leads to an automatic increase

19.   Sufficient conditions for r_p to rise as W_G/W_N rises are as follows: if $F>M$, that $(F-M)/(1-T)$ rises no faster than W_G; and if $F<M$ that $(M-F)/(1-T)$ rises no less fast than W_G.

in the number of graduates.

We now have a very simple explanation of the growth in the stock of graduates. The demand for them grows and the supply is at once forthcoming. Provided the absolute growth in demand increases each year, the demand for entry to higher education will also grow.

3   What is the relation of private supply to manpower need?

But how optimal is this? There is clearly no automatic mechanism whereby the privately-determined supply of graduates will equal numbers 'needed' on manpower grounds. How nearly this happens depends on the relation first between r_p and r_s, and second between $\bar{r}_p$ and $\bar{r}_s$. In most countries private rates of return exceed the calculated social rates, as the high levels of subsidy outweigh the effect of taxes in reducing private returns. The optimal level of subsidy can be readily derived from our model (ignoring psychic and external effects and questions of income distribution). The aim at any time is that $g = g^2$ $(\bar{r}_s, W_N, C, t)$. The instruments available, assuming costs and tax rates cannot be varied, are fees and maintenance grants. And the behavioural assumption is that $g = g^4(\bar{r}_p, W_N, t, T, F - M)$. We then have a relation g^2 $(\bar{r}_s, W_N, C, t) = g^4$ $(\bar{r}_p, W_N, t, T, F - M)$ which determines $F - M$.

Another way of looking at this is shown in figure 6. On the left-hand side are the social and private discount rates. Either of these might be the larger, but the private rate is shown here as higher.[21] On the right-hand side are the actual rates of return. It is desired that $r_s = \bar{r}_s$. But private behaviour will only ensure that $r_p = \bar{r}_p$. Public policy should therefore contrive a pattern of subsidy such that $r_p - r_s = \bar{r}_p - \bar{r}_s$. When this happens, the number of graduates will be optimal.

20.   The optimal level of $F - M$ in our simplified model is in fact $[W_N (\bar{r}_s - \bar{r}_p) + \bar{r}_s C]$ $(1 - T)/\bar{r}_p$ but the approach in the text illustrates the kind of framework that would be needed if one were going to make r_s include external effects and psychic benefits. One may also note that in our simplified model the condition for $r_p > r_s$ is that $(C - F + M)/C > T$, i.e. that public expenditure as a proportion of tuition costs exceed the average tax rate. In this case, of course, the rate of return to public funds $r_f r_s$ since

$$r_f = \frac{(W_g - W_N)T}{W_N T + C - F + M} \quad < \quad \frac{(W_G - W_N)T}{W_N T + CT} = r_s$$

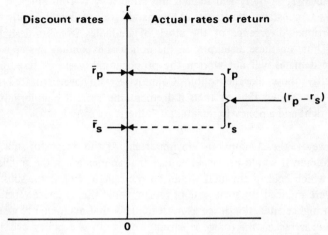

Figure 6

But it may not happen. Actual subsidies may be set at the wrong level and thus produce the wrong number of graduates. How far the actual number differs from the desirable level is a matter for empirical research and for judgement. However, regardless of whether the level is right, it is also relevant to ask: Do *changes* in the private demand for education correspond to *changes* in manpower 'need'?

As before we assume,

$$r_p = \frac{(W_G - W_N)(1 - T)}{W_N(1 - T) + F - M} = \bar{r}_p = constant$$

Now if average tax rates stay constant and likewise the proportion of the total social cost carried by public funds,[22] it follows that

$$\frac{W_G - W_N}{W_N + C} = constant$$

so that the social rate of return is constant. Its (constant) level will probably not equal the social discount rate. But their proportional

---

21. For a host of reasons why private and social discount rates may differ see Marglin, 1963A.
22. A sufficient condition for this would be for F/C, C/W_N and M/W_N to remain constant.

difference $(r_S - \bar{r}_S)/\bar{r}_S$ will remain the same if $\bar{r}_S$ is constant, and so, given a constant elasticity of demand for graduates, will the proportional divergence of the stock of graduates from its desirable level. Thus, on these assumptions, the policy of expanding in step with private demand will not worsen the proportional waste of resources. Implicitly, those, like the Robbins Committee, who have advocated this policy are saying that in their judgement the current equilibrium is about right and a policy to maintain it is therefore sound.

However, the assumptions are important. If the degree of subsidy were altered it would no longer be true that an increase in the graduate stock which held r_p constant would do the same for r_s. If the subsidy rate were reduced the social rate of return would rise, and vice versa. In British higher education it seems most unlikely that maintenance grants will rise as fast as the foregone earnings of youth − a policy decision which *ceteris paribus* is justified only if the present social rate of return on education is too low.

4   Introducing psychic benefits, external effects and individual difference

The reason why we have so far omitted psychic benefits is not because they are unimportant. Indeed in a society where hundreds of millions of pounds are privately spent on the arts, gramophone records, books, travel to centres of culture, and so on, it would be very odd if people did not attach a positive value to having been educated *per se*. For education is complementary to many of the most characteristic forms of modern consumption. And, just as people value (and pay for) the driving lesson which enables them to enjoy a car, they value the (often free) education which enables them to enjoy the Choral Symphony or the Parthenon. In this sense the nation's stock of educational experience is not only an input which helps to produce the standard of living, but is itself a part of the standard of living. The pleasures of having been educated are not however the only psychic benefits which flow from education, and there are three other forms which, though probably less important and possibly negative, should also be considered. First there is the pleasure of acquiring education, as opposed to having acquired it. Secondly, there are the different non-pecuniary advantages of the jobs to which higher education gives access. Third, there is the satisfaction parents may derive from educating their children.

There can be little doubt that the prospect of some of these psychic benefits materially affects the private demand for education. In other words psychic benefits enter into the *ex ante* private rate of return.[23] In full equilibrium we should therefore be able to measure the non-pecuniary benefits of education by the difference between the real rate of return on financial assets (assuming these to convey no psychic benefit) and the financial rate of return on education, which would be lower. Unfortunately, as Becker points out, we are not normally in full equilibrium and financial rates of return on education often exceed those on other capital (Becker, 1964, p. 122). This may be due to capital rationing or other reasons, and only means that the psychic benefits of education are peculiarly difficult to measure, not that they do not exist.

From the policy point of view, cost-benefit reasoning requires psychic benefits to be included also in social rates of return. Blaug argues that to include them involves a political choice (Blaug, 1965, p. 230), but as a matter of principle this cannot be right. Here are benefits which are in principle no less objective than the benefits flowing from the enhanced productivity of educated people. But in practice they are different — they are less measurable. In this sense only, the politicians may have as much to say about their importance as the economists.[24] How far does including them modify our analysis?

Since psychic benefits appear in both private and social rates of return at the same (untaxed) value, their inclusion may not radically alter the relationship between the two rates. However, both numerator and denominator are lower for the private than for the social rate, so that, when psychic benefits are added to the numerators of both rates, the private rate will rise more than the social rate, both absolutely and proportionately. And the greater the psychic benefits are, the greater of course is the proportion of the total social benefit that is unequivocally appropriated by the educated person.

23.   Blaug, 1965, p. 229, suggests that the *ex ante* evaluation of these benefits may be less than their *ex post* value to people who are already educated. The reverse is also possible: that some people are disappointed by education and do not feel that as such it has made them happier. On this point agnosticism may be the best course.
24.   It is sometimes said that allowing for psychic benefits is all right for advanced but not for developing countries. This argument is clearly wrong unless linked to issues of income distribution, which are not discussed in this paper.

We can now, briefly, reformulate the model, including psychic benefits *(P)*, as valued by the man who marginally chooses to be educated, and the net external benefits *(E)* resulting from his education. Now

$$r_p = \frac{(W_G - W_N)(1 - T) + P}{W_N(1 - T) + F - M} = \bar{r}_p = constant$$

and

$$r_s = \frac{(W_G - W_N) + P + E}{W_N + C}$$

Provided the share of external effects and of taxes in the marginal social return remains constant, and likewise the ratio of subsidy to cost, then the social rate of return will remain constant.

However, this depends on the assumption of a constant private discount rate common to all men. Once this is dropped we need to reformulate our explanation of educational growth. This is done in figure 7. As before we measure the private financial rate of return on the vertical scale. But now the supply curve of graduates slopes upward, for three main reasons. People differ in the relative value they put upon the psychic aspects of education: thus when a small financial return would be enough to induce one man to get educated, another will require something more attractive, even if they both have the same discount rate. Similarly, they may vary in the disutility attaching to the risks of educational investment. And finally they may, due to capital rationing, have different discount rates. The supply curve slopes upwards more sharply in the short run than in the long term, due to the limited number of people with qualifications within striking distance of entry to higher education over any one period of time.

As incomes rise the long-run supply curve shifts to the right. The financial rate of return which an individual requires of education falls, since with growing income he puts an increasing value on its psychic benefits. This is one source of the income elasticity of demand for education observed at the economy level.

Equally, or more, important is the effect of income growth in raising the demand for educated people as factors of production. Economic growth increases the number of graduates through both these income effects. To disentangle them is one of the largely unsolved problems of

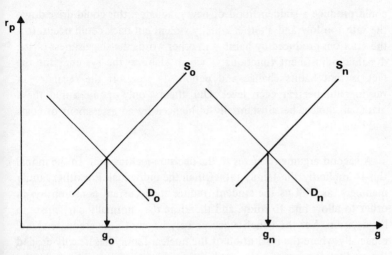

Figure 7

research.[25] But enough has already been said to dispose of the old examination chestnut: Does economic growth produce educational growth or vice versa? Any investment, like education, having a positive rate of return, produces economic growth. But likewise economic growth, however caused, raises the demand for education, both as a financially productive investment and for its psychic benefits.

5   Some sociological objections to the theory of private demand

Finally we must consider some of the main sociological objections to the kind of theory of private demand that has been proposed. One argument, often put forward by people with educated parents, is that people who get higher education have never decided to do so. Once on a certain escalator they get carried on upwards without choosing. To explain their behaviour by a theory of choice is thus said to be impossible.

Now much of human behaviour is certainly a matter of habit. Were it not so, the economic system could be subject to violent fluctuations. A tiny excess of actual private rates of return over their required level

25.   Campbell and Seigel, 1967, pp. 482-94, for example, estimate the income elasticity of demand for U.S. education, but are unable to differentiate these two effects.

could produce a sudden flood of new graduates; this could drive down the rate too low and another equally violent cut-back could occur. It is the frictions produced by habit − in other words the sluggishness of the dynamic adjustment functions − which stabilise the system. But the fact is that habits change and people do step off the escalator in varying numbers at each level. Our theory only requires that these marginal choices be substantially influenced by an assessment of costs and benefits.[26]

A second argument relates to the decision-making unit. In the model this is implicitly the family rather than the individual. For other family members, as well as the student, reduce their current consumption in order to allow him to study, and therefore they normally participate in his decision. Yet the benefits accrue very largely to the graduate alone, especially where the institution of the nuclear family has heavily eroded the graduate's economic responsibility for his parents or siblings. To the individual who gets educated the private rate of return is, strictly, a good deal higher than we have said, because while studying he is subsidised not only by the state but by his family.[27] This gives rise in some families to conflicts between parents and child as to whether the individual should continue his education. In other families the satisfactions which parents get from educating their children may be the main form of benefit, and in these cases there may also be conflicts − with the roles reversed. The fact of such conflicts of interest clearly calls for a more sophisticated theory but should not however undermine our general conclusions.

A third line of criticism comes from those who propose essentially different models for explaining the growth of education. All of these can be broadly termed 'snowball' models, that is they invoke some self-sustaining process of growth.[28] A common idea, for which there is

26. An example of the force of social habit is provided by recent experience in Britain as the population bulge passed through the higher education age group. Presumably the demand for new graduates did not expand abnormally fast in those years, yet the number of new graduates expanded tremendously − at the rate predicted by the trend in the proportion of the age group graduating (Layard, King and Moser, 1969, pp. 35-6).

27. If he had been earning, the student would in some cases have been subsidising the rest of the family. This further reduces the cost to him of studying.

28. We omit *ad hoc* institutional explanations, such as the structural reform of school systems, since there remains the question of why these reforms came about.

some evidence, is that parents' educational level is a major determinant of the educational level of their children.[29] Provided parents make sure their children become better educated than themselves, education must grow. Another suggestion is that information about higher education is a major determinant of the demand for it. The more educated people there are around, the easier is access to such information, not only by direct contact with graduates but also because graduates form an increasing proportion of workers in the mass media and of the mass media's public. Both these two models operate by changing the taste for education, which in our economic model is assumed unchanged. Another model works through the demand for educated people and alleges that graduates like employing graduates. Hence any increase in the supply of graduates leads to an increase in demand for them. In each of these models education is regarded as infectious, and it has been suggested that the time path of its expansion might have the sigmoid form of an epidemic process 'in which changes in the demand for places depend, in part, on the number infected and so liable to infect others and, in part, on the number not yet infected and so available to catch the infection' (Stone, 1965, pp. 179-81).

None of these models purports to be based on a theory of rational individual choice nor to aim at evaluating whether the expansion of education has been desirable. There is however a type of 'Hobbesian snowball' model which has a strong hold over the man in the street and over some academics, and which, to them, both explains the growth of higher education in terms of rational individual choice and shows why it has been a social disaster. As before there is a supply and a demand side variant of the model. On the supply side it is said that people seek higher education for status. Since status is purely relative, the more people have higher education the more others have to have it, simply in order to maintain their relative position. On the demand side the argument is that employers do not fundamentally care about a person's education but only his ability. If the ranking of people by education corresponds broadly to that by ability, then employers can use a person's education as a proxy for his ability. The role of the educational system is thus that of a selective device. But this function could in principle be performed as well if the general educational level were low

29.   See, for example, Committee on Higher Education, 1963, Appendix One, pp. 54-61, 69-70.

as if it were high, provided in each case there was a reasonable spread of education in the population. The Hobbesian character of the situation is that, to attract employers' favours, individuals try to rise in the educational scale, but they thus force other individuals of their level of ability to do the same in self-defence. To get a person of given ability employers have to take, say, a graduate, where before a man with School Certificate would have done.

The wasteful feature of both these Hobbesian situations is that, if only the individuals concerned could get together and agree not to raise the educational requirement for a given status or job, they could all be as well off as before. Then much of the educational growth which has historically occurred would have been unnecessary. Each individual acting singly (as a free rider) can improve his welfare by gaining extra education, either through consumption benefits in the form of higher status or through higher earnings from a better job. But society cannot improve its welfare this way because the education of others adversely affects the welfare of each individual. There are strong external diseconomies from educational expansion, which offset the internal benefits to each of the individuals involved.

What are we to make of these alternative models? They have been crudely stated, but, if suitably modified and combined with other forms of explanation, they each undoubtedly contain seeds of truth. For example a country with a weak educational tradition may be so unaware of the potentialities of education that not all the opportunities for privately fruitful investment in education get taken up. To allow for this we could subject our own model to a 'parental education' constraint, which said that education expands on the lines outlined in the paper provided there are enough children around with adequately educated parents. Alternatively the parental education model could have a rate of return constraint. One hopes that one day really sophisticated models of educational growth will be developed. However at the present stage it seems important to establish which lines of approach promise to yield the greatest explanatory power. The question to be answered is: What causes the number of students to be what it is and to change as it does?[30]

30.   Note that we are not trying to explain *which* people get educated. Economists may have something but not a lot to say on this.

The most obvious criticism of the non-economic models is that they do not seem to explain at all adequately the timing of educational development, which ought according to them to have been happening continuously and without interruption.[31] Yet educational development has not been like that. Since the Second World War there has been an unprecedented educational expansion, accompanied by unprecedented economic growth, in almost every country in the world. Between the wars on the other hand higher education barely grew in Britain and in many other countries — and economies slumped. This is indirect evidence for the economic interpretation in this essay. But there is also direct evidence in that private rates of return (not including consumption benefits) seem in many countries to be surprisingly similar to alternative rates of interest (Psacharopoulos, 1971), and in the USA for which we have time series they have remained astonishingly stable since before the War despite many-fold increases in student numbers. Unless the elasticity of demand for graduates is very high, we do seem to have here an explanation after a fashion of why the number of students is what it is, whereas the other theories would be compatible with its being any number. And if the other theories held, the rates of return would be most unlikely to be what they are.

We must however exempt from this general attack the Hobbesian model which describes education as a selective device. The theory says, after all, that students are each singly pursuing their own advantage which may well be largely financial. What it denies is that the financial return to the student corresponds in any way to a social return deriving from the higher productivity of graduates. The argument is that only ability is productive but that employers cannot tell who is able. So, knowing there is a high correlation (though no causal link) between education and ability, they give educated people the better-paid jobs. In this crude form the hypothesis is contradicted by the evidence of marked pay differences between ability groups within given educational groups (Becker, 1964, pp. 79-88 and Denison, 1964, pp. 86-100). A milder version of the theory says that employers know something, but not everything, about employees' abilities. However, they must surely know more, the longer they have been employing a person. So the effect of education on income (holding ability constant) should di-

31. The 'infection' models can also be criticised because they ignore the cost of education but this is only to say that they differ from the present theory. What is needed is an external test.

145

minish with age; but in fact it increases. We must also count against the theory the tentative evidence from production functions that the marginal productivity of educated people is broadly in line with their pay.[32]

The theory is also weak in explaining the timing of educational development, since the process of self-defeating·expansion could have proceeded indefinitely from any moment of initial disturbance. But a peculiarly subtle version of the theory (Wiles, 1969, p. 195) attempts to pin this disturbance into the post-war period by linking it to the demand for education as consumption. We are now told that education was originally demanded for its psychic benefits, with a high income elasticity of demand, but this then led employers to upgrade jobs thereby raising the financial pay-off to education. Of course the more the theory stresses the psychic benefits of education the harder it becomes to explain the observed level of the financial return, but one must allow that this version broadly passes the historical test. However, as argued above, it does not seem to portray adequately the rationale of graduate pay.

In due course we shall hopefully have complex and validated explanations of educational growth. In the meantime striking things are happening, with surprisingly similar patterns in different countries. It seems appropriate to begin with simple models of explanation. A clear merit of the theory of this essay is that its predictions are reasonably clear, and it can therefore be tested and refined by research.

But we are also interested in affecting change, as well as explaining it. The general argument in Part II has been that, given the right level of subsidy, a system driven by the private demand for education will produce an outcome broadly in line with what is needed on cost-benefit grounds. The Robbins approach is not as uneconomic as many letters to *The Times* would have us think. But does this mean that the arguments in Part I are redundant? The answer is No, for Part II has ignored what for short-run policy purposes may be of great importance — the leads and lags in the system.

32.   See for example Griliches, 1964. This reports an inter-state production function so that, unless there are great ability differences between states, differences in educational level must be taken at their face value.

In a state of steady growth we could with luck find a steadily-changing level of subsidy which equated the social rate of return to its desired level.[33] But in a world of irregular change, private choices under this system might not lead, as we have assumed they would, to stable social rates of return. Unheralded changes in the demand for graduates would, unless demand elasticities are very high, disturb the rate of return. Even if students responded at once to altered private returns, the rate of return would only revert to its proper level after the responding cohort had worked itself through the system. And the chances are that students would respond with a lag. How important these problems are is an empirical matter and varies between fields.

Some forecasting, however, is inevitable and desirable, and should be done both by governments and individuals. The government can use its forecasts to influence individual choice through variable subsidies and by vocational guidance; but also, where it provides education, it may use the pattern of provision as an instrument of policy [34] There may, in the present state of knowledge, be relatively few forecasts inspiring enough confidence for use, but we should use these and try to improve the others.

33.   In principle this could be done without calculating rates of return, by simply allowing for external effects; taxation and the differences between social and private discount rates. But in practice we know little about effective private discount rates and might need to experiment directly with different subsidies and observe the variation in social rates of return.

34.   In strict logic there is an asymmetry here – the provision of places can only reduce the number of students below what it would be, given free choice on the terms offered. However a liberal supply of places does also seem to increase the demand for entry.

REFERENCES

Becker, G.S. *Human Capital,* National Bureau of Economic Research, 1964

Blaug, M. 'The Rate of Return on Investment in Education in Great Britain', *Manchester School,* September 1965 [Reprinted in Blaug (ed.), 1968, to which page numbers refer]

Blaug, M. 'An Economic Interpretation of the Private Demand for Education', *Economica,* May 1966

Blaug, M. 'Approaches to Educational Planning', *Economic Journal,* June 1967

Blaug, M. (ed.) *Penguin Modern Economics. Economics of Education I,* 1968

Blaug, M., Layard, R. and Woodhall, M. *The Causes of Graduate Unemployment in India,* 1969

Bowles, S., *Planning Education for Economic Growth,* 1969

Campbell, R. and Seigel, B.N. 'The Demand for Higher Education in the United States 1919-1964', *American Economic Review,* June 1967

Committee on Higher Education (1963) *Higher Education: Report of the Committee appointed by the Prime Minister under the Chairmanship of Lord Robbins, 1961-63, Appendix One: The Demand for Places in Higher Education,* HMSO, Cmnd.2154-I

Denison, E. 'Proportion of Income Differentials among Education Groups due to Additional Education: The Evidence of the Wolfle-Smith Survey', *The Residual Factor and Economic Growth,* J. Vaizey (ed.), 1964

Dougherty, C.R.S. 'The Optimal Allocation of Investment in Education', in *Studies in Development Planning,* H.B. Chenery (ed.), 1971

Feldstein, M.S. 'The Social Time Preference Rate in Cost Benefit Analysis', *Economic Journal,* June 1964

Griliches, Z. 'Research Expenditures, Education and the Aggregate Agricultural Production Function', *American Economic Review,* December 1964

Hansen, W.L. 'Total and Private Rates of Return to Investment in Schooling', *Journal of Political Economy,* April 1963 [Reprinted in Blaug (ed.), 1968, to which page numbers refer]

Layard, R., King, J. and Moser, C. *The Impact of Robbins: Expansion in Higher Education,* 1969

Marglin, S.A. 'The Social Rate of Discount and the Optimal Rate of Investment', *Quarterly Journal of Economics,* February 1963A

Marglin, S.A. 'The Opportunity Costs of Public Investment', *Quarterly Journal of Economics*, May 1963B

Psacharopoulos, G. 'The Economic Returns to Higher Education in 25 Countries', *World Yearbook of Education 1971*, 1971

Stone, R. 'A Model of the Educational System', *Minerva*, Winter 1965

Weisbrod, B.A. *External Benefits of Public Education: An Economic Analysis*, Industrial Relations Section, Princeton University, 1964

Wiles, P. 'Die Bauchschmerzen eines Fachidioten', *Anarchy and Culture*, D. Martin (ed.), 1969

II. HISTORY OF ECONOMIC THEORY

Lauderdale and the Public Debt
A Reconsideration

B.A. Corry

For some years now there has been a controversy as to whether the early nineteenth century debates on capital accumulation – symbolised perhaps at their most dramatic in the Ricardo-Malthus exchange – are to be regarded as an early rehearsal of 'Keynes versus the Classics'. It was of course Keynes himself, in that fascinating, provocative, and in my view misleading, penultimate chapter of the *General Theory*,[1] who suggested his own lineage in such writers as de Mandeville, Malthus, etc. Most of the discussion has centred around Malthus and contributions have ranged from the extremes of those that argue that Malthus was even more Keynesian than Keynes himself realised,[2] to those that find no obvious theoretical connection: more recently certain other writers have been nominated for a place in the Keynesian Hall of Fame and in particular the case for James Maitland, Eighth Earl of Lauderdale had been advanced.[3] Any attempt to assess the case for or against a particular candidate is bound to be at best a most problematic exercise. In this case much will depend on what is agreed to be the central features of Keynesian economics; on top of this we have the endless problem of interpretation of the earlier writers. This interpretation arises both because of the use of the language of the day and also because of theoretical inconsistencies that occur. As historians of economic thought will know, it is possible by judicious quotation to make any writer a defender of any known position.

A few years ago I argued that in spite of all these difficulties of interpretation it was possible to conclude that none of the English group of early nineteenth century 'underconsumptionists' could be con-

---

1. Keynes, J. M., *The General Theory of Employment, Interest and Money*, ch. 28.

2. Lambert, P., 'Malthus et Keynes', *Revenue d'economic Politique*, 1962

3. McCraken, H., *Keynesian Economics in the Stream of Economic Thought*, ch. 3.

sidered to have grasped even a primitive version of Keynesian economics.[4] I argued rather that their central concern was with the effects of a rapid switch from consumption to saving within a model where decisions to save were automatically translated into expenditure on capital goods. Consequently these models are clearly attempts to grapple with the Harrod-Domar problem rather than the Keynesian short-run macro-equilibrium with its assumptions of a fixed capital stock and the absence of a mechanism to ensure that decisions to save translate into capital expenditures. In spite of the intense debate that continues to rage around this controversy I see no reason to rescind this view. However the true import of a new theoretical contribution is often only seen via its application, with this dictum in mind I now wish to consider the view that if we look at Lauderdale's pronouncements on the question of the Public Debt we will find his position more akin to contemporary (Keynesian) thought.[5]

Lauderdale also commands our attention because he was one of the few of the early underconsumptionists to write before the onset of the post-Napoleonic War depression. Once this had occurred it was quite commonplace to hear remarks that connected the depression with the rapid decrease in government expenditure. He attempted to predict these consequences *ex ante* from his theoretical structure. His main concentration was on debt management and in particular the economics of Sinking Funds; and it is on this aspect of his work that I want to centre this short note.

The literature on the Sinking Fund in the late eighteenth and early nineteenth century was an incoherent mass that grew at a rate that would have delighted both Dr. Price and M. Fortuné Ricard. It is however possible to divide it directly into two broad issues; first of all the straight mechanics of debt reduction and secondly the economic effects of such reductions. After the absurdity of Price and his followers it was soon pointed out that debt redemption could only be achieved from a genuine budget surplus and that, for example, further borrowing — often at higher rates — to add to the fund was not sensible! These

4.   Corry, B.A., *Money, Saving and Investment in English Economics.*
5.   I should add here that the impetus to this particular paper came when looking recently through my notes on Lauderdale I noticed that I had added a marginal comment 'must check LR's view that a much more sympathetic case could be made for Lauderdale if we look at his writings on the Sinking Fund'.

sort of considerations were ably cleared up in studies such as Hamilton's.[6] With all of this Lauderdale agreed — they were obvious — but on the much more complex issue, about the economic effects of a 'properly organised' or rational sinking fund, Lauderdale appears as a violent contrast to the central classical position.

We shall therefore look specifically at Lauderdale's thoughts on the sinking fund and see whether his participation here makes us more sympathetic to the use of the label 'Early Keynesian' than his more general macro-position on the effects of accumulation. In order to set our sights straight let us remind ourselves how in broad terms the extremes of Keynesian and classical models would handle the sinking fund problem. The question is simple. Suppose a government reduces expenditure whilst keeping revenue constant and with the accruing surplus buys up internally held national debt? What happens? In the simplest Keynesian case — as depicted in the Hicksian *IS-LM* cross — there will be a fall in income and the rate of interest. The fall in income will be less than $-dG(1-b)^{-1}$ because of the stimulatory effect on induced investment of the fall in the rate of interest. The total effect will however be deflationary. In the simple classical case there will be no change in income but a fall in the rate of interest. Hence a reallocation of output between investment and consumption will occur. There will be no deflationary effect. In more realistic models the predicted effect of such a policy is a much more complex matter. This is basically an example of what R.A. Musgrave calls a 'mixed fiscal-liquidity' policy and in a standard Keynesian model with allowances for wealth effects the direction of effect is deflationary, but less so e.g. than a decrease in the quantity of money. Since the policy involves a decline in the structure of interest rates the net response depends on how far the secondary decline in expenditure induced by the fall in interest rates can offset the initial decline due to the fall in government expenditure.[7]

We now come onto Lauderdale and his contribution to fiscal theory. The first point of interest to note is that Lauderdale's early writings and speeches on the question of the Public Debt give no hint at all of what is in store. These early views are orthodox; they regard the Debt

6.   Hamilton, R., *The National Debt*.
7.   Musgrave, R.A., *The Theory of Public Finance*, Part 4.

increase as an unmitigated disaster and argue for its immediate reduction if not complete abolition. In these early years he regarded the Debt as an unambiguous burden and the expenditure uses to which it was put unproductive. His first publication — the *Letters to the Peers of Scotland* — in 1794 is straightforward enough.

'We begin to perceive', he writes, 'the rapid diminution of the national debt with which we were loaded, and which forms the only check upon the enterprising spirit of the nation',[8] and of earlier years when the debt was higher, 'all were convinced of the disadvantage under which we laboured, in having so large a part of our wealth employed in unproductive uses; and there were none who did not look forward with alarm, who did not dread the consequences of thus burying any larger proportion of our productive capital'.[9]

The same sentiments are expressed in 1797 in his *Thoughts on Finance, Suggested by the Measures of the Present Session*. The central point here is that public expenditures are wasteful,[10] and inhibit growth. In his discussion of the effects of a possible extension of public loans we read,

> In this country we may pronounce with confidence, that such a measure, if resorted to, must be ruinous. In all opulent and commercial nations there is a variety of uses of capital; and perhaps there is none whose spirit of enterprise has created more channels for the employment of its wealth, and whose, of course, reproduction must be so infinitely varied.[11]

At the macro-economic level that policy implication is one of *laissez-faire;* government expenditure should be reduced to a minimum and the savings-investment mechanism left to the market. Not very Keynesian in outlook you may say!

The apparent *volte face* comes with the first edition of his *Inquiry* of 1804.[12] The position here is still somewhat tentative and does not have

8.   Lauderdale, *Letter to the Peers of Scotland*, p. 23.

9.   Lauderdale, *Letters* . . . . . ., p. 83.

10.   Lauderdale, *Thoughts on Finance* . . . . . ., p. 2. 'It is difficult to find a single individual in the higher or even middling classes of society, who in his own person, or through the medium of some relation or friend, does not habitually prey upon the public revenue'.

11.   Lauderdale, *Thoughts on Finance* . . . . . ., p. 28.

12.   Full title, *An Inquiry into the Nature and Origins of Public Wealth, and into the Means and Causes of its Increase*.

the clear-cut arguments of his post-1815 pamphlets that we shall look at in a moment. As is well known one of the central features of the *Inquiry* is the argument that 'excessive accumulation' may prevent an economy attaining its maximum growth potential. I have already mentioned the point that interpretors of Lauderdale cannot really agree as to whether by 'accumulation' Lauderdale meant 'saving' or capital accumulation. What is clear and uncontrovertible is that in the *Inquiry* Lauderdale still felt that *laissez-faire* at the macro-level was still *the* optimising strategy.

> Fortunately ... for mankind [he tells us] the mechanism of society is so arranged, that the mischief done by the parsimony and disposition to accumulation of one individual is almost uniformly counteracted by the prodigality of some other; so that in practice nothing is found more nearly commensurate than the expenditure and revenue of every society. This enquiry, therefore, if man were left to regulate their conduct by their inclinations, would be rather a matter of curiosity than utility; for if the effects of parsimony are uniformly counteracted by prodigality, the public wealth can be neither increased nor diminished by it.[13]

One major form of 'prodigality' is government expenditure and Lauderdale explains the unprecedented wartime prosperity by the extra demand for goods and services generated by deficit financed government spending. He further goes on in the *Inquiry* to warn of the deflationary dangers inherent in a cessation of hostilities.

In two important pamphlets in the post-war period Lauderdale again grappled with the intricacies of the Sinking Fund. These pamphlets were the *Sinking Fund,* 1822 and *Three Letters to the Duke of Wellington,* 1929.[14] This time of course economic conditions were poles apart from those existing in wartime England — a world then of full employment and rising prices and money wages. In post — 1815 England

13. *Inquiry*, pp. 228-9.
14. Full titles, *Sinking Fund, or, The System Which Recommends the Repeal of Five Million of Taxes, compared with the System which Recommends Levying Five Millions By Taxation, for the Redemption of the Public Debt.* And; *Three Letters to the Duke of Wellington, on the Fourth Report of the Selected Committee of the House of Commons, Appointed in 1828 to Enquire into the Public Income and Expenditure of the United kingdom; in which the Nature and Tendency of a Sinking Fund is Investigated, and the Fallacy of the Reasoning by which it has been Recommended to Public Favour is Explained.*

... it is generally admitted that the people of this country are in a state of unparalleled distress; and those who have official access to the best information, have distinctly, and it is believed, truly stated, that this distress arises from the want of a market, that is, from the want of a sufficient demand for the produce of our country.[15]

In these circumstances he asks, is it wise to attempt to pay off the National Debt by raising taxation? The correct economic strategy, given that its basic troubles arise from deficiency of overall demand, would be to reduce taxation. Apart from the direct relief if taxes were lowered, it would 'ensure infinitely more important relief, by creating an additional demand for commodities to that extent'.[16]

Interest payments on the Debt financed by taxation are not seen affecting the level of aggregate demand but only its composition.

Taxes raised on the People, and paid over to the creditor in the shape of dividend on his capital, certainly cannot fairly be represented as diminishing the demand for the produce of the country. In that case, what is paid in the shape of tax, forms the revenue of the stockholder, and is expended by him in acquiring the objects he wishes to enjoy; though by this means, therefore, the order of expenditure may be altered, it is clear the demand for the produce of the country cannot be diminished.[17]

The use of taxation revenue to buy up Debt via a Sinking Fund involved, on the other hand, a fall in aggregate spending. In Lauderdale's terminology,[18] the deflation was due to the 'conversion of revenue into capital'. The Fund-Holder who has been 'bought out' cannot be 'induced to spend as revenue, that which habit has taught him to regard as capital'.[19] The orthodox reply to all this was via the Smith-Turgot 'saving is spending' theorem which, combined with a flexible structure of interest rates, would ensure that extra saving would induce extra capital formation to the same amount. In these terms Debt redemption was seen as a positive benefit increasing as it did the demand for labour and the growth potential of the economy.

15.   Lauderdale, *Sinking Fund*, p. 7.

16.   Lauderdale, *Sinking Fund,* p. 16.

17.   Lauderdale, *Sinking Fund,* p. 16.

18.   This was general Classical terminology, although the orthodox (e.g. Smith, Ricardo, J.S. Mill) would have disagreed with Lauderdale's view on the consequences.

19.   *Ibid*, p. 10.

In the *Three Letters* the same point is reiterated as only Lauderdale knew how![20] Wealth creation proceeds from demand and not by a reduction of consumer expenditure intended to finance capital formation. 'Parsimony, or abstracting from expenditure in consumable commodities, forcibly to convert a portion of the revenue of a country into capital, impeded the natural progress by which public wealth increases, and was injurious to every community who improvidently adopted such a practice.'[21] The Sinking Fund was such a practice.

And yet the problem of interpretation still remains! Of course, reading Lauderdale (and Malthus) today on the post-Napoleonic war depression, we are bound to feel sympathetic to any writer who even mentions demand deficiency and especially links it up with public expenditure and revenue. Nonetheless by 'expenditure' Lauderdale clearly meant consumption not consumption plus investment. He gives the impression (as Malthus stated explicitly) that hoarding is not part of his model. Hence we are forced to conclude that Lauderdale did think in terms of 'savings leads to capital formation' and consequently it is difficult, once in this framework, to escape from the classical straight-jacket. Whilst it must have been clear to any business man or worker that economic hardship was primarily due to demand deficiency, the revolution in economies that forced the abandonment of the orthodox classical position had to be a theoretical revolution. An alternative theory to 'Say's Law' had to be offered otherwise orthodoxy would reign. Economists have never thought much of empirical evidence anyhow!

20.   The novice should note that the *Three Letters* comprise some 138 pages.
21.   Lauderdale, *Three Letters*, p. 7.

Ricardo's Theory of Distribution

J.R. Hicks

It has been the general impression, ever since Cannan *(Theories of Production and Distribution,* pp. 339 ff.), that there is something wrong with Ricardo's theory of distribution, even on his own assumptions. His arithmetical examples are not sufficient to support his conclusions; they do not show them to be necessary. The matter has been further explored by H. Barkai *(Economica* 1959), whose more sophisticated technique seems to support the Cannan criticism. I accepted it myself, until impelled by some correspondence with Dr. K.V.S. Sastri, of Andhra University (Guntur) India, to look at the matter again. He convinced me that there is more to be said for Ricardo than is allowed by these critics, even when the question at issue is taken as they take it. But I have also beer convinced – and I am now inclined to think that this is a more important matter – that the distribution question on which the critics have fastened is only one of the questions which was in Ricardo's mind. There is another, on which Ricardo's position is stronger; and for his central thesis (his theory of Growth, or Retardation of Growth) it is a more important question. Even for us in our day, when we are interested in that aspect, it is a more important question.

I begin, nevertheless, with the 'conventional' problem, which I do not dispute was one of Ricardo's problems. He says, in his *Introduction,* that he is going to study the ways in which 'the whole produce of the earth ... will be allotted ... to rent, profits, and wages'. It is there in black and white.

The central model, on which the answer that he gives is based, requires neither arithmetical examples nor algebra for its exposition. If we make two *simplifications* (which Ricardo very frequently, but not invariably, allows himself) it can easily be represented on a diagram. I shall begin with this simplified version, but shall not omit before I have done, to consider the adjustments which are needed when the simplifications are removed.

Production, in the Ricardo model, is of two 'goods' — 'food', produced under diminishing returns, and 'manufactures', produced under constant returns. The first of the simplifications is to suppose that the two goods are demanded, throughout, in fixed proportions. Analytically, therefore, they can be reduced to a single good, a 'bundle', which I shall call Output. Output, it will be observed, is produced, by these assumptions, under *diminishing* returns.

The second simplification is to neglect fixed capital, and to make all capital circulate with a uniform fixed period. Input, therefore, is solely input of labour. Wages, however, are advanced to labourers, so that the wage of the labourer is his discounted marginal product. But since the supply of labour is taken to be perfectly elastic at a given (real) wage, a wage that is fixed in terms of Output, the equation of wage to discounted marginal product does not determine the wage, but determines the rate of discount or profit, which is

$$\frac{\textit{marginal product of labour} - \textit{wage}}{\textit{wage}}$$

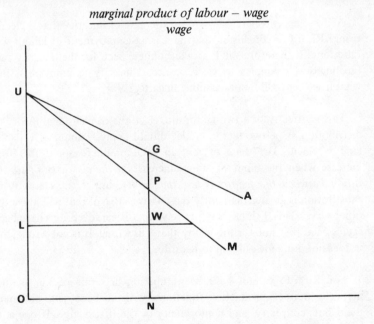

Figure 1

With these simplifications, the diagram is easy. Labour (input) is measured on the horizontal axis. Output on the vertical. *UM* is the

161

curve of the marginal product of labour, *UA* is the curve of the average product. (I have drawn these curves, in figure 1, as straight lines, but I am not assuming that they have this particular form. It is *generally* true that if *UM* slopes downward throughout, *UA* must slope downward throughout.)

When the input of labour is *ON,* the average product of labour is *GN,* the marginal product is *PN,* and the wage is *WN (LW* being the horizontal supply curve of labour). Profit per unit of labour is *PW,* and rent per unit of labour is *GP.* The shares of the factors in the product are therefore proportional to *GP, PW, WN.*

It is at once apparent that since *UA* is falling throughout, the share of wages in total product *(WN/GN)* must be rising. This will be generally true, whatever the form of the curves. It does not depend at all on linearity.

As for the rent-share *(GP/GN)* in the case of linearity that is clearly rising. Ricardo's conclusion that increasing employment of labour will raise rents is therefore valid, as we should expect, for the linearity case (arithmetical examples so easily conceal linearity assumptions). But what if we generalise, not assuming linearity?

This is effectively a two-factor model, so the conventional theory of distribution in a two-factor model should apply. Labour is variable, land is fixed. The share of rent in total product should therefore increase when the input of labour increases *if the elasticity of substitution between the factors is less than unity,* but if the elasticity of substitution is greater than unity the relative share of rent will move the other way.[1] This, I think, is effectively what Ricardo's critics have been saying, and it is not for me to say that it is wrong. It is not wrong, but it does not quite measure up to Ricardo.

For Ricardo cannot have been thinking in terms of our mathematically defined production functions, with no constraint put upon them but 'convexity' and homogeneity of the first degree. If one asks what he is assuming, some of these things are not important; but there are others, on which the mathematical theory does not insist, which are:

1.   J.R. Hicks, *Theory of Wages,* 1932, ch. 6.

> On the first settling of a country, in which there is an abundance of rich and fertile land, a very small proportion of which is required to be cultivated for the support of the actual population, or indeed can be cultivated with the capital which the population can command, there will be no rent.

That is what he says (Sraffa edition, p. 69). So the two-factor production function must be such that when land is plentiful relatively to labour, the marginal product of land is zero. I do not find him saying so explicitly that if the input of labour increased indefinitely, relatively to land, the marginal product of labour would fall to zero; this is indeed, on his assumptions, so fanciful a state of affairs that he would have had no occasion to mention it. But I would have thought that no unprejudiced reader of Ricardo could doubt that it is implied. For it is an implication that can only be avoided, consistently with the diminishing returns that are explicitly assumed, by making the marginal product curve converge asymptotically to some horizontal. Of course Ricardo did not bother about that. If anyone had mentioned it to him, one feels sure that he would have dismissed it as just plain silly!

If the production function is restricted by these *two* extra conditions, that the marginal product of land falls to zero when land is sufficiently abundant, and that the marginal product of labour falls to zero when labour is sufficiently abundant, it follows that at the terminal points, where a factor just ceases to be abundant, the elasticity of substitution between the factors *must* be less than unity. It is unnecessary to give a mathematical proof; for it is obvious that when, as a result of an increase in the input of labour, rent rises from zero to a positive quantity, the share of rent must be rising; so the elasticity of substitution must be less than unity. Similarly at the other end.

If the elasticity of substitution were constant, or even approximately constant, along the whole curve, it would follow at once that it must be less than unity everywhere; Ricardo's proposition about the rent share would then be proved. This is a procedure which may appeal to some; I do not care for it myself. 'CES production functions' have been having a vogue; they are mathematically fairly jolly; but what is the empirical reason why the production function should be of this type? I cannot see any.

Nevertheless, if the elasticity of substitution must be less than unity at each end, it can only become greater than unity anywhere if it has a bulge in the middle; and though we must grant that such a bulge could occur, it might fairly be regarded as 'abnormal'. Ricardo is guilty of no more than the omission of a qualification. Are we doing any more than touching up his theory a little when we put it in?

Notice further just what is implied in it. As the input of labour increases, the relative share of rent begins at zero, rises to a positive fraction, perhaps then slips back a bit, but must 'in the end' resume its rise. If a mountaineer starts at sea-level, and finishes the day at the top of his mountain, he must *on the whole* have been climbing; but it is of course not excluded that he had to get over a smaller range on the way, and was descending for a while as he came down from it.

Even this is not all – by no means all. For though there are many passages (such as that which I quoted from his *Introduction)* in which Ricardo talks in terms of a three-way distribution, it is a question how far it was this distribution which was ultimately his main concern. So long as one is looking at the three-way distribution, the decline in the profit-share seems to be due as much to the rise in the wage-share (which, as we have seen, occurs without exception) as to the rise in the rent-share, which is subject to the qualification we have just been considering. Why does he put so much emphasis on the rise in the rent-share?

The explanation, I think, is to be found in the chapter on'Gross and Net Revenue' (XXVI). Wages (subsistence wages) are for Ricardo a cost, a cost which is necessarily incurred in the earning of the surplus (Net Revenue), from which alone the saving which is the source of capital accumulation and therefore of expansion can be derived. Net Revenue is profits + rents; so if the profit share in Net Revenue falls, the rent share *must* rise, and vice versa.

Now as labour input increases, the wage-share in Gross Revenue (necessarily) rises; so the ratio of Net Revenue to Gross necessarily falls. Thus even if Rent was a constant proportion of Gross Revenue, it would be a rising proportion of Net Revenue. It could even be a falling proportion of Gross, and still be a rising proportion of Net Revenue. Thus when Ricardo is thinking 'net' (as I believe he often is) he can talk of rents gaining at the expense of profits; and though there is still a possible exception (over limited ranges) it has been cut down to a very modest exception.

No doubt it is the fall in the *rate* of profit, diminishing the incentive to save and invest, which is the brake on expansion on which Ricardo laid greatest weight; this (which figures in the diagram as the ratio *PW/WN*) is clearly declining, from the downward slope of the marginal productivity curve, *without exception.* But it is reinforced (fairly certainly reinforced) by the transference of net revenue, which is savable revenue, from a class which looks like having a high propensity to save and invest to one which looks like having a much lower propensity. That they have these propensities is an empirical judgement, but it is not unreasonable. Thus, within the limitations of the model, the retardation is established: securely on the side of incentive, sufficiently on the other.

How much of it remains when we drop the simplifying assumptions — the homogeneous Output and the confinement to circulating capital? So far as the first is concerned, though it bothered Ricardo quite a lot, I do not think it need make any serious difference. While Output remains homogeneous, an expansion in labour input must *necessarily* (as has been seen) imply a rise in the labour share of Gross Revenue; now if (another quite reasonable empirical assumption) labourers spend *relatively* more than other classes on 'food', this shift towards labour will change the 'mix' of Output in such a way as to accentuate the tendency to diminishing returns. The model is harder to set out, but it seems to work in much the same way.

The other assumption (which amounts to making capital-intensity invariable) is much harder to deal with. When we remove it, we make it possible for business to resist the fall in the profit rate by using more capital-intensive methods; but though the decline in the *rate* of profit can be resisted in that way, it cannot be prevented — for it is only because the rate of profit falls that the more capital-intensive methods become profitable. Thus, so far as incentive is concerned, Ricardo's argument still holds; the decline in the rate of profit is slower than it appeared originally, but it is still there — it must be still there. On the distribution side, with which we have been here concerned, there may be more trouble. An increase in capital intensity is a substitution of capital for other factors; the factor for which capital is substituted may be labour, or may be land. If the substitution is heavily for land, it may diminish the share of rent, even the share of rent in the Net Product. Here, therefore, we have another source of exception, more important, perhaps, than the other.

There are two elements in Ricardo's theory: the empirical assumptions and the analytical structure. The empirical assumptions are of his own time; whether they are right or wrong, for that time, is a matter for historians. But the analytical structure is permanent. It has nothing to do with the landlord and tenant system or with the sleepiness of early nineteenth-century landlords (on whom Ricardo may, or may not, have been too hard); it has nothing to do with his (doubtless oversimplified) supply curve of labour. It should be re-stated, for our purposes, in much more general terms. It is solely concerned with the impact of capital investment on an economy with some scarce resources, the scarcity of which the investment of capital does not overcome. There can be such resources in any economy; they are not necessarily 'land', they may be labour. There is a revealing footnote of Ricardo's (Sraffa ed., p. 348), in which he contemplates the probability that, already in his time, a part of Net Revenue was going to wages. He has been identifying wages with the 'necessary expenses of production', but then:

> Perhaps this is expressed too strongly, as more is generally allotted to the labourer under the name of wages, than the absolutely necessary expenses of production. In that case a part of the net produce of the country is received by the labourer, and may be saved or expended by him; or it may enable him to contribute to the defence of his country.

If Ricardo were writing to-day, he would have to expand that footnote. But he would not. therefore be obliged to change his theory, in its analytical structure.

It must be emphasised (an overwhelmingly important qualification, of which Ricardo in several places, as for instance in the chapter on Machinery, shows himself to be well aware) that his apparatus is based upon the assumption of a given technology; the 'declining rate of profit' is a matter of the exhaustion of the expansion which is permitted by *given* technical opportunities. In a progressive economy, in which improvements are continually being made, there is a force which works the other way. But that, though a tempting form of expression, is not the best way of putting the issue. It is more instructive to think of each invention as setting up what might be called an 'Impulse' — which, if it were not succeeded by other

166

Impulses, would peter out.[2] Ricardo's theory is a theory of the working of the individual Impulse. So interpreted, it remains on its throne — an indispensable part of modern economics.

2.   Increasing returns, economies of scale, being treated (so far as they are relevant) as 'inventions'. This is not in fact at all inconvenient.

Thomas Tooke on Monetary Reform [1]

David Laidler

I

The controversy that surrounded the passage of Sir Robert Peel's Bank Charter Act of 1844 has already produced a substantial historical literature, and on the whole this literature has awarded the honours to the Currency School.[2] This is perhaps a little strange since the banking structure created in 1844 failed to mitigate the periodic financial difficulties of the type that had plagued Britain in the 1820s and 1830s, and the very rules under which the system was supposed to work had to be suspended to cope with several subsequent crises. Of course, it is always possible that the suggestions of the opponents of the Act could have led to even worse difficulties but in this essay it will be argued that the recommendations of Thomas Tooke, the leading member of the Banking School, were based on greater insight into the manner in which the monetary system worked prior to 1844, and were very much what a modern economist might suggest within the constrain of the policy goals ruling in the nineteenth century. It will not, however, be argued that Tooke's analysis was logically complete and rigorous for, as we shall see below, there are places where critical pieces of it are missing or badly set out, and where extraneous matters intrude unduly.

1.   I am deeply indebted to Bernard Corry for the many hours he contributed to discussing the subject matter of this essay with me, and to Robert Clower and Harry Johnson for most useful comments on an earlier draft. Nevertheless, all errors, omissions, misinterpretations and quotations taken out of context, are my own responsibility.
2.   The main contributions to this literature are to be found in Gregory [4], Mints [6], Viner [13], Robbins [8], and most recently in Fetter [3]. Of these, it is Fetter, the latest contributor, who is the most sympathetic to the Banking School, and Gregory, the earliest, who goes so far as to refer to the Currency School as 'the elect' ([4], p.77), who is the least so. This literature spans almost forty years, and though it would be a fascinating study in itself to trace the evolution of opinion about nineteenth-century monetary controversy over this period, there is hardly room to do so in one brief paper. As far as possible then, I have tried to avoid debate with these commentators, and to let Tooke's ideas speak for themselves.

In the following pages I will first discuss the policy goals of the time and sketch out the differences of opinion about the problems of achieving them. I will then go into Tooke's analysis of the banking system in order to show that his assessment of the policy problem was not without foundation. Finally, it will be argued that, given this analysis, his very moderate practical recommendations are more appealing than those made by the Currency School.

II

One of the more remarkable facets of nineteenth century British economic doctrine is the almost unanimous agreement that is to be found on policy goals. With the exception of Attwood and his followers the leading economists of the day all took the view that the overriding aim of monetary policy was to maintain the convertibility, both at home and abroad, of Bank of England notes into gold at a fixed price. Tooke himself referred to this as 'the *sine qua non* of any sound system of currency' ([10], Vol 3, p.177) and expressed 'unutterable surprise' that 'any well informed person, not of The Birmingham School could seriously propose to have cash payments suspended, rather than that the mercantile community should be subjected to some inconvenience...' ([11], p.104). To this goal all others were to be sacrificed, and the debate between the Currency School and the Banking School took this for granted. The debate, rather, was about the structure of the institutional framework necessary to guarantee the achievement of this end, and about the costs which competing schemes would impose upon the economy in maintaining the convertibility of paper currency. Nor was there disagreement about the nature of the costs involved, for all saw them as arising from the disruption of credit markets and hence the real side of the economy, that might arise from the monetary measures necessary to correct external drains of specie.[3]

In order to achieve the desired end, the Currency School proposed that the Bank of England note issue should absorb that of the Country Banks, and that, apart from a fixed fiduciary issue, it should fluctuate

3. The whole matter of the so-called 'classical' economists' views on the interaction of monetary and real phenomena is discussed in Hicks [5], chapter 9. On this issue, the 'classics' were a good deal more 'Keynesian' than they are often presented.

exactly with the specie reserve of the Bank's note issue department, which was to be separated strictly from the department handling the Bank's deposit business. This they proposed because they wished to make the monetary system work along the lines of a strict, not to say automatic, price-specie flow mechanism. They took the view that previous crises, in which the suspension of cash payments by the Bank of England had been a very real threat, had had their roots in an over issue of bank notes, both on the part of the Bank of England and of the Country Banks. By linking the note issue directly to specie reserves, they hoped that the system would work exactly as it would under a purely metallic money supply so that any incipient specie drain abroad would immediately set up equilibrating forces. Thus, not only would the convertibility of notes be guaranteed at all times, since the bullion to meet an internal drain would always be available, but also the correction of disequilibrium would be rapid, and, beginning the moment the problem arose, mild in its effects.

It was Tooke's view that this framework, which was of course adopted in 1844, would not achieve the desired effect, for though he agreed that it would ensure the convertibility of the note issue, he was convinced that this would be achieved at too high a price in terms of periodic disruption of domestic credit markets. He did not disagree that too high a price level caused by monetary expansion could cause an external specie drain, but he did deny that this was the only cause.[4] In his view, such drains could equally well arise from shifts in the real conditions of supply and demand for traded goods. Furthermore, such shifts did not have to be permanent. Corn imports in particular were liable to frequent fluctuations, especially given the way in which Corn Laws operated, and in such circumstances he suggested that no monetary action was necessary. Rather, he proposed that the Bank of England should hold reserves of sufficient size to be able to finance temporary deficits of this kind without having a recourse to domestic deflation to combat them, and he regarded the principal cause of previous difficulties to be the Bank's failure to hold adequate amounts of bullion.

4.   It should be noted that by the 1830s the Ricardian practice, of defining too high a price level relative to one which would maintain balance of payments equilibrium regardless of what other factors were operating, had died out.

It was his view that 'not less than ten millions can ever be considered a safe position of the treasure of the Bank of England seeing the sudden calls to which it is liable' ([10], Vol.2, p.330), and he wanted to see for the reserves 'a latitude for variation between fifteen millions and five millions ...' rather than '... as it has recently been, between ten millions and nothing' ([10], Vol.3, p.187). Such an increase in the bank's average level of reserves would enable the economy to ride out temporary disequilibria without serious domestic repercussions, and would also give the Bank ample time to recognise 'the existence of more extensive and deeper seated causes of demand for the metals ...', and to take appropriate action 'without producing alarm and disturbance of the money market on the one hand, or endangering an extreme and unsafe reduction of the Bank treasure on the other' ([10], Vol.3, p.187).[5]

Now it surely needs little argument that these recommendations of Tooke's would meet with approval among modern economists. The distinction between temporary and more fundamental imbalances is now commonplace in the literature on economic policy, and the current international monetary mechanism is based upon it. Moreover, the problems we now face with this system are not ones that could have arisen in the context of nineteenth century policy goals. Debates now

5. The importance which Tooke attached to these passages is attested to by the fact that he quotes them several years after they were first written in [11], pp.114-17.Indeed the theme of the necessity of the Bank of England holding adequate specie reserves is strongly present in Tooke's early *Considerations on the State of the Currency* [9] where it is seen, as in his later work, as being the key to preventing disturbances in the balance of payments being transmitted rapidly and violently to the domestic economy. It is worth pointing out that this earlier essay of Tooke's is much closer to a Currency School position than is his later work, particularly in the stress it lays on the importance of regulating the note issue. However, stress is laid on the regulation of the note issue in this work not only because special monetary characteristics, setting it apart from other forms of paper credit, are attributed to it but also because bank notes are viewed as being the principal store of value used by the poorer members of the society. These are the least able to foresee, and protect themselves from the consequences of, bank failures. Tooke wished to see notes, particularly low denomination notes, replaced by coin, or backed by much bigger specie reserves than were commonly held against them, as much to protect the poor from the consequences of commercial crises as because he expected such a measure to mitigate the causes of such crises. Cf [9], pp.118-27.

are not about the wisdom of financing short-term imbalances without domestic deflation, but arise rather over the choice between deflation and devaluation when disequilibria persist. Since devaluation was out of the question in the 1840s, the problems we face today could hardly have then arisen. Given the overriding need to maintain convertibility at a fixed exchange rate, it is hard to see how modern advice would differ much from that given by Tooke.[6]

This conclusion, however, presupposes a great deal about the monetary institutions existing prior to 1844. Tooke wished to do no more than alter one aspect of the behaviour of one of these institutions, the Bank of England. The Currency School thought it necessary to reform fundamentally the institutional framework itself, and in fact succeeded in doing so. Tooke regarded these reforms as either beside the point, or even likely to worsen rather than better matters; and so, before any firm conclusions as to the superiority of his policy proposals can be reached, we must look at his analysis of the pre-1844 monetary system.

III

The first step in understanding both Tooke's analysis of the banking system, and his objections to the proposals of the Currency School, is to realise that the latter regarded the control of the quantity of currency outside the Bank of England issue department as sufficient to control the level of domestic economic activity. This is a far narrower range of assets than what we would now call 'money', and Tooke, stressing the fact that coin and bank notes were but one component of what he usually referred to as the circulating medium, saw the importance of this factor. As he put it: 'It appears, then, that there is neither authority nor reasoning in favour of the definition which invests

6. There does of course exist the rather serious problem of distinguishing in practice between a fundamental disequilibrium on the one hand and a temporary one on the other. In terms of Tooke's analysis, however, the problem is perhaps not so great as it is in a contemporary framework. First, he tended to associate a temporary problem with a bad harvest, not a difficult phenomenon to recognise, and secondly he offered what amounted to a decision rule for deciding when the Bank should act in other cases. Any time that the Bank's specie reserves, having fallen by five million pounds, continued to fall was an occasion for domestic contraction (cf.[11], pp.115-17).

Bank notes with the properties of money, or paper currency, *to the exclusion of all other forms of paper credit'* ([10], Vol.4, p.163) [Tooke's italics]. Specifically, he thought it necessary to regard bank deposits (or rather cheques drawn upon them, for he was far from clear on this point) and bills of exchange as forms of paper credit with an equal claim to be considered as forming part of what we would now call the money supply (cf.[11], p.32).

It was on the basis of this insight that he argued that control of the note issue alone would be an inadequate policy tool. Indeed he went even further claiming that the volume of notes in circulation at any time depended upon the demand of the public, and was beyond the *direct* control of the banking system. We must be careful not to confuse this doctrine with the so-called 'real bills fallacy', one of whose implications it resembles but to which in this context it is not closely related. Tooke was above all an empiricist, and he noted, as far as country bank notes were concerned, 'that their circulation is devoted and confined to local purposes, chiefly in small amounts, for the retail trade ...'. He further argued that if country bankers were to refuse to issue their own notes, then 'such refusal must be accompanied by offering Bank of England notes or coin, and thus local circulation would be equally filled up' ([11], p.38). Should notes be issued in excess, on the other hand, then 'the law of reflux' would take effect in one of three ways: 'by payment of the redundant amount to a banker on a deposit account, or by the return of notes in discharge of securities on which advances have been made. A third way is that of a return of the notes to the issuing bank by a demand for coin' ([10], Vol.4, p.185). Of these three methods, only the second has anything to do with the workings of bank credit, where the real bills doctrine, which states that the banking system should meet the 'needs of trade' for loans on goods in process, might be relevant. The other two clearly have to do with the way in which the non-bank public desire to hold their assets.[7] The importance of the real bills element here is very minor, particularly when it is realised that it is only a *direct* influence on the

7. As to the real bills element in Tooke's thought at this point, it clearly exists, but as Fetter notes, unlike Fullarton, Tooke never stepped clearly into the celebrated fallacy (cf.[3], pp.191-3). His emphasis on the 'mode of issue' of notes in relation to their effect on prices does suggest that he was not entirely free of erroneous notions on this score, and he clearly attached some importance to this point. Since it does not seem to play a key role in the logic of Tooke's position on policy matters, this writer has chosen not to emphasise the issue. However, cf. fn.

note circulation that Tooke denied the banks. He was perfectly willing to admit that the volume of bank advances could affect the level of economic activity, and hence the volume of notes in circulation.[8]

If we interpret the 'law of reflux' as operating with the level of economic activity given, determined in part by the volume of bank lending, it becomes part of a theory analogous to the modern analysis of the public's demand for currency relative to other assets, rather than a component of some erroneous doctrine of the effect of bank credit. Tooke's views on the determination of the quantity of bank notes in circulation then become propositions about the composition, rather than the size, of what would now be called the money supply, for they amount to the following. At a given level of economic activity the public will find it convenient to hold and use a certain quantity of bank notes. Should these notes not already be in circulation, the public may obtain them by converting their deposits or coin into notes. Should too many notes be in circulation they may be exchanged for deposits, used to pay off debts to the banking system, or should they begin to depreciate they could be exchanged for gold coin, one of the items relative to which their depreciation would have to take place.

However, if Tooke was on the whole correct in his analysis of the demand for currency, his analysis was a good deal less firmly grounded when he came to deal with the 'circulating medium' as a whole, for he argued that its quantity also was the effect, rather than the cause, of the price level. In so arguing, he used reasoning similar to that which he employed in dealing with currency alone, so that even a charitable reader must attribute a fallacy of composition to him on this score. The

8. This comes out clearly from his discussion of the evidence of country and Scottish bankers quoted in [11], chs. 8-9, and in his discussion of the possible manner in which the principles of the 1844 Act would operate. See below, p. 182. In Fullarton's hands the law of reflux becomes more like a component of the real bills doctrine, with his emphasis on the banking system's need only to discount good short-term paper in order never to over-extend its issue. As just noted, Tooke certainly regarded this as good banking practice, but as much because it maintained the system's liquidity in the face of the possibility of sudden demands for redemption of both notes and deposits, as because he viewed it as a safeguard against too much monetary expansion. It is the convertibility of notes into gold that he regarded as the ultimate safeguard here. The fact that he noted it to be a method of reflux 'the least in use' is as well interpreted as evidence that he thought the banking system worked smoothly under the threat of an internal specie drain as that convertibility was unimportant.

basic line of the argument was that just as notes could substitute for coin, so could cheques substitute for notes, and bills of exchange for cheques. If one instrument was not available, then another would take its place. Now, such substitution was doubtless possible, and contractions and expansions of the note issue would to some degree, perhaps a high one, be offset by greater use of other instruments. However, Tooke overlooked several important factors in dealing with it.

In the first place, he never really faced the degree of substitutability between assets on the demand side. Though he noted that coin and small notes would be more difficult to replace with cheques and bills than large notes, he did not go into this too deeply, merely expressing the judgement that there would be little substitution of other forms of paper for one pound notes, but somewhat more for notes up to ten pounds in value. (Notes under five pounds circulated only in Ireland and Scotland in the 1840s.) For notes of higher denomination, the tone of his argument suggests that he regarded them well-nigh perfect substitutes for cheques and bills of exchange (cf.[11], pp.32-3).

However, substitutability on the demand side is not necessarily the most important factor here, for so long as bankers were willing to permit their customers to draw cheques without limit, and businessmen were able to issue bills of exchange in any amount they wished, there would be no reason why a sufficient amount of other instruments could not be created to maintain any level of prices. Substitutability on the supply is the key factor. Bank of England deposits and notes were substitutes in their creation as well as in their use, so in this context Tooke was not so far from the mark. If all that was contracted was the Bank of England's note issue, but not its liabilities, it is far from clear that payments previously made in notes could not have been made almost equally well by cheques on the Bank.

However, with Country Bank liabilities and bills of exchange it is a different matter. They were substitutes in use for Bank of England liabilities, but not in their creation. Though a contraction of Bank of England liabilities might have produced an incentive to use Country Bank liabilities and bills of exchange to finance transactions, it is also probably true that this same contraction would have produced incentives to cut their supply. Tooke, stressing that the motive for issuing bills of exchange lay 'in the prospect of resale with a profit'

([11] , p.79), certainly showed insight into the role of expectations and speculation in private credit markets, but overlooked the fact that emitters of such instruments would presumably wish to hold some form of reserve against the time when they fell due to cover the possibility that the goods so financed might be sold at a loss rather than a profit. Not to have done so would have amounted to speculation on zero margin, and it is hard to believe that this was a very common practice. A similar argument clearly holds for the behaviour of Country Banks.[9] Thus Tooke in this instance overlooked the key role of Bank of England liabilities as a reserve base for other components of the circulating medium, a factor which the Currency School, with their insistence on the fact that bills of exchange and clearing balances between banks had ultimately to be settled in terms of some other means of payment, seem to have had some insight into, albeit perhaps not a very precise one, since the only use to which they put this observation was as a component of the argument that bills of exchange and cheques were not money but merely substitutes for money, and hence could not exert an influence on the price level.[10]

If Tooke erred in one direction, however, his opponents erred in another, for it is Bank of England liabilities, rather than just notes, as they tended to claim, that were the important factor. No one would argue now that control of the note issue of a Central Bank, but not of its deposit business, would be an adequate monetary policy tool, but this is precisely what the Currency School held. The difficulties that both sides of this debate had in understanding the nature of the circulation, and the determination of its magnitude, lies in their lack of a theory of multiple credit expansion, even though versions of such a theory had already been reasonably well worked out by Joplin and Pennington.[11] Presumably the Currency School saw no need for it, since they overemphasised the importance of bank notes, while Tooke

9. The foregoing point is one also raised by Cramp [2], pp.69-74, though not specifically in the context of Tooke's work.

10. Tooke at one point maintains this distinction between money and its substitutes, as Gregory points out. However, he did not carry the argument to the point of assigning all effects on prices to bank notes, and in fact makes no use of the distinction in any analysis (cf.[4] , pp.77-8).

11. Cf. Wood [16] , pp. 35-7. In this context it is interesting to speculate that English economics had to wait until the twentieth century to rediscover this analysis, perhaps because of the influence of the Currency School's emphasis on bank notes and coin as money.

and his followers, because they saw cheques rather than bank deposits as the substitute for notes and bills of exchange, never fully realised the importance of the liability side of the banking system's balance sheet.[12] However, Tooke's lack of clarity on this matter did not lead him too far astray. Having tended to deny any great importance to the circulating medium in the determination of prices, he had to provide an alternative theory, and in the context of the theory to which he appears to have adhered, the above-noted problems lead to difficulty only in the context of short-run disequilibrium situations, and these are more a matter of confused thought than outright error.

IV

Ricardo's work contains two different but not incompatible theories of the price level. In his policy writings during the period of the bank restriction he relied on the quantity theory of money as a short-run theory of prices, but in the *Principles* the price level was viewed as being determined in the long run by the cost of production of gold relative to the cost of production of other goods. Tooke was willing to admit either of these theories as particularly relevant, depending upon the situation to be analysed. The quantity theory was relevant when the money supply was made up of government issues of paper money, 'inconvertible and compulsorily current' ([10], Vol.4, p.176), since such paper could clearly depreciate relative to both goods and gold; and the cost of production of gold theory was relevant when the money supply was convertible on demand into gold.

He regarded any permanent depreciation of the currency as impossible so long as the banks stood ready to buy and sell their notes at a fixed price in gold, just as he regarded any permanent appreciation of paper impossible for the same reasons; the 'law of reflux' (cf. above, p. 173) would prevent this. Though Tooke never explicitly took the step, it is clear that this argument is readily extendible to other forms of paper credit in the circulation. Thus, given that the price of money

12. Wood [16], pp. 56-8, notes Tooke's lack of a theory to connect Bank advances with Bank liabilities and then goes on to argue that this omission precludes Tooke from having a monetary theory of the determination of the level of economic activity. Unless one defines 'monetary' in a particularly narrow sense, this seems to this writer to be going a little too far.

in terms of gold was fixed, in the long run the price of goods in terms of gold and hence money was left to be determined by the 'quantity of money... valued in gold ... destined for current expenditures' ([11], p.71) interacting with the cost of production of goods.[13] If the equilibrium value of gold is given by its cost of production, and so is that of total output, then the equilibrium price of goods coming out of this interaction must be the ratio of the cost of production of goods to that of gold. Tooke, not having any grasp of, or perhaps faith in, an index number concept, does not of course put it in this way, but his discussion of the determination of the prices of various individual goods makes it clear that this is the type of mechanism he had in mind (cf.[11], pp.71-2).

This, as a theory of the long-run equilibrium level of prices in a classical framework, is unimpeachable, and certainly none of the Currency School would have disagreed with it.[14] Indeed Torrens agrees explicitly, and attacks Tooke mainly on what we would now call his 'short-run' theory of the relationship between the quantity of the circulating medium and the level of prices. It was Torrens' view that the third method of reflux, the exchange of notes for specie, could not take place until after an over-issue of notes had depreciated their value, while Tooke argued that the fact of the notes' direct convertibility and

13. In restating this argument in the summary given at the end of *The Currency Principle*, Tooke omitted the words 'valued in gold' which are all-important for the interpretation I am here putting on the analysis. Either this was merely a careless slip in the preparation of a pamphlet which was, after all, put together in a hurry, or, in summarising his argument, Tooke became confused between his analysis of the equilibrium price level and that of the influence of aggregate demand on short-run fluctuations in the price level. The latter element of his thought is taken up below.

14. Morgan [7], p.127 and p.243, notes the general agreement that emerged between the Banking School and the Currency School as to the applicability of this theory to the explanation of the long-run level of prices. The emphasis on cost of production as a determinant of value undoubtedly is responsible for Tooke's apparently extraordinary statement that a low rate of interest leads to low rather than high prices. Though he makes it clear that he is talking of the long-run equilibrium situation here (cf.[11], pp.124-5, particularly the footnote), the statement would still only be true were gold production less capital intensive than that of some representative bundle of other goods. Since he never alludes to this point, one can only conclude that his thought was very confused here. However, note that in the already cited footnote he is quite clear that a rise in the Bank of England's discount rate will lead to a depression of prices in the short run.

other assets' indirect convertibility would prevent them ever depreciating. The debate here, in terms of modern analysis, is best interpreted as being about the cost of converting other assets into gold. Their equilibrium price could never fall below their gold redemption value minus the cost of the redemption transaction. It would take quite a painstaking piece of econometric research to establish the exact value of this cost for various assets but it is hard to believe that it could have been a significant amount. In the case of bank notes, all that was required was to enter a bank and ask for their redemption in gold coin. It is this writer's judgement that, at the very least, the Currency School were not on very strong ground when they argued that the equilibrium gold value of notes could depreciate significantly in the presence of gold convertibility. There is another possible interpretation of the Currency School's position here. They could have been arguing about the possibility of temporary disequilibrium arising, owing to a slowness on the part of the public to realise that notes were depreciating. At best this could be only a short-run phenomenon, and if this is all they meant then a great deal of the debate was about the purely empirical and not very interesting problem of how long was the short run in this case.[15]

However, there is more to the debate than this, for one crucial issue between Tooke and his opponents in this context was that of the causation of disequilibria. Tooke was far from denying that it was impossible for the domestic price level to be, from time to time, too high to maintain external balance. What he did deny was that making the circulation of bank notes fluctuate exactly with the Bank of England's specie reserve would prevent this in any way. If it was true that such disequilibria usually arose in the first place from an over-issue of bank notes, as the Currency School argued, then the reforms they suggested would have dealt with the problem. Tooke, however, thought it as likely, or even more likely, that balance of payments deficits would arise from bad harvests, or from monetary expansion that arose quite independently of the note issue. The latter could arise either from an expansion of the banks' deposit business, or from speculative behaviour in wholesale markets leading to a credit expansion there. If Tooke was right, then rather than preventing a disequilibrium arising, relying on making the note issue fluctuate with the specie stock as

---

15. That much of the dispute between the protagonists in this particular debate centres round the question of how long is the short run is a suggestion already made by Corry [1].

virtually the sole rule of monetary policy meant that no contractionary action would be taken by the banking system until a disequilibrium had been going on long enough for its effects to manifest themselves in an outflow of specie. There is quite a modern touch to Tooke's views here, for he appears to have appreciated, to some extent at least, the importance of lagged responses in the monetary mechanism.

As we have already noted, Tooke's position on the matter of credit expansion occurring independently of the Bank of England is an oversimplified one, since he did not completely appreciate the role of a reserve base in checking such speculative activity. However, so long as the banking department of the Bank of England and the private banks were not subject to any required reserve ratio against their liabilities, and so long as merchants issuing bills of exchange were permitted to make up their own minds as to what size reserve to hold against them, no reserve base could serve as a mechanical check against such speculation.[16] If, in the process of a speculative boom, emitters of the circulating medium permitted their reserve ratios to fall, contraction of the note issue would not automatically offset a monetary expansion. The following passage shows clearly that this was Tooke's view. It also shows his awareness, to which we have alluded earlier, of the short-run effects that the banking system could have on the price level through its lending activities.

The mischief of commercial revulsions from overtrading, whenever traceable to the banks, has been from over advances of capital, on insufficient or inconvertible securities, or both. Banks, whether of issue or not, may, in the competition for business, make advances to persons undeserving of credit, and may discount large amounts of doubtful bills, thus adding to the circulating medium, without adding directly to the amount of the circulation, that is of notes ... prices may experience

16. Tooke, being a staunch advocate of *laisser-faire*, would not have countenanced any legal reserve requirements of the type suggested here: He did not, after all, even envisage implementing his own policy proposals by law, but rather sought to persuade the Bank of England to mend their ways by rational argument. Nevertheless, as Fetter notes ([2], p.191), Tooke's analysis of the evils of over-banking make a very strong case for legal controls on the entire system, let alone on the Bank of England. It is worth noting, though, that legal reserve requirements are always minimum requirements and do not give the Central Bank complete control over commercial banks' liabilities. Contemporary American evidence suggests that this is particularly the case when there are many small banks in a system. Certainly variations in these banks' excess reserves are significant for the behaviour of the monetary sector of the United States even today.

a temporary inflation from credit so unduly extended. A creation of bills of exchange and deposits must be the certain consequence; and while the banks are in credit, might sustain the extended transactions for some time, without the intervention of bank notes. The recoil of the speculation and overtrading would, in most cases, not be caused in the first instance by a want of bank notes, but by a want of demand from a view to the supply and consumption ... Now there is no provision in the proposed measures [i.e. the 1844 Act] to prevent such over advances by banks, whether joint stock or not ([11], pp.158-9).

At the same time, Tooke held that a fall in the Bank of England note issue in response to an external specie drain would not immediately cause any smooth contraction of the circulating medium; he regarded Bank of England banking operations as a much more important factor here than its note issue. He argued that the bulk of any demand for bullion for export 'would fall almost exclusively upon the deposit department' ([11], p.108), so that the notes withdrawn would be from that department's reserves, rather than from those in the hands of the public. As a consequence of this, and 'unless, and upon this, in my opinion, the question hinges, the deposit or banking department were bound to hold a much larger reserve than seems to be contemplated by any of the plans which I have seen' ([11], p.105), in the face of any substantial balance of payments deficit, the Bank 'must sell securities, or allow the existing ones, if short dated, to run off, and they must inexorably shut their doors to all applications for advances or discounts' ([11], p.108). The effect of this, thought Tooke, would go far beyond limiting the power of the Bank to 'overtrade in discounts and loans' as Torrens suggested, and 'under certain circumstances of the trade, it would operate with a degree of violence on the state of credit of which, as it appears to me, Colonel Torrens has no adequate idea' ([11], p.108).

Furthermore, if the demand for bullion came rapidly enough, even a rapid reduction of the Bank's discounts might not be enough to stem the demand, so that 'the deposit department would have no alternative but to stop payment' ([11], p.109). All this, Tooke saw coming about without any large reduction of the quantity of bank notes in the hands of the public, except inasmuch as the restriction of bank advances affected the state of trade and hence reduced the demand for them, and happening, furthermore, when the issue department would still have large stocks of bullion on hand. Written in 1844, the passage from which the above quotations are taken could easily pass as a slightly exaggerated account of the events of 1847.[17]

V

We have now set out what seem to be the key elements of Tooke's views on monetary theory and its application to the policy problems of the 1840s, but it would be as well to attempt to summarise them here briefly before stating any conclusions.

It has been argued that the underlying theory of the price level in Tooke's work is one which related the cost of production of goods to the cost of production of gold, and that this is a long-run theory which implies, in a classical framework, that, if the prices of other elements of the money supply are pegged to gold, then their quantity must adjust and become the consequence rather than the cause of the price level. It has also been argued that there was no real debate on this matter between Tooke and his opponents, but that rather it was the cause of short-run fluctuations that was at issue. There seem to have been two elements to the point of view which he took here.

First, even if the circulation had been made up purely of bank notes and coin, he would have relied on the 'law of reflux' to maintain prices stable over all but quite short periods. Excess notes would either return to the banks in discharge of debts without affecting prices, or, if by any chance they did not, then they would begin to depreciate relative to gold as well as to other goods and would rapidly return to the banks in exchange for coin. In the first of these points there is an element of the real bills doctrine upon which we have commented above (cf. page 173, fn. 7), but the second was accepted by his opponents, who however argued that the reflux in this case would not be rapid. To this extent the debate was purely about how long the short run is.

17. In [10], Vol.4, pp.281- 406. Needless to say, so formidable a controversialist as Tooke did not attribute any exaggeration to himself.
Torrens claimed the events of 1847 as evidence of the success of the Act of 1844, apparently on the grounds that the convertibility of notes was never in danger, which was true, and on the grounds that their quantity in circulation had not fluctuated as greatly as in previous crises. Torrens [12] saw the root of the 1847 crises in the banking department having held too few reserves, rather than as lying in the structure created by the Act of 1844. Though all the evidence he adduces is true, and the arguments he provides are logical, to this writer at least they appear to be beside the point of Tooke's criticism. The latter had, after all, never denied that convertibility would be guaranteed by the Act, and had been arguing for a decade that inadequate reserves were the key factor that had to be cured in order to rid England of financial crises. For a modern account of the events of the 1847 crisis, see Morgan [7], pp.147-57.

However, in the second element of Tooke's thought there is genuine theoretical disagreement with the Currency School, for he saw the problem of the quantity of bank notes in circulation as having to do with the composition rather than the size of what we would now call the total money stock. He denied that the banking system could have any direct influence on the amount of notes in the hands of the public and saw their power to influence this variable as working through the effects of their lending policies on the state of trade. Thus, he argued that regulation of the note issue was neither a necessary nor an effective policy tool.

He tended to apply the same arguments to the determination of the size of the total circulation, and on this point he appears to have been confused. He argued that bills of exchange and the like would be created in anticipation of future prices, and hence were the effect rather than the cause of these prices. He did, however, see that the issue of bills could provide the conditions which would enable predictions of future prices to be fulfilled in the short run. The source of the confusion here is his lack of a theory of the relationship between the lending activities of those institutions and individuals whose debt makes up the circulation, and the quantity of that circulation, and, closely related, his failure to see clearly that deposits, rather than cheques, were the relevant substitute for bills of exchange and bank notes.

However, this confusion did not lead Tooke into serious error. Its principal effect was to lead him to look at bank advances and speculative lending by other institutions and individuals as a source of short-run price fluctuations, rather than to look at the deposits, notes, and bills created in that same process. He may not have understood the credit multiplier process, but he clearly did understand the role that banks, and particularly the Bank of England, could play in altering the level of aggregate demand by changes in the volume of their loans.[18] Though far from a perfect statement of the matter, Tooke's emphasis on bank lending as a key variable in short-run business fluctuations surely put him closer to the truth than did the Currency School's emphasis on the size of the note issue.

Now the main policy problem of the time was the maintenance of the convertibility of the note issue, both at home and abroad, at a fixed parity, and Tooke did not deny for a moment that the plans of the Currency School would achieve this end. Rather he argued that there were other ways of achieving the same goal at less cost. He thought that the structure created in 1844 would work only at the cost of violent fluctuations in credit conditions, and possibly even of the loss of convertibility of Bank of England deposits, unless the government were to intervene. Moreover, he saw such problems arising whenever there was an external specie drain. Had these consequences been necessary to preserve the convertibility of the currency, it is clear he would not have objected to them, but he regarded them as avoidable ones.

In the first place, he did not regard it as necessary to counteract all balance of payments disequilibria with domestic contraction, since temporary problems, especially those arising from the need to import corn in the wake of bad harvests, would in no way endanger convertibility if sufficient reserves were held at the time they started. As to those disequilibria arising from domestic over-expansion, they would provide their own cure with the natural tendency of the banking system to curtail lending in the face of a decreasing reserve of bullion. Moreover, with an adequate reserve base, this could be done without undue haste, and again without financial panic and a danger of a suspension of payments. As to longer-run problems, and Tooke is not very specific as to their cause, they too could be taken care of by domestic contraction carried out slowly.

Given that modern economists are familiar with the distinction between temporary and fundamental balance of payments problems, given that they are extremely conscious of the disruptive effects of sudden contractions of the money supply brought about by rapid cuts in bank lending, and given that they are well aware that a useful definition of money must be wider in scope than bank notes and coin,

18. There are two aspects of this element of Tooke's thought that are worth noting. It must be apparent that he comes quite close to recognising the role of Bank of England deposits as a reserve base for the credit structure of the economy, so that we must conclude that he was unclear about, rather than totally innocent of, this factor as he sometimes gave the impression. Nevertheless, it is changes in the Banks' discounting operations that receive the greatest stress. The volume of its liabilities is not seen as a key variable, except inasmuch as the public's drawing down these will cause changes in Bank lending. The stress on Bank lending as the key factor in short-run fluctuations, here confined to the Bank of England, but elsewhere, as we have seen, extended to the country banks, issuing and non-issuing alike, is also of interest from the point of view of the history of doctrine, since it seems to be one of the roots of Wicksell's thought on the problem, and hence of a great deal of twentieth century monetary theory. Wicksell discusses Tooke in some detail in [14], pp.81-7 and [15], pp.168-90.

they would surely find that Tooke's view, that the key to successfully operating a convertible money supply lay in adequate Central Bank reserves of bullion, has a great deal to commend it. They might also be willing to concede that there was much that was to the point in the analysis that led to this view, despite the flaws that we have noted, and to admit that on the whole Tooke's programme is a more appealing one than that of the Currency School.

REFERENCES

1   Corry, B.A. *Money Saving and Investment in English Economics,* London 1961.

2   Cramp, A.B. *Opinion on Bank Rate 1822-60,* London 1961.

3   Fetter, F.W. *Development of British Monetary Orthodoxy 1797-1875,* Cambridge (Massachusetts) 1965.

4   Gregory, T.E. *An Introduction to Tooke and Newmarch's A History of Prices,* London 1928 (reprinted 1962).

5   Hicks, J.R. *Critical Essays in Monetary Theory,* Oxford 1967.

6   Mints, L. *A History of Banking Theory.*

7   Morgan, E. V. *The Theory and Practice of Central Banking 1797-1913,* Cambridge (England) 1943.

8   Robbins, L. *Robert Torrens and the Evolution of Classical Economics,* London 1958.

9   Tooke, Thomas *Considerations on the State of the Currency,* London 1826.

10 Tooke, Thomas *A History of Prices,* London, Vols. 1 and 2, 1838; Vol. 3, 1840; Vol. 4, 1848.

11 Tooke, Thomas *An Inquiry into the Currency Principle,* (2nd ed.) London, 1844.

12 Torrens, Robert *Sir Robert Peel's Act of 1844 Explained,* London 1847.

13 Viner, J. *Studies in the Theory of International Trade,* New York 1937.

14 Wicksell, K. *Interest and Prices* (tr. R.F. Kahn), London 1936.

15 Wicksell, K. *Lectures on Political Economy* (ed. Robbins), Vol. 2, New York 1935.

16 Wood, E. *English Theories of Central Banking Control, 1819-1958,* Cambridge (Massachusetts) 1939.

Then and Now: The British Problem of Sustaining Development, 1900s and 1960s [1]

E.H. Phelps Brown

I

The mood of disparagement and distrust that the British people have experienced of late had its counterpart at the turn of the century. In recent years, in a world where prestige as well as amenity and power attach to a high rate of growth, we have seen most of our neighbours growing faster than we. Seventy years ago, British opinion was gravely exercised by the faster advance of other economies, an advance signalled not only by statistics of production — in the 1890s the American and German outputs of steel had both overtaken the British — but by the smart of increasingly keen competition in the home market as well as abroad. The country that had led the world in industrialisation was made painfully aware that in some important respects it was in the lead no longer. One reaction, then as now, was to seek to learn from our competitors. In 1902 Mr Alfred Mosley of Manchester took a team of trade unionists to the United States at his own expense, to seek the springs of productivity in their own industries there; and the manager of the biggest engineering works in the United Kingdom sent his foremen to study the organisation of the German shops. It was in the same way, though on a much broader front, that the Anglo-American Productivity Council after the Second World War sent out many teams of managers and workers to observe their opposite numbers in the United States; and such visits continue. In both periods these comparative studies indicated that the United Kingdom was lagging in education for industry: there was talk in the early 1900s of

1. The preparation of this study, as of so many others, has been provided with an indispensable foundation and support in the collaboration of Mrs. Meyrick Browne. It has been the privilege of those who served under Lord Robbins in the London School of Economics to be provided liberally with research assistance. Throughout the last ten years Mrs. Meyrick Browne has entered into my projects with a scholarly skill and unremitting application, of which her contribution to the present paper is only the latest instance.

the need for 'an English Charlottenburg',[2] as there has been latterly of 'an English M.I.T. ' But the development and commercial application of the new technology of the day has been felt to demand a larger scale of enterprise than has obtained in the United Kingdom or could be supported by its existing markets: hence, in recent years, the endeavour to join the Six, and around 1900 much discussion of the advantages conferred by the sheer size of cartel and trust, and a campaign for the sheltering and fostering of the imperial market. International comparisons have also indicated differences amounting to contrasts in the attitudes of labour and the workings of industrial relations. Of late, attention has been focused on overmanning, and the possibility of reducing restrictive practices through productivity bargaining; in 1901-02 a series of articles in *The Times* ascribed 'the crisis in British industry' to an increased enforcement of restrictive practices by the trade unions. In both periods the energies of management have been called in question not less than those of labour: 'the English disease' has been diagnosed in all walks of life.

There have also been some similar political manifestations. The need to adjust themselves to a changed position in the world has been enforced upon the British people of late by the abdication of their imperium and the withdrawal of their garrisons, as well as by the discomfiture of Suez, the slamming of the door of Brussels in their face, and their need to observe in their domestic policy the stipulations of their foreign creditors. A similar need had been enforced when the Boer War revealed at once the inadequacies of the British army and the isolation of the United Kingdom in an envious world, while German naval building began to threaten the Two Power standard. When rebuffs and reverses shake self-confidence, the values of a society are called in question as well as its vigour, and young people hesitate to assume the personal identity that its way of life will confer on them if they follow

2.   The Berlin Technische Hochschule had been set up at Charlottenburg in 1884; by 1896 it had 3000 students. There were six departments: architecture; civil engineering; mechanical and electrical engineering; chemistry and metallurgy; and a general department, including mathematics, in which students spent most of their first year. See a letter to the Lord President of the Council by members of the Commission on Technical Instruction: *Report on a visit to Germany with a view to ascertaining the recent progress of technical education in that country* (C.8301, Parly. Papers 1897, LXXXVIII); and *The Organization of the Instruction in the Berlin technical Hochschule at Charlottenburg,* U.K. Board of Education, Educational Pamphlets No. 9, 1907.

in their fathers' footsteps. In the years before the First World War the stress on the autonomy of the worker in guild socialism, and in syndicalism with its affinities to anarchism, attracted those for whom the accepted aims of an older generation were acceptable no longer. In the last ten years, no less, there has been some breach of continuity in the conception of the personality and style of life that the adolescent is to endue. Strange notions, some of them like anarchism strangely old-fashioned, have attained the prominence that even a small minority can give its creed against a background of widespread misgivings.

Do these likenesses between the two periods only mark the recurrence of a situation such as most countries will experience from time to time in the ups and downs of their affairs, a turn of the wheel of fashion in attitudes and talking-points? Or do they arise out of the persistence of the same malfunctionings of the economy? We can seek an answer in the economists' diagnoses of the troubles of each period.

II

It is now recognised that the main trouble with the British economy of seventy years ago was its slowness to adopt new processes. Old-established industries did not change their locations, lay-outs and equipment as they must have done to keep pace with the new plants of Germany and U.S.A. New industries did not grow up as rapidly in the United Kingdom as they did there. These disabilities showed themselves in reduced competitiveness in the manufactured products that were now the most expansive elements in international trade.

This slowness to innovate has been ascribed to a general decline in the entrepreneurial vigour for which the United Kingdom had once been outstanding. For one thing, the innovations of the time depended increasingly on applied science, but British industrialists distrusted theory. Practical men among their predecessors had not always stood so aloof — in the days of the Lunar Society,[3] Matthew Boulton, James Watt and Josiah Wedgwood met with Erasmus Darwin, Joseph Priestley and Richard Lovell Edgeworth in a free-ranging interplay of money-making business and scientific experiment. It had been clear to

3.   Schofield, R.E. *The Lunar Society of Birmingham: a social history of provincial science and industry in 18th century England,* 1963.

de Tocqueville when he visited England in 1835 that the ultimate reason for its exceptional industrial expansion was the exceptional energy of its people — of those of them at least who were of the Midlands and the North. In Birmingham he wrote,[4] 'We found as much goodwill here as in London; but there is hardly any likeness between these two societies. These folk never have a minute to themselves. They work as if they must get rich by the evening and die the next day. They are generally very intelligent people, but intelligent in the American way.'

He went on to Manchester and Liverpool; in Dublin he concluded:[5]

Looking at the turn given to the human spirit in England by political life; seeing the Englishman, certain of the support of his laws, relying on himself and unaware of any obstacle except the limit of his own powers, acting without constraint; seeing him, inspired by the sense that he can do anything, look restlessly at what now is, always in search of the best, seeing him like that, I am in no hurry to inquire whether nature has scooped out ports for him, and given him coal and iron. The reason for his commercial prosperity is not there at all: it is in himself.

By 1900 foreign observers were less likely to notice the Englishman's restless search for the best: they were more likely to remark on his weekends. Gerhart von Schulze-Gaevernitz, Professor of Political Economy at Freiburg, writing in 1906, had no doubt that the early industrial lead of Great Britain had been due essentially to puritanism: by the high value it set upon the quest for truth it had fostered the natural sciences, and it had inculcated a hardworking, straitly disciplined way of life. He had no doubt either that there had been great changes in these respects in recent years:

The "religion of natural science" fades away as the value set on truth — that exclusive product of the protestant spirit — loses its compelling force; the methodical way of life goes down after its religious backbone has been fractured by the blows of two enemies — luxury and sport.[6]

Alfred Marshall had observed in 1903 how the achievements and advantages of earlier years had encouraged:

the belief that an Englishman could expect to obtain a much larger

4. de Tocqueville, A. *Journeys to England and Ireland,* ed. J.P. Mayer, 1958, p. 94.
5. de Tocqueville, *Journeys,* p. 116.
6. von Schulze-Gaevernitz, G. *Britischer Imperialismus und englischer Freihandle zu Beginn des zwanzigsten Jahrhunderts* 1906, p. 360.

real income and to live much more luxuriously than anybody else, at all events in an old country; and that if he chose to shorten his hours of work and take things easily, he could afford to do it.

These and other causes:

made many of the sons of manufacturers content to follow mechanically the lead given by their fathers. They worked shorter hours, and they exerted themselves less to obtain new practical ideas than their fathers had done; and thus a part of England's leadership was destroyed rapidly.[7]

But if it thus seems clear that in particular firms and families there had been a waning of energy, we have still much to explain. We have to account for what did not happen as well as for what did. There were always Marshall's 'trees of the forest'. Granted that firms grew set in their ways as they aged, and that the will to innovate diminished down the line of succession in management: why did not more new firms grow up vigorously, why did not more young men renew in their own generation the enterprise of their predecessors? The man of enterprise is characterised by the combination of an anxiety that can be assuaged only by incessant work and that demands the reassurance of achievement, with a confidence that is not shaken by uncertainty. These qualities owe something to the prevailing attitudes and values of society at large, but something also to the heredity and upbringing of particular men; and there seems no reason why the statistical distribution of these last circumstances should not have been throwing up as high a proportion of men of enterprise towards the end of the nineteenth century as in earlier years. Charles Wilson[8] has reminded us how many in fact there were who at this time built great businesses up from small beginnings: in civil engineering W.D. Pearson, by the 1890s 'the largest contractor in the world'; in newspapers George Newnes and Alfred Harmsworth: in light industry Lever, Lipton, Cadbury, Rowntree, Guinness, Beecham, Boot, Courtauld; while distribution was revolutionised by Lipton and Boot together with W.H. Smith, Lyons, Harrod, Whiteley, Lewis.

But the concentration of so many names in consumables and

7.   Sec. L. of *Memorandum on Fiscal Policy of International Trade,* House of Commons No. 321, November 1908.
8.   Wilson, Charles 'Economy and Society in late Victorian Britain', in *Essays in Economic History presented to Prof. M.M. Postan, Economic History Review,* 2nd series, 18, 1, August 1965.

distribution showed how times had changed. We need not suppose that there were fewer men of enterprise now: the difference lay in the opportunities their times afforded them. So many of the new processes were science-based; and, more than that, the industrial exploitation of a discovery made in the laboratory might demand long years of costly trials — for synthetic indigo in Germany it had taken twenty. The man who had the skill in his hands and the fire in his belly that could build a great business in the age of Arkwright, Telford and Stephenson lacked both the scientific training for research and the massed resources for development that the new processes required. We need not doubt that the personal qualities of enterprise were renewed in each succeeding generation; where the environment gave them scope, they developed their activities as vigorously as ever; but in much of the field of industry something different was demanded now.

Yet if that explains why the old pioneering spirit seemed to have ebbed away, it does now show why the new requirements of development were not met by established business. More than any of its competitors save the United States, the United Kingdom had the resources to expand training and research in science and technology, and work through the long process of problem-solving in the pilot plant. Yet the resources were not so applied. Contemporaries diagnosed the need clearly;[9] the contrast with Germany showed both that it could

9.   There is a remarkable compendium of the opinions of scientists on the neglect of scientific education by the community and of applied science by industry in Sir Henry Roscoe's paper on 'The Outlook for British Trade, II', in the *Monthly Review,* May 1901. Sir Henry was professor of chemistry in the Victoria University of Manchester. He ends with a plea for the setting up of a University Grants Commission: Rosebery, Chamberlain and Goschen should have absolute disposal of not less than £100,000 a year to promote 'learning and research of the highest university type as applied to industrial pursuits in large centres of population'. But the indictment of British neglect of science that is most striking in its anticipation of later thinking, and powerful in its plea for the development of science as essential to national survival, was made by Sir Norman Lockyer, professor of astronomical physics at the Royal College of Science, in his presidential address to the British Association in 1903, *On the Influence of Brain-power on History,* 1903. 'The school, the University, the laboratory and the workshop are the battle-fields of this new warfare', p. 14. Applied science was needed not in industry alone: if other nations used their scientific spirit and brainpower in all branches of their administration, we too must replace rule of thumb by scientific method throughout the service of the state. If universities as the chief producers of brain-power were the equivalent of battleships for sea-power, we needed eight more universities to reach a two-power standard. But

be met and that it needed to be met urgently; British industrialists did little to meet it.

The trouble seems to have been that they were dominated by the cult of the practical man. In British experience it was he and not the theorist who had built great businesses up and advanced their technique. To have come up through the tools, to have worked in the shops and have the grasp of their processes that only long experience can give, was the industrialist's pride. Our managers, said an editorial in *Engineering* in 1896, had been 'men with no theory about them, but able one and all to show their workmen how to do the job .[10] But a drilling in certain ways of working, without the education that would open mental windows on other ways and instil a questioning habit of thought, engrains a conservatism that is not merely indifferent to innovation but actively hostile to it. Arnold Bennett has left a portrait, sharply drawn yet still this side of caricature, of the small employer who had learned his trade the hard way:

In a community of stiff-necked employers, Julian already held a high place for the quality of being stiff-necked. Jim Horrocleave, for example, had a queer, murderous manner with customers and with 'hands', but Horrocleave was friendly towards scientific ideas in the earthenware industry, and had even given half a guinea to the fund for encouraging technical education in the district. Whereas Julian Maldon not only terrorised customers and work-people (the latter never-theless had a sort of liking for him), but was bitingly scornful of 'cranky chemists', or 'Germans', as he called the scientific educated experts. He was the pure essence of the British manufacturer. He refused to make what the market wanted, unless the market happened to want what he wanted to make. He hated to understand the reasons underlying the processes of manufacture, or to do anything which had not been regularly done for at least fifty years. And he accepted orders like insults.[11]

But a tincture of the same outlook showed itself at a higher level. There is a remarkable paper by Lord Armstrong on 'The Vague Cry for Technical Education' in the *Nineteenth Century* for July 1888. Colleges of physical science, he held, were of minor value, certainly not worth the expenditure of the taxpayer's money. A man of natural capacity will not be defeated by want of knowledge: he will acquire it, as Watt,

the cost should be seen '*as a loan* which will bear a high rate of interest'.

10.   Quoted here from Urwick, L. and Brech, E.F.L. *The Making of Scientific Management*, 1945-48, Vol. 2, p. 114.

11.   Bennett, Arnold *The Price of Love* 1914, c xi.

Stephenson and Telford had done when they were left to educate themselves. It was rare for managers and designers to need more education if they were to get practical results. 'As to the question whether our commerce is to be saved from the effects of foreign competition by a wide diffusion of technical knowledge, I have no faith in any such safeguard.' What he said must have been borne in on him by his own experience. He had developed hydraulic and electrical machines, and been elected to the Royal Society for his work on them; he had designed breech-loading and rifled artillery; he had become the first manager of a great engineering works; but he had been trained only as a lawyer. So in a way it had been too with the great engineer he brought into alliance. Sir Joseph Whitworth was a pioneer of precision in mechanics: he developed standard measurements and gauges, and a uniform system of screw threads; but he had gone into a spinning mill as a boy of fourteen, and run away to get a job as a working mechanic. When he died his fortune went to endow scientific and technical education, but his career might be taken as a demonstration of how well the right man could get on without it. Sir Isaac Lowthian Bell, again, had grown up in the chemical and iron industries, and a father conscious of the importance of science had given him a training in physics and chemistry; but when Siemens at a meeting of the Iron and Steel Institute spoke highly of the continental systems of technical education, this 'provoked Bell to a defence of those untrained heroes, the Corts, the Neilsons and the Darbys'.[12]

The practical man might reject a new process because his test was whether it had proved itself 'commercially desirable', and often in the short run it had not. The Germans worked to a different calculus, one of 'technological rationality', as Landes has called it, 'a different kind of arithmetic, which maximised, not returns, but technical efficiency.[13]

There is thus reason to believe that the slowness of the British

12.   Burn, D.L. *The Economic History of Steelmaking 1867-1939*, 1940, p.66.
13.   Landes, D.S. 'Technological Change and Development in Western Europe, 1750-1914', *Cambridge Economic History of Europe*, Vol. VI, Pt. 1, 1965, p. 581. Richardson, H.W. 'Chemicals', Ch. 9, D.H. Aldcroft (ed.) *The Development of British Industry and Foreign Competition 1875-1914*, 1968, contrasts the German and British attitudes to research and development, and remarks that the German effort after 1870 (and to a lesser extent that of the USA, Switzerland and France) paid off only in the next generation.

economy to adopt new processes was due in part to the conservatism of its managers. But this conservatism had its counterpart in, and was reinforced by, the reluctance of the worker to change. New equipment with more automatic devices and higher speeds was coming in from America, together with the stop watch and the premium bonus: the craftsman resisted them by enforcing practices that were now thrown into relief as restrictive but had long been part of his way of life. They had their roots in his basic needs for job security and job autonomy. The American worker, in a continent whose natural resources kept the door of opportunity open, might take it for granted that men could do better for themselves by working harder. The British worker grew up in a different world, where experience taught him that men who worked harder would get laid off sooner. Hence a variety of provisions to protect a certain territory of employment against the encroachment of other workers and processes, and to regulate the pace of work within it. The skill, moreover, which the craftsman had acquired in years of apprenticeship was not only a marketable asset but a charter of independence and a source of satisfaction in work well done: these gains were lost if new methods were imposed from without. In this attachment to methods acquired and tested by practice, the worker resembled the employer whose own training had so often been on the same practical lines. Their understanding had its benefits, but the price paid was the slowness of the change by which the standard of living of the worker could be raised.

There remains a third cause of the failure to develop new processes as quickly as some other countries were doing – the vicious circle, namely, by which a lag in development impaired international competitiveness, and impaired competitiveness in turn inhibited development.[14] It was at the turn of the century that German competition began to be felt acutely: in the early 1890s German exports of steel and machinery had together amounted in value to a third of the British, in 1894 they began a rise that was to put them 40 per cent

14.   Coppock, D.J. 'The Climacteric of the 1890s: a Critical Note', *Manchester School,* Jan. 1956; Lewis, W.A. 'International Competition in Manufactures', *American Economic Review,* 47, 2, May 1957; but that 'more or less foreign trade is neither a necessary nor a sufficient condition of growth or non-growth' is argued, with reference to these times, by C.P. Kindleberger, 'Foreign Trade and Economic Growth: Lessons from Britain and France, 1850 to 1913', *Economic History Review,* 2nd. series, 14, 2, Dec. 1961.

above the British by 1913. W. Arthur Lewis has given figures, shown
here in Table 1, that summarise the impairment of the position of the
United Kingdom. A reduction in any one country's share of world trade

TABLE 1
Percentage shares in world trade in manufactures, 1890-1913

	1890	1899	1913
UK	35·8	28·4	25·4
France	14·5	12·6	10·6
Germany	17·2	19·5	23·0
USA	3·9	9·8	11·0
Sum of 4 countries	71·4	70·3	70·0

Source: Lewis, W.A., 'International Competition in Manufactures',
American Economic Review, 47, 2, May 1957.

in manufactures is to be expected as other countries become indus-
trialised and develop their exports; but that the development of the
manufactured exports of Germany and the USA at this time went
beyond that is enforced by their ability to penetrate the British home
market – after 1900 the United Kingdom was importing more cars,
more electrical equipment, and more of some kinds of chemical, than it
exported. It has been shown, moreover, that British exports were not
handicapped by an initial concentration on the types of product or
market that were to prove less expansive in the world trade of those
years.[15] In an article with the reassuring title of 'The Commercial
Supremacy of Britain', in 1894, A.W. Flux[16] in fact showed just what
was going wrong. Other countries, he said, 'failing to seriously encroach
on the mass of our trade in well-secured and accustomed markets, have
had to develop new lines of trade with fresh countries'.

The British failure to contribute proportionally to those new lines of

15.   Maizels, A. *Industrial Growth and World Trade* 1963, Table 8.5, p. 200,
and Saul, S.B. 'The Export Economy 1870-1914', *Yorkshire Bulletin of
Economic and Social Research,* 17, 1, May 1965, pp. 13-14.
16.   *Economic Journal,* 4, 15, Sept. 1894, and 16, Dec. 1894; the quotation is
from p. 605.

trade may be ascribed largely to the resistances to innovation that we have already discussed. But one particular kind of innovation was required if the new types of product were to be exported. The 'commercial supremacy' of the United Kingdom had been attained by exporting products which for the most part could be sold in bulk through organised produce markets or through merchant houses who bought from the British manufacturer at his own gates. At one time, again, the British producer had had such a lead in some products that 'the world beat a path to his door'. He continued to sell largely to customers who were habituated to his dimensions, nomenclature, and solid standards of quality. But the new products were more differentiated and complex: they required the manufacturer to develop his own marketing, with technically instructed salesmen, stockists, and after-sales service; and the new markets required the seller to meet the customer in his own language and on his own ground. These techniques of marketing the British were slow to develop. By a paradox of history they had become pre-eminent in international trade while retaining their insularity of outlook. By 1897, A.W. Flux, though holding that British trade was still 'the envy of the world', was stressing the need to remedy our shortcomings in salesmanship.[17] Our marketing of textile and agricultural machinery was effective;[18] but when the Board of Trade Committees of 1917-18 surveyed the performance of British industries, they were to find much to criticise in the lack of enterprise by salesmen in foreign markets,[19] and the unwillingness of manufacturers to adjust the quality of the article to the purse of the customer.[20]

Thus slowness to innovate in marketing was mounted upon slowness to innovate in processes and products, to check the extension of British exports. This in turn checked the growth of the new industries: the slow expansion of their sales denied them the economies of scale and discouraged investment in them, especially in those processes of research and development on which they depended. Hence in turn a loss

17.   Flux, A.W. 'British Trade and German Competition', *Economic Journal,* 7, 25, March 1897.
18.   Saul, S.B. 'The Engineering Industry', D.H. Aldcroft (ed.), *The Development of British Industry and Foreign Competition: Studies in Industrial Enterprise,* 1968, pp. 191-94, 208.
19.   Cd. 9035, para 97, British Parly Papers 1918, Vol. XIII.
20.   Cd. 9073, pp. 24-25, British Parly Papers 1918, Vol. XIII.

of competitiveness against other countries whose new industries, thanks to their exports, were growing faster, and a renewed check to British exports.

Such are the three factors to which the inadequate performance of the British economy of seventy years ago now appears to have been chiefly due: the quality of management, especially the conservatism induced by the remarkable success of the practical man in earlier years; the parallel conservatism of labour; and the failure to develop export trade in the products and markets that were expanding most rapidly.

III

In recent years the performance of the British economy has been under scrutiny not only by the academic analyst but by those international bodies that are concerned with development at large or with the solvency of a borrowing country. British governments meanwhile have acted upon what diagnosis seemed most convincing from time to time, and assessment of the effectiveness of their actions has helped to improve the diagnoses. Out of this experience and debate a large measure of consensus has now emerged. A view of the whole field of the evidence and the conclusions to which it leads has recently been provided by the report of a team of American and Canadian economists commissioned by the Brookings Institute.[21] In any full account such as this team has drawn up, much must be qualified, and not a little left undecided. Though the diagnosis now to be presented owes much to the team's report, they must therefore not be held responsible for what is categorical in it; and in its assessment of devaluation it differs from them radically.

At the outset, some negative findings serve to clear the ground.[22] It does not appear that the growth rate of the United Kingdom, having been lower than that of most other western countries, can be attributed to any of those quantifiable factors that make up macro-economic systems. The one apparent exception is the comparatively low level of British industrial investment; but the reason for this investment not having ruled higher has been found not in interest rates or the supply of

21.   Caves, Richard E. and Associates: *Britain's Economic Prospects,* 1968.
22.   See Beckerman, W. 'The determinants of economic growth', Henderson. P.D. (ed.) *Economic Growth in Britain* 1966.

funds, but in the way investment decisions are taken, and the low yield obtained from the operation of the equipment that has been installed. Again, it is not the case that British exports have been handicapped because twenty years ago they were concentrated upon those markets and commodities in which international trade has grown more slowly since.[23] Nor does it appear that the insufficient rise of British exports, or what, given this, has been the too great rise of the imports of manufactures, can be accounted for by relative costs and prices alone. True that among the twelve principal exporters of manufactures, it is the United Kingdom whose unit values of exports rose most between 1954 and 1966; but the evidence is also clear that exports were kept down by political changes in buyers' preferences, and by the slow rate of growth of the output of manufacturing industry for home and export markets combined. As for manufactured imports, their rising trend of recent years, not absolutely only but as a proportion of home output, has been common to most industrial countries, and has yet to restore the proportion to what it was in 1920s: the trend is unlikely to have been set up by relative prices alone. From these findings it appears probable that the parity of sterling maintained from 1949 to 1967 was no major source of difficulty to the balance of payments; and, consequently, that no sharp change of course is to be expected from devaluation.

That government policy in respect of sterling thus appears not to have exerted a great influence either for good or ill is of a piece with the assessment of government policy generally. Because the balance of payments and domestic activity were often out of phase, the timing of stabilising measures was difficult, and in the event sometimes perverse in its effects. But the economic strategy of government, whether monetary or fiscal, does not appear to have missed any clear opportunity of doing good, or persisted in any line that clearly did harm.

These negative conclusions receive support from the study of other western economies. Odd Aukrust's review[24] of research into the causes of the differences in their rates of growth concludes that the role of the quantity of capital has been overestimated, and that it is actually the

23. *Export Trends,* National Economic Development Council, 1963.

24. Aukrust, 'Odd Factors in Economic Development: a Review of Recent Research', *Weltwirtschaftliches Archiv,* 93, 1, 1964.

TABLE 2

Six countries, 1949-59; average annual rate of growth of GDP, and estimated contributions thereto of increase of the labour force, increase of the stock of capital, and 'technical progress'.

(per cent per annum throughout)

	Period	rate of growth of GDP	Estimated contribution to growth of GDP of		
			increase of labour force	increase of stock of capital	'technical progress'
UK	1949-59	2·5	0·4	0·9	1·2
Sweden	1949-59	3·4	0·3	0·6	2·5
Netherlands	1949-54	4·9	1·0	1·2	2·7
	1954-59	4·1	0·8	1·7	1·6
France	1949-54	4·8	0·1	0·9	3·8
	1954-59	4·1	0·1	1·2	2·8
Italy	1949-54	6·4	1·1	0·9	4·4
	1954-59	5·7	0·6	1·0	4·1
W. Germany	1950-54	8·3	1·3	1·4	5·6
	1954-59	6·6	1·0	2·1	3·5

Source: Aukrust, Odd, 'Factors in Economic Development: a Review of Recent Research', *Weltwirtschaftliches Archiv*, 93, 1, 1964, Table 4.

human factor — technical progress, organisation and the advance of 'know how' — that has made most of the difference. In the long run 'it is the ability of man to devise new technological possibilities ...(and) increasing insight and cleverness alone which determine the speed of technical progress', whether 'the rate of capital accumulation is being kept permanently high or permanently low'. Many factors enter into technical progress, and we do not know their relative importance, but the root of the matter is human competence, resulting from education, training and research. Aukrust assesses the contribution of 'technical progress' in this sense by fitting to the GDP of eleven countries in the 1950s a Cobb-Douglas function in which the exponents of labour and capital are set *a priori* in all countries at 0.7 and 0.3 respectively. Table 2 reproduces his findings for three countries in which the contribution of 'technical progress', so estimated, has been relatively low, and the three countries of outstanding growth in which it has been relatively high. His findings indicate not only that the contribution of human competence to growth has been largely relative to that of the physical factors in most countries, but also that its contribution has been lower in the United Kingdom than in all but one of his other ten countries.

The diagnosis of the recent performance of the British economy is therefore on international ground when it moves on from the quantitative factors to the qualitative. One of these to which more than one train of analysis has led is the professional quality of management. We now have data that enable us to compare the profitability of American-managed plants in the United Kingdom with that of British manufacturing generally,[25] and, similarly, that of British-managed plants in the United States with that of American manufacturing:[26] in both comparisons it is under American management that the higher rate of return on capital has been obtained. One difference noted is that American subsidiaries in the United Kingdom spent a higher proportion of their sales revenues on marketing and distribution than did their British competitors. It seems also that British managers make less use of professional qualifications. Joan Woodward in her study of management in a hundred firms in the industrial outskirts of London found that 'attitudes to professional qualifications were prejudiced, and in some firms the possession of academic or professional qualifications was regarded as a handicap.'[27] One is reminded of the evidence given to the Tariff Commission of 1906 by Joe Benn of Bradford, where a Technical School had been set up as early as 1875: 'All applications from young men who apply to me with their gold medal certificates and so on, I put in the waste paper basket.'[28]

The performance of British management has been bound up with the

25.   Dunning, J.H. U.S. subsidiaries in Britain and their U.K. competitors', *Business Ratios*, No. 1, Autumn 1966.

26.   Reddaway, W.B. *Effects of U.K. Direct Investment Overseas*, 1967.|

27.   Woodward, Joan *Industrial Organization: Theory and Practice*, 1965, p.14.
28.   Quoted here from Sigsworth, E.M. and Blackman, J.M. 'The Woollen and Worsted Industries', D.H. Aldcroft (ed.), *The Development of British Industry and Foreign Competition: Studies in Industrial Enterprise*, 1968, p. 147.

state of British industrial relations. It is dangerous to generalise from striking instances, or to attribute a distinctive influence to pressures exerted by British workers when similar pressures are in fact exerted in some measure by the workers of most free countries. The assessment of British practice by an observer deeply versed in American industrial relations is correspondingly valuable. Lloyd Ulman has contributed to the Brookings report a study of British collective bargaining and industrial efficiency. He finds among the workers 'a proletarian spirit which seems conservative even by the standards of a traditionalist society. It appears to be compounded of an unfading memory of pre-war unemployment and a deep-seated mistrust of employer motives and capability.[29] The 'occupational striation' of British trade unionism involves the complications of multi-union bargaining, and increases resistance to changes in the allocation of work. The tradition of relying upon industry-wide negotiations, while actual earnings are settled piecemeal in the firm, has denied management control of its wage structure and of the possibility of obtaining changes in working practices in return for higher earnings. Here as elsewhere much depends on how much management is concerned to exert itself. A report drawn up for the Ministry of Labour by some directors and senior managers of Midland firms held that 'overmanning in much of British industry stems more from managerial weaknesses than from trade union restrictive practices'.[30]

International comparisons have brought out a third factor that differentiates the British performance of recent years. Very widely, the rate of growth of productivity has been positively correlated with that of exports. There is reason to believe that this relation is not merely contingent,[31] and that a reciprocal influence has been exerted between the slow rates of growth of productivity and exports in which the relation has manifested itself in the United Kingdom. Domestic expansion brings an increase of imports, not merely of consumables, but of materials and semi-manufactures for stock, and equipment for

29. Caves, Richard E. and Associates, *Britain's Economic Prospects,* 1968, p. 332.
30. Ministry of Labour, *Efficient Use of Manpower,* 1967, p. 5.
31. Beckerman, W. 'The determinants of economic growth', P.D. Henderson (ed.) *Economic Growth in Britain,* 1966; Aukrust, Odd 'Factors in Economic Development: a Review of Recent Research', *Weltwirtschaftliches Archiv,* 93, 1, 1964.

investment. Unless this rise in imports is accompanied by a growth of exports it must itself exert some deflationary effect, and in the absence of sufficient reserves the passive balance of payments will oblige the government to impose additional restraints. Growing exports do not merely ward off these checks to expansion, they positively foster it by encouraging managers to expect a greater and more sustained rise in output than the home market alone could promise and so inducing a higher rate of investment and innovation. This will tend to lower costs, through the economies of scale and technical progress, and lower costs in turn will promote exports. Hence a circle of forces, virtuous or vicious, operating to improve the performance of those who enjoy an initial advantage in exporting or exert themselves to obtain it, and holding back the performance of those whose exports rose slowly in the first place. For the United Kingdom 'the first place' here must mean the early 1950s, when the first great increase of British exports above the pre-war level had been accomplished, and other countries whose economies had been more disturbed by the war had restored and renewed their industrial capacities. At that time they were distinguished from the United Kingdom by the limited size of their home markets, which made exporting a condition for their industrial expansion as it was not for the British. But that British exports did not rise more at this time kept down the rate of investment and innovation in British industry; hence an increase over time of British relative costs, which in turn did something to reduce the rise in British exports. This spontaneous interplay was intensified by the restraints imposed from time to time by governments to meet crises of the balance of payments.

Such are the three factors on which the diagnosis of the unsatisfactory performance of the British economy in recent years has come to put most weight: the quality of management, the conservatism of labour, the failure to develop exports more. But these, by title at least, are the same three as have been held chiefly responsible for the difficulties of the economy seventy years ago. There are differences, it is true, in the particular manifestations of these factors. A major defect of British management at the earlier date was its neglect of science, and of research and development: no one could charge British management with such neglect today – indeed, the Brookings report has shown that as a proportion of GNP the British expenditure on R & D is half as big again as the American. Again, whereas 1900 began a run of years through which, down to the war, productivity in British industry as a whole failed to rise at all, through the last twenty years it has been rising faster than over any such previous period for which we have estimates. On the other hand, in the years after 1900 the failure to develop exports of the new manufactures exerted no such restraint on the economy as has been exerted in recent years: for at that time traditional exports continued an expansion that both made possible and was promoted by a great export of capital. Yet after we have taken account of all these and other differences, a similarity remains that we can now see to be much more substantial than a mere recurrence of a contagion of mood. Can it really be that the selfsame needs for change that made themselves felt in 1900 have persisted, and kept ahead of the response and adaptation of the economy meanwhile, so that they remain to be met, now as then?

IV

Certainly there are grounds to expect that response and adaptation would have been more difficult in the British economy than in others whose industrialisation had not yet gone so far. An economy whose industrial infrastructure and superstructure alike have been built up as densely as those of the United Kingdom had been by 1900 will find more difficulty in adopting new processes than one that has more resources to commit freshly and more room in which to site them. There will be some sheer physical constraints on the expansion of existing plants and the carrying of more traffic on existing lines of communication. Much new equipment will be installed within old layouts that prevent its being used efficiently. It will often be more profitable for the time being to go on working in an existing location than to move to another where costs will be lower ultimately. The part of the labour force currently available for new developments, without transplantation from existing industrial employment, will be relatively small where the sectors of agriculture and self-employment have been drawn down so far already. To these physical constraints there are mental counterparts. The sheer extent of industry, and the length of its experience, will have made it harder for managers who had grown up in it to challenge its methods and ask, How else could this be done? A labour force habituated to and organised within existing processes is less adaptable to new ones than are workers entering industry for the first time. Generally, where the stream of activity runs long enough on the same course, it cuts a channel that in turn confines and directs it.[32]

None the less, the changes in the British economy in the twentieth century have been radical. The facts are familiar, but it is worth reminding ourselves how far they go.

We can form one impression of this from the changes in the deployment of the working population that are indicated by Table 3. One can say only 'indicated', because the classifications of censuses as far apart as those of 1901 and 1961 are hard to match; but the comparisons presented are close enough to represent at least the relative size of the changes significantly. We see that sectors which together contained half the whole labour force of 1901 contained only a third of it sixty years later; while just the opposite change in relative size occurred in the group composed of metals and engineering, the public utilities, and the professional, technical, administrative and clerical

32.   On 'the legacy of precocious urbanisation' see Landes, D.S. 'Technological Change and Development in Western Europe, 1750-1914', Ch. V in the *Cambridge Economic History of Europe,* Vol. VI, Pt. 1, 1963. On the inefficiency of investment by accretion; see the *Report of the Departmental Committee of the Board of Trade* on the position of the engineering trades after the war (Cd. 9073 of 1918), and Lamfalussy, A. *The United Kingdom and the Six: an Essay on Economic Growth in Western Europe, 1963,* pp. 105-07. The consequences of earlier development in Great Britain for the efficiency of buildings, layout and machinery were assessed by comparison with Germany and the USA in Shadwell, A. *Industrial Efficiency,* Vol. II, 1906, ch. VI. Ashworth, W. 'The Late Victorian Economy', *Economica,* NS 33, 129, Feb. 1966, brings out the costs of adhering to the existing location of industry, especially in iron and steel, on which he cites Burn, D.L. *The Economic History of Steelmaking 1867-1939,* 1940, pp. 167-74, 179-82, 233-36. The resistance to the adoption of new processes exerted by mental and physical investment in earlier ones has been instanced by neglect of the gas and diesel engines (Saul, S.B. 'The Engineering Industry', D.H. Aldcroft (ed.) *The Development of British Industry and Foreign Competition,* 1968) and in the obstruction of the Solvay process by the Leblanc (Richardson, H.W. 'Chemicals', Aldcroft (ed.), *British Industry and Foreign Competition,* 1968) and of electricity by gas (Clapham, Sir John *An Economic History of Modern Britain,* Vol. III, 1938, pp. 130-138). An association between a rapidly rising industrial labour force and a high rate of rise of productivity has been noted for western economies in recent years by Aukrust, Odd 'Factors in Economic Development: a Review of Recent Research', *Weltwirtschaftliches Archiv,* 93, 1, 1964, and Kindleberger, C.P. *Europe's Postwar Growth: the Role of Labor Supply,* 1967, but is called in question by Beckerman, W. 'The Determinants of Economic Growth', P.D. Henderson (ed.) *Economic Growth in Britain,* 1966.

occupations outside industry. The figures here are for both sexes: if we take women alone, even sharper changes appear. Table 4 indicates the extent of the redeployment of women from manual to clerical and administrative, and from less to more skilled occupations. We can add evidence of the mobility of the labour force, and not least its mobility between regions.[33] It is noteworthy that in recent years 'if anything, reallocations towards the faster-growing industries seem to have gone along more speedily in the UK' than in the USA.[34]

TABLE 3

Great Britain, 1901 and 1961: proportions of the total working working population in certain industries

	1901 %	1961 %
Agriculture and fishing	9·0	4·2
Mining and quarrying	5·6	2·3
Textiles	7·2	2·2
Transport & communications	9·0	6·8
Service & entertainment	14·0	10·7
Construction	7·0	6·9
Sub-total in above	51·8	33·1
Metals & engineering	9·4	16·0
Gas, water & electricity	0·4	1·4
Government (excl. Forces); professional, administrative & clerical; commerce & finance	20·4	34·2
Sub-total in above	30·2	51·6
TOTAL	82·0	84·7

Sources. 1901: Census of England & Wales, Vol. X, Pt. 1, Tables 26 & 27; Scotland, Vol. 2, Table D.1: both after removal of 'dealers', because in later Censuses these are included in 'Commerce, etc.'.

1961: Great Britain, 10 per cent Sample, Summary Tables, Table 31; and, for gas, electricity and water, Industry Table 36.

33. *Labour Mobility in Great Britain,, 1953-63,* Govt. Social Survey, SS.333, March 1966. Brown, E.H.Phelps *The Growth of British Industrial Relations,* 1960, I.3.
34. Caves, Richard E. and Associates, *Britain's Economic Prospects,* 1968, p.294.

We have laid stress on the failure, then and now, to develop exports more; but Tables 5 and 6 show how much change has in fact come about in the composition of British exports by both commodity and destination.

But if change has gone so far, why has it not been able to go that little bit farther which would make so much difference today? And why are the kinds of change that are still needed so similar to those that were needed in 1900? Two reasons suggest themselves, corresponding to the different kinds of change required.

The one kind is in attitudes – in the assumptions, expectations, traditions and training that govern the approach to work by both managers and employees. Here some slowness to change seems due to the sheer continuity of British social history. The endeavour to get

TABLE 4

Great Britain, 1901 and 1961: numbers of females in certain industries or occupations as proportions of all occupied females

	1901 %	1961 %
Private domestic service	29·9	4·3
Other service, sport & recreation	12·3	17·2
Textiles	15·2	4·0
Dress	11·9	5·0
Sub-total in above	69·3	30·5
Metals & engineering	1·6	4·7
Transport & communication	0·6	1·9
Professional, administrative, commerce & finance	22·9	23·6
Clerks	1·8	25·4
Sub-total in above	26·9	55·6
TOTAL	96·2	86·1

Sources. *1901:* Census of England & Wales, Vol. X, Pt. 1, Table 26; Scotland, Vol. 2, Table D.1: both excluding 'dealers'.

1961: Great Britain, 10 per Cent Sample, Summary Tables, Table 31.

development going in some backward countries has driven home the fact that their peoples have not been brought up to approach the day's work in the same way as Americans or Swedes. Observers at the turn of the century had little doubt that the approach of the Germans then was very different from that of the British. True, we must beware of explaining a people's economic performance by the innate propensities of their culture: these supposed causes cannot always be observed apart from the behaviour to which they are held to give rise, and there is a consequent danger of falling into a circular argument, in which the existence of a propensity to behave is first inferred from the fact of the behaviour, and then used to account for it. But this danger does not dispose of the possibility that performance is in fact dependent upon attitudes, nor does it prevent us from asking what independent observations can be made of the extent of change in attitudes over time. That they have been more tenacious in Great Britain than in many other industrial economies seems likely because the country has undergone no such upheavals as they. European observers remark that the British never had a revolution, and think they see the effects of this in the persistence of class attitudes — in that peculiarly British

TABLE 5

United Kingdom, 1898 (incl. all Ireland), 1966: proportions of total value of all visible exports made up by given classes of product (classification as in 1966)

	1898 %		1966 %	
Mineral fuel & lubricants	8.4		2.7	
Manufactured goods other than machinery and transport equipment	59.7		24.8	
of which: textiles		41.5		5.2
iron & steel		9.7		4.3
Chemicals	4.8		9.3	
Machinery and transport equipment	9.3		43.2	
All other	17.8		20.1	
TOTAL	100.0		100.0	

Sources. *1898:* 46th Statistical Abstract of the UK, Table 37.
1966: Annual Abstract of Statistics, 1967, Table 27.

combination of the avoidance of overt conflict with an unquestioning assumption of a clash of interests, which makes it so often necessary to keep to the beaten path, because a new line would be a collision course. The British people have not been brought together in relatively recent times from diverse migrations, like the Americans, nor have they pioneered their way across a continent. They have not been defeated in war in the present century, or occupied by a foreign power since 1066. Of course this does not mean that their attitudes have not been and do not continue to be altered as time goes on; but it does suggest that the approach of British managers and employees to their working life will be influenced by a greater force of tradition, and show a greater persistence of old ways through new circumstances, than are found in countries the thread of whose social history has been broken off at some point by revolution or invasion.

TABLE 6

United Kingdom, 1898, (incl. all Ireland), 1966: proportions of total value of all visible exports sent to given regions

	1898 %	1966 %
Asia	19·8	9·7
Australia & New Zealand	9·0	7·8
Latin America	8·4	3·3
Russia[1]	3·9	3·0
Sub-total of above	41·1	23·8
Africa South of the Sahara	6·1	8·6
North America	8·8	17·2
W. Europe & Scandinavia	32·8	38·4
Sub-total of above	47·7	64·2
TOTAL	88·8	88·0

[1] In 1966 includes other Soviet economies.

Sources. 1898: 46th Statistical Abstract for the UK, Table 35.
1966: Annual Abstract of Statistics, 1967, Table 273, and UK Overseas Trade Accounts, Dec. 1967, Table IV.

The other reason that suggests itself for the failure of the British economy to change enough concerns exports. We have seen the power of the vicious circle, by which an initial slowness to export checks the rise of productivity, and this in turn checks the rise of exports. But the initial slowness needs its own explanation; and even after the circle has been joined, a sufficient determination to export on the part of managers could still break out of it. But British managers, it seems, have too often lacked the tradition, whether of putting plant down that was intended from the first to find outlets overseas, or of seeking achievement and recognition through the ever higher turnover that only an international market can accommodate. In the absence of such built-in propensities to export, British governments have used exhortation, with some prospect of honours and awards for those who hear the call; but since the days of import licensing they have had no stronger incentives at their disposal. This is not merely a matter of the rules of GATT and EFTA. Rather, the lack of incentives to export that will be brought into play automatically by an external deficit is common to all advanced economies. It marks a gap in the mechanism of the contemporary market economy. The difficulty is not that national monetary systems do not allow an external deficit to reduce the purchasing power of an economy in the same way as that of one region within it will be reduced if its balance of payments with the rest of the economy is in deficit: for even did this come about, the difficulty would remain that the exporting of manufactures today is not a matter of merchants diverting cargoes to the markets in which for the time being prices are higher. On the contrary, to most manufacturers today the development of an export trade must present itself as a form of diversification, similar to the launching of a new product, and requiring an extensive investment in the modification of designs, the recruitment of agents and training of salesmen, the building up of stocks and the provision of after-sales service. Where this is so, the effect of an external deficit may be actually perverse: when restraints are imposed and home sales are checked, it seems to be no time for risky investments, even in markets free of those restraints. There is no remedy save a change in the aims and values of management: instead of insularity, the assumption that one sells abroad as a matter of course; and the drive to exploit the opportunity of doing so as a means to recognised achievement.

III. ECONOMIC POLICY AND APPLIED STUDIES

The Background of Ratio Control
by Central Banks

R.S. Sayers

Although there are roots of central banking deep in the nineteenth century, the core of central banking as we know it to-day — the function of controlling monetary conditions in accordance with the broad economic policy of a nation — is mainly a twentieth century development. The historical tasks of protection of government finance from catastrophe and of maintenance of the external value of the currency continue to be important preoccupations of the central bankers, but they are nowadays seen as particular aspects of the wider tasks rather than as ends in themselves. In terms of personal activities inside central banks, these matters of government finance and foreign exchange indeed appear as a very large part of the whole; nevertheless, the central bankers themselves, the academic economists and the outside public all regard control of the domestic monetary situation as the heart of the business. It is with this basic task that the first part of my paper is concerned.

The traditional operation of the central bank as lender of last resort is of course part of the technique employed by the central bank for the purpose of controlling internal monetary conditions. The bank lends at last resort in order to prevent a restriction of credit from operating so sharply as to have disastrous effects on the domestic economic situation. A willingness to operate as lender of last resort carries the implication of a continuing selective interest in ordinary financial institutions, and this can lead the central bank into a considerable volume of routine activity. All this is well understood, and I need not dwell on it; I mention it here simply to emphasise that in what follows we shall be taking it for granted that the central bank is operating efficiently as lender of last resort, with all that this implies.

To the task of controlling the domestic monetary situation there are two approaches: the rate of interest approach and the supply of credit approach. My old teacher Dennis Robertson always insisted that the one implies the other, that a chosen rate of interest policy implies a certain supply of credit, and alternatively that a chosen supply of credit implies a certain rate of interest. I acknowledge this as an important element of truth which monetary authorities ignore at their peril, but it is not sufficient in a world where all sorts of imperfections characterise financial markets and the economists' curves are as kinked as a Picasso abstraction and never have the Botticelli smoothness that habitually appears when the teacher gets to work on the blackboard. The basic truth is that a central bank cannot simultaneously choose a dear money policy and an abundant credit policy, nor can it simultaneously choose a cheap money policy and enforce severe contraction of credit. The central bank must make up its mind whether fundamentally contraction (implying dear money) or expansion (implying cheap money) is appropriate. But, having made this basic choice, it must decide whether it wants to operate primarily through interest rates, with supporting action on the supply of credit, or primarily through the supply of credit, with supporting action on interest rates.

It so happened, as a matter of history, that the rate of interest approach acquired a kind of dignified precedence because, early in this century, the Bank of England had adopted this approach and the leadership of London as an international financial centre made it look as though the Bank of England's ways must be the right ones. London relied on 'Bank Rate policy' – London was successful – therefore the manipulation of Bank Rate was the major concern of the central bank: this was the common attitude. Actually there should be a great many more steps in the arguments and particularly a close examination of the judgement that 'London was successful'. This is an historical problem that has never been tackled in sufficient detail. For myself I can only say here that it is possible to argue that the Bank of England's approach, though certainly consistent with fixity of the gold value of the pound and reasonable stability of its purchasing power, may have made for unnecessary fluctuation in economic activity and strain on the international gold standard. Whatever the truth on that question – and it is one of the most interesting unresolved questions in economic history – the world certainly began this century with a prejudice in favour of what I am calling very roughly 'the interest rate approach' in central banking.

Between 1910 and 1930 there was a quite considerable development of the alternative view: the idea that the central bank should think of the supply of credit (an idea never absent from the more theoretical English discussions) gained ground. This development came very naturally as people began to think much more comprehensively and systematically about central banking, a process in which an important part was played by the American enquiry (the National Monetary Commission) preceding the foundation of the Federal Reserve System. Two economists of worldwide fame had much to do with the change in thought. Irving Fisher published in 1910 his *Purchasing Power of Money,* the centrepiece of which was a straightforward Quantity Theory of Money, and for many years this was probably the world's most widely read textbook on money. Then, in the inflation period after the first war, Gustav Cassel's writings on comparative inflation found a wide readership in a world of monetary disorder. By 1923 the Federal Reserve System was finding its feet as a central bank, and was feeling its way towards the policy of controlling by open market operations the supply of bank credit. The Bank Rate technique of the Bank of England continued to be venerated, but there was now a broadening of central banking theory to take in the alternative approach. The state of play in the later 1920s can be seen in Keynes' *Treatise on Money* (1930) for Keynes, brought up in the English tradition, had become a close observer of developments on the other side of the Atlantic. He wanted, moreover, to integrate the strangely independent strands there had been in Marshallian teaching on the working of the monetary system. The result was a model – a slightly untidy model – in which interest rates were seen as crucial influences on capital spending and so on movements of prices, and in which the central banks thrust on markets their views of interest rates by open market operations which could alter the volume of bank credit via the volume of the cash reserves of the commercial banks.

Since 1930 this has remained the core of central banking theory, although the range of important central bank activities has substantially widened. The complexities of foreign exchange policies, especially, have driven central banks into foreign exchange activities on a scale quite unforeseen in 1930; and the establishment of central banks in the less developed countries has given altogether new emphasis to the need to encourage the growth of healthy financial institutions and markets. I do not intend to belittle these aspects of modern central banking in choosing, in the remainder of this paper, to concentrate on one part of the

Keynesian 1930 model: the dependence of the central bank's influence on the asset structures – the *ratios* – of the commercial banks.

The simplest model of central bank control of the supply of bank credit consists of an assumed fixed cash ratio in the commercial banks, coupled with a freedom in the central bank to regulate the absolute volume of cash by buying and selling securities which have to be paid for ultimately by cash transactions between the central bank and the commercial banks. This has been, in a very broad way, the model relevant to the USA system throughout the history of the Federal Reserve System, and it was the model believed to be relevant to the English system through the first half of this century. More elaborate models arise from the complexity of contemporary aims of central banks and their reliance on other liquidity conventions of the commercial banks. The current English system is of this more complicated kind. Even in this more complicated model, however, the central bank relies on certain rigidities in the asset ratios of the commercial banks: on 'liquid assets ratios' or 'secondary liquidity ratios'. These liquidity ratios – both the cash ratio and the secondary liquidity ratios – have become of increasing interest in a wide range of countries in which central banks have been emerging and commercial banking systems have been becoming more sophisticated. At the same time, in the older systems themselves new questions have arisen on old ratios, especially in relation to the problems of controlling a wider range of financial firms. It is therefore high time for us to look at the foundations and the nature of these asset ratios which have traditionally played a vital role in the analysis of central banking.

It is well to begin by remembering the origin of these ratios. They began not as bright ideas of central bankers but as the rules of thumb evolved by prudent commercial bankers: and this applies not only to the cash ratio but also to the ratios of other liquid assets. The prudent banker had to keep instantaneously available enough cash to meet without hesitation his customers' requirements, and he found it wise also to carry normally enough other assets that could be quickly turned into cash to deal with any extraordinarily persistent demand that would otherwise have threatened to exhaust his cash reserve. The circum-stances of individual banks would naturally lead to different ratios in different banks, but when, in the latter part of the nineteenth century, some publication of balance sheets became normal, such variations as previously existed tended to be ironed out. The habits of the larger and more successful banks came to set the pattern, for other banks dared not face the loss of public confidence in themselves which might have followed their exposure of much lower ratios, and at the same time they could feel — especially in England, where secondary reserve assets were readily available — that it would be extravagant to show much higher ratios than the big banks were showing. And so in England, by the time the structure settled down, in 1917-18, to a 'Big Five plus', cash ratios of something like ten to fourteen per cent had become the rule. In other countries — notably in the USA — it became common practice for the government to step in and, for the protection of depositors, to require banks to hold certain ratios of reserve cash.

Once things had reached this pass, the original anchorage in the requirements of prudent banking was lost. Cash ratios — and sometimes other ratios as well — had become conventionalised or even legalised; in one way or another they had acquired a stickiness not inherent in their origin. This stickiness was eventually carried to the extreme point in England, where since 1946 there has been a cash ratio which is not a minimum but is fixed at eight per cent. That is to say, the cash has ceased to be a reserve; instead, the banks depend completely on the central bank (in England operating through the discount market) for such elasticity as they require in order to meet variations in the public's need for cash. Substantially the same extreme position has almost been reached in the USA, where the development of the Federal Funds market has tended to the elimination of the so-called 'excess reserves'; here again, the variable element — the cushion in the system — could be eliminated from the commercial banks themselves only because there is an effective central bank operating to avert any uncomfortable shortage or glut of cash in the system. The central bank has then been able — if it so chose — to turn round and, depending on the fixity of the cash ratio, to use it as a fulcrum for control of the volume of the commercial banks' total of lending to their customers. The central bank has been able to do this because the original cushion, or buffer, in commercial banking has ceased to be a cushion.

One step further along this road, the second line of liquidity — of short-term interest-earning assets — has in some countries gone through the same metamorphosis. In earlier English banking, with its high degree of dependence on London as an effective financial centre with a central bank that early learned to be a ready lender of last resort, this secondary liquidity reserve played a particularly important role. In English country banking, indeed, it almost superseded the cash ratio as the primary ratio; many a country banker learned his trade on the basis of a one-third reserve of liquid assets (including cash) rather than on any settled rule of ten or fifteen per cent cash. In the first three decades of the twentieth century it seems that the principal English banks may have been watching their liquid assets ratio — the 30 per cent, as it came to be called — more rigorously than their actual (as opposed to their window-dressed) cash ratio. When, in later years, the English authorities went to great lengths to keep the Treasury Bill rate under close control, it suited them to absorb into their system of control this secondary liquidity ratio, and it became, at least for a time, rather the primary fulcrum upon which the central bank could operate. (The authorities gradually embarrassed themselves even in this control by their sensitiveness to the moods of the market in longer-term government paper — but that is another episode in the story, which we cannot cover here.)

The upshot of all this is that the central bankers have taken over from the commercial bankers certain ratios, which had been evolved as the rough and ready rules of prudent banking, and have integrated them, in very rigid forms, into their own systems of control — and at the end have compromised their own use of them in the apparatus of control. For the central banks began by making the ratios even more rigid than they had grown of themselves, and then found that the rigidity was leaving the central bankers with less power than they had supposed. In all this long travelling from the origins, certain aspects of the original backcloth have been forgotten, and I must now touch upon these, in order to point some of the problems with which the central bankers now find themselves left.

When commercial banks themselves first began, it was by a gentle process of distinction from more generalised trading businesses: some merchants (and others) came to specialise in the financial part of their business. It was difficult, at that stage, to say who was and who was not a banker. But the bankers did become, over the decades, decidedly specialised, and when it came to direct or indirect access to facilities provided by the central bank, and of subjection to rules imposed by it, there was no doubt whether any firm was or was not a bank. When, therefore, the cash ratio — or any other ratio — had become a matter of ruling by the central bank, the scope, in terms of banks, of that rule could be perfectly clear. Nor, given the normal adoption by the central bank of ratios at which the commercial banks had already arrived, could there by any question of unfairness or imposition of unreasonable burdens. The authorities were doing no more than to insist that each commercial bank should strictly maintain the rules of prudence at which their own fraternity had arrived.

Now it so happened that circumstances had historically led to the convention that the central bank does not pay interest on the balances placed with it by the commercial banks. To have a balance at the central bank brought to the member bank certain facilities and other advantages (including prestige) that were highly valued by the member bank, so that the central bank was able to hold these very large deposits without having to pay any interest on them. What had begun as an ordinary commercial practice, arising from the balance of advantage between willing parties, became one of the fixed rules: that the central bank does not pay interest on its deposit liabilities became an accepted principle.

When the idea of compulsory secondary reserves was developed, a similar course was followed, with a different result. On these secondary reserves of non-cash but highly liquid assets, the member banks had of course been earning interest — generally at relatively low rates, but in absolute terms an important contribution to the normal profits of their business. Once again, in most cases, the authorities were simply calling upon the member banks to adhere strictly to their normal practices, and it was perfectly fair that the member banks should be allowed, on any compulsory secondary reserves, rates of interest comparable to those on any comparable marketable securities. (Not always, for there have been some very special cases, as in the Belgian system after the war, when the secondary reserves arose from the extraordinary circumstances of the moment.) When the banks have been allowed to go on holding, as these secondary reserves, exactly the same market instruments as before, the arrangements were simple enough: the banks earned market rates on these reserves, just as they had done when the holding of them was a matter of free choice on their part. No question of any unfair burdens, resulting from the enforcement of rules by the central bank, arose in these circumstances. Moreover, as with the cash ratios, there was no doubt about the identification of the banks to which the rules should be applicable.

But now a quite different position seems to be developing: to have been reached, indeed, in some countries, and to be approaching in others. We have virtually forgotten that these so-called 'reserves', whether of cash or other liquid assets, were ever reserves in the true sense of acting as compressible cushions whereby banks could face variations on their customers' requirements. The element of elasticity required in the system is provided by the operations of the central bank, whether in action as lender of last resort or in its open market operations; and the ratios have become purely devices for ensuring that the member banks should closely follow the policy of the central bank. Because the central bank is not always able to operate in the market on a sufficient scale, we now accept the right of the authorities to raise the ratios from time to time. Anyway their original anchorage in prudent banking practices has been lost, for changes in the structure of the commercial banking system and in the financial markets would by now have generally allowed much lower ratios consistently with the old standards of prudence. The old argument that no interest should be paid on the bankers' deposits at the central bank has lost its cogency. The erstwhile fairness of the yield on secondary reserves has been brought into question both by the willingness of the authorities to raise the ratios above conventional levels and by adherence to conventional categories of liquid assets in spite of great changes in the range of market instruments among which the banks might nowadays be choosing their first lines of liquid assets.

There is also another kind of change driving the most highly developed systems further and further away from the simplicity and fairness of a generation ago. With the continuing development of financial markets — especially now that all of them are centred around the unfailing support of a central bank — the distinction between what is a bank and what is not a bank is becoming blurred. The old assurance that we knew exactly to what firms — being banks — the central bank's edicts about ratios were applicable, has gone. Issues of fairness — of justice between competing businesses — have emerged, of which there was no trace in the financial structures characteristic of the previous generation. I must emphasise, too, that there were not only questions of justice: the broad economic case for equality of regulation, of restriction, of burdens, for competing firms is one that is relevant to the efficiency in the distribution of financial resources, and therefore of real resources.

There have thus arisen elements of artificiality in the ratios which, for the sake of central banking control — and, one should mention, for the sake of national debt policy — imply questions of equity between competing financial institutions and therefore imply also questions of efficiency in the distribution of real resources. Something of this new range of problems is, I suspect, being perceived by central banks, and particularly by the Bank of England, as it seeks to elaborate, for a wider structure of financial institutions, a system of regulation of 'reserve ratios'.

This turn of circumstances leads on to some practical questions. The foundation of the principle that the central bank should pay no interest on deposits (which enter into the cash ratio) has gone; and, if required secondary reserves are to include artificially restricted classes of assets, perhaps the rates of interest on these also have been brought into question. At any rate, we need to take a fresh look at a whole range of questions on the income and profit relationships of the central bank, the commercial banks and that wider — and widening — range of other financial institutions that have thrust themselves into the purview of the central bank.

On Regional Economic Policy in the United Kingdom

G.C. Archibald

I INTRODUCTION [1]

1   It is customary to discuss alternative cures for a balance of payments deficit under the headings 'Expenditure Damping', 'Expenditure Switching', and 'Direct Control'. Since fiscal measures, imposed changes in relative prices, and controls do exhaust the policy instruments open to governments, in mixed economies at least, it seems reasonable to adopt the same taxonomy in our discussion of regional economic policy. Assume for the moment that the problem is persistently high unemployment in some region or regions.[2] We may distinguish:

(1)   *Expenditure policy.* This is basically the application at the regional level of the Keynesian cure for unemployment due to deficient aggregate demand: regionally directed public works expenditures and measures of that sort. Generally, we include here any regional variation in the government's vector of final demand designed to alter expenditure injections on a geographical basis.

(2)   *Price policy.* By price policy, I mean differential subsidy and tax rates designed to alter relative prices between regions: geographically discriminatory investment grants and payroll taxes are obvious

1.   A first draft of this paper was written during my tenure of a Ford Foundation Faculty Fellowship at Northwestern University and delivered to the 1968 meetings of the Midwest Economics Association and the Staff Seminar at the University of Essex. I am indebted to all participants and particularly to Professors R.B. Heflebower and T. Hardie Park for valuable comment. I am responsible for all remaining errors. The estimate given below of the extent to which the Phillips Curve might be shifted to regional policy is based on work done in 1968. Subsequent estimates (see University of Essex Discussion Paper No. 34 by Kemmis, Perkins and myself) suggest much less favorable results.
2.   In what follows, the division of the country into regions is taken for granted without discussion. I hope to make the location of regional boundaries the subject of a future paper.

224

examples. These examples are of policies directed to changing relative factor prices on a geographically discriminatory basis; but differential taxes or subsidies in product markets may also be regionally discriminatory. Price policies work, of course, by providing incentives and disincentives to independent decision-takers.

(3) *Controls* might be regarded as extreme cases of price policy: either permission is granted at zero price (save any cost of dealing with the bureaucracy), or it is not granted, effectively putting an infinite price on the forbidden activity. It is, however, convenient as well as conventional to discuss controls separately. They may obviously be used on a geographically discriminatory basis. An example is the Industrial Development Certificate.

Missing from this list is the well-known prescription, 'improve the infra-structure'. Improvement of the infra-structure on a regionally discriminatory basis is a particular case of expenditure policy. What requires attention is the possibility that public expenditure on the infra-structure not only has Keynesian effects, but stimulates growth in a fashion that justifies departures from usual criteria. This possibility will not be discussed here, due largely to ignorance.[3] This paper, in fact, will be largely confined to a static, or a least short-run, discussion of Expenditure and Price Policies. Some discussion of Controls is, of course, unavoidable.

2   Before proceeding, it would be well to have some idea of what the problem is, what the rewards to curing it might be, and even of what the causes might be. It would be impossible to deal adequately with all these questions, on which there is a large literature, but a few remarks may be in order.

As for the problem, or rather, the phenomenon, it is taken to be persistent unemployment in parts of the UK. Strictly, the case is that the dispersion of regional unemployment rates round the national rate is not trivial; *and* regions have remained obstinately in the same position in the distribution; *and* such trends as can be observed do not

3.   The question has recently been discussed by A.J. Brown in his 'Note of Dissent' to the Report of the Hunt Committee, 1969.

suggest that a correcting process is at work, or at least working with reasonable speed. This is all well documented and the evidence need not be repeated here.[4] (There are, of course, other regional problems that may deserve notice, such as slow growth rates. The measures tend to be associated; and it will simplify discussion to concentrate on the 'traditional' problem to which regional policy has been directed.)

3 Reasons for thinking that the prevailing pattern of regional unemployment imposes costs and is objectionable have often been discussed: attention has concentrated on the waste of resources and the plight of the long-term unemployed. Recently two further suggestions have been made, that development of the Development Areas would be a source of additional growth, and that reduction of the regional dispersion in unemployment would improve the trade-off between unemployment and wage inflation for the country as a whole. The first suggestion is beyond the scope of this paper.[5] Something more may, however, be said about the second.[6]

In a recent paper[7] on the Phillips' curve, I endeavoured to test Lipsey's disaggregation hypothesis.[8] The suggestion is, briefly, that, if the function relating the rate-of-change of money wages to excess demand (or unemployment) in each market is steeper for low levels of unemployment than for high, then the greater is intra-market dispersion the faster will average money wage rates increase for a given national unemployment rate. This result holds if the reaction functions are steeper in the markets with greater excess demand. Since we do not have data for 'true' labour markets (even if we know what they are), two proxies for the dispersion were constructed, the industrial variance of unemployment and the regional variance. Each was used in an ordinary time-series regression equation for the Phillips' curve. For reasons discussed in the original paper, the regional version works better than the industrial version. The preferred equation is

4.   But for the time-series behaviour of the 'structural' component in regional unemployment see Brechling, 1967.

5.   See, e.g. Mackay, 1968, N.E.D.C., 1963.

6.   The suggestion was made by Archibald, 1967, Brechling, 1967, and Brown, 1967. It appeared to be taken up by Whitehall: see the Green Paper, 1967 and the White Paper, 1967.

7.   Archibald, 1969 See also Thirlwall, 1969.

8.   Lipsey, 1960.

$$\frac{\dot{W}}{W} = 4.40 + 8.32U^1 + 0.3\frac{\dot{P}}{P} + 1.7\sigma^2 \tag{1}$$

$$(1.96) \quad (2.32) \quad (0.13) \, (0.55) \quad \frac{w}{R^2} = \cdot 81$$

(where $\frac{\dot{W}}{W}$ is the first central difference of the twelve-month average of the Index of Weekly Wage Rates, $\frac{\dot{P}}{P}$ the first central difference of the twelve-month average of the Index of Retail Prices, U is the national per cent unemployment rate, and

$$\sigma_t^2 = \Sigma_i f_i (U_{it} - U_t)^2$$

where f_i is the proportion of the labour force in the ith region, and U_{it} is unemployment rate in the ith region at time t. Figures in parentheses are Standard Errors. The model was fitted to annual data, 1950-66).

We may use equation (1) to obtain some measure of the shift in the Phillips' curve that would result from reducing regional dispersion in unemployment. To avoid the problem of the long-run shift in the curve consequent upon the expectation of inflation induced by continuous inflation,[9] we wish to estimate the shift in the unemployment level consistent with price stability. We therefore require some assumption about productivity growth. To illustrate, let us assume that productivity grows at 3 per cent, and that this is consistent with stable prices if $\frac{\dot{W}}{W} = 3$ per cent also. Then rearrangement of (1) gives

$$U^* = \frac{a_1}{3\% - a_0 - a_3\sigma^2} \tag{2}$$

where U^* is the unemployment level consistent with price stability, and the a_i are the coefficients of (1) taken in order. We can now proceed in several ways. We may compute from (2) the values of U^* for alternative values of σ^2, with results given in Table I, where $\bar{\sigma}^2$, denotes the mean value for the period of observation, and 'min.' and 'max.' the minimum and maximum in that period, respectively. We may also differentiate (1) totally, putting $\frac{\dot{P}}{P} = 0$, and set $d(\frac{W}{W}) = 0$ to compute the marginal rate of substitution between the variables, giving

$$\frac{dU^*}{d\sigma^2} = \frac{a_3}{a_1} U^2 \tag{3}$$

(approximately equal to 0.4 *at U* = 1.4 %). And from (2) we may calculate the partial elasticity of *U* with respect to σ^2 as

$$\eta_{u:\sigma} = \frac{a_3 \sigma^2}{\frac{\dot{W}}{W} - a_O - a_3 \sigma^2}$$

Taking $\frac{\dot{W}}{W}$ = 3%, this gives us

$$\eta_{u^*:\sigma^2} = \frac{a_3}{a_1} U^* \sigma^2 \tag{4}$$

some values of which are reported in Table I.

TABLE I

Alternative values of U^* and $\eta_{u^*\sigma^2}$, assuming $P = \frac{\dot{W}}{W}$ = 3% and

$$\frac{\dot{P}}{P} = o$$

(1) *Value of σ^2*	(2) U^*	(3) $\eta_{u^*\sigma^2}$ at cols. (1) and (2) values
$\sigma^2 = \bar{\sigma}^2 = 1.26$	1·59	0·41
$\sigma^2 = 0$	1·12	–
$\sigma^2 = \frac{1}{2}\bar{\sigma}^2 = 0.63$	1·32	0·17
$\sigma^2 = min = 0.67$	1·33	0·18
$\sigma^2 = max = 3.21$	4·35	2·87

On the whole, Table I suggests that reductions in σ^2 do have some effect on U^*. Reducing σ^2 from its mean value to zero (an extreme assumption) reduces U^* by nearly half a percentage point, or over a quarter of its initial value. Reducing σ^2 from its maximum observed value to its mean reduces U^* by about one and three-quarter percentage points. (Due to the non-linear form of the relationship, σ^2 obviously has more 'leverage' at higher than at lower levels of U^*: see (3).) What we should like, however, is some notion of the confidence that should be attached to these estimates. The non-linear form of (2), however, presents serious difficulties in finding the distribution of estimated U^*, even given the distribution of a_i, and the matter will not be pursued here.

4   It remains to say something about the causes of the persistent pattern of regional unemployment. Two popular candidates in recent literature are deficient aggregate demand and/or the industrial structure.[10] Economic theory suggests, however, that excess supply of labour in some regions only should have relative price effects, inducing capital to move in (thus increasing aggregate demand, and 'correcting' the industrial structure) while at the same time some outward migration of labour helps to correct the disequilibrium. The duration of the unemployment pattern is apparently inconsistent with this argument, unless one is willing to use virtually indefinite lags as alibis. There is, however, another possibility, that market imperfections in fact prevent the required changes in relative prices from taking place. It appears to the present author, at least, that this is a very serious possibility in the UK, and deserves some attention.[11]

Let us start from the familiar proposition of linear programming that resources that are not fully used in the optimal solution have zero shadow prices. Now, workers (with given locations and skills) would have zero shadow prices if, and only if, they were complementary in every activity with a scarce resource that was more valuable in another use. It seems hard to believe that the persistent pattern of regional unemployment in the UK is due to groups of workers having zero shadow prices (particularly bearing in mind the duration of the phenomenon and the possibility of substituting labour for capital, i.e. altering coefficients, in the long run). The alternative explanation is simply that market wages for certain groups of workers (with given locations and skills) are above shadow prices. This is indeed obvious; but we note that there must be a persistent discrepancy to account for observation. The suggested explanation is therefore that market imperfection operates persistently to maintain the market wages of

10.   See NIESR, 1968, but cf. Holmans, 1965.

11.   The argument that follows owes much to a paper by Johansen, 1967, that will be discussed in greater detail in III below. Borts, 1966, appears to reach similar conclusions by different techniques but fundamentally similar arguments.

certain groups of workers above their shadow prices, and therefore persistently impedes the adjustment mechanism from working. We may notice at once that this is a general hypothesis: if it is correct, then there is no need for any special or 'structural' explanations of bad regional performance. A 'bad' industrial structure, for example, remains so because what would otherwise be induced incentives to change do not operate. From this point of view, structuralist and 'local' explanations are not explanations at all; at the most, they record the results of an impeded adjustment mechanism.

There is no possibility of settling the matter here, but a few points may be made, chiefly intuitive. It seems hard to believe that the 'extra' unemployed in the high unemployment areas have been worth chronically less than their unemployment benefit (a measure of their minimum supply price). It is not hard to believe, however, that their shadow prices may be generally less than market prices determined by national wage bargaining.[12] It is, indeed, hard to think why else they should remain unemployed (unless their shadow prices are indeed zero, or at least less than unemployment benefit). And it is hard to see how the rates of change of earnings could have kept pace, as they have, in regions with different unemployment experience, if the market price of labour were free to vary locally.[13] At least one may say that the prevalence of national wage bargaining in Britain is consistent with this explanation.

If wages cannot adjust, workers can at least move. It is well known that there has been 'a lot' of migration in Britain. What is undetermined is whether migration is fast or slow as a response to market stimuli. It is clear that there exist some serious market imperfections that must deter migration. Council housing and rent control, leading to waiting lists, and a 'two-tier' system of pricing, must be a deterrent,[14] although the quantitative effect cannot presently be measured. It is clear, however,

12. Thirlwall, 1970, finds that the national rate of change of wages (earnings) is almost perfectly explained by unemployment in the LSE area. If wage rates are determined by the excess demand for labour in the area of highest excess demand, and enforced elsewhere, the argument of the text appears obvious.
13. It is well known that there are regional differences in per capita income, family income, etc. But this is not the point. The point is rigidity in *prices*.
14. So also must be other barriers to entry, such as closed shops, restrictive apprenticeship rules, and the like.

that many unemployed workers cannot reduce their supply prices where they are, and cannot go where the demand price meets the supply price without accepting what is, in effect, a real wage discriminatorily lower than that enjoyed by those already present, due to housing. It is also, of course, true that the existence of unemployment benefit always makes the private return on movement less than the social return.

None of the forgoing should be taken as implying any policy prescription. I shall not, for example, ask how the government might discourage national wage bargaining. On the contrary, in the discussion of Price Policies in III below, we shall ask how, given that there are discrepancies between market and shadow prices, the government can bring accounting prices into line with the latter rather than the former.

II EXPENDITURE POLICIES

1 Expenditure Policies are defined as regionally-discriminatory variations in the government's vector of final demand, or, more loosely, the obvious Keynesian remedies for regional unemployment: regionally-directed public works expenditures, and measures of that sort. It unfortunately turns out that they are not very effective, and that they have side-effects which inhibit their use in times of generally high employment. The reason for this is that regional multipliers tend to be low, the local-income/government-expenditure ratios lower still (due to import content in the expenditures), and the spill-over effects to other regions (due to import content in both the exogenous and the endogenous expenditures) non-negligible.[15]

2 We can illustrate and clarify further the difficulties of Expenditure Policies by consideration of a simple input-output model. For simplicity, we consider only two sectors, but we close the model with respect to households. The coefficient matrix is given in Table II. We assume that labour 'belongs' to a sector (or region) in the short-run, although it may be mobile in the long-run. The simplifying assumption that households do not buy labour from other households does not detract from the generality of the argument. We also simplify by

15.   See Archibald, 1967, and also Brown, 1967, and Steele, 1969. A classic on spill-over effects is Chenery, 1953.

assuming no final demand for direct labour. If we wished to alter that assumption, we should have to add a third group of workers, specific to the third (government service) sector, but should gain nothing in generality. Yet another simplifying assumption is that the consumption coefficients, c_1 and c_2, are independent of the region of origin of the income. We could replace the c-vector by a *2 x 2* matrix of consumption coefficients without altering anything of substance: so long as the A-matrix is not diagonal the argument to follow does not require that the consumption matrix be non-diagonal.

TABLE II

	1	2	3	
Sector 1	a_{11}	a_{12}	c_1	Y_1
Sector 2	a_{21}	a_{22}	c_2	Y_2
Households	l_1	l_2	0	0

It will be noticed that, in describing Table II, the words 'region' and 'sector' have been used interchangeably. This is deliberate, and will, I think, shortly be seen to be legitimate. We may now consider some very obvious propositions.

If we can solve for required outputs, given Y_1 and Y_2, we can solve for required labour inputs, L_1 and L_2. Vice-versa, if we have a vector of desired labour inputs, $\bar{L}_1$ and $\bar{L}_2$ (say, 'full employment') we can solve for the *required vector of final demands* (assuming that no constraints imposed by the available quantities of factors complementary to labour are effective). The usual properties of an input-output transformation suffice to assure us that this is *unique*.

Suppose now that we have unemployment in one sector, but not in the other, i.e., $L_1 < \bar{L}_1$, but $L_2 = \bar{L}_2$. We already know that there exists a final demand vector that will cure this unemployment, but it is unique. The implication of this is that no arbitrary multiple of Y_1 and Y_2 will do. Specifically, it will be necessary to *reduce* Y_2 if excess demand and inflation are to be avoided in Sector 2, while unemployment in Sector 1 is reduced by increasing Y_1. This is an important constraint on Expenditure Policies, and its practical implications for Britain will be discussed further below.

To illustrate further, suppose that full employment is disturbed by an autonomous fall in Y_1. The *only* non-inflationary Expenditure Policy that will restore full employment is that the government exactly restore Y_1. Alternatively, suppose that a coefficient is altered, specifically that l_1, expenditure on labour per unit of good one produced, falls (due, say, to technical change). If Y_1 and Y_2 are unchanged, employment falls in *both* sectors. Shall we call this 'structural' or 'demand deficient' unemployment? It is *caused* by a structural change, and *could be cured* in the short-run by a change in final demand. We notice again, however, that a unique vector of final demands is required: in particular, neither an increase in Y_1 alone, nor any proportionate increase in Y_1 and Y_2, will restore zero excess demand for labour in both sectors.

3 The case of particular interest here is that in which we have full employment in one sector but not in the other. The Expenditure cure for unemployment in say, the North East, is to increase the programme of public works expenditure there. Given full employment in the Midlands and London areas, we know that this programme will cause inflationary pressure in those areas unless there is an offsetting reduction (less, of course, than one-for-one) in final demand for the products of those areas. But social policy dictates that expenditures on housing, schools, sanitation, transport, etc., take place where they are required: the population growth in the growth regions itself induces public expenditures. Thus the policy maker is faced with a choice: if he spends more to reduce unemployment in Region A, he must trade-off 'socially desirable' expenditures in Region B. In the ordinary one-sector macro-economics of unemployment this choice does not occur. The appropriate analogy is perhaps to the choice problems presented in an open economy.

In the circumstances, it is not at all surprising that Expenditure Policies sufficient to solve the regional unemployment problem in Britain have not been adopted: governments have not been willing to make the required offsetting cuts in other components of their final demand vectors.

The conclusion is that, although there has doubtless been some use of regional expenditure policy, it has not been, and for good reason is not likely to be, used sufficiently extensively to solve our regional problems.

III   PRICE POLICIES

1 Price Policies are defined to be regionally discriminatory subsidies and tax rates (whether applied to inputs or outputs), such as favourable tax treatment for investment carried out in designated areas. To help to evaluate such policies, I shall now borrow heavily from Johansen, 1967, and start by presenting his linear programming analysis in some detail. He assumes two production processes in each of two regions, two regionally-specific but industry-mobile factors in each region, and one 'common factor', i.e., a factor completely mobile between the two regions. The notation is:

x_1, x_2 the output from the two production process in Region A

y_1, y_2 the output from the two production processes in Region B

V_1, V_2 the amounts available of the two regional factors in Region A

W_1, W_2 the amounts available of the two regional factors in Region B

F the amount available of the common factor (a factor that is not tied to any particular region).

The constraints are

$$a_{11}x_1 + a_{12}x_2 \leqq V_1$$
$$a_{21}x_1 + a_{22}x_2 \leqq V_2$$
$$b_{11}y_1 + b_{12}y_2 \leqq W_1$$
$$b_{21}y_1 + b_{22}y_2 \leqq W_2$$
$$g_1x_1 + g_2x_2 + h_1y_1 + h_2y_2 \leqq F$$

and

$$x_1 \leqq 0, x_2 \leqq 0, y_1 \leqq 0, y_2 \leqq 0.$$

The maximand is

$$R = P_1 x_1 + P_2 x_2 + Q_1 y_1 + Q_2 y_2$$

where the P's and Q's are the product prices.

We write the dual:

$$r_1 a_{11} + r_2 a_{21} \qquad\qquad\qquad + u g_1 \gneqq P_1$$

$$r_1 a_{12} + r_2 a_{22} \qquad\qquad\qquad + u g_2 \gneqq P_2$$

$$s_1 b_{11} + s_2 b_{21} \qquad + u h_1 \gneqq Q_1$$

$$s_1 b_{12} + s_2 b_{22} \qquad + u h_2 \gneqq Q_2$$

and

$$r_1 \gneqq 0, r_2 \gneqq 0, s_1 \gneqq 0, s_2 \gneqq 0, u \gneqq 0;$$

minimise

$$R^* = r_1 V_1 + r_2 V_2 + s_1 W_1 + s_2 W_2 + uF$$

where r_1, r_2, s_1, s_2, u are the shadow prices. Johansen's Rule is fairly obvious and may be quoted immediately:

> The accounting prices which indicate the optimal set of processes must be such that each common factor has the same accounting price in every region, while regional resources (even if they are physically the same) generally have accounting prices which differ from region to region. 1967, p.69.

It is clear that the shadow prices of physically similar but spatially different regionally specific factors are likely to be different. Problems arise if market prices differ from shadow prices. Existing capital presents no difficulty, since rents are residuals. The case of interest is that regionally specific labour may receive the same wage in both regions, but have different shadow prices. We have here a very simple case for intervention: we can get the market solution closer to the optimal solution by intervening to make accounting wages closer to shadow wages, i.e., by regionally discriminatory subsidies to employment. Thus we have a case *for* the Regional Employment premium, and an immediate case against regionally discriminatory treatment of investment for tax purposes (if we may interpret new capital as the common or mobile factor), which has been the main instrument of British regional Price Policy.[16]

2 Before taking up any details of policy, let us consider the model a little further. In the first place, Johansen's rule follows simply from the circumstance that in the primal problem there is a single constraint involving F: the total supply of the common factor (new capital available in the planning period, say), whence there is only one corresponding unknown in the dual problem. The statement of a second constraint is a necessary condition for a different result (we shall consider some other constraints below). Thus it is not necessary to vary the objective function, introduce migration, etc., in order to show that the rule is 'robust'. Johansen in fact considers a variety of interesting cases which we need not rehearse.

Next we notice that employment is not an argument of the objective function in this model. Johansen suggests that (un)employment may be redundant as an argument of the utility function: the target of maximising output may be sufficient.[17] This will be the case if all labour is fully utilised in the optimal solution. Thus Johansen assumes that in Region A, say, there is an activity, the first, say, that uses only labour, the first resource. Then $a_{21} = g_1 = o$, and the first line of the dual gives

$$ r_1 a_{11} \quad P_1, \quad i.e. \quad r_1 \geqq \frac{P_1}{a_{11}} . $$

In this case, labour will be fully utilised if output is maximised, but not if decision-takers have to accept a market wage above r_1. A positive subsidy less than the market wage is required for maximum output and employment.[18]

16.   The effect of this policy on the so-called Grey Areas, which has recently received attention, will not be pursued here. If Johansen's Rule is accepted, then the policy is mistaken *in toto,* and its effect on the Grey Areas requires no special attention. Application of *any* policy requires that regional (or Area) boundaries are correctly located, which is a separate issue. It may be remarked that in some recent discussion of the Grey Areas it is not clear whether it is assumed that total investment is invariant to geographical tax concessions, in which case there is obviously only a relocation effect, or responds to the tax concessions, in which case matters are more complicated.

17.   In this case the favourable shift in the Phillips' curve discussed above is also a consequence of output maximisation, and need not be adopted as an additional target.

18.   There remains the possibility that P_1/a_{11} is less than unemployment benefit and/or National Assistance. Crudely, one might say that the workers for whom this is true are the unemployables. They must be smaller in number than the unemployed workers for whom P_1/a_{11} is less than the market wage.

We may now take up another question: given inequality between the shadow and the market prices of *inputs,* would discriminatory taxes and subsidies on *outputs* be a substitute for taxes and subsidies on the inputs? The answer is, in general, no. Suppose for the moment that the optimal solution of the primal problem required full utilisation of all resources. Then we could proceed as follows: substitute strict equalities for the inequalities in the dual; substitute the known market prices of inputs for the shadow prices; finally solve the dual for the *P's* and *Q's.* These would be the full employment product prices, given existing factor prices, i.e., those that give rise to shadow prices equal to existing market prices. Comparison of this vector of product prices with market prices would then give the required tax-subsidy vector for products. But this procedure is possible only in the special case in which the optimum requires full utilisation of *all* resources, including all existing capital. We notice that the assumption made in the last paragraph, though sufficient to ensure full employment of labour, was by no means sufficient to ensure full employment of all resources: the programme still has five constraints and only four activities. We therefore conclude that Price Policy should generally be directed to input rather than output prices. We also notice, of course, that alteration of the values of the *P's* and *Q's* leaves Johansen's Rule unaffected: it alters only the values of the required input subsidies. Full employment of all resources is simply the special case in which there exists a *P,Q* vector such that all input subsidies should be zero.

What if a regional wage subsidy to employers causes the market wage to alter? We should normally expect this to occur. The answer, of course, is that while it makes the required subsidy harder to calculate, it does not alter any principle except in the limit case in which the alteration is always equal to the subsidy.

3 Against this background, the Regional Employment Premium[19] looks like a good idea, at least more hopeful than reliance on Expenditure Policies.

The fact is, however, that the subsidy is paid *in respect of employment in manufacturing only.* This seems so remarkable that it is

19.   For discussion of a payroll tax (subsidy) in place of a specific premium, see Hutton and Hartley, 1968.

worth a little discussion.[20] It follows from the prior imposition of a Selective Employment Tax, intentionally discriminatory between sectors, rather than regions, i.e., to be negative in manufacturing and non-negative elsewhere. The New Physiocrats[21] of Whitehall are at least consistent. The decision to impose the SET seems quite irrational (revealed preference: it is virtuous to make automobiles, but bad to service them) unless we assume that manufacturing differs from all other activities in certain monopoly and monopsony characteristics, and that these differences are more significant inter-sectorally than intra-sectorally. In Johansen's model the shadow price of each regionally-specific resource is the same in both activities, whence a decision to subsidise employment in only one activity is wrong. We should therefore now recall an important assumption, that regionally immobile resources are activity-mobile. Does the conclusion change if we assume that some resources are activity-specific as well as regionally specific, in spite of being 'physically' the same? This has the effect of increasing the number of factors, and we see that shadow prices of workers are likely to differ by activity as well as region. To justify policy, however, we must believe that serious discrepancies between shadow and market prices arise only in manufacturing. This amounts to saying that whatever forces make regional wage differentials less than

20. The official arguments in favour of this decision will be found in the Green Paper, 1967, and the White Paper, 1967. Space does not permit a detailed critique of all the arguments employed (some of which are sound, and some quite specious) but one is so perverse as to be worthy of note. In the Green Paper, p. 16, we are told that the objection to simple relief of SET in Development Areas is that it frustrates the purpose of SET to 'broaden the tax base by selective imposition of the tax on the service industries, which are not subject to the purchase tax and revenue duties levied on the output of manufacturing industries'. Even if all manufacturing outputs were so taxed (which they are not) the argument would be: we used a tax (SET) to offset a bad tax, and get a third (bad) tax (REP) because we can't repeal the other two. The authors of the Green Paper talk as though any existing taxes that do discriminate against manufacturing were acts of God.

21. By a New Physiocrat I mean one who believes (or whose actions apparently make sense only if he is assumed to believe) that manufacturing is the only really productive activity, and that all others, particularly services, are essentially non-productive or even parasitic. In defence of the New Physiocrats it has been argued that productivity growth is faster in manufacturing than elsewhere, whence shifting resources into manufacturing is conducive to faster growth. To conclude that this shows the policy to be good is, at the least, to confuse measured growth with real, or welfare, growth. Also c.f. Baumol and Bowen, 1965.

regional shadow-price differentials in manufacturing do not operate elsewhere. In view of the existence of strong national unions in government service, fuel and power, railways, etc., this extreme position is hard to accept, although it may well be true that there is little or no monopoly element in wage-setting in distribution and some other service trades (employing a high proportion of females).[22]

Arguments for the REP stress its prospective influence on growth, *via* its effect on location decisions for new investment. We cannot assess such arguments within the framework of our simple static model (and we are very ignorant about location decisions anyhow). Two points, however, seem worth making. The first is that the short-run or impact-effect of the Premium in some regions will be negligible. The Western Development Area (Cornwall and North Devon) contains at present virtually no manufacturing, neither do the Highlands of Scotland. The second is that the argument implicitly neglects comparative advantage. The notion that regions whose comparative advantage is obviously in tourism should only be saved by manufacturing development seems grotesque.

4 So far we have assumed without discussion that the common, or mobile, factor, F, can be interpreted as new capital. Johansen suggests two interpretations. The first causes no difficulty: if the common factor is, say, fuel, the interpretation is obvious. The second, and more interesting, is more difficult: to interpret the mobile factor as new capital

... is only possible when the problem is considered as a planning problem; over the period to which the plan refers we expect a certain supply of capital which can be made available to the one region or the other and which consequently does not already exist as physical capital equipment, with a specific geographical location. (Already existing real capital can be included among the regional resources.) 1967, p. 66.

Now, in all Johansen's experiments one part of the Rule is unaltered, for a reason we have already discussed: the shadow price of the mobile factor is the same in both regions. If we accept the 'new capital' inter-

22.   In the White Paper, 1967, we are told, p. 8, that 'most changes in standard wage rates are negotiated at the national level, and, outside London, regional variations in wage rates are relatively uncommon'. This seems to be contrary to what we need to assume to justify the payment of REP in manufacturing only.

pretation on a planning basis, the inference is clear: we should not give regionally discriminatory investment subsidies. Regionally discriminatory treatment of investment for tax purposes has been, at least up to the introduction of the REP, the chief instrument of British regional policy since the War.[23] Since these subsidies are also activity-discriminating (like REP) they appear to offend in all possible ways. As Johansen notes, however, the Rule does change if we introduce a further constraint, e.g., '... if we introduce the requirement that in a given region there shall be a certain minimum utilisation of a common factor, though a regional preference of this kind would seem rather odd', (p. 81). In the next section, I shall suggest a reason for preferring that a region does not use *too much* of the common factor, if this is interpreted as new capital. We shall then see how this preference alters the Rule, and our assessment of policy.

IV CONTROL POLICY

1   Let us now assume what is widely believed, that the social costs of migration into the fast-growing and congested areas are large, and in excess of private costs. (Illustrations such as traffic congestion, overcrowded schools, hospital queues, pressure on recreational space, and the like, are obvious.) We now ask how our discussion of policy is modified if we assume that migration imposes social costs not reflected in market prices to individuals, and that policy should therefore be directed to encouraging solutions that lessen migration and, by obvious implication, to discouraging socially expensive capital-widening investment in the congested areas.

If we start by adding migration to the objective function (with a negative coefficient if it is the 'wrong' direction), Johansen's Rule is unaltered for reasons already discussed. All that happens is that, instead of finding that accounting prices should differ regionally by private transfer costs, we obviously find that they should differ by transfer costs *plus* the assumed additional social cost. Hence the conclusion would merely be that REP should be larger than it should otherwise be.

Now suppose that we add a new constraint, that not more than some given amount of the common factor, interpreted as new capital, should

23.   For detail, see, e.g. Thomas, 1969.

be employed in Region B. This is a very crude way of getting at the problem, since we should distinguish between capital-widening ('bad') and capital-deepening ('good') investment in Region B, but it will serve to illustrate an exception to the Rule. We alter the constraints in the programming problem of III.1 above by adding a new constraint, say, $h_1y_1 + h_2y_2 \leqq \lambda F$ where $O < \lambda < 1$. We know that in forming the dual we have a shadow price corresponding to each scarce resource, and λF, for fixed λ is effectively an additional scarce resource. (The same result obtains if in place of λF we introduce a limit B, $B < F$, otherwise independent of the amount of the capital available.) Now the shadow price of the mobile factor is generally different in the two regions, and, if market prices are the same, a regionally discriminatory policy towards investment is at once justified.[24] Unfortunately, of course, we have no idea of the *amount* by which social costs differ from private costs in the congested regions, what the value of λ should be, or what the subsidy should be. We have not, of course, come any nearer to justifying activity as well as regionally-discriminatory treatment of the common factor (which, by definition, cannot be activity specific).

2 We may now consider an instrument of Control Policy, the Industrial Development Certificate. By giving or withholding a Certificate the Board of Trade may permit or prohibit a proposed new development in a certain place.[25] Prohibition amounts to putting an

24.   It is easily seen that the same result obtains, if, instead of introducing a new constraint, we alter the objective function. If we put utilisation of F in region B into the objective function, with a negative coefficient of $-c$, say, we naturally find that, assuming full utilisation, the optimum requires the price of F to differ between the regions by exactly c.

25.   This instrument seems to introduce *droit administratif* in an alien and objectionable way. The description of policy given in the White Paper, 1967, p. 15, is very revealing:

The basis of Industrial Development Certificate policy is to treat each application on its merits. The Board of Trade is required to have particular regard to the need for providing appropriate employment in Development Areas. Subject to this proviso, the Board of Trade does approve applications for Industrial Development Certificates for projects outside Development Areas if they are appropriate to the needs and resources of particular localities. Indeed it has been pointed out on a number of occasions that policy on Industrial Development Certificates can be and is conducted with every shade of flexibility as between the most congested areas and the Development Areas.

Is it uncharitable to think that administrative 'flexibility' in this sense is the antithesis of 'due process', and that, just as the applicant cannot know what rules govern his own case, neither can the critic know what policy can be inferred from the rules?

infinite price on a given development in a given place (the nature of Control Policy). Social costs may exceed private, but presumably not by an infinite amount. Let us suppose that the social costs of development in Region B do exceed the private costs, although by an unknown amount, and ask if we could not do better. The first thing to notice is that if a Certificate *is* granted, the lucky recipient makes no contribution to his externalities (the nature of Control Policy again). This immediately suggests that we try to use the price mechanism: a (continuous) Development Tax in Congested Areas instead of a (discontinuous no-yield) tax of zero or infinity. This scheme has certain obvious advantages, at least in principle:

(1) When development takes place, government agencies automatically become endowed with additional resources to meet the additional social costs, i.e., to build schools, extend transport systems, combat air pollution, etc.

(2) Development does take place if it shows a net social return, but not otherwise.

The difficulty is obviously to find the 'right' tax rates. Discussion of this cost-benefit problem is beyond the scope of this paper; but a starting point might be to require the relevant agencies (Education Authorities, Transport Boards, etc.) to estimate their resource requirements to maintain a constant standard of services per thousand new families in the area.[26] One is inclined to guess that almost any arbitrary but uniformly positive tax rate would be better than the arbitrary application of a zero or infinite rate!

V CONCLUSION

The arguments presented above do not appear to require summary. One point, however, may be pursued a little further. It has been argued, implicitly and explicitly, that the long-run 'regional problem' is the consequence of market imperfections. In assessing REP and SET, much depends on whether discrepancies between shadow prices and market prices are more serious inter-regionally than inter-activity, intra-regionally. That both discrepancies exist is obvious. The use of Price

26. Due to the specificity of sites, it is hard to see how an auction system, which would otherwise be attractive, could in fact work.

Policy then implies that whatever laws, institutions and other policies occasion these discrepancies are accepted as prior constraints. (Compare the use of Price Policy to alter the balance of payments, given that a disequilibrium exchange rate is not to be altered.) Thus it is obvious that the whole problem is one of alternative second best solutions. But there are two questions to ask. Must *all* arrangements that contribute to the discrepancies be accepted as unalterable? And, if some contribution is made by other policy instruments, is not simultaneous solution for the values of the instruments likely to produce better results than piecemeal solution?

The first question will not be pursued here. We merely note that some fundamental social arrangements, such as collective bargaining and unemployment relief, are involved. As for the second, it is easy to illustrate. Housing subsidies (and rent control) contribute to the discrepancies (as was argued in I.4 above). The subsidies and controls are, however, policy instruments, which influence regional targets. To determine their levels *first*, and *then* to determine the levels of the specifically regional instruments, is clearly suboptimal: interdependence of targets and instruments requires simultaneous solution for the optimal values of the latter. Thus we might conclude that the British approach to regional problems has been unduly parochial, and we might turn our attention to the decision models of the modern Dutch school (e.g. Theil, 1968).

REFERENCES

Archibald, G.C. 'Regional Multiplier Effects in the UK', *Oxford Economic Papers,* 19, No. 1, March 1967

Archibald, G.C. 'The Phillips Curve and the Distribution of Unemployment', *American Economic Review,* LIX, No. 2, May 1969

Baumol, W.J. and Bowen, W.G. 'On the Performing Arts: the Anatomy of their Economic Problem', *American Economic Review,* LV, No. 2, May 1965

Borts, George H., and Stein, Jerome L. *Economic Growth in a Free Market,* Columbia University Press, 1964

Borts, George H. 'Criteria for the Evaluation of Regional Development Programs', in *Regional Accounting for Policy Decisions,* The John Hopkins Press, 1966

Brechling, F.P.R. 'Trends and Cycles in British Regional Unemployment', *Oxford Economic Papers,* 19, No. 1, March 1967

Brown, A.J. and others 'The "Green Paper" on the Development Areas', *National Institute Economic Review,* May 1967

Chenery, Hollis B. 'Regional Analysis', in *The Structure and Growth of the Italian Economy,* U.S. Mutual Security Agency, Special Mission to Italy for Economic Co-operation, Rome 1953 eds. Chenery H.B., Clark P.G., and Cao-Pinna, V.

Friedman, M. 'The Role of Monetary Policy', *American Economic Review,* Vol. LVIII, 1968

Green Paper: 'The Development Areas — A Proposal for a Regional Employment Premium', *Department of Economic Affairs and H.M. Treasury,* April 1967

Holmans, A.E. 'Inter-Regional Differences in Levels of Income: are there "Two Nations" or One?', in *Papers on Regional Development,* ed. T. Wilson, Basil Blackwell, 1965

'The Intermediate Areas — Report of a Committee under the Chairmanship of Sir Joseph Hunt', Cmnd. 3998, April 1969

Hutton, J.P. and Hartley, K. 'A Regional Payroll Tax', Oxford Economic *Papers,* Vol. XX, November 1968

Johansen, Leif 'Regional Economic Problems Elucidated by Linear Programming', *International Economic Papers,* 12, 1967

Lipsey, R.G. 'The Relation between Unemployment and the Rate of Change of Money Wage Rates in the United Kingdom, 1862-1957: a further analysis' *Economica,* N.S. 27, 1960

MacKay, D.I. 'Industrial Structure and Regional Growth: a Methodological Problem', *Scottish Journal of Political Economy,* Vol. XV, June 1968

Conditions Favourable to Faster Growth, National Economic Development Council, 1963

'Regional Problems and Regional Policy', *National Institute Economic Review,* November 1968

Phelps, E.S. 'Phillips Curves, Expectations of Inflation and Optimal Unemployment over Time', *Economica,* N.S. Vol. XXXIV, 1967

Phelps, E.S. 'Money-Wage Dynamics and Labour-Market Equilibrium' *Journal of Political Economy,* LXXVI, No. 4, Supplement, August 1968

Steele, B.D. 'Regional Multipliers in Great Britain', *Oxford Economic Papers,* Vol. XXI, July 1969

Theil, H. *Optimal Decision Rules for Government and Industry,* North-Holland Publishing Co., and Rand McNally and Co., 1968

Thirlwall, A.P. 'Demand Disequilibrium in the Labour Market and Wage Rate Inflation in the United Kingdom', *Yorkshire Bulletin of Economic and Social Research,* XXI, No. 1, May 1969

Thirlwall, A.P. 'Regional Phillips Curves', *The Bulletin of the Oxford University Institute of Economics and Statistics,* XXXII, Feb 1970

Thomas, Roy 'The Financial Benefits of Expanding in the Development Areas', *Bulletin of the Oxford University Institute of Economics and Statistics,* Vol. XXXI, May 1969

White Paper: 'The Development Areas — Regional Employment Premium', Cmnd. 3310, June 1967

Equality of Opportunity, Fairness and Efficiency *

Kurt Klappholz

Lionel Robbins has been aptly described as teaching economics as 'part of the main stream of social philosophy'.[1] In a book of essays to honour him on his seventieth birthday it may be appropriate to consider a moral principle of social philosophy, the principle of equality of opportunity. Most economists seem to favour equality of opportunity, but rarely discuss it in a systematic manner, as they have tended to confine their discussion to the conditions which would satisfy one moral norm, that of Pareto-optimality. The arguments in favour of equality of opportunity invoke additional norms.[2]

The reasons for advocating equality of opportunity include (a) that it would promote distributive justice; (b) that it would promote economic efficiency. Section I examines some proposals for equality of opportunity which aim to secure distributive justice. My argument will be that these proposals are devoid of merit. The principle of equality of opportunity is irrelevant to distributive justice, but it deserves respect in such contexts as access to occupations and education. Section II examines the efficiency argument for equality of opportunity in (pre-university) education. It will be shown that although this argument has substance it turns out on careful examination to be more limited than is often supposed. Yet even this limited argument tends to

*   Earlier versions of this paper were read to the general staff seminar in Economics at Manchester University, and to the LSE Students' Economics Society.
I wish to thank my friends and colleagues, L.P. Foldes and J.R. Gould, for reading more than one draft of this paper, and for being more helpful than one could reasonably expect. I am also indebted to Ray Richardson for his helpful comments.

1.   *LSE Magazine,* No. 35, June 1968, p. 10.

2.   For a criticism of the Pareto norm as the only basis of political judgement see, for example, [26], ch. 1; for a criticism of the view that economists must confine themselves to the Pareto norm. see [17].

be unjustifiably ignored in some recent proposals for educational reform.

I

Discussing 'equality of opportunity' a recent writer reminds us that '... it is not easy to say exactly what it means or to find in it consistent identity'.[3] Such a reminder ought to be unnecessary, as this and other broad principles of social philosophy are always vague and acquire more precision only when applied in particular contexts.

Often when we complain that certain individuals, or groups, do not have 'equality of opportunity' we have in mind that they lack certain opportunities, that this is 'unfair' and ought to be remedied. In such a context the noun 'equality' is often misplaced. When such a complaint is made, we are usually aware that to improve the situation would require the diversion of resources. Yet, when social or political philosophers discuss 'equality of opportunity' they sometimes do so as though the opportunities with respect to which equality is demanded were not scarce. For example: 'Men equally have a right to full opportunity to do, each of them, what his life calls for, if it is to be lived successfully. No man has a greater right to full opportunity, or a right to fuller opportunity, than another man, and no man has less'.[4] If men have a right to 'full opportunity' in this sense then scarcity must be abolished. In the absence of scarcity opportunities would be available 'equally' and the demand for equal opportunities would be redundant. The demand is relevant only if opportunities are scarce, and its fulfilment requires some rule of 'equality' for the distribution of these opportunities. Differences between various formulations of the principle of 'equality of opportunity' can be reduced to the differences in the factors or characteristics with respect to which the rule of equality is proposed. People differ in the value they attach to various kinds of equality, so that it is not surprising that equality should be demanded with respect to different characteristics, for 'equality in respect of one quality (say, colour or sex) is perfectly compatible with great inequalities in respect of other qualities'.[5]

3.   [29], p. 50.
4.   [13], p. 121.

247

Sometimes — though one imagines this is due to careless expression rather than deliberate intention — equality of opportunity is formulated as demanding that '... everyone ... has an equal chance of scaling the heights'.[6] This presumably implies that social life is organised on the principle of a lottery, in which each individual should have the same tickets, each with a chance of winning a wide range of prizes. Such an arrangement would indeed make for a mobile society, but presumably is not seriously proposed.[7] In contrast to this view, which would make everyone's chances unconditionally the same, we have the classical principle of *la carriere ouverte aux talents*. According to Hayek, this principle

> ... was a demand that all man-made obstacles to the rise of some should be removed, that all privileges of individuals should be abolished, and that what the state contributed to the chance of improving one's conditions should be the same for all. ... It was understood that the duty of government was ... merely to make available to all on equal terms those facilities which in their nature depended on government action. That the results were bound to be different, not only because the individuals were different, but also because only a small part of the relevant circumstances depended on government action, was taken for granted.[8]

Two related points may be made about this principle, which suggest why policies based on it were held not to ensure 'equality of opportunity'. First, although Hayek does not say what it was that 'the state contributed to the chance of improving one's conditions', it is clear that the state's contribution was *not* 'the same for all', precisely because an individual's chance of benefiting depended on other factors, which differed among people. For example, if the state provided free tuition at universities 'to all on equal terms', but made no other financial provisions, the chance of benefiting from the state's contribution would be strongly affected by family income. Secondly, Hayek wishes to remove only those obstacles to the rise of some people which fall within 'the small part of the relevant circumstances' which depend on government action. Here again, due, for example, to family circumstances, obstacles to the rise of many would remain unless the state went outside 'the small part' reserved for it by Hayek. These

6.   [6], p. 218.

7.   For a brief criticism of this proposal see [27], p. 143. The proposal is taken seriously in [12], ch. 6.

8.   [12], p. 92.

arguments apply with particular force to equality of opportunity in education and are considered in greater detail in the next Section. Formulations such as Hayek's have also been criticised on the ground that 'equality of opportunity involves ... reward in strict correspondence with desert'[9] and this would not be ensured by Hayek's proposal.

A

Distributive principles need not necessarily rely on notions of 'desert' or 'merit'.[10] But when one talks of 'rewards in correspondence with desert' one is appealing to a distributive principle based on 'desert'. The content of the principle will then depend on how the term 'desert' or 'merit' is used, and usage here differs widely.[11]

Despite the variety of senses given to the term 'desert' it seems possible to indicate, in a general way, the kind of ethical theory on which the 'desert' approach to distributive principles is based. Without proposing mutually exhaustive classifications, we can think of ethical theories as falling into two broad classes: (a) those according to which we should appraise 'events', or proposed courses of 'action', by their consequences;[12] (b) those according to which we should appraise things 'in themselves' *(an sich)*. These respective approaches can be subdivided according to whether they recommend that each individual 'action' should be judged by its consequences or 'in itself', or whether only moral *rules* should be judged in this way (an example is the distinction between 'act' utilitarianism and 'rule' utilitarianism). It seems clear that the 'desert' approach to distributive principles belongs to class (b) of ethical theories.[13]

As is well known, the moral recommendations which may be derived from (a) or (b) need not always conflict. Nevertheless, the two

9.   [11], p. 18.

10.   See, for example, [1], pp. 43-7.

11.   For a brief review of notions of 'desert', see [1], pp. 106-15.

12.   The implicit dichotomy between 'actions' and 'consequences' – like the dichotomy between 'means' and 'ends' – can be misleading. It is therefore preferable to regard these approaches to ethics as recommending that we balance '... the total results, as far as they can be foreseen, of one course of action against those of another' [25], Vol. I, note 6, ch. 9, pp. 286-7. See also [26], ch. 5.

13.   'It follows ... that to say that "S deserves X because giving it to him would be in the public interest' is simply to misuse the words "deserve".' (Quoted in [1], p. 111.)

approaches differ methodologically. (a) might perhaps be called 'moral nominalism' and (b) 'moral essentialism'.[14] This is not the place for a general criticism of moral essentialism. We might merely note the general difficulty of criticising *isolated* moral recommendations. Nevertheless, where possible we may point out the consequences of such moral prescriptions, and we may also try to show inconsistencies where the proposals do not consist of isolated utterances.

Sometimes 'desert' is regarded as warranting merely praise or blame, rather than reward or punishment. We shall ignore this interpretation and consider 'desert' only in connection with reward. Here the question arises whether 'desert' is regarded as necessary or sufficient for reward, or both. This appears to depend on particular contexts and no general rule seems to have been proposed. For example, in a mild defence of the 'desert' approach it has been suggested

... that a person's having been able to have done otherwise is a *necessary condition* of ascribing desert... We can paraphrase this principle as follows: specially strong countervailing reasons must be forthcoming before it is ever justifiable to connect advantages and disadvantages with anything except a person's voluntary actions and their consequences.[15]

The paraphrase makes 'desert' neither a necessary nor a sufficient condition for reward.

We now turn to consider briefly some proposals for rewards in accordance with desert.

B

Hayek uses the term 'merit' 'exclusively to describe the attributes of conduct that make it deserving of praise, that is, the moral character of the action and not the value of the achievement'.[16] Hayek has no difficulty in showing the consequences of attempts to base rewards on merit in his sense. They would convert social life into a continuous Day of Judgement, and would be incompatible 'with freedom to choose one's pursuit'. In any case 'we do not wish people to earn a maximum of merit but to achieve a maximum of usefulness at a minimum of pain and sacrifice and therefore a minimum of merit'.[17]

14. By analogy with Popper's distinction. See [25], Vol. II, ch. 11.
15. [1], pp. 108-9. Italics in original.
16. [12], p. 94.

Equality of Opportunity, Fairness and Efficiency

While Hayek uses the term 'merit' to refer exclusively to the motives for a person's action, others include the results of the action. For example: 'To ascribe desert to a person is to say that it would be a good thing if he were to receive something (advantageous or disadvantageous) in virtue of some action or effort on his part or some result brought about by him'.[18] According to this view, a person's 'productivity', or, to use Hayek's term, his 'usefulness', is sometimes regarded as an index of his desert. Although economists long ago repudiated J.B. Clark's moral interpretation of the theory of marginal productivity,[19] this version is occasionally still endorsed by others. Thus it is sometimes said that '... in a liberal society ... each person's worth (desert) can be precisely ascertained — it is his net marginal product and under certain postulated conditions (which it is conveniently assumed the existing economy approximates) market prices give each factor of production its net marginal product'.[20] It is worth restating why marginal productivity cannot provide a criterion of 'desert'. In general, values of marginal products depend on the distribution of factor endowments. Thus we cannot regard a particular set of factor prices (= the value of marginal products) as corresponding to 'desert' unless we also regard the distribution of factor endowments as being in accordance with 'desert'.

Marginal productivity tells us nothing about the 'appropriate' distribution of factor endowments. It may be said that this criticism merely shows that marginal productivity is not sufficient to provide a principle of distributive justice. But *if* we can always obtain an 'appropriate' distribution of factor endowments, *then* payment according to marginal productivity is necessary for distributive justice. This

---

17. [12], p. 96. Strangely, Hayek provides no references to any writer who clearly advocated rewards on the basis of merit in this sense.
It is also surprising that Hayek appears to accept merit as a suitable basis for moral appraisal. For a brief criticism of a morality of 'judgements' see [25], Vol. I, note 18 to ch. 5, p. 237.

18. [1], p. 106.

19. See [14], pp. 253-56.

20. [1], pp. 112-13. As recently as 1955 Eucken, for example, seemed to hold this view:
'We should seek social justice through the creation of an efficient social order, and particularly by ensuring that the distribution of income is subject to the strict rules of competition, risk and liability'. ([7], p.317. Translation by present author.)

condition, however, cannot always be satisfied. First, we can never redistribute endowments of ability. Second, it may also not be possible to obtain a 'just' distribution of physical endowments, e.g. for reasons of incentives. Hence reward according to marginal productivity is not only insufficient for distributive justice; it is also not necessary.

The principle of 'equality of opportunity' has been formulated so as to include considerations of a 'just' or 'fair' distribution of factor endowments (an 'equal' start) which would ensure 'fair' rewards. One possible version of 'equality of opportunity' in this sense is as follows:

> If differences in innate abilities are accepted ... the requirements ... are that holdings of property and benefits of formal education and general environment be such that the equal exercise of equal abilities (directed toward money-making) will result in equal incomes, and that the equal exercise of unequal abilities will result in incomes proportional to talents.[21]

This version of 'equality of opportunity' is meant to ensure 'fairness' in the sense of establishing a relationship of equality or proportionality between some characteristics of individuals and the rewards accruing to them. Such a relationship has often been regarded as a condition for rewards according to 'desert'.[22] Although this is not explicitly stated it seems clear that 'fairness' here is equivalent to reward according to 'desert'. Such proposals for ensuring 'fairness' are usually criticised on the ground that their implementation '... must be restrictive of human activity',[23] but there are additional criticisms which are sometimes overlooked.

The 'fair rule' which awards income in relation to effort and ability is said to be analogous to the rules for awarding prizes in competitive games of sport (sometimes regarded as paradigms of equal opportunity).[24] Now, in sport, prizes are awarded for performance measured

21. [21], p. 62. For some reason it is held (see, e.g. [21], p. 63) that the required 'benefit of formal education', given differences in abilities, is equal education. Given equal 'abilities' equal education would make rewards proportional to effort. But with unequal abilities equal education would make rewards proportional neither to effort nor to initial abilities, because an equal amount of education will add more to the 'abilities' of some than to others.
22. See [13], pp. 116-119.
23. [21], p. 65.
24. See [21], p. 61.

according to agreed rules, e.g. knocking out one's opponent in boxing, or arriving first at the finishing line in swimming or running. What is the relationship between such measurable performance on the one hand and psychological aspects such as 'effort' and 'ability' on the other? In the present state of knowledge no general answer seems available, although even the common assertion that some people 'have great ability but no will to win' suggests that the relationship is not a simple one. Moveover, in so far as 'effort' means, not the measurable expenditure of calories, but psychological effort, comparisons of effort are on the same footing as interpersonal comparisons of utility. Thus, statements about the connection between prizes in sport and effort and ability cannot be subjected to any tests. From the point of view of equality of opportunity the important feature of sport is not any such alleged relationship, but rather that in sport prizes are awarded by reference only to certain criteria deemed to be relevant.[25] Abandoning the untestable version of equality of opportunity, we may ask instead whether we believe that there are 'irrelevant factors' which should have no effect on relative incomes, for example, that 'all inequalities that rest on birth and inherited property ought ... to be abolished, and none remain unless it is an effect of superior talents or industry'.[26] (We might note in passing that the view that remaining inequalities must be due only to the 'effect of superior talents or industry' is also either untestable, or true by implicit definition. As Knight pointed out long ago, the factors which determine an individual's income are 'affected to a large if not overwhelming extent by all sorts of imponderables and contingencies...')[27]

Leaving aside other advantages of birth, this version of the principle of equality of opportunity would require that (absolute) differences in income be independent of differences in inherited property. To implement this would require equal absolute inheritance including, as a special case, zero inheritance.[28]

A proposal to abolish inheritance might have as its aim an increase in

25. 'Equality of opportunity is the elimination of "irrelevant factors" from having any influence on the result of the contest" [1], p. 304.

26. [24], p. 100.

27. [19], p. 151.

28. Although it is often interpreted as requiring no inheritance, e.g. 'Inheritance incompatible with equality of opportunity', [11], p. 133.

social mobility, but this does not appear to be the main purpose behind proposals such as we have just quoted. Their main object seems to be to ensure rewards in accordance with 'desert' by ensuring the absence of 'undeserved' initial endowments. This calls for further comment.

Assume that the abolition of inheritance implies that no income can be obtained without 'some effort' ('he who does not work shall not eat'). Since differences in abilities are part of 'deserved' endowments, the consequences of the proposal may be summarised as follows: 'some effort' is a necessary condition for any reward. Differences in effort are sufficient for differences in rewards, but they are not necessary, as differences in 'abilities' without differences in effort will also produce differential rewards. The implied notion of 'desert' thus treats as crucial the distinction between zero effort and any 'positive amount' of effort. It is not surprising that economists should have been critical of such a principle of distributive justice. Knight, for example, pointed out that 'there is no visible reason why anyone is more or less entitled to the earnings of inherited personal capacities than to those of inherited property in any other form'.[29] Reward for 'ability' would appear to be no more 'deserved' than reward for inherited property. Moreover, we do not know how to distinguish 'ability' from 'effort'. For example, we often say of someone that he has the ability to engage in sustained effort. In the context of economic rewards, the attempt to distinguish, on grounds of 'desert', between 'effort', 'ability' and inheritance thus seems to break down.[30]

We have interpreted 'equality of opportunity' as a principle which demands the exclusion of 'irrelevant' factors in determining the outcome of a 'contest'. We then considered the view that, on grounds of 'desert', inheritance of property ought to be considered irrelevant, while effort and ability ought to be considered relevant. Our argument has been that this moral view will not withstand critical examination. This criticism can be generalised to various doctrines which regard 'equality of opportunity' as a principle of distributive justice. In the case of a race, for example, the criteria which are to determine the

29.   [19], p. 151. See also [10], p. 164.
30.   Knight maintained that, of the 'mixture of inheritance, luck and effort ... none but the effort can have ethical validity'. He also seemed to support the principle of 'distribution according to ... *conscientious* effort' (see [18], p. 56 including note. Italics in original).

outcome are clear and everything else is irrelevant: 'The right result is for the side with most of the quality which the contest is supposed to be testing to win'.[31] From this point of view the 'contest' for income is analogous, not to that in one competitive sport, but to all games taken together, including, for example, beauty contests. In the 'contest' for income there are no particular qualities that are to be tested, apart from the ability to make money. Thus, we cannot specify what are to be regarded as 'irrelevant factors' in determining the outcome,[32] and we cannot specify the characteristics of individuals which should lead to their 'equal' treatment in the receipt of income. If we interpret 'equality of opportunity' as a principle which demands that the outcome should be independent of 'irrelevant' factors, then this principle seems to have nothing to say as regards distributive justice, i.e. appropriate relative incomes.

C

'Desert' is sometimes used in a different sense from that considered so far:

...there is a use of 'deserve' which only claims that *given* the prize is so much, so-and-so 'deserves' it more than anyone else in that he fulfils the conditions laid down better than anyone else. The prize may have been set up not to reward desert but to stimulate productions of suitable kinds ...[33]

'Desert' in this sense would seem to be identical with equality of opportunity. We have suggested that the principle of equality of opportunity has nothing to say about appropriate relative incomes. If we ask 'on what grounds, given the principle of equality of opportunity, should doctors earn more or less than opera stars?' we cannot specify any 'irrelevant' factors which should have no effect on their relative earnings.[34] But when we ask 'what are the factors which should

31. [1], p. 304.
32. This argument is analogous to the suggestion that 'parity of bargaining power' has nothing to do with equality of opportunity, because parity 'cannot be specified independently of the desired result' (see [1], pp. 303-5). It is often said that a free market '... separates economic efficiency from irrelevant characteristics'. But this is immediately qualified with the observation that 'there are real problems in defining ...' what are 'irrelevant' characteristics. (see [10], pp. 109-10).
33. [1], p. 112. Italics in original.
34. We might wish to say that relative earnings should not be affected by 'restrictive practices'. But here we are concerned with the kind of characteristics of *individuals* mentioned earlier, i.e. effort, ability.

be irrelevant in determining whether an individual may become a doctor or an opera star?' the principle of equality of opportunity comes into its own. In an attempt to answer this question we may call upon criteria of relevance which, though less precise than those in sport, are nevertheless susceptible to specification. For example, it is both reasonable to claim, and in conformity with the principle of equality of opportunity, that an individual should not be prevented from becoming a doctor or an opera star due to such 'irrelevant' factors as his parents' social status or his colour. In this sense the principle has been well stated:

> Man, as a worker, has equality of opportunity with other men when he is free to choose any occupation he is fit for, and when his chance of acquiring that fitness is limited only by defects of nature or morals and not by lack of education or wealth or social prestige. Tests of fitness must be the same for all men, and they must be genuine. They must seek to discover only whether a man has the qualities which experience teaches are needed in that occupation; they must be relevant tests ... they must never require of a man that he should have qualities that he does not need to enable him to do the work he has applied for.[35]

II

Although the references given in the preceding Section suggest that notions of 'equality of opportunity' in the sense of a principle of distributive justice are still prevalent (and therefore still warrant criticism) they are no longer at the forefront of discussion. As Hayek points out,[36] the emphasis now is on equality of opportunity in education. This, like distributive justice, is advocated on grounds of 'fairness', but unlike distributive justice it is also advocated on grounds of efficiency.[37]

Whether equality of opportunity in education is advocated on grounds of efficiency or 'fairness', the principle always demands that the opportunities available to children be independent of certain factors, such as parental income and expenditure preferences. The criteria according to which educational opportunities should be allocated will depend on the different grounds for advocating equality

35. [24], p. 104.
36. [12], p. 91.
37. See, for example, [26], p. 76.

of opportunity.

Before considering the criteria for allocating educational expenditure where equality of opportunity is advocated on grounds of efficiency, a few comments may be made about 'fairness'.

Differential education may lead to differential 'rewards' in terms of income, non-pecuniary benefits from occupations, etc. It is frequently claimed that these rewards ought to be independent of certain factors, e.g. parental expenditure on education, and depend only on other factors, e.g. ability. If this claim is based on 'desert', it suffers from the deficiencies examined in the previous Section. On grounds of 'desert', there is no more reason for treating children equally with respect to their abilities than with respect to their parents' income. However, there are 'fairness' arguments for equality of opportunity in education which do not identify 'fairness' with 'desert' — for example, when it is urged that the educational needs of a mentally handicapped child should be met despite the poverty of its parents. In this example, the noun 'equality' is usually redundant since the demand does not imply that the education of all mentally handicapped children should be independent of their parents' income. Another example of a 'fairness' criterion for allocating educational expenditure might be what Professor Meade calls the 'distributional principle' which '... would be to use the available resources in education in such a way as to equalise the future earning power of different students'.[38] In general this aim would require that educational expenditure on children be independent of parents' incomes. However, it is clear that an educational policy based on the distributional principle would conflict with economic efficiency as ordinarily understood. Indeed, most ordinary 'fairness' criteria would seem to conflict with economic efficiency.

In the remainder of this Section I wish to consider the question of how educational resources should be allocated if equality of opportunity in education is advocated only on grounds of efficiency. In other words, I wish to appraise equality of opportunity in education solely on the basis of the Pareto criterion, but I do not wish to suggest that efficiency is the only aim of people seeking to promote equality of opportunity. I should now like to outline some reasons for appraising

38.   [20], p. 62.

equality of opportunity in terms of the Pareto criterion. First, although equality of opportunity in education is frequently advocated on grounds of efficiency, the relationship between the two has not as far as I am aware been systematically examined. When it is examined, the claim that inequality of opportunity leads to inefficiency is only partially confirmed. Secondly, this claim has been ignored, and implicitly denied, in some recent writings concerning the optimality of (pre-university) educational expenditure. These writings serve as the theoretical basis for the advocacy of vouchers as a means of (partially) financing pre-university education. It therefore seems appropriate to examine proposals for vouchers in the light of the efficiency arguments for equality of opportunity in education. I shall be concerned exclusively with pre-universtiy education, the recipients of which cannot, as a rule, control the resources which finance it.

A

The claim that inequality of opportunity in education leads to inefficiency seems to contain two arguments: (a) that inefficiency results if the family is the sole source of educational finance; (b) that efficiency requires that educational expenditure on any child be independent (in a sense explained below) of parental resources and expenditure preferences, and (given an 'appropriate' discount rate) depend only on the child's 'abilities' and preferences. We will consider the two propositions in turn.

Proposition (a) may be derived from the necessary conditions for optimality and the inadequacies of the family as the sole source of educational finance. We are referring here to 'first-best' optimality, i.e. the maximisation of welfare subject only to the constraints of resource endowments and production functions. It is a necessary condition for 'first-best' optimality that (marginal) rates of return on all investments should be equal.[39] For our subsequent discussion only one point need be made about this condition, namely that it applies irrespective of whether individuals wish to bequeath assets to subsequent generations. If this condition does not hold 'somebody' can be made better off without 'anyone' being made worse off. It is a commonplace that certain institutional or legal arrangements may prevent the attainment of 'first-

39. Ignoring inequalities associated with corner solutions.

best' optimality. This is the case with an institutional arrangement in which the family is the only source of educational finance. For example: '... because our laws prohibit slavery, even if voluntarily entered into, investment in human capital tends to be very inefficient by comparison with investment in non-human capital'.[40] If the family is the only source of educational expenditure, rates of return on the educational investment of different children will not be equal to rates of return on other assets. Education is a 'most important capital-goods-producing industry' where, in the circumstances postulated, the 'selection of material for processing is strongly influenced by the irrelevant consideration of family capacity to pay'.[41] Thus, a necessary condition for efficiency will not be fulfilled. This confirms, qualitatively, the first part of the argument that inequality of opportunity leads to inefficiency.

The second part of the argument − (b) − would appear to be a plausible inference from the first. If dependence of educational expenditure on parental resources is sufficient to cause inefficiency, then independence might be thought necessary to ensure efficiency. Before examining the validity of this inference, it is necessary to explain what must be meant by 'independence' in this context.

1) 'Independence' does *not* mean statistical independence and therefore also does not mean absence of correlation. If the 'appropriate' amount of education is to depend only on 'abilities' and preferences, as is suggested, and if these are correlated with parental income, then educational expenditure will also be correlated with parental income;

2) Sometimes 'independence' is taken to *mean* that private parental expenditure on education must be prohibited. This interpretation

40.   [15], p. 184.
If we *exclude* the child's future income, the argument that inefficiency results if the family is the sole source of educational finance applies whether we are thinking of current family earnings or family life earnings. The reason for mentioning this is that it was recently suggested that, with a perfect capital market, educational expenditure on any child would be a function of parental life earnings (see [31], p. 61, note 1). From the theory of a perfect market nothing follows about the relationship between parental resources and the educational expenditure on any child.
41.   [15], p. 192. In this quotation Johnson is referring to university education, but see below, subsection E.

confuses an (alleged) condition for efficiency with the institutional arrangements which may, or may not, ensure its fulfilment. It is analogous to the confusion of competition with the Pareto criterion.

Independence' in the present context must mean 'invariance of educational expenditure to permutations of parents while the childrens' preference functions and abilities remain unchanged'. This implies that any two children with identical abilities and preferences would receive the same education[42] irrespective of their parents' resources or expenditure preferences. It seems that the independence requirement is usually designed to ensure this result.

In what circumstances would independence, in the sense just explained, be a necessary condition for efficiency? One obvious circumstance is if investment in education were the same as investment in machines. [43] With a perfect capital market an individual's decision to invest in a machine is independent of his income and endowments and of his time preference, though these affect his borrowing-lending decisions. This is one of the conditions which ensures optimal investment in a perfect market. The optimal investment is determined by the productivity of the asset and the discount rate. If investment in education were governed by the same criteria as investment in machines, the optimal investment in any child would be determined by the child's 'ability' and the discount rate, irrespective of parental resources and preferences.

From the point of view of optimal resource allocation there are, of course, differences between investment in physical assets and invest-

42. In this discussion we make the usual 'perfect knowledge' assumption, while in no way denying Hayek's observation that 'it is probably undeniable that we have no certain methods of ascertaining beforehand who among the young people will derive the greatest benefit from ... education'. [12], p. 382.
Sometimes equality of opportunity in education is interpreted to require equal education for all. If different children have different capacities to 'absorb' education, equal education would in general conflict with efficiency. In the present context it is appropriate to select that interpretation of equality of opportunity which is relevant to efficiency.
43. The discussion applies only to 'machines' which produce output for sale and do not produce any non-pecuniary returns such as are produced by durable consumer goods, for example.

ment in education. First, educational investment yields non-pecuniary returns either directly, or through the occupations to which it may give access. Second, the optimal amount of educational investment for any particular individual will depend, among other factors, on his work-leisure preferences. In other words, physical assets have no preferences, human beings do. These preferences must be taken into account in discussing the optimality of human capital formation. Then it is immediately clear that the optimal amount of educational investment for any child depends not only on its abilities and preferences, but also on its endowment of assets (other than ability). Parental resources and expenditure preferences often determine these endowments. In general, therefore, efficiency does *not* require that educational investment in any child be independent of parental resources and expenditure preferences. In general, such a requirement would be incompatible with efficiency.

It is not easy to generalise (in qualitative terms) about the relationship between endowments (other than 'ability') and the optimal amount of educational expenditure. Consider, for example, two children with identical 'abilities' and preferences but with different endowments. Suppose also that the non-pecuniary returns from education and leisure are both normal goods. The child with the greater endowments would choose more education in order to enjoy its non-pecuniary returns; but it would also want to consume more (future) leisure, which would indicate less education on the grounds of its pecuniary returns. In the absence of quantitative assumptions, no conclusion follows.[44]

This example shows that 'equal education for children with equal abilities and preferences' could be a requirement for efficiency. This is so in the trivial case in which these children also have equal endowments. Despite its triviality, the example serves two purposes. First, it should lead us to question the merits of a proposal which is often made, namely that private expenditure on education should be prohibited, but inheritance apparently not.[45] Second, the proposal – if it were made – that 'children with equal abilities and preferences' should have equal endowments is not as devoid of merit as the proposals examined in

---

44. Here we are considering only the returns from education to the child. There may be (and often are) returns to the parents. See below, subsection C.

45. See below, subsection E.

Section 1. For example, such a proposal would allow the advantages of 'ability' in some to be offset by advantages of endowments in the case of others.

In the remainder of this Section we shall be concerned with the argument that inefficiency results if the family is the sole source of educational finance. In general, this argument holds irrespective of initial endowments, and can therefore be discussed within the confines of Pareto optimality. Concern with Pareto optimality does not imply that it is the only relevant principle for appraising policies. Nor does it imply indifference with respect to alternative distributions of initial endowments.

B

We have considered the proposition that inefficiency results if the family is the sole source of educational finance. General theoretical considerations lend support to this proposition and it does not seem to have been explicitly criticised. But inefficiency − in this case the non-equalisation of marginal rates of return on educational expenditure − can always be viewed as implying the existence of externalities, defined as discrepancies between private and social costs and benefits. However, the externalities involved here, like those, for example, in the case of simple monopoly, do not derive from interdependent utility functions or 'neighbourhood effects'.[46] Yet, in some recent discussions, the welfare justification of government support of pre-university education is based solely on the consideration that 'persons other than the direct consumers of education (the child, or, more generally, his family unit) derive benefit from that child's consumption of educational services'.[47] The presence of such 'neighbourhood

46.   Although a recent writer treated inequality of opportunity *as such* as an externality by suggesting that 'if equality of opportunity is a social good, then education pays social returns over and above the private returns to the recipients of the education' (quoted in [29], p. 50). West criticised this view on the ground that such a 'return' is 'something so intangible as to be inaccessible even to the most ambitious of statisticians' ([29], p. 50) while Blaug interpreted West as having shown 'that "equality of opportunity" as a social good cannot be logically considered a neighbourhood benefit of education' ([2], p. 28). This is an error, since what is, or is not, an externality depends on people's utility function and is not simply a matter of logic. However, in what follows we shall ignore this possible inefficiency which may result from inequality of opportunity.

effects' or externalities seems to be regarded as a *necessary* condition for government support,[48] not only in an economy with 'perfect' capital markets, but also in the absence of 'perfect' capital markets, so that 'families with low incomes will be consuming small amounts of education and families with large incomes large amounts'.[49] Thus, in his well-known paper on the financing of education, Friedman advocates equity-type loans for *university* students on the grounds, among others, that these would '... do much to make equality of opportunity a reality'[50] and would tend to equalise rates of return on human capital with those on other assets. Yet, he justifies government help in the financing of *pre-university* education *solely* on the ground of 'neighbourhood effects' and does not mention equality of opportunity as one of the aims of government education policy.[51] Similarly, West examines various aspects of the 'neighbourhood effect' argument for government support of pre-university education and tentatively suggests that this argument, together with the protection of minors principle, would seem to justify no more than selective help to 'problem families'. He considers underinvestment in education only where 'there are "spillover" benefits to society as a whole which would not be taken into account by people acting privately'.[52] These 'spill-over' effects derive from interdependent utility functions and are not the same as the inefficiencies resulting from the failure to equalise rates of return on the educational investment of different children. Finally, as noted above, Pauly holds that the only reason for the non-optimality of purely private parental expenditure on education is the fact 'that some kinds of education — citizenship or literacy oriented education — generate spillover or neighbourhood effects'.[53]

47.   [22], p. 121.

48.   [29], p. 30.

49.   [22], p. 123.

50.   [9], pp. 142-3. By 'equality of opportunity' Friedman meant, not Hayek's version of the principle, but rather equal educational opportunities for people with 'equal abilities'.

51.   In a later version of this paper Friedman mentions the incidental effects on equality of opportunity of alternative ways of organising pre-university education. Yet, in deploring the use of public funds for such items as 'courses in basket weaving, social dancing ...' he asks' 'Wherein are the "neighbourhood effects" that justify such use of tax money?' ([10], p. 94).

52.   [29], p. 225, also Part IV.

53.   [22], p. 121.

All the writers quoted above advocate some kind of voucher scheme for the finance of pre-university education. Among the advocates of vouchers only Peacock and Wiseman explicitly note that 'education may confer direct economic benefits upon individuals or families; it may also confer benefits upon the community at large ... Reasons for government action in the provision of education arise in respect of both kinds of benefit'.[54] However, their discussion of the first kind of benefit fails to take into account the considerations with which this Section is mainly concerned.

The writers we have quoted appear to ignore one aspect of inefficiency which results from purely private educational expenditure, namely the failure to equalise (marginal) rates of return. We shall ignore from now on the aspect which they stress, i.e. 'neighbourhood effects'.

C

At this stage it is appropriate to consider a question which does not appear to have been considered in the literature. Can we derive any qualitative conclusions regarding the direction in which purely private parental expenditure on education can diverge from the efficient amount? We may begin by asking whether, in the absence of 'distorting' taxes on capital transfers between parents and children, private expenditure can exceed that amount. Such a possibility is suggested by the observation that '...family pride coupled with money can result in expenditure on education yielding a low or negative rate of return...'[55]

There are many reasons why parents may wish to spend on their children's education. Given 'perfect knowledge' and divisibility of expenditure, parents who wish to maximise the child's welfare according to the child's own preferences (subject to the constraint of the total resources to be devoted to the child) will not spend more than the optimal amount,[56] but they may spend less. If more than the

54.   [23], pp. 16-17.
55.   [15], p. 185. The quotation continues: 'especially as ... educational investment is a fool proof way of beating the inheritance tax'.
Educational investment is usually a capital transfer *inter vivos*. Taxes on gifts *inter vivos* (excluding education), frequently advocated, would give incentives towards excessive expenditure on education, but it is difficult to see why death duties should have this effect in the absence of a gift tax.

optimal amount were spent, the marginal rate of return on this expenditure (allowing for non-pecuniary returns to the child) would be less than the return on other assets. Given the aims attributed to the parents, this would be irrational behaviour.

In our previous discussion of the efficiency conditions for educational expenditure (above, subsection A) we supposed that any possible non-pecuniary returns from education directly affect only the child.[57] This assumption is the same as that just made about parental aims, i.e. that parents wish to maximise the child's welfare according to the child's own preferences, subject to the constraint of the total resources to be devoted to the child. The claim that parental expenditure on education can yield 'a low or negative rate of return' either presupposes 'irrationality' on the part of the parents, or implicitly only takes into account the returns from educational expenditure valued according to the preferences of the child.[58] If we rule out parental irrationality, then 'a low or negative rate of return' according to the preferences of the child implies one of two conditons: a) that parents behave 'paternalistically', or b) that parents derive direct non-pecuniary returns from the educational expenditure on their children. Let us briefly consider whether, given such parental behaviour, parental expenditure on education can be such that a reduction in it would make both the parents and the child better off.

a) By 'paternalism' we usually mean that the decision taker (in the present case parents) acts, not according to the actual preferences of the individual on whose behalf decisions are being made (the subject), but according to the preferences which the decision taker thinks are appropriate. It is always a consequence of paternalistic decisions that they lead to a use of *given* resources which make the subject less well off, according to his own preferences, than he could be. Paternalism may thus lead to 'a low or negative rate of return' if measured according to the subject's own preferences, but not if measured according

56. The 'unrealistic' assumption of 'given preferences' for the child is made for the simple reason that I cannot see how it can be dispensed with in a welfare economic discussion of these issues.

57. If the only concern is efficiency it is immaterial whether the pecuniary returns accrue to the child or the parents.

58. We are ignoring erroneous decisions, as the quotation does not appear to refer to these.

to the paternalistically imposed preferences.[59] Whether or not parental expenditure in this case can exceed the efficient amount depends on which preferences we use for the definition of efficiency.

b)   It does not seem possible to distinguish 'operationally' paternalism from the case in which parents derive direct non-pecuniary benefits from the educational expenditure of their children. The reason for distinguishing one case from the other is in order to take account of the different motivations which give rise to them. The parent who says: 'I shall insist that my son stay on at school after fifteen, even though he does not wish to, because to do so would be better for *him*' has a different motive from the parent who says: 'I shall insist that my son stay at school after fifteen, even though he does not wish to, because otherwise my neighbours will think I cannot afford to continue his education'.

We may distinguish two cases in which parents derive direct non-pecuniary benefits from the expenditure on their children:

b_1) parents wish to maximise the child's welfare (from given resources) taking into account not only its own actual preferences, but also parental preferences among the particular uses to which the child can put the resources it receives;

b_2) parents' expenditure decisions are unaffected by their consequences for the child's welfare (i.e. are determined only by the direct satisfaction to parents).

Consider (b_1) and suppose that parents never extend educational expenditure to the point at which the child would be better off if it received less education and no more of any other good. In this case it may be true (as in the case of paternalism) that the child might be better off if the total resources it receives were allocated differently,

<hr/>

59.   For a discussion of the subtle issues connected with the notion of paternalism, see the forthcoming work by L.P. Foldes.
Here we might note the curious habit of some writers of describing advocates of state education as 'paternalists' with the implication that advocates of parental choice in education are non-paternalist (see, for example, [2], [23]. [29]). The implicit suggestion that parents always behave non-paternalistically, according to our definition, is hardly supported by experience. Opponents of state education do not advocate that children make their own educational choices.

but this would make the parents worse off (it *may* be true, as joint products are involved). Since the parents are assumed to wish to maximise the child's welfare, they will make the child as well off as possible for any given utility level of the parents. Expenditure therefore cannot exceed, but may still fall short of, the Pareto-efficient amount.

Case (b_1), however, does not exclude the possibility that expenditure may be extended to the point at which the child would be better off if it received less education and no more of any other good. If we take it as given that parents have the power to compel the child to accept any amount of educational expenditure, expenditure still cannot exceed the Pareto-efficient amount. If one thinks that parents should not have that power, one would regard the level of expenditure as exceeding the Pareto-efficient amount. This leads directly to case (b_2).

In order to decide whether expenditure can exceed the Pareto-efficient amount in case (b_2) it is necessary to specify whose preferences are to count in the definition of efficiency. If we count only parental preferences on which, in this case, decisions are exclusively based then expenditure cannot exceed the efficient amount. If, for the same level of expenditure, we take into account the preferences of both the parents and the child, expenditure may exceed the efficient amount.

Advocates of equality of opportunity would define efficiency so as to include the preferences of the child, so that case (b_2) could lead to 'a low or negative rate of return'. Indeed, for equality of opportunity it would seem appropriate to measure rates of return to educational expenditure according only to the preferences of the child, so that case (b_1) could also lead to 'a low or negative rate of return'.

For the sake of brevity we shall say, from now on, that parents behave 'non-paternalistically' only if they seek to maximise the children's welfare according to the children's own preferences, subject to the constraint of the resources to be devoted to them. We shall describe all other behaviour as 'paternalistic'.[60] From now on we shall assume

60. Perhaps it should be pointed out that, although 'paternalistic' behaviour can lead to 'a low or negative rate of return' (according to the child's preferences) the child may be better off if parents behave 'paternalistically' than if they do not, because 'paternalism' may lead parents to transfer more resources to the child.

that parents behave 'non-paternalistically'. On this assumption the question regarding the conditions in which private parental expenditure would be appropriate reduces to the question regarding the conditions in which it would not be too small.

We have made a simple assumption of maximising behaviour which, together with knowledge of the child's abilities and preferences and divisibility of expenditure, is sufficient to ensure that parental expenditure on education does not exceed the amount required for optimality. We can make some rather more complex assumptions which might be sufficient to ensure that parental expenditure is optimal, and I shall consider them below. First it may be useful to try to guard against a possible misunderstanding which has sometimes occurred in the literature, for example, in that on externalities. Private expenditure on education may generate external economies which are not taken into account in the private calculus of costs and benefits. This implies that there is no market mechanism which would ensure an optimal result. It does *not* imply that in these circumstances private expenditure must be non-optimal.[61] Such an inference would rest on a confusion of necessary with sufficient conditions. Similarly, the failure of the conditions which are sufficient to ensure that parental expenditure on education is optimal does not imply that parental expenditure must be non-optimal. After all, it is, for example, conceivable that, due to accident or possibly genetic and environmental factors, children and parents are matched in such a way that the parental expenditure on each child's education ensures the equalisation of rates of return on educational expenditure.[62]

We have shown that parents who wish to maximise the child's

61.   See [29], pp. 225-6.
62.   In a recent analysis of optimal (pre-university) educational expenditure 'all children are assumed equally capable of benefiting from education' yet in the optimal solution they receive different amounts of education as an increasing function of parental income (see [22]). Neglecting parental paternalism, the optimal educational expenditure on any child depends on its abilities, preferences and endowments. 'Equally capable of benefiting from education' would seem to suggest identical abilities *and* preferences, leaving only differences in endowments. It was pointed out above that there appears to be no simple qualitative relationship between endowments, *ceteris paribus,* and optimal education. The optimality of the solution in [22] must therefore depend on specific, but unstated, assumptions about preferences.

welfare according to the child's own preferences (subject to the constraint of the resources to be spent on the child) will not spend *more* on education than the optimal amount. *Given this assumption,* we can state conditions for ensuring that parents spend the optimal amount. The conditions to be stated would seem jointly sufficient, but not individually necessary.

First, that all parents bequeath some divisible assets, other than education, to all of their children; also that educational expenditure be divisible. To reach the conclusion that parents would not spend too much we made the assumption of 'perfect knowledge' (on the part of the parents) of the child's abilities and preferences and of future relative prices.[63] Now we suppose, in addition, that parents' future income is known and can serve as the basis for borrowing. Otherwise parents could, and often do, come into money long after their children have been inadequately educated. We also suppose that parents can insure against future contingencies and therefore do not need to accumulate assets to meet them. Otherwise parents may leave a bequest which they had not intended to leave because, for example, their contingency provisions – in terms of accumulated assets – made allowance for later death. In this case the fact of bequest would again not ensure that enough had been spent on education.

The above are examples of the kinds of conditions which would ensure (given our assumption about parental aims) that the fact of bequest implies that the optimal amount has been spent on education. If such conditions hold and all parents bequeath some assets to all of their children the situation would be the same as with a perfect capital market.[64] Given the assumptions about the aims we have attributed to

63. See [20], pp. 19-21.
64. Non-pecuniary returns would also be fully taken into account.
Friedman seems to have this in mind when he says that if returns on non-human capital were higher than on human capital '... parents or benefactors would have an incentive to buy such capital for their children instead of investing a corresponding sum in vocational training, and conversely' ([9], p. 136). But he immediately adds that this equalisation of rates of return does not appear to have occurred, and attributes this to 'imperfections in the capital market'. If these transactions were to be based on loans, repayable out of the children's future earnings, they would hardly be described as the work of 'benefactors'. 'Benefactors' are normally those who finance benefactions from their own resources and in this case the market imperfections at issue here would be irrelevant.

parents, the conditions connected with bequest would seem to be the only ones which ensure that private parental expenditure on education is optimal.[65]

The conditions with respect to bequest are clearly not fulfilled in a country like the UK. Nevertheless, some writers take the view that, if the state withdrew from the provision of education and taxes were correspondingly reduced, 'most' parents would voluntarily spend enough on education.[66] Such a view is of necessity difficult to appraise, as we lack the factual knowledge necessary for its appraisal. For example, our definition of optimal expenditure includes consideration of non-pecuniary returns, and we do not know what would be optimal expenditure in the light of this definition. Allegations about 'untapped pools of ability' may not be regarded as relevant evidence, as these refer to expenditure under the present system. However, in so far as government expenditure can be explained by the 'economics of political choice' they may be relevant. Given the outcome of political choice as regards, for example, educational expenditure, there will generally be some voters who would prefer to spend less.[67] Among them one would expect to find parents of children who are now alleged to be members of the 'untapped pool'.[68] Evidence regarding fees paid by parents of public school pupils would also seem to go against the view that purely private parental expenditure would ensure optimal results. If the fees paid by these parents do not exceed the optimal amount, then there must be many more children for whom such amounts would also not exceed the optimum (see above, note 62), but whose parents would not spend such sums. The conjecture that purely private expenditure would be insufficient for first-best optimality is certainly not contradicted by any available evidence.

65. The conditions could be modified to refer, not to bequest at death, but to transfers *inter vivos* at the end of the education period.
The preceding discussion of parental expenditure owes much to conversations with L.P. Foldes and M. Perlman.
66. See, for example, [29], esp. chs. 13 and 14. In [29], however, 'enough' does not mean 'sufficient to equalise marginal rates of return' and is not clearly defined.
67. See below, subsection F.
68. I am assuming that the definition of the 'untapped pool' excludes the possibility that '... the costs of removing ... [it] ... may be much higher than the extra revenue to be expected by concentrating resources on ...' other uses ([29], p. 58).

Equality of Opportunity, Fairness and Efficiency

It may be asked whether private parental expenditure would satisfy the conditions for 'second-best' optimality, i.e. optimality subject to the constraint that '... the bright child of poor parents cannot be sold to a capitalist who wants to invest in his talents, nor can his future earning capacity be tied up as security for a loan'.[69] The notion of 'second-best' optimality needs to be approached warily as it is necessary to specify precisely what actions are followed. If, in our example, we do not allow any collective action, then the situation is indeed 'second-best' optimal, as there are no possibilities of further gains from trade. However, once we do allow for collective action, while retaining the constraint of an 'imperfect' capital market, possibilities for improvement present themselves. We shall compare, in a purely qualitative and taxonomic manner, the effects of two kinds of collective action: a 'free' state school system with state-provided education vouchers. The observations to be made are rather obvious, but seem to have been overlooked.

D

There are two preliminary points to be mentioned. The first is this. As we have seen, writers who advocate vouchers to finance pre-university education wish to use collective action to deal only with those inefficiencies the removal of which will '... confer benefits upon the community at large' but apparently not with inefficiencies whose removal would 'confer direct economic benefits upon individuals or families'. Since this point is not explicitly stated we can only consider how it might be rationalised. One possible argument is found in the view that 'there is a legitimate question concerning the justice of requiring broad, public support for education insofar as the benefits are narrow and private ...'[70] In other words, while it may be reasonable to require me to contribute to the financing of the education of my neighbour's children if that education benefits my family, it is unreasonable to make this requirement solely in order to raise the future income of my neighbour's children. This view may perhaps help to explain why Friedman regards equality of opportunity as a proper aim of a policy for university finance, where its pursuit does not require redistributive taxation. According to him, as we have seen, equality of

69. [15], p. 184. The absence of this constraint may not ensure optimality because of the non-pecuniary returns from education.

70. [28], p. 180.

271

opportunity is not to be regarded as an aim of a policy for pre-university education, for in that case its fulfilment would in general require redistributive taxation.

This is not the place to discuss the merits of the benefit principle of taxation. It is sufficient to note that if an inefficiency cannot be removed by the application of the benefit principle of taxation – as in the case of pre-university education[71] – this cannot be taken to imply efficiency.

The second point is this. It is often taken to follow from welfare economics that, in the absence of 'neighbourhood effects' or paternalism, the aim of improving the distribution of income never justifies the provision of subsidies on specific goods.[72] If this view is to be derived from welfare economics, its application must be restricted to situations when the optimality conditions hold and where every optimum is also an equilibrium.[73] The point about educational expenditure in the context of an imperfect capital market is that the optimality conditions cannot be assumed to hold. Even so, this view is sometimes extended to cover the case of (pre-university) education. For example, Peacock and Wiseman consider the argument 'that the government must intervene in the education process because the demand of ... families for education is limited by their available resources of income and capital', and conclude that '... the distribution of income and capital affects ability to purchase not only education but all kinds of goods and services. For those who believe the distribution to be wrong, the appropriate policies would appear to be those that alter capital and income distribution directly; education policy becomes even potentially relevant only if such general redistributive policies are technically impossible'.[74] If there were a perfect capital market in education this view could, perhaps, be justified on the basis of welfare economics. The writers quoted do not make this counter-factual assumption, but give no indication of what would be an 'appropriate' distribution of income and capital to ensure efficient educational investment. They do not, for example, recommend a

71. See, for example, [23], p. 66.
72. For a criticism of this view, see [8] and his forthcoming work.
73. See [8].
74. [23], p. 21.

redistribution of capital which would result in the universal inheritance of assets other than education, and themselves note that '... if there were a high correlation between means and demand for education ... many of the problems of education policy would be much simpler'. Moreover, their own proposals for education vouchers and earmarked maintenance grants for children between the school leaving age and University entrance contradict the view that the only requirement is a policy of general redistribution of income and captial.

E

We shall now compare a 'free' state school system with a voucher scheme. The comparison will be based on the preceding discussion, and will therefore deal almost exclusively with the effects on the efficiency of educational expenditure. One need not hold that there is any 'fundamental' difference between the 'economic' and the 'non-economic' aspects of welfare to be aware of the limitations of such a comparison. The debate about vouchers encompasses issues which cannot be expressed in terms of rates of return to educational expenditure.

Johnson outlined some of the reasons which may prevent families from spending optimal amounts on their children's education. He ignored proposals for vouchers then already current and observed that:

The first need is for as good an elementary and secondary education as the individual can absorb. The free provision of such education is our accepted way both of equipping the child to take a place in our ... economic system and of compensating, in part at least, for the inequalities of family circumstance into which children are born.[75]

The advocates of vouchers assert that there are better ways of achieving the above aims than 'our accepted way'. Their proposals can be summarised briefly as follows: instead of providing 'free' state owned and administered schools, the government will issue vouchers to parents. Schools would charge fees and would have to cover costs without government subsidy. The vouchers would be encashable at any school which meets government imposed standards and parents would be free to supplement the voucher. How the value of the voucher for any child is to be calculated is an open question. Friedman [9], for

75.   [15], p. 190.

example, proposed a flat-rate voucher for every child, the value of which would apparently not be added to taxable income; Peacock and Wiseman [23] proposed a flat-rate voucher the value of which would be added to taxable income; Pauly [22] argued that welfare-economic considerations require that the government's subsidy to parents 'varies inversely with income'.

In order to compare the effects of a voucher scheme with the present system it is useful to distinguish various dimensions of educational expenditure, in particular:

1) the duration of education;

2) the intensity of education (e.g. staff/pupil ratios, other resource/ pupil ratios as well as the quality of staff);

3) content or type of education (e.g. religious or not, academic or vocational).

Efficiency requires that marginal equalities hold with respect to (1) and (2). But efficiency is not only a matter of marginal adjustments but also a matter of 'total' conditions.[76]

As regards (1) — the duration of education — the difference between the two systems will depend on the minimum school leaving age and on policy regarding the allocation of vouchers between the minimum school leaving age and university entrance. Voucher advocates generally propose to maintain a compulsory school leaving age, and the fixing of that age can perhaps be regarded as independent of the system.[77] If the minimum school leaving age coincides with the age for university

76.   We once again ignore the crucial consideration that one of the purposes of education may be to influence the child's preferences, since otherwise the application of the usual welfare economic criteria becomes impossible. We would then require a valuation of the preference-forming attributes of alternative systems of education. (see [23], p. 22ᐟ

77.   Friedman suggests that 'the social gain from education is presumably greatest for the very lowest levels of education, where there is the nearest approach to unanimity about the content of the education, and declines continuously as the level of education rises' ([9], pp. 126-7). It would therefore seem that, *if* public support of education is advocated solely on grounds of 'neighbourhood effects', there could hardly be a case for a minimum school leaving age of sixteen/eighteen. The appropriate minimum age could hardly exceed twelve or eleven, though advocates of vouchers do not seem to have noticed this particular consequence of their view.

entrance — as is the case in many states in the USA — there would be no difference between the two systems. In the UK the result would depend on whether, and how, vouchers would be allocated after the minimum leaving age. Peacock and Wiseman proposed '... that vouchers sufficiently large to meet basic fees be provided for all children able to benefit from remaining at school'.[78] If such a policy were followed there would appear to be no difference — as regards (1) — between the present system and a voucher scheme. Advocates of vouchers concentrate their criticisms of the present system as regards its effects under (2) and (3) above, and maintain that a voucher system would be unambiguously preferable.

(2) and (3) are not independent of one another, since the optimal resource input will generally vary with the kind of education provided.[79] If the introduction of vouchers led to a change in the 'mix' of educational output, as its advocates predict, there would be no clear way of comparing expenditure under the two systems. *Faute de mieux* we shall therefore consider the two aspects of educational expenditure separately.

As regards (2) advocates of vouchers seem to be agreed that the provision of educational *services* is deficient under the 'free' school system. However, they attribute this deficiency at least in part to the inefficiencies resulting from the absence of competition, and therefore not necessarily to a deficiency in resource *inputs*. For example, it is pointed out that

... the criterion is the amount of education obtained before and after, not the amount of money spent on it; for it is possible ... that parents could ... purchase for themselves the same amount of education that the government now provides, but at a lower total cost.

Indeed, when collectively provided, education 'will be much more expensive'.[80] On this view the introduction of vouchers would lead nearer to the production frontier. As far as I am aware, no attempt has been made to support this view by evidence regarding the relative

78.   [23], p. 66. They also proposed the provision of 'finance for parents to offset the cost of maintaining the child at home'after the minimum school leaving age. Such a scheme, which would be most desirable, could also be introduced under the present system.

79.   See [16], p. 306.

80.   [29], pp. 210-11. See also [23], p.46.

efficiency of private and state schools. Again, 'greater efficiency' is often interpreted as relating to aspect (3) above, namely that 'educational resources will be more satisfactorily related to individual needs',[81] an aspect we are now ignoring. At the same time voucher advocates stress the political constraints on educational expenditure which lead to 'the financial starvation of education' and claim as an advantage of the voucher scheme that 'it offers a prospect of total expenditure on education larger than "normal" '.[82] Thus it is not clear whether one argument for a voucher scheme is that it would increase resource input to education, or merely that, whatever the changes in resources input, vouchers would be an improvement because (a) of the increased efficiency of resource use due to competition, and (b) the allocation of resources in education would better reflect 'parental preferences' than can be the case in a 'free' state system. Sometimes this latter view is suggested when it is

> ... pointed out that there is no need to concern oneself with some concept of a welfare ... 'optimum' – a conception unnecessarily imported into the present discussion ... – in order to distinguish between a situation in which parents can make direct choices about education and situations in which they can not.[83]

It is true that we must be able to distinguish different institutional arrangements independently of their consequences for optimality. Unless this can be done we could not appraise them in the light of optimality considerations. In so far as the 'direct choice' relates to aspect (3) above, the question, from our point of view, is whether 'direct choice' by parents would take into account better the 'abilities' and 'preferences' of children than does a 'free' school system, a question we do not propose to consider, although, as was suggested before, welfare economic considerations are not irrelevant to it. As regards 'direct choice' with respect to aspect (2) – educational expenditure per period of time – its merits presumably need to be tested against the usual criteria of efficiency. The appraisal of the changes in educational expenditure which may result from the introduction of vouchers must be part of the appraisal of the merits of a voucher scheme.

81.   [23], p.46.
82.   [31], p.48.
83.   [32], pp. 379-80.

We shall confine our discussion to aspect (2) of educational expenditure and ignore aspect (3), despite the *caveats* entered above. For simplicity we shall also ignore the efficiency argument for competition and assume that a given 'output' of educational services is produced at lowest cost both under the 'free' school system and under a voucher scheme.

We have already analysed the effects of purely private parental expenditure on education. We concluded that, if parents do not behave 'paternalistically' with respect to educational expenditure on their children, they will not spend more than is required for efficiency, but they may spend less. If we ignore considerations of the economics of political choice this would appear to furnish a strong argument in favour of vouchers, although this argument is not usually derived in the way it has been here. Under the 'free' state school system parents can generally spend more on their children's education only by transferring them from the state to the private sector, which means that they confront a large discontinuity in their expenditure opportunities. With a voucher scheme this discontinuity would be removed, or, at any rate, greatly reduced. This would provide incentives to increased parental expenditure, which are stressed by advocates of vouchers.

Let us first assume that the total amount of government expenditure on pre-university education is independent of whether it is distributed through a 'free' state school system or through vouchers, and similarly let us assume that there is no change in the relative prices of educational inputs, so that the voucher can be fixed in real terms. In this case, simple economic theory suggests that total expenditure on pre-university education would be larger under a voucher scheme than under a 'free' state school system. One objection to vouchers (apparently given the assumptions stated) has been put as follows:

inasmuch as education creates future earning capacity, the more education is sold to the highest bidder rather than rationed out in equal amounts, the more the inheritance of a good education approximates the inheritance of real wealth, systematically favouring the rich at the expense of the poor.[84]

Quite apart from the fact that, as voucher advocates always stress, education is not now 'rationed out in equal amounts', the conclusion

84.   [2], p. 35. Blaug himself does not appear to endorse this objection.

that vouchers would 'worsen' the distribution of income does not follow as it stands. This is so for the simple reason that no-one has proposed that the amounts which would be privately added to vouchers should be taxed away when schools are 'free'. If these amounts are not spent on education they can be invested and transferred to children as gifts *inter vivos*. Nevertheless, vouchers could 'worsen' the distribution of earning capacity because they imply 'distributing education in accordance with purchasing power'.[85] The personal distribution of income is a function of many variables, and there do not appear to be any necessary conditions for a 'worsening' of that distribution. One could state a set of conditions which would be jointly sufficient for vouchers to lead to greater inequality in the distribution of income. One of the conditions in this set could be that rates of return on educational investment are substantially higher than rates of return on other assets.[86] Given this condition, children who had hitherto attended 'free' state schools and also received income-yielding assets from their parents would now enjoy a higher future income if those assets are used to purchase additional education. If we suppose that, given under-investment in education, additional educational expenditure can be obtained only from parental sources, there would be a conflict between distributional aims and efficiency. For in this case ordinary welfare rules would appear to suggest that additional expenditure on education should be encouraged. This is the view of advocates of vouchers.[87] However, we must consider whether this view is correct, i.e. whether an increase in educational expenditure is sufficient to ensure greater efficiency when the 'free' school system was accompanied by under-investment in education.

We have assumed that the introduction of vouchers does not affect the total amount spent by the government on pre-university education. Let us now assume that the voucher is of the kind proposed by Friedman, that is, a flat-rate voucher equal in value to the average cost per child in the previous 'free' state system. As is well known, in the 'free' state system in the UK more than the average tends to be spent

---

85. [2], p. 35.

86. Empirical studies appear to suggest '... that there is substantial under-investment of resources in secondary education ...' in the UK ([3], pp. 253-4).

87. 'If parents will provide supplements to the state-financed amount, to allow such payments is *clearly* Pareto-optimal, since only those parents making the expenditure need bear the incremental costs'. ([22], p. 123, italics added).

in grammar schools, and less than the average on those of more modest abilities (e.g. secondary modern schools).[88] We have made the assumption that under the 'free' state system, pre-university educational expenditure is too small. To simplify the exposition, let us now make the stronger assumption that expenditure on each child is too small. We can immediately summarise the possible directions of change in educational expenditure resulting from the introduction of vouchers. On our assumptions, any reductions in educational expenditure on any child is a deterioration and any (small) increase an improvement. Any large increase will also be an improvement given the assumption that parents behave non-paternalistically and therefore will not spend too much. We divide children in the 'free' state system into two groups: (a) those on whom more than the average is spent; (b) those on whom the average or less is spent. The introduction of the flat-rate voucher postulated can lead to a deterioration only in expenditure on children in group (a). This trivial case is enough to show that an increase in expenditure is not sufficient to ensure an improvement in educational investment. If vouchers are inversely related to parental income we can ignore any changes in total expenditure and again say, tautologically, that children who receive a voucher of greater value than the education previously received must gain. As regards all others the result depends on the amounts parents add to the voucher.

The preceding comparison of the voucher scheme with the present school system would suggest that the advocates of vouchers are right, i.e. that, on plausible assumptions regarding parental additions to vouchers, additional expenditure would more than offset any possible reductions.[89] However, the comparison so far made fails to take into account certain important considerations.

There is, first, the fact that a voucher scheme and the attendant competition among schools would lead to relative price changes in educational inputs, particularly teachers' salaries (and presumably also site values). Indeed, one of the advantages claimed for the voucher scheme is that competition would produce '... salary differentials within

88. These remarks are not meant to imply approval of the 'tripartite' system.
89. Although among the children on whom less could be spent might well be '... the exceptional few ... who are the hope of the future ...' (see [10], p. 93) and for whose benefit Friedman particularly urged the introduction of vouchers.

teaching ... more nearly in keeping with the scarcity of particular teaching ... skills'.[90] At present, of course, better state schools tend to attract better teachers because of the non-pecuniary advantages they offer. With a voucher scheme they would have the choice of offering better salaries. The quality of teachers would thus become more strongly correlated with expenditure on education than it is at present. To this extent the previous comparison of educational expenditure under the present system with that under a voucher scheme must be modified, for that comparison assumed no change in the relative prices of teaching inputs. The point under discussion is sometimes referred to as the 'creaming off' or 'pirating threat' and it is alleged that this 'threat' presupposes a perfectly inelastic supply of teachers.[91] This is an error. The point presupposes that teachers are not homogeneous, and that under the present system many of the better teachers do not earn the rents they would earn under a more competitive system.

A second point was also omitted from our initial comparison, which was concerned exclusively with possible increases or decreases in educational expenditure. The present point relates to the response in educational expenditure on a given child to changing knowledge of that child's capacity – the central point of the debate surrounding the eleven-plus examination. The question is simply whether this response would be 'better' or 'worse' under a voucher scheme than in a 'free' state school system. Put in terms of the efficiency of educational investment, the question is whether any given amount of expenditure would be re-allocated more efficiently in response to changing knowledge of children's capacities. Parents may, and sometimes do, adjust expenditure to changing knowledge about the child. But it is probably true that the main determinant of expenditure is parental resources which, in general, do not vary with the child's educational requirements. In a state system like that envisaged, for example, by proponents of comprehensive schools, educational 'inputs' can be varied directly in response to changes in the child's revealed capacities.

There is, finally, a point related to the one just made which is commonly overlooked. The preceding discussion concentrated on the qualitative changes in the *absolute* 'amount' of education which might

90.   [23], p. 51.
91.   See, for example, [31], p. 40-42.

result from the introduction of vouchers. When university places are rationed changes in relative amounts may be important. That is to say, a child who, under the present system, would have gained entry to university and who continued to receive the same 'amount' of education under the voucher scheme might not gain entry to the university because he now received *relatively* less. The consequence might be a 'worse' selection of university entrants. To avoid this contingency there would have to be no rationing of university places. It should be pointed out that advocates of vouchers also advocate loans for university students and university fees which would cover 'costs'.

The preceding purely qualitative comparison of a 'free' state school system with a voucher scheme suggested questions rather than answers. These questions tend to be ignored by voucher advocates who appear to ignore the valid efficiency argument for equality of opportunity.[92] When that argument is considered the points made above simply provide another example of a well-known proposition from second-best welfare economics, namely that the removal of one or more 'constraints' when others remain need not be sufficient for an increase in welfare. In the case under discussion the introduction of vouchers would remove the discontinuity in the costs of additional private expenditure on education and would make factor prices in education equal to opportunity costs.[93] However, the 'imperfections' of the capital market would remain (and rationing of university places, perhaps, also). We have tried to show that such a change need not be sufficient for an increase in welfare, although it may lead to that result.

So far we have assumed that the amount of public expenditure on education is independent of the method of financing education. Just as it is not clear what voucher advocates predict regarding the effects of vouchers on total educational expenditure, so it is not clear what they predict, or recommend, regarding the relationship between vouchers and public educational expenditure. For example, in his initial proposal Friedman recommended that public expenditure remain unchanged.[94]

92.   See above, subsection A.
93.   One 'constraint' does not imply the other. For example, it would be possible for factor prices in the state system to equal opportunity costs while at the same time parents would get no refund when removing their children from the state system.
94.   See [9], p. 130.

In a later version of his proposal he observed that a voucher scheme 'might well mean smaller governmental expenditure on schooling'.[95] Peacock and Wiseman '... would ... assess the voucher-level high enough alone to provide adequate finance for families in lower income brackets'.[96] Pauly argued that, on welfare-economic grounds, the introduction of vouchers should be accompanied by a reduction in public expenditure.[97] As was noted above, however, he was concerned only with 'neighbourhood effects' and did not consider the political effects of the introduction of vouchers. West initially proposed only selective help to problem families, which would entail a reduction in public expenditure. Later he observed that vouchers could be '... of equal value or graded inversely with income or according to "need" ',[98] which leaves open the questions of the effects of vouchers on total public expenditure. Yet these must also be considered, since a change in public expenditure will generally alter the incidence of educational expenditure. Take a trivial example: suppose public expenditure falls, but total expenditure remains the same. In general this would imply a reduction in educational expenditure on some children matched by an equal increase on others. If we further suppose that (a) all children are of equal 'abilities' and 'tastes', and optimal education is independent of endowments, (b) all had previously received equal 'amounts' of education, and (c) there are diminishing marginal returns, then it follows that expenditure under the voucher scheme will be less efficiently distributed. It is therefore useful to compare the outcome of political choice regarding the amount of public educational expenditure under a 'free' state school system and a voucher scheme

F

We shall not try to derive the outcome of a vote from individuals' preferences and the prevailing voting rule. We shall merely ask whether the introduction of vouchers may cause voters to change their preferences for alternative amounts of public expenditure and, if so, in what direction.

For the sake of illustration we make the following assumptions:

96. [23], p. 65.
97. See [22].
98. [31], pp. 47.

a) voting takes place on single issues, e.g. the amount of educational expenditure;

b) voters are non-paternalistic and interested only in the 'amount' of education received by their own children, i.e. there are no 'neighbourhood effects' and voters do not take into account the inefficiencies due to any failure to satisfy marginal conditions in educational expenditure (an assumption apparently made by voucher advocates);[99]

c) all children are of equal 'ability';

d) voters are indifferent between public and private education as such, and a 'free' state school system is exogenously given;[100]

e) the financing of education involves no redistribution of income, i.e. each family contributes to the cost of education what it receives by way of educational services;

f) the introduction of vouchers leaves relative prices of educational inputs unchanged.

Given our assumptions, what qualitative inferences can be made about the efficiency of public expenditure under a 'free' school system? There has been much discussion of whether the provision of goods through the public sector falls short of or exceeds the requirements of efficiency.[101] In that discussion it is usually assumed that, given no 'strategic' behaviour, efficiency requires that collective action must not prevent people from spending the amounts they would most prefer to spend.[102] Our previous discussion (above, subsection C) has shown that this view requires modification as regards educational expenditure in the context of an 'imperfect' capital market. On our assumption about parental aims, efficiency requires that parents must not be 'forced' to spend *less* than their most preferred amount.[103] If they are forced to spend more, then, in general, this may or may not lead to excessive expenditure. Given our assumptions, we can easily construct

99.   See, for example, [29], p. 211.

100.   As, for example, is the Health Service, in a recent analysis of the political determinants of expenditure on health. See [5].

101.   See, for example, [4].

102.   Whence it is shown that collective action cannot ensure efficiency in the Pareto-sense unless there are 'side payments'. (see, for example, [4]).

103.   We assume 'single-peaked' preferences (see, for example, [31], pp. 48-9).

an example in which the fact that some parents are forced to spend more than their most preferred amount does not imply excessive expenditure. In addition to (b), (c) and (e) we may assume that differences in endowments do not affect the optimal amount of educational expenditure. In this case, educational expenditure under our 'free' school system (like purely private parental expenditure) cannot be excessive, but only too small. Unless we make a restrictive assumption of this kind we cannot specify whether expenditure will be too large or too small. For our purposes we do not need to be able to specify this. All we need to suppose is that the outcome of the vote leads some parents to spend less than their most preferred amount and some to spend more (ignoring any who may be in their most preferred position).

Now consider the effect of the introduction of vouchers on the preferences of the two classes of voters as between alternative amounts of public educational expenditure. Parents who (most) preferred to spend less would have no reason to change their preferences. Parents who (most) preferred to spend more are now indifferent – given assumption (d) – as to whether they obtain additional education privately or through the political process. Their most preferred amount of public expenditure cannot increase. We may note in passing that, under the 'free' state system and the attendant discontinuity in the costs of additional private expenditure, such parents would have an incentive to try to persuade others to vote for more expenditure. Parents who preferred to spend less would be unaffected by the change. This point merely adds an argument from 'the economics of political choice' to the old proposition that, when 'contracting out' is allowed, political pressure to maintain or increase public expenditure will diminish.

The introduction of vouchers thus cannot lead to a greater preference for public educational expenditure. Moreover, since, by assumption, the voucher scheme does not redistribute income, there are gratuitous costs of collection which should make the 'rational' voter prefer a lesser amount than he did under the 'free' school system. Indeed, since we are ignoring interdependent utility functions, the voucher scheme should collapse, unless voters take into account the inefficiencies resulting from inadequate expenditure on education.

284

Now suppose that the financing of education is accompanied by redistribution both under the 'free' school system and under the voucher scheme. We must also suppose that this redistribution can be achieved only through educational finance, since, if it can be achieved in other ways, redistribution and educational finance are independent and the previous comparison holds. The extent of redistribution for any given level of educational expenditure is determined by a *given* tax structure.

The difference, as regards the two systems, between the case with no redistribution and the case with redistribution is this: with no redistribution, the cost of the education actually received by any family is the same whether financed collectively or privately. Under collective provision the family may not be able to secure the most preferred amount, which it can secure under the voucher scheme, provided that amount exceeds the value of the voucher. With redistribution the costs of collectively financed and privately financed education will differ. Vouchers remove the discontinuity in the costs of additional private expenditure and thus provide incentives, where applicable, to escape the higher costs of collective provision. We may note that the presence of redistribution *may* help to make expenditure on education 'excessive', both under the 'free' school system and under the voucher scheme.[104]

We consider the effects of the introduction of vouchers on the voting preferences of the two classes of voters distinguished before: (a) those who, under the 'free' school system, would have (most) preferred less education than is actually provided and (b) those who would have (most) preferred more. We must also consider possible directions of redistribution.

1) Those who prefer less education (class a) subsidise those who prefer more (class b).

In this case voters in class (a) have no reason to *change* their preferences, nor have voters in class (b). The latter now receive the subsidy via the voucher and can add to it from their own resources.

2) Those who prefer more education (class b) subsidise those who prefer less (class a).

104. This is sometimes claimed to be a general feature of collective provision of goods. See [4].

Voters in class (a) once again have no reason to change their preferences. But voters in class (b) will now prefer less, for they can obtain the same amount of education at lower cost,[105] if it is financed purely privately.

Thus, the introduction of vouchers can only lead to voters preferring less public educational expenditure. A change in voters' preferences need not change the outcome of a vote. But, if preferences can change in only one direction, then, if the outcome of the vote changes, it, too, can change in only one direction. Case (2) also suggests that, where the introduction of vouchers leads to a reduction in public expenditure, the 'free' school system is likely to redistribute income in the 'right' direction. There is '... evidence that "free" state education conforms to ... egalitarian ideals',[106] in the UK, which suggests that vouchers would reduce public educational expenditure.

This comparison of the political 'determinants' of public expenditure on education under a 'free' school system with those under a voucher scheme supposed constant relative prices of educational inputs, as did our initial, purely arithmetic, comparison. We have already mentioned some possible consequences of the introduction of vouchers on the relative prices of educational inputs, and of changes in the relative amounts of education received by different children.

G

The main premise of this Section has been that *one* of the arguments for equality of opportunity is part and parcel of the traditional and respectable aim of efficient resource allocation (ignoring some exceptions noted above (Subsection C).) This aim appears to be accepted by the advocates of vouchers[107] although, as has been pointed out, they fail to take into account the conditions required for its fulfilment. The results of our qualitative comparison of of 'free' school system with a voucher scheme are hardly surprising. They confirm the commonplace

---

105. Case (2) would appear to apply in the UK. See, for example, [2], pp. 39-41. Redistribution can, and no doubt does, take place within the respective classes, but this does not alter our conclusions.
I am grateful to M. Perlman for a most helpful discussion of these points.
106. [2], p. 42.
107. [2], p. 39.

view that a 'free' school system does not, and a voucher scheme would not, achieve complete efficiency in educational expenditure, '... but no participants in the debate believe it to be attainable'.[108] If this were the only conclusion it would be otiose to state it. Our comparison, however, also shows that, for a voucher scheme to be an improvement over the present system, even in terms of our extremely limited frame of reference, a number of conditions would have to be fulfilled. These conditions are ignored by the advocates of vouchers, who therefore write as if their scheme constituted an unambiguous improvement over the present system. Admittedly, they sometimes point out that their view does not take into account certain possible aims with respect to education, but if so, then these must be 'authoritarian' aims, and not the aims considered in the present paper.[109] However, some advocates of vouchers insist that even if such illiberal aims are taken into account, vouchers are still unambiguously superior. Blaug, in reviewing the debate over vouchers, seemed to conclude that the only argument for a 'free' state system was the argument from 'social cohesion'. If that were indeed the case a liberal would have to be in favour of vouchers. West claimed that even the illiberal aim of 'social cohesion' could be achieved by vouchers: 'once it is seen that public provision is technically a less efficient instrument for the promotion of "social cohesion", Dr. Blaug is left with nothing at all on one side of his scales ... If the voucher is correctly "priced" ... all children would benefit'.[110] In fact, Blaug had not quite agreed that there is 'nothing at all on one side of his scales'. At one point he did conclude that: 'if we favour equality of educational opportunity, we should be advocating more vigorous use of state finance in aid of education. To call for state provision ... is to demand a peashooter to fight an elephant'.[111] Yet, by the time he came to the end of his paper he had second thoughts: 'In the final analysis the voucher scheme stands or falls on questions of fact ... will educational opportunity be more equally distributed?'[112] A modest part of the purpose of this Section was to argue, on the basis of elementary economic theory, that Blaug's second thoughts deserve serious consideration and that the merits of the voucher scheme may be questioned from the point of view of traditional liberal policy aims.

108. [31], p. 31.
109. See, for example, [32], pp. 380-1.
110. [30], p. 85 and p. 83.
111. [2], p. 43.
112. [2], p. 46.

REFERENCES

[1] Barry, B.   *Political Argument,* 1965

[2] Blaug, M.   'Economic Aspects of Vouchers for Education', in *Education: A Framework for Choice,* IEA, London 1967

[3] Blaug, M.   'The Rate of Return on Investment in Education' in *Economics of Education 1,* ed. M. Blaug, 1968

[4] Buchanan, J.M. & Tullock, G.   *The Calculus of Consent,* 1962

[5] Buchanan, J.M.   *The Inconsistencies of the National Health Service,* I.E.A. Occasional Paper 7, 1965

[6] Crosland, C.A.R.   *The Future of Socialism,* 1956

[7] Eucken, W.   *Grundsaetze der Wirtschaftspolitik,* 1955

[8] Foldes, L.P.   'Redistribution in Money and in Kind', 'A Note on Redistribution', 'Redistribution: A Reply', *Economica,* Feb., 1967, May 1967, May 1968

[9] Friedman, M.   'The Role of Government in Education', in *Economics and the Public Interest,* ed. R.A. Solo, 1955

[10] Friedman, M.   *Capitalism and Freedom,* 1962

[11] Graham, F.D.   *Social Goals and Economic Institutions,* 1942

[12] Hayek, F.A.   *The Constitution of Liberty,* 1960

[13] Hofstadter, A.   'The Career Open to Personality' in *Aspects of Human Equality,* eds. L. Bryson et al., 1956

[14] Hutchison, T.W.   *A Review of Economic Doctrines 1870 - 1929,* 1953

[15] Johnson, H.G.   *Money Trade and Economic Growth,* 1962

[16] Kershaw, J.A.   'Productivity in American Schools and Colleges', in *Economics of Education 2,* ed. M. Blaug, 1969

[17] Klappholz, K.   'What Redistribution May Economists Discuss?' *Economica,* May 1968

[18] Knight, F.H.   *The Ethics of Competition,* 1935

[19] Knight, F.H.   *Freedom and Reform,* 1947

[20] Meade, J.E.   *Efficiency, Equality and the Ownership of Property*, 1964

[21] Oliver, H.M., Jr.   *A Critique of Socio-economic Goals*, 1954

[22] Pauly, M.V.   'Mixed Public and Private Financing of Education', *American Economic Review*, March 1967

[23] Peacock, A.T. &   *Education for Democrats*, IEA Hobart Paper
     Wiseman, J.   25, 1964

[24] Plamenatz, J.P.   'Equality of Opportunity' in *Aspects of Human Equality*, eds. L. Bryson et al., 1956

[25] Popper, K.R.   *The Open Society and its Enemies*, 2 Vols, third edition, 1957

[26] Robbins, Lord   *Politics and Economics*, 1963

[27] Wallich, H.C.   *The Cost of Freedom*, 1960

[28] Weisbrod, B.A.   'External Effects of Investment in Education' in *Economics of Education 1*, ed. M. Blaug, 1968

[29] West, E.G.   *Education and the State*, IEA, London, 1965

[30] West, E.G.   'Dr. Blaug and State Education: A Reply' in *Education: A Framework for Choice*, IEA, London, 1957

[31] West, E.G.   *Economics, Education and the Politician*, IEA Hobart Paper 42, 1968

[32] Wiseman, J.   'Vouchers for Education: Counter-Reply' in *Economics of Education 2*, ed. M. Blaug, 1969

Do Monopoly and Near-Monopoly Matter?
A Survey of Empirical Studies

B.S. Yamey

I

The monopolist restricts output and raises price as compared with the competitive norm, secures profits in excess of normal competitive profits, and brings about a misallocation of resources entailing a loss of economic welfare. This formulation and the corresponding formulation for monopsony constitute the standard economic indictment of monopoly or near-monopoly conditions in industrial, commercial and financial activities; and the ingredients of the charge, or at least the first two of them, reflect popular views of monopoly for several centuries. It is only quite recently that disinterested observers have come to question the general validity of the condemnation of monopoly, and of the economic theory underlying it, so much so that in the last decade or two economists have begun to give serious attention to the systematic empirical testing of the theory — an activity which would have appeared supererogatory in the years when the doctrine of the economic mischiefs of monopoly held virtually undisputed sway.[1]

Today there are economists who would argue that the traditional theory is basically inadequate in that it ignores such matters as the application of resources to the improvement of knowledge, which favourably affects prices and economic welfare. There are others who, while willing to accept the adequacy of the traditional analysis, would say that in the real world of growing and changing advanced economies there are few industrial, commercial or financial activities to which the theory of monopoly can be applied properly. 'Monopolistic' firms are constrained to act as if they were operating in competitive conditions because of the ease with which viable competitors (including estab-

---

1.   It was always conceded that in some situations monopoly was inevitable because of marked decreasing cost conditions. Even then, however, orthodoxy expressed itself in the form of scepticism about the frequency of such conditions.

Do Monopoly and Near-Monopoly Matter?

lished firms extending their range of operations) can emerge either in the same activity or in activities producing closely-substitutable goods or services, despite apparent barriers to entry. Prices and profits will be much the same whether there is only one firm, a few firms or many.[2] Yet others, while accepting that the traditional analytical approach is appropriate, as well as applicable, might say that the economic ill-effects of monopoly are so small in advanced economies that the monopoly problem should at best have but a low priority on the agenda of public policy measures, unless so-called non-economic effects are thought to be relevant and important.

This paper surveys the character and findings of a number of postwar studies, almost all referring to the United States, bearing on the question whether monopoly and near-monopoly matter because of their undesirable economic effects. It surveys a number of studies designed to establish the nature and to indicate the (quantitative) extent of the effect of monopoly or near-monopoly conditions on prices, profits, economic welfare and inventive and innovative activities. It need hardly

2.   Marshall in his *Industry and Trade,* first published in 1919, noted that most monopolies, other than those endowed by the state with exclusive rights, were 'conditional', and that the modern monopolist in his price policy 'will keep a watchful eye on the sources of possible competition, direct or indirect'. As to the reality of barriers to entry as a protection to the monopolist, allowing him to pursue monopolistic policies, Marshall made two points. On the one hand, increasing requirements of capital and organising effort meant that 'some kinds of monopolies, which even a generation ago would have been properly classed as provisional, have now become so strong as to give grounds for raising the question whether authority should be called in to exercise a control, which competition might have been trusted to do in earlier times'. On the other hand, the protection of monopolists provided by the *vis inertiae* 'is being constantly diminished by the influences of modern technique, no less than those of modern habits of thought and life: and accordingly some monopolies, so strongly fortified by large capitalistic resources, advanced methods, high ability and large business connections that they would have been practically impregnable not long ago, are now often quickly impaired'. *Industry and Trade,* third ed., 1932 reprint, pp. 396-9.
    Present-day exposition of the view that at best only a few industries are effectively insulated against competition by high capital requirements includes the view that there are many large, well-financed business firms in, say, the United States, each able to break through such entry barriers without difficulty; moreover, such firms are not subject to the constraints imposed by the imperfections of the capital market. For a strong expression of such views, see McGee, John S., 'Discussion: Vertical Mergers, Market Power, and the Antitrust Law', *American Economic Review,* Vol. LVII, 1967, Papers and Proceedings, pp. 269-70.

291

be mentioned here that the authors of the various studies to be considered are all aware of the limitations of the methods of inquiry adopted and the data used, and of the degree of tentativeness in the inferences to be drawn from their results. These limitations will not be considered in this paper, save in general terms in respect of major issues; and the interpretations and suggestions put forward here are subject to reservations similar to those entered by the authors of the various studies surveyed. The main objective here is to provide a brief guide to a number of published but scattered pieces of empirical work, many of which are likely to have escaped the attention of the general economist, although they relate to one of the central and longest-established themes in economics.

Since pure monopoly is rare except when created by the power of the state, since 'monopoly and free competition are ideally wide apart, yet in practice they shade into one another by imperceptible degrees',[3] and since the degree of market control cannot be measured directly, empirical research has had to make do with indirect and imperfect measures of monopoly power. Measures of concentration, notably the concentration ratio, have been used commonly as a surrogate for the degree of monopoly power or market control. The imperfections of the concentration ratio as a proxy for monopoly power are well known, and need not be rehearsed here; and one may agree with Professor Fellner that here, as in other contexts, 'an uncomfortable gap exists between the concepts to which the theory relates and the concepts that can be made operational in the *actual* practice of empirical researchers'.[4] No one would dissent from the statement that 'we have no theory that allows us to deduce from the observable degree of concentration in a *particular* market whether or not price or output are competitive'.[5] High concentration does not invariably denote a position close to the monopoly end of the spectrum stretching from atomistic competition to pure monopoly; and there are other characteristics of market structure as well as other factors influencing the degree of competition which are not reflected in an index of concentration. The

3.   Marshall, *Industry and Trade*, p. 397.
4.   Fellner, William, 'The Adaptability and Lasting Significance of the Chamberlinian Contribution', in Robert E. Kuenne (ed.), *Monopolistic Competition Theory: Studies in Impact*, 1967, p.6.
5.   Demsetz, Harold, 'Why Regulate Utilities?' *Journal of Law and Economics*, Vol. XI, 1968, pp. 59-60; emphasis added.

latter consideration is recognised, indeed, in the emphasis placed on barriers to entry in economists' discussions of monopoly and competition. Nevertheless, one does have some confidence in the view that industries with high concentration will *tend on the average* to be closer to the monopoly end of the spectrum than industries with low concentration. The confidence derives from the reasonable belief that the concentration ratio is directly related to the market position of the largest firm, and, further, that the structural characteristic measured by the ratio has a direct bearing on the ease of collusion among firms and of the development of non-collusive but non-competitive business policies; and this confidence is not undermined by the recognition that there is no simple one-to-one relationship between numbers of firms or size-distribution of firms, on the one hand, and market behaviour, on the other. Should a number of otherwise acceptable tests using concentration ratios for randomly chosen groups of industries go against the predictions of standard price theory, ordinarily one would not wish to argue that the tests tell us nothing useful because the concentration ratio is an imperfect measure of degree of monopoly.[6] In the absence of a more soundly-based measure of the degree of monopoly (or of degree of departure from 'free competition'), the concentration ratio (or some other analogous measure of industry structure) will continue to be used and to be relied upon in empirical work, as has been done in the studies reviewed in this paper.

The next section is concerned with studies of the effect of monopoly and high concentration on price; and profits are the theme of Section III. In Section IV estimates of the welfare loss from the misallocation of resources are considered briefly. Section V looks at the evidence of changes in industrial concentration over time. It is somewhat of a digression from the main theme, but its inclusion is explained in Section IV. Finally, in Section VI studies of the relation between concentration and inventive and innovative activity are examined.

6. The qualification 'ordinarily' is added because one would question the relevance of a study, especially one involving a small number of industries, if sensible precautions have not been taken to minimise the impact of the technical-statistical limitations of concentration ratios based, as they generally are, on census data: ordinarily one expects – and finds – that attention is given to such matters as the appropriateness of industry classifications, adjustment for industries with distinct local or regional sub-divisions of the national market, and the elimination of industries with low specialisation or coverage ratios.

II

There are only a few studies which have attempted to measure the effect of monopoly or monopsony on price, no doubt because of the major difficulties posed by differences in products as well as by differences in cost conditions in different periods, regions or countries.

An ingenious enquiry into the effect of monopoly on price was carried out by D. Schwartzman.[7] He took advantage of the fact that manufacturing industries in Canada tend to have higher levels of concentration than their counterparts in the United States; and also of the reasonable presumption that demand conditions and the availability of technologies are fairly similar in the two neighbouring countries. Differences in factor prices were dealt with by concentrating the investigation on the ratio of price to average variable cost — that is, by concentrating not directly on inter-country differences in price but, instead, on inter-country differences in the degree of uplift imparted to average variable cost. Differences in cost conditions, not caught in the measured average variable cost, were allowed for by calculating the average inter-country difference in the price-cost ratios for a number of industries which were unconcentrated in both countries, and using this as an adjustment factor. The average difference in the ratios for a group of industries with high concentration in Canada and low concentration in the United States was calculated, and reduced by the adjustment factor. The main finding, for a group of fourteen industries (including three industries where there were substantial imports into Canada), was that the ratio for Canada was higher than for the United States, that the difference was significant at the 1 per cent level,[8] and that the difference could be translated (under certain assumptions) into an estimate that the monopoly effect on price was 11·2 per cent of average variable cost or 8·3 per cent of the competitive price.[9]

The effect of concentration on the prices of banking outputs has

7.   Schwartzman, David, 'The Effect of Monopoly on Price', *Journal of Political Economy,* Vol. LXVII, 1959, pp. 352-62.
8.   It is interesting that the average Canadian ratio for five exporting industries was lower than that for their United States counterparts. (These five industries were not included in the fourteen.)
9.   See correction of error in original article: Schwartzman, David, 'The Effect of Monopoly: A Correction', *Journal of Political Economy,* Vol. LXIX, 1961, p. 494.

been the subject of several statistical studies in the United States. The geographical sub-division of the national market, with a wide range of degrees of concentration among sub-divisions, has made possible such studies.[10] By mid-1965 four studies had been reported. Two of these found no identifiable relationship between concentration ratios and the level of interest rates on business loans. The remaining two disclosed a statistically significant positive relationship between concentration and output prices. The findings of the most recent (fifth) study supports the hypothesis of a positive relationship. The estimates presented in this study suggest that on the average 'a 25 percentage point increase in concentration results in a 25 basis point rise in average loan rates ...'[11]

A study by Stigler on the theory of oligopoly includes some statistical evidence of the relation between the number of suppliers of a service and its price. The expected negative relation is reported: rates for advertising space in newspapers and 'spot' commercial rates of radio stations tend to be lower where the number of suppliers is greater, allowance having been made for other influences on price such as newspaper circulations and population.[12]

There have been a few studies of the effect of *monopsony* on the prices of purchased inputs. These all find a negative relationship between degree of monopsony and the level of purchase prices, thus supporting the analysis of standard price theory.[13] None of these studies concerns industrial products.

10.   A particular complication which may affect the interpretation of the findings of the banking studies is the effect of official regulation – a point made in Greenbaum, Stuart I., 'Competition and Efficiency in the Banking System – Empirical Research and its Policy Implications', *Journal of Political Economy*, Vol. LXXV, 1967, Supplement, p. 475. Data problems affecting banking studies are considered in Alhadeff, David A., 'Monopolistic Competition and Banking Markets', in Kuenne (ed.), *Monopolistic Competition Theory*, pp. 367-73.

11.   See Edwards, Franklin R., 'The Banking Competition Controversy', *National Banking Review*, Vol. 3, 1965, pp. 1-34, for references and summary, and the details of the fifth study. One of the earlier studies, finding a positive relationship between concentration and price, was unpublished in 1965; it has since been published: Kaufman, George G., 'Bank Market Structure and Performance: The Evidence from Iowa', *Southern Economic Journal*, Vol. XXXII, 1965-66, pp. 429-39.

12.   Stigler, G.J., 'A Theory of Oligopoly', *Journal of Political Economy*, Vol. LXXII, 1964, pp. 44-61, p. 56.

13.   The banking studies, discussed in an earlier paragraph, also include

A study of the effect of number of trader-buyers on the prices paid to producers for groundnuts in Nigeria in the late 1940s was made possible by the official prescription of (minimum) producer prices: from this base line over-payments could be measured and related to number of buyers; and distance effectively broke up the national market into a number of separate sub-markets. The available statistics showed that there were no over-payments in a large region in which barriers to entry limited the number of buyers to two established firms, while there were large over-payments in many parts of the rest of the country where varying numbers of buyers operated. (In 1949-50 the average over-payment at thirty-two buying stations exceeded 5 per cent of the average prescribed price. Over-payments of the order of 20 per cent were common.) There was also evidence that the level of over-payments tended to be quite markedly associated with the number of buyers.[14]

Similar results were found by W.J. Mead in a more elaborate study of the prices paid by buyers for timber sold by the United States federal authorities. The use of the price data for the study was made possible by the seller's practice of fixing a reserve (appraisal) price for each lot sold. The effect of the number of buyers — and of other independent variables introduced in the multiple regression analysis — could be measured in terms of the ratio of the actual transaction price to the reserve price. It was found that there was a statistically significant positive relationship between the number of bidders and this

estimates of the effect of concentration on the level of interest paid to depositors. The findings follow the same pattern, *mutatis mutandis,* as that for output prices.

The exploration of the relation between concentration and level of wages has been the subject of a number of largely inconclusive studies in the United States: Lewis, H.G., *Unionism and Relative Wages in the United States,* 1963, esp. pp. 284-5; also Weiss, Leonard W., 'Concentration and Labor Earnings', *American Economic Review,* Vol. LVI, 1966, pp. 96-117. The study of the relation is complicated, *inter alia,* by differences in the degree of monopoly power of organised labour in different industries, and by the possibility that part of monopoly profits of business firms may be distributed voluntarily to employees. On the latter, see Alchian, A.A. and Kessel, R.A., 'Competition, Monopoly, and the Pursuit of Money', in *Aspects of Labor Economics,* NBER, 1960, pp. 70-81.

14.   Bauer, P.T. and Yamey, B.S., 'Competition and Prices: A Study of Groundnut Buying in Nigeria', *Economica,* Vol. XIX, 1952, pp. 31-43; reprinted in the authors' *Markets, Market Control and Marketing Reform: Selected Papers,* 1969, pp. 69-81.

ratio.[15]

Paul W. MacAvoy's study of prices paid for natural gas supplies in various gas fields in the United States is interesting both for the inventiveness shown in its theoretical underpinnings and also for the richness of its empirical work. MacAvoy develops a series of predictions as to how the presence of monopoly or competition among buyers would affect the structure of price differences among contracts differing among themselves in relevant details such as distance of reservoir from consumption centre and duration of contract. Statistical tests applied to prices in different fields and periods yield findings in broad conformity to the predictions. Where monopsony prevailed, the price-depressing effect of monopsony expressed itself not only in lower prices for the typical contract but also in a pattern of largely uniform prices for contracts with different characteristics; by contrast, where competitors were present, prices were higher, and the structure of prices reflected differences in the 'productivity' of different contracts.[16]

The studies referred to in this section generally suggest that monopoly or monopsony, indicated by a small number of firms or a high level of concentration, has the effect on prices predicted by traditional price theory. All of them suggest further, of course, that the observed differences in prices cannot be explained wholly in terms of the influence of monopoly.

III

It is a commonplace that what the economist means by 'profits' is not what the accountant measures as profits or net income. Yet enquiry into the effects of monopoly or high concentration on the level of

15.   Mead, Walter J., *Competition and Oligopsony in the Douglas Fir Lumber Industry*, 1966, ch. 11; for a summarised version, see Mead, Walter J., 'The Workability of Competition in the Lumber Industry', in Paul L. Kleinsorge (ed.), *Public Finance and Welfare: Essays in Honor of C. Ward Macy*, 1966, pp. 227-54.

For empirical evidence (simple regressions) of the positive relation between number of bidders and the 'high bid' for state gas and oil leases in Alaska and for federal leases in the Gulf of Mexico, in the 1960s, see the same author's 'The Competitive Significance of Joint Ventures', *Antitrust Bulletin*, Vol. XII, 1967, p. 844.

16.   MacAvoy, Paul W., *Price Formation in Natural Gas Fields*, 1962.

profits generally has to be based on accounting data. Moreover, differences among firms in the accounting treatment of various items of cost or revenue complicate the task of the enquirer — such differences in treatment occur notably in the depreciation of fixed assets, the valuation of inventories, and the apportionment of such outlays as are likely to include current expense as well as investment elements (e.g. expenditure on research or on sales promotion). Since he lacks the information necessary to adjust the available accounting data so that they conform to his concepts of profit and capital, by and large he is obliged to make do with what he finds and to take refuge in the belief or hope that the 'errors' are randomly distributed and not related systematically to industries according to their different levels of concentration. The enquirer can take some comfort from the fact that empirical research has not revealed any source of serious measurement error of a kind which biases the data in favour of the theory of a positive relation between rates of return and concentration and which cannot be allowed for specifically (e.g. by the exclusion of classes of firms whose reported figures are known or thought to be materially distorted).

Reliance on the assumption of randomness is also generally necessary in some measure in another connection. Price theory is largely concerned with equilibrium situations; in particular, these are the relevant situations when one is concerned with establishing whether competition among established firms in high-concentration industries or the entry (or potentiality of entry) of new firms reduces profits to the competitive norm. Firms for which accounting or similar data are available are, save accidentally, not in equilibrium situations; and at any date industries differ in the extent to which their actual situations deviate from the long-term equilibrium situations. The enquirer need not, however, rely entirely on a hoped-for random distribution of deviations from equilibrium. Where availability of data permits, a long period of 'normal' conditions may be selected for analysis, or the statistical exercise can be repeated for each of several years or periods. Alternatively or additionally, allowance can be made by incorporating in the analysis some measure or measures likely to be related to the direction and size of the deviations. The rate of growth of the industry is one such measure which has been used.

A further difficulty stems from the fact that inter-industry differences in risk might be expected to give rise, other things being equal, to inter-industry differences in the long-run rate of return on capital. No statistical study of profits and concentration has attempted to allow for the risk factor; and the difficulties involved in devising a suitable statistic are apparent. There is no reason, however, to expect that differences in the degree of risk are systematically related to the level of concentration so as to impart an upward bias to the profits of highly-concentrated industries. The creation or emergence of a market structure yielding effective market control to the established firms might seem to be one way of dealing with unusually risky situations; on the other hand, frequent and severe unforeseeable changes in supply or demand tend to weaken the group cohesiveness even of small-number groups, and so reduce the attractiveness of this method of adaptation to particularly risky conditions. Moreover, the likelihood of such changes also militates against large firm size, and hence high concentration.[17]

In spite of these and other difficulties a number of studies has been made into the relation between concentration and level of profits as a percentage of capital employed in manufacturing industries. Seven published studies, all relating to the United States economy, are considered first. They will be referred to by name of author.[18] These

17.   For a discussion of risk premiums and of attempts to measure them, see Stigler, George J., *Capital and Rates of Return in Manufacturing Industries*, 1963, pp. 62-4.

For a group of sixty-four consumer-goods industries Schwartzman developed a measure of demand uncertainty based on the markdown experience of department stores. He found that degree of uncertainty was negatively associated with average size of firm and also with concentration. Schwartzman, David 'Uncertainty and the Size of the Firm', *Economica*, Vol. XXX, 1963, pp. 287-96.

In a recent paper risk premiums are estimated in terms of the variance (and skewness) of distributions of rates of return. Fisher, I.N. and Hall, G.R., 'Risk and Corporate Rates of Return', *Quarterly Journal of Economics*, Vol. LXXXIII, 1969, pp. 79-92. Data in Stigler, *Capital and Rates of Return*, p. 70, suggest that unconcentrated industries have a more volatile pattern of rates of return than concentrated industries.

It may be noted that the estimation of risk premiums from profit variability does not allow for the possibility that high profits in oligopoly can be associated with competitive behaviour which gives rise to high variability of profit rates over time. High profits may produce profit volatility, and *vice versa*. See Caves, R.E. and Yamey, B.S., 'Risk and Corporate Rates of Return: Comment', *Quarterly Journal of Economics, Vol. LXXXV, 1971, pp. 513-7.*

studies differ in period of observation, specification of profit rate, measure of concentration, number and range of industries and fineness of industry classification, and method of approach. They have it in common that they are concerned with differences among industries (not individual firms), and the profits examined are the averages for all firms or at least several firms in each industry. Here it is convenient to group the findings according to their methods of approach, of which three can be identified: dichotimisation of industries into groups of high and low concentration, and comparison of profits between the groups; simple regression analysis; and multiple regression analysis including additional independent variables. (Some studies include more than one approach.)

For the period 1936-40 Bain found average profit rates of 12·1 per cent for the high-concentration group as against 6·9 per cent for the low-concentration group of industries, the difference being statistically significant at the 1 per cent level. For postwar periods, Mann's study shows a substantially similar picture, while that of Comanor and Wilson shows a somewhat smaller difference — all three studies make use of the

18.　The seven studies are, in chronological order of publication, as follows, the detail in parentheses referring to the number of industries and the period of the profit data studied:

(i)　Bain, Joe S. 'Relation of Profit Rate to Industry Concentration: American Manufacturing, 1936-1940', *Quarterly Journal of Economics* Vol. LXV, 1951, pp. 293-324 (42 industries; 1936-1940);

(ii)　Fuchs, Victor R. 'Integration, Concentration, and Profits in Manufacturing Industries', *Quarterly Journal of Economics,* Vol. LXXV, 1961, pp. 278-91 (38 industries; 1953-54);

(iii)　Weiss, Leonard W. 'Average Concentration Ratios and Industrial Performance', *Journal of Industrial Economics,* Vol. XI, 1963, pp. 237-54 (22 industry groups; 1949-58);

(iv)　Stigler, George J. *Capital and Rates of Return in Manufacturing Industries,* ch. 3 (99 industries; 1938-57);

(v)　Mann, H. Michael 'Seller Concentration, Barriers to Entry, and Rates of Return in Thirty Industries, 1950-1960', *Review of Economics and Statistics,* Vol. XLVIII, 1966, pp. 296-307 (30 industries; 1950-60);

(vi)　Miller, Richard A. 'Marginal Concentration Ratios and Industrial Profit Rates: Some Empirical Results of Oligopoly Behavior', *Southern Economic Journal,* Vol. XXXIV, 1967, pp. 259-67 (118 industries; 1958/ 59-1961/62);

(vii)　Comanor, William S. and Wilson, Thomas A. 'Advertising, Market Structure and Performance', *Review of Economics and Statistics,* Vol. XLIX, 1967, pp. 423-40 (41 consumer-goods industries; 1954-57).

Further studies are referred to briefly in the Addendum to this section.

same line of division between the two groups of industries. Stigler's findings are different. Although the differences in profit rates between concentrated and unconcentrated industries in the periods 1951-54 and 1955-57 were statistically significant at the 5 and 2 per cent levels, respectively, and there was some difference over the period 1947-54, 'if one adjusts the returns [in the raw data] for excess withdrawals of officers of small corporations, which are important in the unconcentrated industries, the differences almost vanish'.[19] (It should be explained that Stigler makes an adjustment, considered briefly in footnote 27, in order to allow for the unknown extent of understatement of profits of small companies resulting from the tendency of owner-managers to take part of their entrepreneurial reward in the form of inflated managerial remuneration.)

Simple regressions of profit rates on concentration, the concentration ratio being treated as a continuous variable, are reported in the Bain, Fuchs, Stigler, Comanor and Wilson and Miller studies. All the studies except Stigler's show a positive relationship between the two variables, the relationship varying in strength. (The simple correlation coefficients, where reported, are: Bain + 0·33; Fuchs, + 0·28 [the relationship is much stronger when, appropriately, some correction is made for differences in the 'regionality' of industries]; Comanor and Wilson, + 0·36.)[20] Correlation analysis applied by Stigler to his data, adjusted for excess withdrawals in small companies, conforms with his finding, noted above, of no significant relation between concentration and rates of return.[21]

Both methods of approach considered in the two preceding paragraphs suffer from the drawback that they make no allowance for factors, other than concentration, which may be expected to have some influence on inter-industry differences in profitability, and may therefore either understate or overstate the strength of the relationship

19. Stigler, *Capital and Rates of Return*, pp. 67-8.
20. Stigler was able to match sixteen of his industries with their counterparts in Bain's group of forty-two industries. Using a different profit statistic, Stigler found a statistically significant correlation coefficient of + 0.53 for 1938-40. For the period 1947-54, the coefficient did not differ significantly from zero. Stigler, *Capital and Rates of Return*, p. 68, n. 22.
21. For various subdivisions of his industries, Stigler reported that the correlation coefficient between rates of return and concentration in no case was significant at the 10 per cent level.

between concentration and profits. Multiple regression analysis attempts to repair this omission by the introduction of additional explanatory variables; and this approach is used in the Weiss, Comanor-Wilson and Miller studies.[22] The rate of growth of the industry is introduced as an additional variable in two of the studies, and in each case the regression coefficient of the growth rate is reported to be positive.[23] Various other independent variables purporting to measure the height of various barriers (or combinations of barriers) to entry are introduced in one or more of the studies.[24]

The detailed findings of the various multiple regression analyses are too complex to be presented conveniently. It must suffice to note that the concentration ratio emerges in these studies as a more or less important partial 'explanation' of differences of profitability among industries when allowance is made for the impact of other influences: in this respect the findings of the simpler kinds of analysis are not thrown into question by the findings of the more complex. Estimates of the distinctive influence of concentration or of other factors on the

22.   See also George, K.D., 'Concentration, Barriers to Entry and Rates of Return', *Review of Economics and Statistics,* Vol. L, 1968, pp. 273-5. This study extends that of Mann.

23.   Also reported in Fuchs and George.

24.   The Miller study differs from the others in that it introduces as the only other independent variables the combined market shares of such groups as the fifth to eighth biggest firms. Miller extended his own analysis in a later article, by introducing two further industry-structure variables. Concentration remains a significant explanatory variable. 'Market Structure and Industrial Performance', *Journal of Industrial Economics,* Vol. XVII, 1969, pp. 104-118.

25.   The finding of a strong positive relation between concentration and proxies for the entry barriers associated with production economies is not surprising. Nor is it complicating in the present context, because both concentration and entry barriers are generally recognised as bearing on monopoly and competition.

Comanor and Wilson report low and statistically non-significant correlations between their proxies for the product-differentiation barrier to entry (derived from expenditure on advertising) and the concentration ratio. This finding is in line with that by Telser for the three years 1947, 1954 and 1958. Telser, Lester G., 'Advertising and Competition', *Journal of Political Economy* Vol. LXXII, 1964, pp. 537-62.

The inclusion of entry barriers as independent variables raises the question of the appropriateness of the proxies chosen. The question is perhaps most acute with the so-called product-differentiation barrier, whose analytical significance, moreover, itself is the subject of dispute. This matter cannot be pursued here.

rate of return are, however, complicated by inter-relations among some of the independent variables.[25]

In summary, the findings of the seven studies, differing though they do in many respects, build up towards the conclusion that concentration and profit rates are positively related,[26] and that differences in concentration are among the factors accounting for inter-industry differences in profit rates. It is the Stigler study alone which provides no support for it.[27]

26.   The two most recent banking studies, noted in footnote 11 above, both report a positive relation between concentration and profits.

27.   Each of the seven studies naturally has its limitations, if only in its necessarily limited scope. It is not possible to pursue this matter here. In view of the divergent nature of the findings of the Stigler study, however, three comments on it are in order.

(a)   The study adjusts specifically for one source of bias tending to understate the profits of unconcentrated industries relatively to those of concentrated industries - the excess withdrawals of profits as salaries by owners in small companies. No adjustments are attempted for sources of bias tending in the opposite direction, i.e. tending to understate the profits of concentrated industries. These include the possible capitalisation of monopoly profits in accounting asset valuations either by internal accounting revaluations or when companies change hands in mergers and acquisitions. They also include the possible conversion of part of monopoly profits into costs, for example, by the 'spending' of such profits on items which are not necessary for the earning of the profits but give satisfaction to the decision-makers in the company. See, for example, Williamson, Oliver E., *The Economics of Discretionary Behavior: Managerial Objectives in a Theory of the Firm*, 1964, especially pp. 129-34, 173. These sources of understatement are relevant where the focus of interest is the price and allocational effects of business policies.

(b)   The method of adjusting the raw data for the under-statement of profits by way of excess withdrawals as officers' remuneration *may* have over-corrected. The adjustment made use of a regression of the unadjusted rate of return on the importance of small companies (expressed as the share of total industry sales receipts accounted for by companies with less than 250,000 dollars assets). Since small companies are relatively more important in the less concentrated industries (Stigler, *Capital and Rates of Return*, pp.59, 68n.2), the adjustment *may* have eliminated part of the effect of concentration itself. (Stephen Peck drew my attention to this point.)

(c)   Stigler suggests that the concentrated industries (in his sample), 'which are few in number', may 'include enough essentially competitive industries to mask the higher rates of return of the truly monopolistic industries' (p.70).

Two further cross-industry studies are noted briefly, although in them the dependent variable under examination is not the rate of profit. The chosen variable in each case might be expected to be related to the profit rate, although the relationship might not always be so close that the former variable can be taken as a reliable substitute for the latter unless some suitable adjustment can be made. The first of these two studies, by Collins and Preston, concerns thirty-two industries in food manufacturing in the United States in 1958.[28] The study explores the relationship between the price-cost margin (roughly, value added *minus* wages and salaries, repair costs, insurance and rent) expressed as a percentage of sales revenue, and concentration, with a capital-output ratio and an index of industry growth included as additional independent variables in the regression analysis. The analysis suggests the presence of a positive continuous (and in this case curvilinear) relationship between the margin and concentration.[29] The second of the two studies is a pioneering analysis of data for the United Kingdom, by Hart. The 'rates of return', measured for each industry as value added *minus* employee compensation and expressed as a percentage of capital employed (based on the fire insurance values of the assets of a sample of companies in that industry), were calculated for thirty-seven industries in 1954. Simple regression analysis shows a small positive association between concentration and rate of return, but the coefficient is not significantly different from zero. In addition to data limitations (e.g. several of the industry classifications are wide), the analysis may suffer from the absence of independent variables such as rate of growth of industry and a proxy for the relative importance of capital as a factor of production.[30]

Yet two more studies may be noted, although they are of greater interest in other contexts than the present one. These relate to analyses of differences in the profit rates among large firms, and in which the

28.   Collins, Norman R. and Preston, Lee E., 'Concentration and Price-Cost Margins in Food Manufacturing Industries', *Journal of Industrial Economics*, Vol. XIV, 1966, pp. 226-42.

29.   An analysis of concentration ratios and 'gross' profit margins (value added minus payrolls divided by value of shipments) in 137 manufacturing industries in the United States, 1958, shows 'the expected relation if one interprets concentration as measuring competition and [the margin] as reflecting the return on capital'. Telser, L.G., 'Cutthroat Competition and the Long Purse', *Journal of Law and Economics*, Vol. IX, 1966, p. 274. Telser points out that the profit margin 'reflects the effects of both capital intensity and the return on capital' (p.273).

concentration ratio appears as one of the independent variables examined. The first, by Hall and Weiss, discloses a significant positive relation between concentration and profits over a period of years in a group of over 300 of the largest companies in the United States.[31] The second study, by Kamerschen, relating to a sample of forty-seven of the 200 largest non-financial companies in the United States in 1963, shows a significant positive (simple) correlation between concentration and profit rates. This relation disappears when other variables are included in the analysis. The author draws attention to the problem of collinearity, and points out that there is a strong positive relation between concentration and a variable representing the height of barriers to entry, the latter being 'an important force in "explaining" firm profit rates'.[32] It should be noted that both studies refer to inter-firm and not to inter-industry differences in profit rates.

Addendum: Some further studies concerning the relation between rates of return on capital and concentration have been published or have come to my notice after the text of this paper had been completed. This addendum summarises and comments briefly on these studies.

In Norman R. Collins and Lee E. Preston, *Concentration and Price-Cost Margins in Manufacturing Industries,* 1968, the authors report a positive relation between profits (expressed in various ways) and concentration in respect of twenty industry-groups for the year 1958 and the period 1956-60. The industry groupings used are, however, too broad for the particular findings to be of much interest. The authors

30. Hart,P.E., 'Competition and Rate of Return on Capital in U.K. Industry', *Business Ratios,* Vol. 2, 1968, pp. 3-11.

    A second part of the study refers to (accounting) rates of return on capital in 1958-60 and 1960-63. These data were obtained for fifty dominant companies in highly concentrated trades, and compared with corresponding data for large samples of companies. Analysis suggests that there was no significant difference between the proportion of dominant companies earning profits above the sample averages and the proportion of all companies in the samples earning such profits. The 'control' samples appear to include companies, both dominant and others, in highly-concentrated industries.

31. Hall, Marshall, and Weiss, Leonard, 'Firm Size and Profitability', *Review of* Economics and Statistics, Vol. XLIX, 1967, pp. 319-31.

32. Kamerschen, David R., 'The Influence of Ownership and Control on Profit Rates', *American Economic Review,* Vol. LVIII, 1968, pp. 432-47: and 'Correction', *American Economic Review* Vol. LVIII 1968, p. 1376.

also refer to two other studies not noted in the present paper, one by Harold M. Levinson and the other by Howard J. Sherman, both of which report a positive relation between profits and concentration.

In their book Collins and Preston extend their earlier investigations (noted on p. 304) into the relation between concentration and the price-cost margin (expressed as a percentage of sales) to cover each of nine additional groups of four-digit industries for the year 1958. This part of their study reports a positive relation between the two variables except in those groups in which the possibilities of inter-industry substitution of resources and products are relatively strong. In a yet more recent study, 'Price-Cost Margins and Industry Structure', *Review of Economics and Statistics,* Vol. LI, 1969, pp. 271-86, the two authors investigate the data for 1963 on a similar basis for all four-digit industries; and they elaborate their analysis of the data for both 1958 and 1963. An interesting result is that the positive relation between concentration and the price-cost margin is markedly stronger for (primarily) consumer-goods industries than for producer-goods industries – a result which tallies with that, for profits, of Miller's study noted in footnote 24.

In Robert W. Kilpatrick, 'Stigler on the Relationship between Industry Profit Rates and Market Concentration', *Journal of Political Economy,* Vol. 76, 1968, pp. 479-88, the author makes critical comments on Stigler's adjustment procedure for the upward adjustment of the recorded profits of small companies. He also presents the results of an independent enquiry into the profits of manufacturing industries in 1950, 1956 and 1963, the problem of withdrawals of profits in the form of additional management remuneration being dealt with in two alternative ways: (i) the relative importance of small companies is introduced as an additional independent variable; (ii) small companies are excluded (as they have been in other studies such as those of Bain and Comanor and Wilson). In each case two alternative definitions of small companies are used. The multiple regression analysis – in which the rate of industry growth is an additional variable – shows that, whilst the inclusion of the 'small company' variable in its various specifications does 'reduce the estimated strength of the relationship between profit rates and concentration', the results nevertheless support the hypothesis that concentration and rates of return are positively related.

Do Monopoly and Near-Monopoly Matter?

Yale Brozen, 'Significance of Profit Data for Antitrust Policy', *Antitrust Bulletin*, Vol. XIV, 1969, pp. 119-39, refers, *en passant*, to two studies not noted in the present paper, by J.R. Felton and F.J. Kottke respectively, both of which report a positive relation between rates of return and concentration. The major part of the article is a lengthy criticism of the use of accounting data in such studies. Particular stress is placed upon the importance of an accounting practice which, it is claimed, tends to bias upwards the reported accounting rates of return of the more concentrated industries. The practice involves the treatment of certain expenditures as current costs although part of them should properly be treated as investment, that is expenditure on the acquisition of an asset subject to depreciation over time. It is said that such expenditures are relatively more important in large than in small companies, and hence in more than in less concentrated industries. However, the practice may lead either to understatement or to over-statement of rates of return, the direction and extent of the 'error' being dependent upon a complex of factors.[33] There is no *a priori* reason for supposing that, for any year or period of observation, there should be a bias of the kind asserted. Moreover, studies confined to large companies point to a positive relation between concentration and rates of return on capital. In addition to such studies referred to in the present paper, reference may be made to Stigler, 'A Theory of Oligopoly', *Journal of Political Economy*, Vol. LXXII, 1964, pp. 57-8. Finally, as is discussed in Hall and Weiss, 'Firm Size and Profitability, *Review of Economics and Statistics*, Vol. XLIX, 1967, p. 321, there are several reasons why profitable firms, and particularly large and profitable firms, might *under-state* their accounting profits; some of these matters have been noted in footnote 27.

Brozen refers to an article by Peter Asch, 'Industry Structure and Performance: Some Empirical Evidence', *Review of Social Economy*, Vol. XXV, 1967, pp. 167-82. This study refers to twenty-one manufacturing industries for the period 1951-60. Simple correlation analysis shows a positive relation between profit rate and concentration. Multiple regression analysis does not confirm the presence of such a relation. One of the additional independent variables introduced is a

33.   See Telser, Lester G., 'Theory of the Firm: Discussion', *American Economic Review* Vol LIX, 1969, Supplement, pp. 121-3 [formula (3) suffers from misprints] : and Weiss, Leonard W., 'Advertising, Profits, and Corporate Taxes', *Review of Economics and Statistics*, Vol. LI, 1969, pp. 421-30.

proxy for barriers to entry, and this is positively associated with concentration. Of the twenty-one industries, eight had both high entry barriers and high concentration, and nine had both low entry barriers and low concentration. In the first sub-group, seven had 'high' rates of return on capital; in the second, eight had 'low' rates of return.

Finally, in an elaborate and ingenious study covering the manufacturing sector of the United States in 1963, L.G. Telser has reported a statistically significant positive relation between rates of return and concentration, and an especially strong 'effect' of concentration on rates of return among industries with high levels of concentration — those with four-firm concentration ratios above 50 per cent. (L.G. Telser, 'Some Determinants of the Returns to Manufacturing Industries', Report 6935, Center for Mathematical Studies in Business and Economics, University of Chicago, 1969, mimeographed.)

The studies noted in this addendum give general support to the main conclusion of this section. A further study by Brozen, however, has discordant findings, and in my view is the only evidence so far which casts some doubt on the relation between concentration and profitability. (Yale Brozen, 'The Antitrust Task Force Deconcentration Recommendation', *Journal of Law and Economics*, Vol. XIII, 1970, pp. 279-92.) Brozen repeated for a later period in each case the experiments reported in Bain, Mann and Stigler (1964). In each case the relation was found to be much weaker than it had been in the earlier period. However, Brozen's enterprising follow-up test shares the weakness in the original studies in that no allowance is made for differences in the rate of growth of the market in the different industries; and two of the studies are based on small numbers of industries. Taken in conjunction with the findings of other studies, his particular findings should serve more as a further note of caution rather than as convincing counter-evidence.

IV

The difficulties, already alluded to, of isolating and measuring at all precisely the effects of monopoly or high concentration on the level of prices or profits might seem to rule out the possibility of expressing quantitatively the economic ill-effects of monopoly in an economy. It might be thought, moreover, that the ill-effects, being both complex and also not uniform in their incidence on different individuals in the economy, would defy useful aggregation and estimation. Nevertheless, Harberger, accepting and building upon the analytical structure of modern welfare economics, and adopting heroic simplifications so as to be able to use available data, has made an ingenious and interesting attempt to quantify the 'welfare loss' occasioned by the misallocation of resources associated with monopoly in the United States for a particular year, 1953.[34] Schwartzman, using different data and a modified approach, arrived at much the same estimate as Harberger's of the welfare loss.[35] Harberger derives the welfare loss by means of a calculation, using a simple price-theory model, based on the observed 'excess' profits of firms in industries classified as being monopolistic on the basis of having had above-average rates of profit in the period of observation. Schwartzman uses the same model; but his starting-point for the calculation is the observed difference in the price-cost ratios of concentrated and unconcentrated industries (as explained above, p.294).

Both methods of approach involve the critical assumption that unit costs (average total and average variable costs, respectively) are not affected by the degree of monopoly. This assumption, probably unavoidable when any such computation of the welfare loss is attempted, side-steps an issue which, although it tends to be by-passed also in current analytical treatment, was in the forefront of earlier discussions of the monopoly problem; and there is reason to believe that it remains relevant today. The question is whether firms which are not subject to the persistent pressure of competition from numerous established competitors follow up possibilities of reducing costs as fully as where such pressure is present, and whether the threat of take-over by more efficient firms is a sufficient alternative inducement to efficiency when the pressure of competition is weak. A similar consideration relates to the assiduity with which firms in different market structures adapt their products to the varied and varying needs of customers. Again, both methods of approach involve the assumption

34.   Harberger, A.C., 'Monopoly and Resource Allocation', *American Economic Review*, Vol. XLIV, 1954, Supplement, pp. 77-87.

35.   Schwartzman, D., 'The Burden of Monopoly', *Journal of Political Economy*, Vol LXVIII, 1960, pp. 627-30; and 'A Correction', *Journal of Political Economy*, Vol. LXIX, 1961, p. 494.

that the only welfare loss of monopoly is that which is associated with the smaller output of monopoly. The attitudes of many business and final consumers suggest that dependence on one source or a few sources of supply itself is sometimes a cause of disutility.

However, it is not the present intention to examine the appropriateness for purposes of public policy of the underlying welfare theory, or the detail of the basic data used and the simplifying estimation procedures applied. The data and procedures have been subjected to considerable detailed scrutiny,[36] and the authors themselves are careful to draw attention to possible biases and deficiencies. Present concern is with the possible inference — not drawn by Harberger or Schwartzman — that because the welfare loss is estimated to be so small, nothing much would be lost by not doing anything about monopoly.

Harberger estimated that in 1953 the welfare loss due to monopoly in the United States was $225 million. Schwartzman's estimate, following Harberger on a critical assumption, was $202·5 million. A doubling of this latter figure produces a welfare loss less than one-seventh of 1 per cent of the national income. It would clearly require a very considerable upward adjustment of the estimate, or the application of the method of estimation to a much smaller economy with a much larger monopolistic sector, to achieve a sum which would look at all striking when expressed as a percentage of national income.

But the expression of the estimated welfare loss in the form of a percentage of the national income is not helpful when one is concerned with the merits of public policy intervention. The possible achievements of most individual public policy measures at the micro-economic level are likely to be insignificant when related to so large an aggregate as the national income. It would be no less helpful, and possibly more relevant, to relate the welfare loss — noting that it refers to only one

36. See Mack, Ruth P., discussion of Harberger's paper, *American Economic Review*, Vol. XLIV, 1954, Supplement, pp. 88-92; Stigler, George J., 'The Statistics of Monopoly and Merger', *Journal of Political Economy*, Vol. LXIV, 1956, pp. 33-40; Worcester, Jr., Dean A.,*Monopoly, Big Business and Welfare in the Postwar United States*, 1967, ch. IX; and Comanor, William S. and Leibenstein, Harvey,'Allocative Efficiency, X-Efficiency and the Measurement of Welfare Losses', *Economica*, Vol. XXXVI, 1969, pp. 304-9.

aspect of the effects of monopoly and assesses it in terms of a particular theoretical construct — to the costs of the policy measures; and then the quantum of welfare loss may look more impressive. Moreover, it is conceivable that the estimated welfare loss itself may be affected by the fact that a public policy and programme concerning monopolies is in operation. Firms in highly concentrated industries, and *a fortiori* firms with dominant market positions, may moderate their price policies for fear of the sanctions they might attract. Part of the 'welfare gain' of monopoly policy may take the form of a reduction in the magnitudes from which estimates of the 'welfare loss' of monopoly are derived. It should be recognised, on the other hand, that the formulation and implementation of monopoly policy are likely to be imperfect in an imperfect world, and some welfare loss may result from ill-informed or ill-conceived activity.

Whatever view one may take of the extent of the ill-effects ascribed to conditions of monopoly and high concentration in industry at a particular time, one's attitude towards public policy measures might be influenced by the evidence of medium-run or even long-run changes in the extent of the high-concentration sectors and in the levels of concentration in a changing and growing economy; one might be prepared to play down the importance of having deliberate public policy measures which have their own costs and inefficiencies if time, change and growth all tended to work favourably and reasonably briskly. Some of the available data are therefore considered in the next section, the main emphasis being placed, as seems appropriate, on the influence on concentration of the secular growth of the market.

V

Summarising developments in the United States over several decades, Adelman remarked: 'The extent of concentration shows no tendency to grow, and it may possibly be declining. Any tendency either way, if it does exist, must be at the pace of a glacial drift'.[37] Nutter, in a study which includes a painstaking reconstruction of market structures in the United States economy in 1899, estimated that whereas in 1899 32·0

37. Adelman, M.A., 'The Measurement of Industrial Concentration', *Review of Economics and Statistics*, Vol. XXXIII, 1951; reprinted in R.B. Heflebower and G.W. Stocking (eds.), *Readings in Industrial Organization and Public Policy*, 1958, pp. 3-45, quoted at p. 44.

per cent of the manufacturing sector was 'effectively monopolistic', in 1937 the corresponding figure was 28·0 per cent [38] — an estimated decline of 4 per cent in forty years. For more recent decades, a further slight decline in the relative extent of monopoly has been reported.[39] There are no comparable estimates for the United Kingdom covering a number of decades. In the short period 1951 to 1958, for which data are available, there appears to have been an increase in the share of the high-concentration sectors of manufacturing industry: industries with (three-firm) concentration ratios of 70 per cent or more produced 5·2 per cent of industrial net output in 1951 and 14·2 per cent in 1958.[40]

Estimates of the kind referred to in the preceding paragraph are useful for giving a general sense of perspective, and for indicating whether the general 'monopoly problem' is waxing or waning. They do not, however, isolate the effect on concentration of the passage of time or of changes in the size of the market: changes in the relative importance of the various component industries, including the emergence of new industries, obscure their effect. Comparisons of the structures of the same industries in different countries give some relevant information. The scope for such comparisons is limited by international differences in census classifications which affect many industries. Here two sets of inter-country comparisons are noted: between Canada and the United States, and between Britain and the United States. Concen-

38. Nutter, G. Warren, *The Extent of Enterprise Monopoly in the United States, 1899-1939*, 1951, p. 40. The basis of classification and possible biases are discussed in detail in the book. See also Stigler, George J., *Five Lectures on Economic Problems*, 1949, lecture 5.

For a study with a different approach, but with reasonably similar findings (for the period 1901-1958), see Adelman, M.A., 'Monopoly and Competition: Comparisons in Time and Space', in Bagiotti, Tullio (ed.) *Essays in Honour of Marco Fanno*, 1966, esp. pp. 6-7.

39. On the basis of a less stringent definition of 'monopoly', Nutter estimated that in 1937 38·3 per cent of the manufacturing sector was subject to monopoly. Using the same definition, Einhorn has estimated a figure of 37·8 per cent for 1958. Einhorn, Henry A., 'Competition in American Industry, 1939-58', *Journal of Political Economy*, Vol. LXXIV, 1966, pp. 506-11. See also Rosenbluth, G., 'Measures of Concentration', in *Business Concentration and Public Policy*, NBER, 1955, pp. 79-83.

40. Corresponding figures for industries with concentration ratios above 50 per cent were 12·7 and 21·7 per cent in 1951 and 1958, respectively. Shepherd, W.G., 'Changes in British Industrial Concentration, 1951-1958', *Oxford Economic Papers*, Vol. XVIII, 1966, pp. 126-32.

tration ratios tend to be higher in Canada than in the United States with its larger markets,[41] suggesting an inverse relation between extent of market and degree of concentration. Several studies have been made comparing concentration in Britain and in the United States. The most recent of these, by Pashigian, relates to ninety-two paired industries in 1951. The average of the four-firm concentration ratios for the United States was 43 per cent as against an average of 51 or 54 per cent for Britain. Measured in terms of labour force, the average size of the group of American industries was about twice that of their British counterparts.[42] This again suggests that the extension of the market is likely to have some moderating effect on concentration, although large differences in size of market appear to be associated, in general, with quite modest differences in concentration.

The more direct approach to the question of the effect of the extension of the market on concentration is the examination of inter-temporal changes in concentration in the same industries in a particular country. Changes in census classification limit the data that can be used, a disability which is serious for the study of long-term tendencies. For the United States, Nelson was able to trace changes in concentration for 101 (out of a total of over 400 four-digit) industries for the two decades from 1935 to 1954. Change in the concentration ratio was found to be negatively related to an index of change in the size of the industry (the ratio of value added in 1954 to value added in

41. Rosenbluth, G.,*Concentration in Canadian Manufacturing Industries*, 1955, esp. pp. 70-76. See also Bain, Joe S., *International Differences in Industrial Structure*, 1966, pp. 103-6.
42. Pashigian, Peter, 'Market Concentration in the United States and Great Britain', *Journal of Law and Economics*, Vol. XI, 1968, pp. 299-319.

The two figures for the British average result from two alternative methods used to transform three-firm into four-firm concentration ratios.

Earlier studies are: Florence, P. Sargent, *The Logic of British and American Industry*, 1953; Rosenbluth, G., 'Measures of Concentration', in *Business Concentration and Price Policy*, pp. 70-77; Shepherd, W.G., 'A Comparison of Industrial Concentration in the United States and Britain', *Review of Economics and Statistics*, Vol. XLIII, 1961, pp. 70-75; Bain, J.S.,*International Differences ...*, pp. 76-81. Florence concluded that concentration was broadly the same in the two countries in 1935; Rosenbluth, that concentration was higher in Britain in that year; Shepherd, that there was a tendency towards rough similarity in the two countries, 'or somewhat higher American concentration', in 1951; and Bain that, for a sample biassed towards high-concentration industries, concentration was 'roughly the same' in the two countries in 1951.

1935, not adjusted for changes in price level). The regression equation suggests that a ten-fold increase in the value-added ratio was associated with a reduction in the four-firm concentration ratio of just over 6 per cent, and a five-fold increase with a slight increase in the ratio.[43] Analyses of data for the shorter post-war period 1947-1958 also reveal a negative, but weak, relationship between change in concentration and the extent of growth of the industry or market,[44] whilst the most recently published study of post-war changes, covering periods of varied length terminating in 1963, provides no positive support for the existence of a negative relationship.[45]

There are few studies of changes over time in the concentration ratios of the more highly-concentrated industries alone, or of industries generally recognised to be markedly oligopolistic in their business behaviour; and their conclusions are tentative. The general impression to be gained is that concentration in these industries has tended to be stable in the postwar period in the United States.[46]

The experience of the United States has to be interpreted with care

43.   Nelson, Ralph L., *Concentration in the Manufacturing Industries of the United States,* 1963, pp. 50-56.
44.   Nelson, Ralph L., 'Market Growth, Company Diversification and Product Concentration, 1947-1954', *Journal of the American Statistical Association,* Vol. 55, 1960, pp. 640-9; Shepherd, W.G. 'Trends of Concentration in American Manufacturing Industries, 1947-1958', *Review of Economics and Statistics,* Vol. XLVI, 1964, pp. 200-12; Telser, 'Cutthroat Competition and the Long Purse', *Journal of Law and Economics,* Vol. IX, 1966, p. 272, n. 13.
45.   Kamerschen, David R., 'Market Growth and Industry Concentration', *Journal of the American Statistical Association,* Vol. 63, 1968, pp. 228-41.
      Studies by the Staff of the Cabinet Committee on Price Stability, Washington, D.C., January 1969, appeared after this paper had been written. Study Paper Number 2 includes the following findings: (i) The average of the four-firm concentration ratios of 213 manufacturing industries hardly changed between 1947 and 1966 (p. 58). (ii) A multiple regression analysis of changes in four-firm concentration between 1947 and 1963. in eighty-one consumer-goods industries showed that a doubling of size of industry (measured by sales) was associated with a 3 per cent decrease in the concentration ratio. The other independent variables were the level of concentration in 1967 and the extent of product differentiation (as indicated by the ratio of advertising expenditure to sales) (pp. 63, 96).
46.   See Shepherd, W.G., 'Trends of Concentration ... 1947-1958', *Review of Economics and Statistics,* Vol. XLVI, 1964; and Kamerschen, David R., 'An Empirical Test of Oligopoly Theories', *Journal of Political Economy,* Vol. 76, 1968, pp. 615-34.

in the present context because anti-trust policy and its implementation may have had some effect, not necessarily always in the same direction, on concentration.[47] British experience is not subject to this influence, at least not until, say, 1960. Analysis of data for thirty-five industries in the years 1935 and 1951 — both years falling within abnormal periods — suggests that an increase in the size of an industry (measured in terms of employment) was not associated with a reduction in the concentration ratio.[48] Examination of the census data for the short period 1951-1958, on the other hand, points to a negative relation between change in concentration and rate of growth of the industry.[49]

The weight of the evidence considered in this section favours the view that growth of market or industry does tend to have some dampening effect on concentration ratios, but that this effect is weak. In general, although the composition of the groups of leading firms changes over time, there do not appear to be powerful obstacles preventing the average size of leading firms from growing at much the same rate as the industries in which they are leaders. There appears to be no hidden hand serving to reduce concentration levels with the passage of time and the growth of the economy.

VI

It was part of the traditional indictment of monopoly that the

47.   Before the intensification of control over mergers in 1950, anti-trust measures, by their early outlawing of inter-firm restrictive agreements, may have served to encourage some merger activity although they may have inhibited horizontal mergers by market leaders, perhaps more notably in industries which had attracted the attentions of enforcement agencies in the past. Moreover, anti-trust policy generally may have caused some large firms to deflect their energies and resources away from growth in their main industries towards establishment and subsequent expansion of capacity in other industries new to them.

        For an interesting attempt to assess the effects of anti-trust policy in the United States, see Stigler, George J., 'The Economic Effects of Antitrust Laws', *Journal of Law and Economics,* Vol. IX, 1966, pp. 225-37. See also Eis, Carl, 'The 1919-1930 Merger Movement in American Industry', *Journal of Law and Economics,* Vol. XII, 1969, pp. 267-96.

48.   Evely, Richard and Little, I.M.D., *Concentration in British Industry,* 1960, ch. XI.

49.   George, K.D., 'Changes in British Industrial Concentration 1951-1958', *Journal of Industrial Economics,* Vol. XV, 1967, pp. 200-11.

monopolist, not being subjected to the pressures of competition, was likely to be content with the established methods of production and products which gave him his monopoly profits. He was therefore not likely to be greatly interested in putting resources into research, invention, development and innovation (for brevity referred to here as 'innovative activity'). Today, however, it is often argued or implied that high levels of concentration in industry, sometimes including single-firm monopoly, are favourable for innovative activity and in this respect superior to more competitive industrial structures. This source of superiority is not comprehended in the formal analytical models of contemporary price theory, which therefore mislead.

The theory that concentration is good for innovative activity rests on a variety of bases which may be characterised in the following terms, which implicitly compare a situation of high concentration with an otherwise similar situation of low concentration. Firms in more concentrated situations have more resources, or better access to funds, to conduct expensive innovative activity: this is an aspect of higher profits. Such firms individually also are in a more secure position because competition, especially price competition, is damped down, at least in the short run: the greater security allows the firms to make risky expenditures extending over long periods such as are involved in innovative activity. But neither higher profits nor greater security in the short run leads to sluggishness and lack of enterprise inimical to innovative activity; for even where competitors are few in number, as they tend to be in highly concentrated industries, actual and potential competition constrains each of them to behave competitively so as to be able to achieve satisfactory profits and market shares in the long run. Competitive pressures, although apparently weak or muffled in the short run, do operate powerfully; and they serve to induce the firms to compete, *inter alia*, in innovative activity — more especially as price (and possibly some forms of non-price) competition in respect of established products is not likely to be available as an effective method for firms individually to increase profits or market shares. Incentives, moreover, work in the same way as do competitive pressures. The circumstance that there are relatively few firms means that each has a large share of the market to which to apply the results of innovative activity, thereby increasing the profitability of the activity and sharpening the incentive to engage in it. The same circumstance further sharpens incentive by making it possible for the innovating firm to appropriate to itself more of the fruits of its enterprise; there are fewer firms immediately available to imitate a successful innovation.[50] Finally, where the size of firms influences innovative activity favourably, because of economies of scale or in other ways, the beneficial effects of high concentration are reinforced.

Since 1960 a number of published studies, based on data for industries in the United States, have explored the statistical relationship between size of firm and/or level of concentration on the one hand, and various aspects of innovative activity on the other. These studies come up against the major difficulty of expressing, in quantitative terms, the differences in volume and intensity of innovative activity among firms or industries. A variety of indices have been used, each with its evident limitations. Some measure innovative activity in terms of inputs, such as expenditure on research and development or the labour force engaged in them. Others measure innovative activity in terms of some aspect of its results, for example, the number of patents issued. Fortunately the findings of the various studies fall into a general pattern and there is some reassuring evidence that various measures of innovative activity are closely related to one another.[51]

Before coming to concentration and innovation, the principal findings of the more numerous studies relating size of firm to innovative activity are summarised.[52] These studies differ in their coverage of industries, classification of industries, range of firm-size included, specification of the relationships tested, and aspect of innovative activity examined. Availability of data has restricted most of the studies to the larger firms. From them emerges the reasonably clear conclusion — to state it cautiously — that the industry leaders in size, with one or two exceptions (the chemicals industry being one, although not an invariable, example), perform no better in innovative activity than do other firms which, although large, are small relatively to the leaders. (In one study Comanor calculated the elasticity of innovative activity — the latter represented by the number of professional research personnel

50. The last two considerations clearly would not apply if property rights in the fruits of innovative activity were fully protected and could be marketed efficiently.
51. See Comanor, William S. and Scherer, F.M., 'Patent Statistics as a Measure of Technological Change', *Journal of Political Economy*, Vol. 77, 1969, pp. 392-8, for a study of the pharmaceutical industry.

Do Monopoly and Near-Monopoly Matter?

employed — with respect to firm size in twenty-one industry groups. In six groups the elasticity exceeded unity, but in none of these cases did it differ significantly, at the 5 per cent level, from unity. In seven groups the elasticity was below unity, with the difference statistically significant.)[53] The few studies which cover all the firms and not only the larger firms in an industry reinforce this general conclusion, and point to such industries as steel and pharmaceuticals where comparatively small firms have performed better than much larger firms. Thus the theory linking concentration and innovative activity derives no support from the studies of the relationship between size of firm and innovative activity in the United States economy. This conclusion does not, of course, dispose of the theory.

The earliest studies of the relationship between concentration and innovative activity did not attempt to allow for those large inter-

52.   Schmookler, Jacob 'Bigness, Fewness and Research', *Journal of Political Economy*, Vol. LXVII, 1959, pp. 628-32; Villard, Henry H., 'Reply' *Journal of Political Economy*, Vol. LXVII, 1959, pp. 633-5; Worley, J.S., 'Industrial Research and the New Competition', *Journal of Political Economy*, Vol. LXIX, 1961, pp. 183-6; Mansfield, Edwin, 'Size of Firm, Market Structure and Innovation', *Journal of Political Economy*, Vol. LXXI, 1963, pp. 556-76; Hamberg,D., 'Size of Firm, Oligopoly and Research: The Evidence', *Canadian Journal of Economics and Political Science*, Vol. XXX, 1964, pp. 62-75; Scherer, F.M., 'A Comment', *Canadian Journal of Economics and Political Science*, Vol. XXXI, 1965, pp. 256-66; Mansfield, Edwin, 'Industrial Research and Development Expenditures: Determinants, Prospects and Relation to Size of Firm and Inventive Output', *Journal of Political Economy*, Vol. LXXII, 1964, pp. 319-40; Comanor, William S., 'Research and Technical Change in the Pharmaceutical Industry', *Review of Economics and Statistics*, Vol. XLVII, 1965, pp. 182-90; Scherer, F.M., 'Firm Size, Market Structure, Opportunity, and the Output of Patented Inventions', *American Economic Review*, Vol. LV, 1965, pp. 1097-1125; Scherer, F.M., 'Market Structure and the Employment of Scientists and Engineers', *American Economic Review*, Vol. LVII, 1967, pp. 524-31; Comanor, William S., 'Market Structure, Product Differentiation and Industrial Research', *Quarterly Journal of Economics*, Vol. LXXXI, 1967, pp. 639-57; Grabowski, Henry G., 'The Determinants of Industrial Research and Development: A Study of the Chemical, Drug and Petroleum Industries', *Journal of Political Economy*, Vol. 76, 1968, pp. 292-307.

For a (non-statistical) discussion of a large number of inventions, see Jewkes, John et al., *The Sources of Invention*, 2nd ed., 1969
53.   The use of an alternative index of innovative activity, the number of all research and development personnel employed, gave substantially the same results. Comanor, 'Market Structure, Product Differentiation and Industrial Research', *Quarterly Journal of Economics*, Vol. LXXXI, 1967, pp. 640-5.

318

industry differences in levels of innovative activity which reflect differences in the technological opportunities to develop new processes and new products by research and development and not differences in industrial structure or typical size of firms. Two such studies reported moderate positive correlation between concentration and innovative activity.[54] Scherer, in an elaborate study published in 1965, allowed for inter-industry differences in innovative opportunity, partly directly and partly indirectly, by excluding from his sample industries with meagre innovative opportunity. His finding was that the analysis 'revealed a positive but very modest and statistically insignificant influence on patenting [the measure of innovative activity used in this study] for the market share variable [four-firm concentration ratio]'.[55] A later study by the same author, published in 1967, used a different measure of innovative activity (employment of scientists and technical engineers) and included industries with limited opportunities for technological advance. Allowing 'crudely' for inter-industry differences in innovative opportunity, a 'modest positive correlation' was found. However, 'technological vigor appears to increase with concentration mainly at relatively low levels of concentration. When the four-firm concentration ratio exceeds 50 or 55 per cent, additional market power is probably not conducive to more vigorous technological efforts and may be downright stultifying'.[56]

The most recently-published study, by Comanor, is interesting because it attempts to analyse the impact of concentration on innovative activity in different market settings. His main conclusion, for present purposes, is as follows. Concentration is not a significant factor in industries in which a main form of competition (regardless of industry structure) is differentiation in product characteristics or product design: here, both low and high-concentration industries tend to have similar levels of innovative activity. In industries where there is little scope for such differentiation, however, there is evidence of a

54. Horowitz, Ira, 'Firm Size and Research Activity', *Southern Economic Journal,* Vol. XXVIII, 1962, pp. 298-301; Hamberg, 'Size of Firm, Oligopoly and Research: The Evidence', *Canadian Journal of Economics and Political Science,* Vol. XXX, 1964.

55. Scherer, 'Firm Size, Market Structure, Opportunity, and the Output of Patented Inventions', *American Economic Review,* Vol. LV, 1965, p. 1119.

56. Scherer, 'Market Structure and the Employment of Scientists and Engineers', *American Economic Review,* Vol. LVII, 1967, p. 530.

positive correlation between concentration and innovative activity. The study does not allow for inter-industry differences in technological opportunity within the two broad categories of industries. Comanor believes that this omission may well cause the degree of correlation to be over-stated in the second category of industries. Another interesting but 'highly tentative' finding is that innovative activity tends to be relatively low, regardless of degree of concentration, both where entry into an industry is difficult because of high barriers to entry stemming from large economies of scale in production, and also where entry is easy because such barriers are absent.[57] This finding accords with the implication in Scherer's study that 'too much' competition as well as 'too little' competition may be inimical to innovative activity.

It is fair to summarise by saying that the positive relation between concentration and innovative activity is modest on a generous inter-pretation of the findings, and that there is no firm supporting evidence for it on a stricter interpretation;[58] and that any beneficent effect of concentration[59] is likely to be exhausted before high levels of concen-tration are attained.

The case for concentration would be strengthened if firms in more concentrated industries tended to adopt innovations more rapidly than firms in less concentrated industries — regardless of the origins of the innovation. Little systematic enquiry has been made into this aspect of the subject. Mansfield's work suggests, however, that although large firms tend to be quicker at adopting innovations than small firms,[60] the limited evidence suggests that innovations tend to be adopted faster in more competitive industries.[61]

57. Comanor, 'Market Structure, Product Differentiation and Industrial Research', *Quarterly Journal of Economics*, Vol. LXXXI, 1967.

58. Williamson's analysis, limited in that it pertains to three industries and two time-periods, suggests a strong *negative* relationship both between degree of con-centration and total industry innovative activity and also between the former and the innovative activity of market leaders. Williamson, Oliver E., 'Innovation and Market Structure', *Journal of Political Economy*, Vol. LXXIII, 1965, pp. 67-73.

59. It is possible that innovative activity influences concentration in some cases, i.e. that the causation does not necessarily run the other way, as is assumed in the text discussion in accordance with the theory under examination.

60. Mansfield, Edwin, 'The Speed of Response of Firms to New Techniques', *Quarterly Journal of Economics*, Vol. LXXVII, 1963, p. 310.

It may be added that there is no systematic evidence to show that independent inventors and research organisations find it preferable to work in fields where the results are applicable in more rather than in less concentrated industries. *A priori,* one would expect any bias to be in the other direction.[62]

VII

The present survey of a number of empirical studies, almost all of which relate to the United States economy, suggests that the traditional theory relating to competition and monopoly points in the right direction and concerns itself with relevant issues. From this survey of the present state of systematic enquiry — and the results of additional and more refined studies are currently being reported at a brisk rate — one may conclude that higher levels of concentration in industry tend to be associated with higher prices of products and lower prices of purchased inputs, and with higher profits; that especially high levels of concentration show the 'monopoly' effects most strongly; and that differences in concentration seem to have little bearing on industry performance as reflected in the improvement of processes and the development of new products. The studies of rates of return on capital, when combined with studies showing the relative stability of concentration over time, suggest, moreover, that even in an economy in which business firms generally are eager to extend their activities and diligent in the search for profitable opportunities, the entry of new competitors cannot be relied upon to serve as a solvent of situations of monopoly or near-monopoly; and the solvent, where present, appears to operate slowly and incompletely.[63] The fact that the studies yield different

61. Mansfield, Edwin, 'Technical Change and the Rate of Imitation', *Econometrica,* Vol. XXIX, 1961, p. 763; and 'Industrial Research and Development: Characteristics, Costs, and Diffusion of Results', *American Economic Review,* Vol. LIX, 1969, Supplement, p. 70.
62. For some discussion and references, see Yamey, B.S., 'Monopoly, Competition and the Incentive to Invent: A Comment', *Journal of Law and Economics,* Vol. XIII, 1970, pp. 253-256.
63. See also Telser, Lester G., 'Abusive Trade Practices: An Economic Analysis', *Law and Contemporary Problems,* Vol. XXX, 1965, pp. 497-8; and Stigler, *Capital and Rates of Return in Manufacturing Industries,* 1963, pp. 70-71. (This part of Stigler's statistical investigation is not affected by the adjustment made for the profits of small companies.) But see now Brozen's paper, noted on (p. 307), above.

estimates of the strength of the generally-observed positive relation between profitability and concentration is not surprising in view of the multiplicity of factors affecting rates of return and of the difficulties of measurement; this fact, moreover, is less important than the near-unanimity of the studies in pointing to the presence of the positive relation itself. (In the practical implementation of monopoly policy, moreover, account could be taken of some of the factors which are omitted in the statistical cross-industry studies and which are likely to weaken the association between concentration and profits; for example, particular cases of high concentration might be properly disregarded where there is reason to believe that the elasticity of demand for the product is relatively high or where circumstances outside the control of the firms are likely to prevent the development and maintenance of effective non-competitive practices, understandings or patterns of behaviour.)

It is more difficult to say whether the vindication of the traditional approach means that monopoly and high levels of concentration are so serious a matter that public policy intervention is imperative. An answer to this question would involve an assessment both of the costs of monopoly and also of the costs of formulating and implementing public policy measures. No good purpose can be served by attempting to answer this kind of question in general terms. Moreover, the studies surveyed in this paper are concerned with effects, at the micro-economic level only — and then not all such effects, favourable or unfavourable.[64] Some economists and other observers are concerned also with certain adverse macro-economic effects which they attribute

---

64. Two omitted 'effects' of market structure may be noted briefly. (i) The relation between concentration and stability of investment has been explored in a pioneering paper by Scherer, who reports that 'investment outlays tend to be more unstable relative to their trend values in concentrated than in atomistically structured industries, *ceteris paribus*'. Scherer, Frederic M.,'Market Structure and Stability of Investment', *American Economic Review,* Vol. LIX, 1969, Supplement, pp. 72-9. (ii) An interesting study of the presence of sub-optimal manufacturing capacity in a number of industries in the United States suggests a negative relation between the percentage of industry output supplied from sub-optimally sized plants and the concentration ratio. Weiss, Leonard W., 'The Survival Technique and the Extent of Suboptimal Capacity', *Journal of Political Economy,* Vol. LXXII, 1964, pp. 246-61. A similar finding, for the United Kingdom, is presented in Sutton,C.J.,*Optimum Size and the Survivor Technique,* D. Phil. thesis, University of Bristol, 1968, ch. VII.

to monopoly and oligopoly.[65] Nevertheless, although the survey can provide no more than a contribution to part of the answer to the question whether monopoly matters seriously, it shows at least that a general attitude of vigilance towards monopoly and high levels of concentration can be founded on something more substantial than economic dogma or a mistaken appreciation of the realities of contemporary industrial and commercial markets.

65.   The relation between concentration in industry (oligopoly), pricing decisions and inflation has been much debated in the United States. For a recent discussion, with the results of a statistical study for the period 1953-63, see Weiss, Leonard W., 'Business Pricing Policies and Inflation Reconsidered', *Journal of Political Economy,* Vol. LXXIV, 1966, pp. 177-87. Weiss found a small positive relationship between concentration and price changes for 1953-59, but no relationship for 1959-63. Findings similar to the latter are reported for 1958-65 for Belgium, the Netherlands and France, in Phlips, Louis, 'Business Pricing Policies and Inflation', *Journal of Industrial Economics,* Vol. XVII, 1969, pp. 1-14.

Indicators of Direct Controls on the United Kingdom Capital Market 1951 – 1969

R.F.G. Alford

In the United Kingdom the term monetary policy is commonly used to include two different classes of policy measures: action upon interest rates and direct controls upon the capital market. The latter controls have played a major role in the management of aggregate demand, allowing as they do some selectiveness in the categories of demand to be influenced.[1]

This selectiveness has been achieved partly through the choice of the capital market channels to be directly subjected to control (hire purchase borrowing for the purchase of cars, for example, but not mortgage borrowing for the purchase of houses) and partly through the use of qualitative restrictions on their own (as in the case of the Capital Issues Committee) or in conjunction with direct qualitative limitation on certain types of lending (as in the case of the banks). The effectiveness of such policies depends upon the imperfections of the capital market. The more imperfect is the capital market, the more difficult it is for a would-be borrower to switch his borrowing from an obstructed capital market channel to an unobstructed one. To the extent that expenditure plans depend upon the availability of borrowed funds, the more imperfect the capital market the greater will be the effect of any given capital market control measure upon expenditure.[2]

While these direct controls have been heavily used by the authorities,

1.   This article was completed in February 1970. For an earlier survey of these controls see Brewis, T.N. 'Selective credit and investment controls in the United Kingdom', *Journal of the Institute of Public Administration of Canada*, March 1962.

2.   The use of direct controls creates an awkward divergence between the short run interest of the authorities in maintaining the imperfection of the capital market in order to maintain the effectiveness of these controls, and the general long run interest of making the capital market more perfect as one means of assisting economic efficiency and growth.

very little has been done in the way of incorporating these measures into econometric models of the economy as a whole,[3] or into models of the monetary system; and what has been done in the way of econometric work on the effects of such measures upon particular markets or groups of institutions has been done almost exclusively upon the effects of hire purchase terms controls (see below). One reason for this situation is that direct controls very often do not lend themselves to expression as time series, so that seldom are they readily available for use in econometric work. But until these variables are incorporated into a variety of econometric models, we shall continue to lack any real basis upon which to assess their effectiveness as policy measures. The problems likely to arise in any work of this kind are formidable, but the dangers of ignorance in a field so closely bound up with the management of the economy are if anything even more formidable; the conclusion must be that anything that can be done to reduce the area of our ignorance is well worth doing.

This article does no more than attempt to provide some material which is necessary for work of this kind. It sets out the main direct controls that have been used in the period 1951-1969[4] with a bare minimum of background information and expresses each of them in the form of a quantitative time series (in all cases a step function of some sort). With some measures (such as hire purchase terms controls) this is no more than a matter of collecting the material. But with others it requires considerable imaginative effort to produce anything at all in quantitative form, and what has been produced may well prove to be defective in various ways. For this reason the material has been set out to make reasonably clear how the quantitative interpretations have been arrived at and to allow any user to make his own amendments fairly easily if these seem desirable for any reason. To assist this, some of the tables and parts of the text contain a mixture of quotation, paraphrase and precis of statements by the authorities or reports of these in our sources.

One further point that should be made is that only readily available published sources have been used in compiling these quantitative

3.   For a model which does incorporate one variable of this type see Stone, 'Private saving in Britain, past, present and future', *Manchester School*, May 1964.

4.   The material in this article is believed to be complete to the end of November 1969.

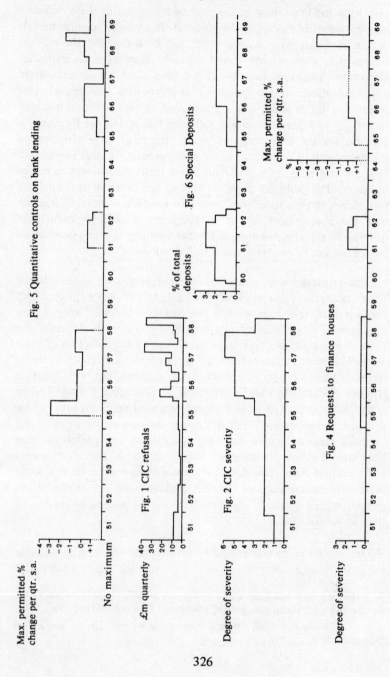

Fig. 5 Quantitative controls on bank lending

Max. permitted %
change per qtr. s.a.

No maximum

Fig. 1 CIC refusals

£m quarterly

Fig. 2 CIC severity

Degree of severity

Fig. 4 Requests to finance houses

Degree of severity

Fig. 6 Special Deposits

% of total
deposits

Max. permitted %
change per qtr. s.a.

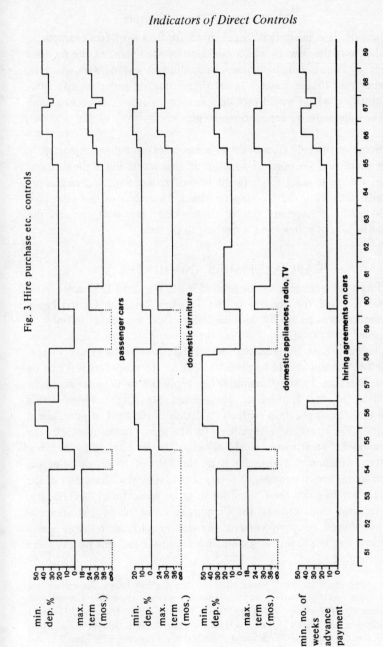

Fig. 3 Hire purchase etc. controls

passenger cars

domestic furniture

domestic appliances, radio, TV

hiring agreements on cars

min. dep. %
max. term (mos.)

min. dep. %
max. term (mos.)

min. dep. %
max. term (mos.)

min. no. of weeks advance payment

Sources: Tables 1–6. Note that all these series are plotted (some inversely) so that the higher the step function, the more restrictive the policy.

indicators. It is likely that there is room for field work (for example, in finding out the way in which banks interpreted some of the requests made to them), and in the use of unpublished material (for example, memoranda to the Capital Issues Committee) in order to gain fresh information which would provide a sounder basis for interpreting some of the statements we are concerned with.

Some of the indicators of direct controls set out below are obviously very crude and are open to criticism on that score. But if the relationships we are looking for with the help of econometric techniques are robust, then even quite poorly constructed variables of this kind may yield useful preliminary results. In any case, we must try and the material set out below gives something to try with.

CAPITAL ISSUES COMMITTEE

From the beginning of the Second World War until 1959 any capital issues required the consent of the Treasury, and the Capital Issues Committee was set up by the Chancellor of the Exchequer in order to consider individual applications for consent to make new issues (including private mortgage borrowing) and to advise the Treasury upon whether consent should be given.[5] In outline the procedure was that on first applying to the Committee an applicant to borrow would be referred to the appropriate government department which would consider the application with all its details in the light of government policy. The application, together with the report made upon it by the government department, would then go to the Capital Issues Committee, which would consider it in the light of letters of guidance, memoranda and statements of policy sent to it by the Chancellor of the Exchequer to guide the Committee in giving its advice to the Treasury. In applying these criteria, the Committee could advise that an application should be given consent, consent in part, or refused; where consent was given, this was valid for six months and this period could be extended.

5. For more detailed information on the Capital Issues Committee see Committee on the Working of the Monetary System (Radcliffe Committee), *Memoranda of Evidence*, Vol. I, pp. 103-5, 177-8 and 232, *Minutes of Evidence* particularly Q. 1191-1283 and 6087-6248, and *Report* (Cmnd. 827, 1959) particularly paras 965-977; *Midland Bank Review* February 1960, pp. 3-8; and Dow, *Management of the British Economy 1945-60*, pp. 242-6. The Committee was dissolved in November 1967.

Indicators of Direct Controls

Here we shall set out two possible indicators of the effect upon would-be borrowers of the control operated through the Capital Issues Committee. First, we have quarterly for 1954-58 figures of applications, consents and refusals. This information is cross-classified by number and value, by overseas borrowers, domestic financial borrowers, and domestic commercial and industrial and private mortgage borrowers; and by issues which provided new money to borrowers and those that did not (issues to redeem other securities, capitalisations of reserves, conversions, renewals etc). The most suitable series for our purpose appears to be the value of refusals of applications by domestic commercial and industrial and private mortgage borrowers for new money issues, as this is likely to be the best indicator of the frustration of direct expenditure on real resources through the denial of funds by the action of the Capital Issues Committee. Some proportion of this frustrated demand was in all probability made good in one way or another; the more stable this proportion, the better this indicator will be. The one obvious disadvantage is that the series does not commence until 1954, and even then the first two years provide only annual figures. Earlier figures appear to be available only on an annual basis and for all applications.[6] These have been used to estimate quarterly figures for 1951-53 for our indicator series;[7] these are shown in brackets in the table to emphasise their shortcomings (Table 1, Figure 1).

There is some case for including domestic financial new money refusals in our indicator series, on the grounds that some proportion of these would represent frustrated demand for real resources directly or at only one remove, and such a series could be estimated back to 1951 on the same basis as above. The larger and more stable this proportion, the better would be the case for including these refusals; as we have no means of judging either size or stability, we have chosen to exclude these refusals from our indicator series.

The second possible indicator of the effect of the control operated

6.   The source used here is *Midland Bank Review*, February 1960, p. 7.
7.   The method was to take the new money refusals series for 1954-58 and to calculate these refusals as a proportion of all refusals. The resulting proportion was then applied to all refusals annually for 1951-53 to get annual estimates of domestic non-financial new money refusals; division by four then gives the quarterly figures shown in Table 1. The possible sources of error are all too evident, and the very large figure for overseas issue refusals in 1957 and 1958 are rather worrying indications of the possible importance of these errors.

through the Capital Issues Committee is a series showing the severity of the criteria applied by the Committee at different periods. This is necessarily a subjective matter, and here the procedure has been to scrutinise the published information upon the criteria used by the Committee, and by interpreting this to construct a crude quantitative indicator of its severity. By no means all changes in criteria have been judged important enough to be included; those that have been taken into account are set out in the briefest possible form (Table 2, Figure 2).[8]

TABLE 1
Capital Issues Committee
Refusals of applications for new money issues by domestic commercial and industrial borrowers, private mortgages etc.

		£m			£m
1951	I	(8·1)	1955	I	2·2
	II	(8·1)		II	2·2
	III	(8·1)		III	2·2
	IV	(8·1)		IV	2·2
1952	I	(2·6)	1956	I	8·7
	II	(2·6)		II	22·1
	III	(2·6)		III	13·3
	IV	(2·6)		IV	4·2
1953	I	(0·9)	1957	I	12·5
	II	(0·9)		II	15·6
	III	(0·9)		III	11·8
	IV	(0·9)		IV	38·9
1954	I	1·5	1958	I	5·8
	II	1·5		II	8·5
	III	1·5		III	9·4
	IV	1·5		IV	37·5

Sources: 1951-53 calculated from *Midland Bank Review*, February 1960, p. 7.

1954-58 *Monthly Digest of Statistics*. (Figures for 1954 and 1955 are derived from annual data).

See Figure 1 on p. 326.

The first indicator above has the advantage of using figures (some estimated, but most actual) for refusals and so is largely based upon firm data. The second indicator, however, although necessarily subjective does allow the possibility of picking up the effect arising from would-be borrowers being deterred from even applying to the Committee in the belief that they would in any case be refused consent.[9] This effect could be a significant part of the influence of the working of the Capital Issues Committee, and so worth looking for even if it means using the imperfect indicator proposed here.

HIRE PURCHASE TERMS CONTROLS

Terms control on hire purchase contracts was first imposed by the Board of Trade in February 1952,[10] and except for the two periods July 1954 – February 1955 and October 1958 – April 1960, these controls have remained in force (although in all probability for a considerable part of the period 1961-65 they were at levels sufficiently close to the normal commercial terms to mean that they were hardly significantly restrictive). The controls set a minimum percentage downpayment and a maximum term for the main classes of goods bought on hire purchase. Econometric studies on the effect of these controls indicate that they have had significant influence upon expenditure on the goods concerned.[11]

8.   According to the Treasury (Radcliffe Committee *Minutes of Evidence Q* 1273) the severity of the Committee's criteria underwent a certain relaxation in 1953 and 1954 followed by a tightening in 1955, 1956 and 1957. The tightening is evident from the published sources, but the known relaxations (which occurred in February, July and December 1953 and August 1954, the last being included in table 4) have been judged insufficiently important for inclusion in table 2.

9.   The change in criteria in July 1955 was not made public until October 1955. However, it has been included here since most applications appear to have been made with the help of professional advisers (Radcliffe Committee *Minutes of Evidence Q*. 6194-6) and we assume that this tightening would have been evident to those concerned fairly soon after it occurred.

10.   See Radcliffe Committee *Memoranda of Evidence*, Vol. I, pp. 234-6 for the Board of Trade's account of these controls.

11.   Ball and Drake, 'The impact of credit control on consumer durable spending in the United Kingdom',1957-61, *Review of Economic Studies*. October 1963; Silberston, 'Hire purchase controls and the demand for cars', *Economic Journal*, March 1963. See also Ali, 'Hire purchase controls and the demand for cars in the post-war United Kingdom', *Journal of Economic Studies*, Winter 1965. Dow, *Management of the British Economy 1945-60*, pp. 275-282, comes to the same conclusion.

TABLE 2

Capital Issues Committee

Severity of criteria

			Estimated degree of severity	
			effect of change	*resulting level 1**
1951	4 Dec	new letter of guidance; more restrictive instructions	+1	2
1955	25 July†	postponement of projects where possible	+1	3
1956	17 Feb	recommend consent only if definite urgency	+1	4
	14 Mar	minimum requiring permission reduced to £10,000	+1	5
1957	19 Sept	CIC to be more critical	+1	6
1958	3 July	criteria eased — consent possible for anticipated needs; minimum requiring consent restored to £50,000	−3	3
1959	5 Feb	general consent under Control of Borrowing Order 1958; end of all significant domestic restrictions	−3	0

*   assumed level at 1 January 1951
†   change not made public until October 1955

Sources: Radcliffe Committee, *Memoranda of Evidence,* Vol I, pp. 103-5. *Midland Bank Review,* passim.

See Figure 2 on p.326.

The proportions in which hire purchase finance outstanding is concerned with different classes of goods can only be estimated, and what figures are available go back only to 1957.[12] Using the figures for the second quarters of 1958, 1963 and 1968 the percentage of hire purchase debt outstanding for the main classes of goods over this period appears on average to have been:

vehicles	50%
domestic furniture	21%
other durables	21%
farm, industrial and building equipment	8%
	100%

These averages conceal an apparently significant downward trend in debt outstanding for domestic furniture (perhaps as low as 15 per cent in 1968) and an upward trend in farm etc. equipment (11 per cent in 1968). Of the figure for vehicles, the only readily available guidance upon its composition relates to the very end of our period — the third quarters of 1966 and 1967 — and gives the following proportions: new cars 28 per cent; used cars 51 per cent; commercial vehicles 17 per cent.[13] The terms controls for the main classes of goods shown by this — passenger cars; domestic furniture; and domestic appliances, radio and television sets[14] — are set out in Table 3 and Figure 3. Also shown there are the controls on hiring agreements for passenger cars; these specify the minimum number of weeks rental etc. payments that have to be paid in advance.[15] The terms shown in Table 3 for hire purchase and hiring agreements for passenger cars applied also to commercial vehicles under 30 cwt until August 1963; then commercial vehicles under 30 cwt with 'C' licenses (those used by commercial operators) were exempt, others remaining subject to the terms for passenger cars.

12.   The Board of Trade very kindly made available their quarterly estimates of finance house debt by category of good and debt outstanding to durable goods shops by type of shop. These are the figures which have been used here.

13.   See *Credit,* September 1967, table on p. 93 which gives figures for new instalment credit extended, as opposed to credit outstanding. Possibly the chief effect of using this basis is to underestimate the share of commercial vehicles in the figures for outstanding credit.

14.   These do not include all domestic appliances — cookers, washers and water heaters, for example, have been subject to control, but since 29 April 1960 their terms have remained at 10 per cent and forty-eight months. Even so, the terms given in Table 3 are judged to account for the bulk of 'other durables'.

15.   For other consumer durables controls on hiring agreements began on 18 February 1956.

TABLE 3
Hire purchase terms controls and hiring agreement controls

effective date	Passenger cars* min.% dep.	Passenger cars* max. term mos.	Domestic furniture min.% dep.	Domestic furniture max. term mos.	Domestic appliances radio, T.V. min.% dep.	Domestic appliances radio, T.V. max. term mos.	Hiring agreement min. advance payment cars* weeks of rental
1 Feb. 52	$33\frac{1}{3}$%	18	no control		$33\frac{1}{3}$%	18	no control
14 Jul. 54	no control		no control		no control		no control
25 Feb. 55	15%	24	15%	24	15%	24	no control
26 Jul. 55	$33\frac{1}{3}$%	24	15%	24	$33\frac{1}{3}$%	24	no control
18 Feb. 56	50%	24	20%	24	50%	24	39 weeks†
21 Dec. 56	20%	24	20%	24	50%	24	no control
29 May 57	$33\frac{1}{3}$%	24	20%	24	50%	24	no control
16 Sept. 58	$33\frac{1}{3}$%	24	no control		$33\frac{1}{3}$%	24	no control
29 Oct. 58	no control		no control		no control		no control
29 Apr. 60	20%	24	10%	24	20%	24	13 weeks
20 Jan. 61	20%	36	10%	36	20%	36	13 weeks
5 Jun. 62	20%	36	10%	36	10%	36	13 weeks
4 Jun. 65	25%	36	10%	36	15%	36	20 weeks
28 Jul. 65	25%	30	10%	36	15%	30	20 weeks
8 Feb. 66	25%	27	15%	30	25%	24	32 weeks
21 Jul. 66	40%	24	20%	24	$33\frac{1}{3}$%	24	42 weeks
8 Jun. 67	30%	30	20%	24	$33\frac{1}{3}$%	24	32 weeks
31 Aug. 67	25%	36	15%	30	25%	30	26 weeks
20 Nov. 67	$33\frac{1}{3}$%	27	15%	30	25%	30	36 weeks
2 Nov. 68	40%	24	20%	24	$33\frac{1}{3}$%	24	42 weeks

* from 12 April 1967 relates only to cars with more than three wheels.
† came into effect on 1 October 1956, and ended on 21 December 1956. This minimum advance payment applied to hiring for a definite period of over nine months or for an indefinite period.

Sources: *Credit*, December 1968, pp. 117-18.
         Information provided by the Board of Trade.
See Figure 3 on p.327

The terms of hire purchase contracts on commercial vehicles over thirty cwt. were controlled only between 18 February 1956 and 21 December 1956, the terms being 50 per cent and twenty-four months. Terms on plant and machinery (that is, farm etc. equipment) were controlled only between 18 February 1956 and 16 September 1958; the terms were 50% and 24 months to begin with but then eased to 33⅓ per cent and twenty-four months on 29 May 1957.

REQUESTS TO FINANCE HOUSES

Besides being faced with hire purchase terms control, the finance houses have also been subject to requests aimed directly at limiting their outstanding hire purchase lending or, later, the whole of their outstanding lending. The chief changes are set out in Table 4, and fall into three phases. The first (1951-59) was one in which the Capital Issues Committee, under its guidance from the Chancellor, placed restrictions on finance house borrowing from the public by means of new issues (but did not restrict them from borrowing by taking deposits from the public). The second phase (1961-62) consisted of direct requests to the Finance Houses Association and the Industrial Bankers Association for their members to co-operate in the requests made to the banks to limit lending for personal consumption, including hire purchase. For these first two periods we can show in Table 4 only a crude indicator of the degree of severity of these restrictions. It needs to be borne in mind that we do not include here restrictions on bank borrowing by finance houses, as these were imposed not on the finance houses directly but on the banks as part of the qualitative restrictions upon their lending (see Table 7). There is a problem here in how to treat such restrictions on transactions between financial institutions so as to avoid double counting and maintain some degree of consistency.

The third phase began in May 1965[16] with an explicit quantitative request addressed by the authorities to the two associations of finance houses;[17] this request was for them to restrict to a specified ceiling the

16. In December 1964 the authorities made warning noises on bank and finance house lending similar to those in 1961-62. However, these did not amount to a request as we are using the term here.
17. 'Subsequently the Bank approached a number of leading finance houses which were not members of one of these associations drawing their attention to the Governor's letter and asking them to cooperate similarly.' *Bank of England Quarterly Bulletin*, September 1965, p. 218.

volume of their outstanding lending, excluding lending to the UK public sector and lending specifically identified with exports. There are no published figures for either of these exempt categories, but on general grounds we shall guess that both are small enough to be ignored here. Similarly we ignore the change in May 1968 which included lending specifically identified with exports in the restricted total of lending.

Two of the quantifications in Table 4 require some comment, those of May 1965 and November 1968. Each of these requires the estimation of a seasonally adjusted series of finance house lending in order to calculate the maximum permitted change over a period of only part of a year, and the method of estimation is outlined below.[18] In these cases (as in the corresponding cases for quantitative controls on bank lending, in the next section) we assume that the restriction is not merely a ceiling level to be achieved at a future specified date, but that it creates a new upper limit to lending, running from the existing level at the time it is imposed to the ceiling level at the specified future date; this upper limit is linear and is expressed as the maximum permitted change (positive or negative) per quarter, seasonally adjusted, expressed as a percentage of the level existing when the new future ceiling level was imposed. It will be seen that this could be an over-restrictive interpretation of what the authorities were asking for. Finally it will be seen that the maximum permitted changes for March 1966 and November 1967 are both 0·0 per cent in Table 4. Since finance house lending was falling from March 1966 (using the quarterly seasonally adjusted data referred to above),[19] the first ceiling became redundant a few months after this, while the second one was imposed when lending was recovering from a lower level.

18.   Here we take finance house lending which was subject to restriction as hire purchase outstanding *plus* advances and loans (source: *Financial Statistics*). This series has been seasonally adjusted using a conventional deviation from moving average method, and using data from I 1963 to III 1969.

19.   In both March and June 1966 the finance houses were above the limit requested in May 1965, see *Bank of England Quarterly Bulletin*, June 1966, p. 112, where however it is also noted that expected trends 'would help the finance houses to cut back their lending, *as they must,* to the 5% limit.' (italics added).

20.   Apart from the sources quoted in Table 5, see Dow, *Management of the British Economy 1945-60*, pp. 235-242.

TABLE 4
Requests to finance houses

			Estimated degree of severity	
			effect of change	resulting level
				0*
1954	Aug	no rigid ban on finance house issues following the end of terms control	–	0
1955	Feb	more stringent examination by CIC of applications by finance houses	+0·5	0·5
1958	July	finance house issues more acceptable if they strengthen stability of cos.	–	0·5
1959	Feb	requests withdrawn	–0·5	0
1961	July	restraints on lending for consumption/HP; HP not to rise through borrowing from public	+2·0	2·0
1962	May	modest relaxation	–0·5	1·5
	Sept	requests withdrawn	–1·5	0
			maximum permitted % change per qtr. s.a.	
1965	May	total outstanding lending at Mar 1966 to be limited to 105% of the level at end Mar 1965 (lending for exports and to public sector excluded)	+0.9%	
1966	Feb Mar	request of May 1965 to hold indefinitely (see above)		
1967	Nov	outstanding lending, seasonally adjusted , not to exceed level of end Oct 1967	0.0%	
1968	Nov	lending at end Mar 1969, s.a., not to exceed 98% of level at end Oct 1967	–3.1%	
1969	Mar	required level for end Mar 1969 assumed to remain as ceiling	0·0%	

Indicators of Direct Controls

* assumed level at 1 Jan 1951

Sources: Radcliffe Committee, *Memoranda of Evidence,* Vol. 1,
             p. 103-4.
             Midland Bank Review, passim.
             Bank of England Quarterly Bulletin, passim.
             Credit, Dec 1968, p. 118.
See Figure 4 on p.326.

QUANTITATIVE CONTROLS ON BANK LENDING

In the early 1950s bank lending had been subject to qualitative guidance or control since the beginning of the Second World War, and these measures had clearly been expected to have some quantitative effect upon particular categories of lending; but it was not until the middle of 1955 that the banks were requested to observe restrictions aimed directly at the level of their outstanding advances. The main quantitative restrictions that have been placed upon the banks from that time are set out in Table 5,[20] which interprets these restrictions in terms of the maximum percentage change per quarter, seasonally adjusted, which they permit in the level of outstanding lending; these maximum permitted rates of change are shown in Figure 5.

To express the requests in Table 5 in quantitative terms means that for the periods 1955-58 and 1961-62 we have to make precise interpretations of a number of imprecise statements by the authorities, on the assumption that the authorities had some fairly clear idea of the quantitative effect upon bank lending which they wished to see (and that the banks would have been made aware of this). How these interpretations have been arrived at is set out briefly below, so that any user can readily amend them if this should seem desirable. Amendment could, of course, involve bringing into Table 5 some policy changes (such as those of 28 April 1960 and 8 December 1964) which have been excluded here as in some way falling short of a quantitative request as we are using the term here, or excluding changes included here.

It is useful to look at the coverage of quantitative requests on bank lending under the following four headings: the types of lending; the customers concerned; the banks concerned; and any specific exemptions from the restrictions. Since one aim is to secure comparability over time for our indicator, under each of these headings we shall look at the situation in each of the three periods of restriction:- 1955-58, 1961-62 and 1965 onwards.

1 *Type of lending.* The main target of the requests in each period of restriction has been bank advances in sterling. Commercial bills (including refinanceable credits) were not included in the first period. but were mentioned at the time of the call for special deposits in April 1960 and in the request of July 1961, although in a somewhat oblique manner; the fact that they were singled out for mention seems to indicate that it is best to regard commercial bill finance as having been covered from July 1961. It was explicitly included in the request of May 1965, both commercial bill purchases (which should presumably be read as holdings) and acceptances being mentioned. Since then bill finance and advances have always been treated upon an equal footing.[21]

2 *The customers concerned.* Here it is useful to distinguish between three groups of borrowers: a) the UK public sector (which consists of local authorities and nationalised industries, which for present purposes borrow from the banks almost entirely through advances, and central government, which for all practical purposes does not borrow from the banking system through advances); b) the overseas sector; and c) the UK private sector. In 1955-58 and 1961-62 the restrictions covered bank lending to all these borrowers. From 1965, the UK public sector was excluded from the restrictions.[22]

3 *The banks concerned.* It is evident that from the beginning quantitative requests were intended to cover all banks in the United Kingdom. The first request of July 1955 covered 'the British Bankers' Association and other bodies concerned' while that of July 1956 was

21. One difficulty with the inclusion of commercial bill finance is that local authority bills and Treasury bills of the Northern Ireland government are not normally distinguished from commercial bills proper. This could cause some difficulty, particularly in the case of the discount houses, which seem quite likely to hold proportionately more of these bills than do other groups of banks.

22. However, the authorities did not leave the public sector entirely free; in May 1968 they asked the London clearing banks and the Scottish banks to ensure that their lending to local authorities, which had risen appreciably since November 1967, returned to normal levels.

Indicators of Direct Controls

TABLE 5

Quantitative controls on bank lending

			Estimated maximum permitted change (per qtr. seasonally adjusted)
1955	25 July	request for a positive and significant reduction in advances over the next few months	−3.0%
1956	18 Jan	(see text)	−0.5%
	17 Feb	continue efforts to reduce advances	
	25 July	contraction of credit to be resolutely pursued; no relaxation in present critical attitude towards applications for bank finance	−0.5%
1957	7 Feb	no relaxation meant by cut in Bank Rate	0.0%
	19 Sept	hold advances in coming 12 months to average level in last 12 months	−0.65%
1958	3 July	end of restraint on total of advances from 31 July	control ceases
1961	25 July	recent rate of rise in advances to be greatly reduced; undesirability of any continued rise in bill finance which would weaken effect of this	+0.5%
1962	31 May	limited easing of credit restriction	+1.0%
	27 Sept	request withdrawn	control ceases
1965	5 May	lending to private sector to rise by not more than 5% in 12 months to make-up date in Mar 1966, bill finance included	+1.25%
1966	1 Feb	level of advances and commercial bills not to rise above level set for Mar 1966	
	16 March	(see preceding entry)	0.0%
	12 July	present ceiling of 105% of Mar 1965 to remain till Mar 1967 at earliest	
1967	11 Apr	withdrawal of lending restrictions on clearing and Scottish banks and discount houses (a). More active use of Special Deposits in future if necessary. Present limit remains for other banks (b) till comparable arrangements agreed	+1.9%

with them.
(a) actual rate of growth +2.35%
(b) 0.0%
weighted average = +1.9%

	18 Nov	banks' latest published figures of sterling lending by advances and commercial bills to UK private and overseas sectors, with exemptions, to become new ceiling. Exemptions = +0.5%	+0.5%
1968	23 May	bank lending as above not to exceed the level of May (seasonally adjusted). No exemptions.	0.0%
	22 Nov	Restoration of some exemptions. Allowing for these, clearing and Scottish banks to reduce lending to 98% of Nov 1967 level by 19 Mar 1969. (a) Other banks and discount houses to limit lending at end Mar 1969 to 102% of level of Nov 1967. (b) (a)−1.5% (b)−4.2% weighted average = − 2.3% *less* exemptions + 0.6% = −1.7%	−1.7%
1969	19 March	(ceilings as specified in November 1968, with exemptions) exemptions = +0.6%	+0.6%
	31 May	clearing banks reminded of great importance of early compliance with request of Nov 1968; interest rate on Special Deposits to be halved from 2 June till compliance achieved.	

Sources: Radcliffe Committee, *Memoranda of Evidence,* Vol 1, pp. 28-32, 104-5.
Radcliffe Committee, *Minutes of Evidence,* p.969.
Midland Bank Review, passim.
Bank of England Quarterly Bulletin, passim.

See Figure 5 on p.326.

addressed to 'representatives of the clearing banks and the main banking associations'. Later requests tended to become more explicit in their coverage, that of July 1961, for example, covering the London clearing banks. Scottish banks and 'other banks in the United Kingdom, including the associations of the overseas and foreign banks and the Accepting Houses Committee', while that of May 1965 had a similar coverage but, on account of their commercial bill holdings, included also the London Discount Market Association, representing the discount houses.[23] As will be seen, the authorities have tended to approach the banks through their representative associations: more recently, at least, all banks which are not members of associations appear to have received direct notice of any changes in lending restrictions.

The Bank of England noted in evidence to the Radcliffe Committee that the foreign banks in London 'are certainly expected to act in accordance with official policy. The various requests made by Chancellors of the Exchequer about bank advances have on each occasion been passed to the organisations representing the foreign banks in London. In response, these organisations have on all recent occasions confirmed their readiness to cooperate with Government policy'.[24]

For our purposes it is useful to divide the British banking system into three parts: the London clearing banks and the Scottish banks; the discount houses; and all other banks. Then in the first period, the London clearing banks and the Scottish banks and the group of other banks would have been restricted, but not the discount houses which do virtually no advances business. In the second period we are taking commercial bill finance to be covered as well as advances; but while the rest of the banking system was subject to the restrictions the discount

23. The quotations in this paragraph come respectively from Radcliffe Committee, *Memoranda of Evidence*, Vol. 1, p. 28, para 89; *ibid.* p. 31 para 114; *Bank of England Quarterly Bulletin*, September, 1961, p. 6; and *ibid.* June 1965, p. 111 for the request covering the London Discount Market Association.
24. Radcliffe Committee, *Minutes of Evidence*, p. 952, Note by the Bank of England to Q. 1301 (Treasury). One's attention is caught by the use of the word 'recent'. It is perhaps worth bearing in mind that new overseas banks opening in London may ask for, and receive, some degree of exemption from restrictions to allow them to get their relatively very small sterling business on to a viable footing.

houses were not explicitly mentioned. In the third period all banks including the discount houses were taken account of in the restrictions, although different groups of banks were treated differently at times. Here we shall assume that discount houses are to be included in the restrictions in period 2, so that coverage is the same for periods 2 and 3, while differences of treatment between groups of banks are dealt with below by ad hoc adjustments.

4   *Exemptions.*   In period 3 certain classes of lending were exempt over certain sub-periods, and restrictions applied to the level of bank lending after the exclusion of these classes. The exempt classes of lending and the sub-periods were:

18 November 1967 – 22 May 1968
a)   medium term fixed rate finance for exports.
b)   medium term fixed rate finance for shipbuilding.
c)   short term export finance at Bank Rate
d)   any other lending specifically identified with export transactions.

22 November 1968 onwards
    classes a) and b) above only.

These exemptions are dealt with below by ad hoc adjustments.

This survey of the coverage of the restrictions in 1955-58, 1961-62 and 1965 onwards shows that the scope of the controls changed between periods 1 and 2 (with the inclusion of commercial bills and, we are assuming, the discount houses) and between periods 2 and 3 (with the exclusion of lending to the public sector), these changes in basis are shown by the dotted lines between the periods in Table 5.[25] This leaves in period 3 the different restrictions placed upon different groups of banks, and the exemptions, to be dealt with by ad hoc methods. The

25.   In econometric work these changes in basis could be allowed for by using two on/off variables, but they could also be dealt with by ad hoc adjustment on the basis of the following data. In 1955-58 commercial bills were some 10-12 per cent of advances + commercial bills for all banks and discount houses, compared with about 11 per cent in 1961-62 and 12 per cent rising to about 15 per cent in 1965-69. Lending to the UK public sector in 1965-69 was some 2¼-4 per cent of total bank lending on advances + commercial bills to all sectors (excluding the abnormally high levels of 3rd quarter 1967 – 1st quarter 1968) while the comparable figures for 1955-58 were an estimated 8 per cent falling to 5 per cent, and 2¼-3½ per cent in 1961-62.

aim of these methods in every case is to estimate the percentage change in total UK banking sector lending, by advances and commercial bills, outside the UK public sector, which is due either to some groups of banks being uncontrolled or to some lending categories being exempt. Then by adding this unrestricted element of growth to the maximum permitted percentage change in the restricted categories of lending,[26] to reach a maximum permitted percentage change per quarter, seasonally adjusted, in total bank lending outside the UK public sector.

We come now to the requests themselves. In the case of the first one, in July 1955, the 'positive and significant reduction' appears to have been interpreted by the banks as a cut of at least 10 per cent,[27] and here we have interpreted 'the next few months' as six months. We assume also that the request was not made on a seasonally adjusted basis, and since advances would have fallen seasonally over this six month period by perhaps 4 per cent, this means that the request was for a fall of (at least) 6 per cent seasonally adjusted over this period. This request of July 1955 therefore appears in the right hand column of Table 5 as − 3·0 per cent per quarter, seasonally adjusted.

The request of February 1956 really gives no basis at all for a quantitative interpretation. We therefore resort to an ad hoc solution, assuming that the actual rate of change in advances in the following few months was the one requested, − 0·5 per cent in Table 5. We date this back to the clearing banks' make-up date in January, which we took as roughly the terminal date for the preceding request. The request of July 1956 appears to ask for a continuation of the preceding downward trend in advances, and again appears as −0·5 per cent in Table 5. Finally we interpret the request of February 1957 as requiring no rise in advances, 0·0 per cent in Table 5. At the time of the next request in September 1957, bank advances had risen over the preceding twelve months. Using unadjusted figures from the Statistical Appendix to Vol 2 of the Radcliffe *Memoranda of Evidence,* the average level of advances for the preceding twelve months was £2076m, and the level for September 1957 £2102m. Spreading the required fall in advances

26. For a note on the method of estimating this, see the last paragraph in the section on *Requests to finance houses,* p.336.

27. See Dow, *Management of the British Economy 1945-60,* p. 239. The *Radcliffe Report* (para 422) referred to this request as 'a loose quantitative restriction'.

over the coming twelve months would therefore lead to a fall of 2·5 per cent or −0·65 per cent per quarter, seasonally adjusted. If seasonally adjusted figures are used, the required fall can be nearly double the above, but here we shall follow the result from the unadjusted figures.[28]

The first call for special deposits in April 1960 was accompanied by some warning noises from the authorities, but it was not until July 1961 that the next request was made, accompanying the third call for special deposits and the rise in Bank Rate from 5 to 7 per cent. The request gives very little ground for any quantitative interpretation. In the preceding twelve months clearing bank advances had risen by about 10 per cent and those of some other groups of banks by much more, while acceptances and commercial bills had also risen sharply. It has been assumed here that a rise of 2 per cent per annum for each of these categories would be a reasonable interpretation of a 'great reduction' on the preceding rate of increase (0·5 per cent in Table 5). On 31 May 1962 there was a release of special deposits and some limited easing of credit restrictions, interpreted here as allowing a rise in lending of 4 per cent per annum (+1·0 per cent in Table 5).

The requests of May 1965 and February 1966 (extended in July 1966) were unequivocal[29] and applied to advances, commercial bills and acceptances each taken separately. In April 1967 these restrictions were lifted from the clearing and Scottish banks and the discount houses, whose lending was expected to rise only very moderately in the coming year. In fact it rose at an actual rate of 2·35 per cent per quarter seasonally adjusted. The remaining banks continued under the preceding request which at that point permitted no rise in lending. Using sterling lending through advances and commercial bills to the UK private and overseas sectors by the two groups of banks as weights, we arrive at a weighted average of 1·9 per cent.

The request of November 1967[30] specifically exempted certain

---

28.   At the time of its announcement by the Chancellor, this request was said to be 'subject to special considerations which might arise with respect to export credits' (Bank of England *Report,* 1958). What this may have involved is not clear and has not been taken into account here.

29.   But not successful so far as commercial bills were concerned, see *Bank of England Quarterly Bulletin,* June 1966, p. 113.

categories of lending from the total which was being restricted; these categories have been set out under the section above dealing with exemptions. Here it is estimated that the actual rise in exempt lending would have led to a rise in total lending of 0.5 per cent per quarter, seasonally adjusted, in the period after this request, and since other lending was not permitted to rise at all, +0.5 per cent is the figure which appears in Table 5.[31]

The request of May 1968 allowed no exemptions and is quite clear, but the request of November 1968 did permit exemptions (although excluding two categories allowed in the request of November 1967), and treated the clearing and Scottish banks differently from the other banks. We shall assume that the discount houses were treated in the same way as these other banks. Further, the request relates to different dates in March (19th and 30th respectively) for the two groups of

30.   On this occasion and subsequently, advances and commercial bills were taken together and not separately as in 1965 and 1966, and lending through leasing facilities was also included. The banks were also asked that personal loans for the purchase of goods which were subject to HP terms control should be on terms no easier than those permitted under the control. The same points on leasing facilities and terms for personal loans were repeated in May 1968.

31.   Calculations of exempt lending under the requests of November 1967 and November 1968 are as follows:

Fixed rate lending schemes for exports and (since mid 1967) shipbuilding (£m).

	amount rediscountable	total amount	growth p.a.
March 67	114[a]	280	
			104 (37%)
March 68	156[a]	384	
			212 (55%)
June 69	264[b]	650[b]	

Sources:

a: from Bank of England *Report*, 1968, p. 22.

b: from *BEQB*, Sept. 1969, p. 239. Other figures calculated from these by simple proportion.

November 1967: we assume that the growth of lending covered in the table is the same absolutely (£104m p.a.) from November 1967 as between March 1967 and March 1968, and that other lending specifically related to exports (including short term lending at Bank Rate) grows at half this rate, £52m p.a. This gives growth in all exempt lending of £156m p.a., + 2.0 per cent p.a. on total banking sector lending in sterling outside the UK public sector, + 0.5 per cent per quarter s.a.

November 1968: only lending shown in the table was exempt. We assume that the absolute annual growth from November 1968 is the same as between March 1968 and June 1969, £212m p.a., + 2.5 per cent p.a. on total banking sector lending in sterling outside the UK public sector, + 0.6 per cent per quarter s.a.

banks. Since the first group is the larger, the 19th has been taken as the effective date for both groups. The figure of −1.7% shown for this request in Table 5 is to be treated cautiously, since it is rather sensitive to the assumptions made in calculating it. The allowance for the growth of exempt lending is taken from footnote 31, and the same figure is carried forward for the period after March 1968.

SPECIAL DEPOSITS

The special deposits scheme was announced on 3 July 1958, the role of special deposits being to enable the authorities 'to adjust the liquidity of the banking system'; special deposits would 'serve as a general control of credit, used periodically in the same way and after the same sort of consideration as Bank Rate'.[32]

In our period only the London clearing banks and the Scottish banks have been subject to calls for special deposits, and the figures for calls and releases, in percentage form, give an objective series of direct control measures taken by the authorities (Table 6, Figure 6).[33] Since special deposits are intended to have a liquidity effect, it should be noted that the feelings of the clearing banks, and of the Bank of England, about liquidity have changed over our period. An agreed minimum of liquid assets equal to 30 per cent of gross deposits had emerged from a less formalised situation before the introduction of the scheme, while in September 1963 this minimum was reduced to 28 per cent, first as a temporary measure but later as standard practice. The Scottish banks, although they have adopted an agreed definition of liquid assets and publish a liquid assets ratio for their group of banks as

32.   Radcliffe Committee, *Memoranda of Evidence*, Vol. I, p. 41 particularly paras 36, 38. Details of the scheme were given in *Bank of England Quarterly Bulletin*, December 1960, p. 18.

33.   The way in which the authorities have used special deposits makes it more suitable to plot calls/releases at the date of announcement rather than at the date(s) of payment. This is done in Figure 6.

34.   See 'Bank liquidity in the United Kingdom', *Bank of England Quarterly Bulletin*, December 1962, particularly p. 252; and *Bank of England Quarterly Bulletin*, December 1963, p. 257, June 1964, p. 91 and December 1964, p. 263. See also Wadsworth, 'Banking ratios past and present', in *Essays in Money and Banking in honour of R.S. Sayers,* particularly p. 240 ff. It is worth recalling that the 'forced funding' of November 1951 was a measure which acted upon bank liquidity in the hope of some effect upon bank lending: see *Radcliffe Report* para 406.

TABLE 6
Special deposits with the Bank of England

		London clearing banks, percentage of total deposits			
announced	date of payment	called	released	cumulative total
1960	28 April	by 15 June	1		1
	23 June	by 20 July	½		1½
		by 17 Aug	½		2
1961	25 July	by 16 Aug	½		2½
		by 20 Sept	½		3
1962	31 May	on 12 June		½	2½
		on 18 June		½	2
	27 Sept	on 8 Oct		½	1½
		on 15 Oct		½	1
	29 Nov	on 10 Dec		½	½
		on 17 Dec		½	0
1965	29 April	by 19 May	½		½
		by 16 June	½		1
1966	14 July	by 20 July	½		1½
		by 17 Aug	½		2

Calls and releases of special deposits for the Scottish banks in this period were at half the rate for the London clearing banks.

Source: Financial Statistics

See Figure 6 on p.326, where the cumulative series is plotted by date of announcement of call/release.

a whole, do not attach the same importance to these as do the London clearing banks.[34]

On 11 April 1967, when the clearing banks, Scottish banks and discount houses were released from restrictions upon their lending to the private sector, the Bank of England stated that it would 'stand ready to adjust the calls [for special deposits] more frequently than in the past to keep credit conditions continuously in line with the changing needs of the economy.',[35] implying a change in the tactical use of special deposits. In fact, as can be seen from Table 5 above, the authorities did not pursue policy along this line later in 1967, but instead resorted again to direct restrictions on bank lending.

Finally, on 31 May 1969 the Bank of England announced that from 2 June the rate of interest paid on special deposits made by the London clearing banks would be halved until these banks complied with the ceiling on bank lending imposed in November 1968.

In general, observers have not been impressed by the use of special deposits as a means of controlling bank lending;[36] and even the Bank of England felt it necessary to make clear to the banks that it wished the calls of July 1961 and April 1965 to affect bank lending,[37] thus using requests and special deposits together.

QUALITATIVE GUIDANCE ON BORROWING AND LENDING

Over the greater part of our period the authorities gave guidance to the Capital Issues Committee, the banks, and other financial institutions upon the emphasis in the pattern of lending which they regarded as desirable from the point of view of economic policy. This consisted of setting out some fairly general categories to which priority should be given and other categories for which lending should be restricted to a greater or lesser degree. An indication of the guidance given to the Capital Issues Committee and the banks is set out in Table 7. This has been compiled from readily available published sources (given in the table)[38] and notes the occasions when particular categories of lending were mentioned in statements by the authorities.

35. 'Credit restraint in 1967/68', *Bank of England Quarterly Bulletin*, June 1967, pp. 164-5. At the same time the Bank of England announced coming discussions with the banks remaining subject to restrictions from which were to emerge the Cash Deposits scheme; see *Bank of England Quarterly Bulletin*, June 1968, pp. 166-70.
36. See for example Wadsworth, *op. cit.*, p. 244 ff. and Gibson, 'Special deposits as an instrument of monetary policy', *Manchester School*, September 1964, particularly p. 256.
37. *Bank of England Quarterly Bulletin*, September 1961, p. 6 and June 1965, p. 111.

The table is certainly not exhaustive; there are likely to have been many occasions when statements of policy were reiterated in Parliament but which are not included here and which do not significantly alter the picture given in the table. But there are other known and likely omissions some of which are dealt with below.

Three phases appear in Table 7: 1951-59, 1961-62 and 1964 onwards. In the first phase the Capital Issues Committee was in operation and received guidance from the Chancellor of the Exchequer; the banks were expected to observe this guidance, but were also given further guidance related more closely to their role as chiefly short term lenders to a whole range of industrial, commercial and personal borrowers. The guidance given to the Capital Issues Committee late in 1947 still stood at the beginning of our period, but in April 1951 a new letter of guidance was issued[39] to take account of the defence programme, and this was followed in December 1951 by another letter of guidance to take account of the new monetary policy. This letter of guidance of December 1951, with the additional guidance to the banks, and as amended by later memoranda and requests, stood until the issue of a new letter of guidance to the Capital Issues Committee in July 1958, on the occasion of a general easing of credit restrictions. This guidance was withdrawn in February 1959, marking the end of the first phase.

Looking at the first phase in Table 7, the presumption is that the guidance of December 1951, as amended, continued in force until replaced by the guidance of July 1958. It would seem, however, that outdated restrictions were quite likely to be quietly eased off and that this is one source of missing entries in the table. On the other hand a deliberate omission relates to finance for investment and unit trusts. A previous ban on this was lifted in July 1953, but such finance was not

38.   The Radcliffe Committee received the texts of the published guidance given to the Capital Issues Committee since 1951, but these were not included in the volumes of *Memoranda of Evidence*. These published texts appear to have covered all the guidance given with the exception of that covering finance for private house ownership in 1956-57 (see Radcliffe Committee *Minutes of Evidence*, Q. 1193). The references to the working of the Capital Issues Committee have already been given above.

39.   It is not altogether clear how far a new letter of guidance entirely superseded preceding letters. See Radcliffe Committee, *Minutes of Evidence*, Q. 1191.

given explicit priority or disapproval; the ban was later reimposed and lifted again in July 1958, with some reservations.

In the second phase, July 1961-September 1962, the Capital Issues Committee had effectively ceased to function so far as domestic borrowing was concerned, and guidance or qualitative requests were made direct to the banks by the authorities. This was the case also in the third phase, from December 1964 onwards, and in both there was a tendency for the guidance to be reiterated or re-stated with amendments at relatively short intervals.[40]

This information on qualitative guidance could be used to construct on/off variables for the encouragement and discouragement of finance for the various forms of activity covered. Some disaggregation of our single category 'Improvement of the UK balance of payments' might be helpful here, if only to show the phases in official policy. It is not easy to see how any further quantification of these variables could be achieved.

The restrictions imposed by the authorities through their guidance to the Capital Issues Committee and the banks naturally led would-be borrowers to seek alternative and unobstructed channels through which they could borrow; and to the extent that these channels seemed likely to make possible significant avoidance of the obstructions imposed by policy, the authorities had some incentive to extend their requests to obstruct these alternative channels also. These additional requests are not included in Table 7. but are outlined below.

In the letter of guidance of December 1951, the Capital Issues Committee was given criteria by which capital expenditure was to be judged; at the same time the banks were requested in general not to lend for capital expenditure (although in any case lending of this kind above the exemption limit had to go to the Capital Issues Committee). One way around these restrictions on capital expenditure was by leaseback transactions, in which a would-be spender with capital assets in the form of property would sell it to an investor, taking a lease on

40.   One characteristic of this third phase was the increasing emphasis on the primacy of improvement in the UK balance of payments within the priority categories.

TABLE 7

Qualitative guidance on borrowing and lending

Priority Categories

		Improvement of UK Balance of Payments[2]	Improvement of Sterling Area Balance of Payments[3]	Basic Industries[3]	Defence	Assisting Government's Regional Policy	Productive Investment in Manufacturing Industry	Finance for Private House Ownership
1947		c	.	c	.	.	.	.
1951	Apr (n)	cb	.	cb	cb	.	.	.
	Dec (n)	cb	.	c	cb	.	.	.
1953	Feb	.	c	.	.	.	.	.
	Dec	.	.	.	.	.	.	.
1954	Aug	.	.	.	.	.	.	.
1955	Feb	.	.	.	.	.	.	.
1956	Feb	.	.	.	.	.	.	c
	Jul	.	.	.	.	c	.	.
1958	Jul (n)	c	c	.	.	c	.	.
1959	Feb (w)	—	—	—	—	—	—	—
1961	Jul	b	.	.	.	.	.	.
1962	May	b	.	.	.	.	.	.
	Sept (w)	—	—	—	—	—	—	—
1964	Dec	b	.	.	.	b	b	.
1965	May	b	.	.	.	b	b	.
1966	Feb	b	.	.	.	b	b	.
	Nov	b	.	.	.	.	b	b[8]
1967	Apr	b	.	.	.	b	b[6]	b[8]
	Nov	b	.	.	.	b	.	b[8]
1968	May	b	.	.	.	.	.	.
	Nov	b	.	.	.	.	.	.
1969	Jan	.	.	.	.	.	.	.

(n) : new letter of guidance
(w) : requests withdrawn

Indicators of Direct Controls

TABLE 7 (cont.)

Qualitative guidance on borrowing and lending

Disapproved Categories[1]

Property Development	Speculative Purposes	Hire Purchase	Personal Consumption/ Personal and Professional	Production of Inessential Goods[4]	Capital Expenditure			
		.	.	.	.			1947
.	b	.	.	.	.	(n)	Apr	1951
.	b	b	.	c	b	(n)	Dec	
.	.	.	.				Feb	1953
.	b	.	.				Dec	
.	.	e	.				Aug	1954
.	.	c	.				Feb	1955
.	.	.	.				Feb	1956
							Jul	
c	c	e	.	.	.	(n)	Jul	1958
—	—	—	—	—	—	(w)	Feb	1959
b	b	b	b	.	.		Jul	1961
b	b	e	e	.	.		May	1962
—	—	—	—	—	—	(w)	Sept	
b[5]	.	b	b	.			Dec	1964
b	.	b	b	.			May	1965
b	.	b	b	.			Feb	1966
.	.	.	.				Nov	
b[7]	.	.	b	.			Apr	1967
.	.	.	b[9]	.			Nov	
.	.	.	b[9]	.			May	1968
.	.	.	b[9]	.			Nov	
.	.	.	b[9]	.			Jan	1969

b : guidance direct to banks

c : guidance to CIC (covering banks also)

e : eased

for further notes and sources, see over

353

Indicators of Direct Controls

1. finance for imports has been a disapproved category on a number of occasions; this is subsumed here under the first priority category – improvement in the balance of payments.
2. chiefly assisting exports but also at various times reducing imports of primary products and manufactured goods and promoting invisible earnings.
3. from December 1951: relief of basic deficiencies (particularly raw materials), technical development of industrial production and more economical use of resources.
4. especially those for the home market and which use metals.
5. from December 1964, excludes development related to productive manufacturing investment.
6. including investment in agriculture.
7. credit for house building is included in the priority category.
8. bridging finance for housing.
9. lending for all non-priority purposes to be severely restricted.

Sources: Dow, *Management of the British Economy 1945-60*, pp 238n, 243; Radcliffe Committee, *Memoranda of Evidence*, Vol. 1, pp 103-4; Bank of England *Annual Report*, 1953; *Midland Bank Review*, passim; *Bank of England Quarterly Bulletin*, passim; Radcliffe Committee, *Minutes of Evidence*, Q. 1193, 1235.

the property at the same time. This made capital available to the seller at the cost of the rental payments, but leaving him occupying his factory or office building as before, although as a tenant instead of the owner. The potentialities of this type of transaction led the authorities in March 1956, when the exemption level for Capital Issues Committee applications was lowered, to request the insurance companies (which were buyers of real property) to examine with special care transactions of this type as, in the official view, they tended to weaken the effectiveness of the restrictions on finance for capital expenditure. The insurance companies appear to have given an undertaking to do this; they were released from this undertaking in September 1958.

In July 1961 the authorities requested that the members of the British Insurance Association should observe, in respect of their own lending, a policy similar to that of the banks. The important category in the case of the insurance companies would seem to be speculative building and property development on which, amongst other things, the banks were asked to be particularly severe. This request was reiterated in May 1962 and withdrawn in September 1962.

In December 1964 much the same thing occurred, but this time in addition to the British Insurance Association, the Building Societies Association was requested to cooperate (it being made clear that this was not intended to affect finance for the owner occupier). In May 1965 this guidance was reiterated and the request extended again, this time to include the members of the National Association of Pension Funds. The guidance was again reiterated in February 1966 and still stood at the end of our period.

Marginal Cost Pricing: Then and Now

Ralph Turvey

Some twenty years ago Lionel Robbins' seminar devoted a year to the economics of TVA and we found ourselves discussing public utility pricing. At the time there was also a good deal of theoretical discussion on the subject in the journals. After the early fifties, however, interest faded out and it is only recently that it has again become relatively popular. Looking back at the discussions we used to have, it is clear that our understanding has developed considerably since then. As my contribution to this volume, I propose to review some of the problems which we used to discuss and some more recent problems which have since arisen.

I do not propose to give a narrative of developments, surveying the literature and seeking the earliest antecedents of doctrines now current. Instead I shall simply pick out a number of problems and see where we have got to now. We probably had some of the answers then and probably already foresaw some of the new problems, but since the seminar had the great merit of generating and developing ideas corporatively it is impossible to look back and remember who said what.

The major problem which concerned us was whether marginal cost pricing was desirable and practicable in decreasing cost industries. This was linked with the problem of choosing between long-run and short-run marginal cost as the basis for pricing, since we wondered whether short-run marginal cost pricing might not avoid a loss even when long-run marginal cost was lower than long-run average cost. Even if we knew the answer to this problem in Vinerian terms we were less sure when it came to industries with peak and off-peak outputs where the jointness of capacity costs created complications.

It now looks as though one of these problems was not a very interesting one. Whether marginal cost pricing will generate a problem of financing a deficit depends on whether the revenue it generates falls short of total accounting cost. The relationship between this and marginal cost is a matter of the technical and financial history of the industry and of the movement of the general price level in past years. It is, in other words, a relationship which is historically determined and is not just a matter of a unique production function and a set of factor supply curves. To speak, as we did then, of an average long-run cost curve was to speak of the costs of alternative sizes of a non-existent industry which could be newly built with today's technology and at today's factor prices.

Abandoning the notion of average costs, as being uninteresting except, when measured by accountants, in a purely financial context, has not meant abandoning the economists' notion of marginal cost. Indeed we now see that long-run and short-run marginal cost must be equal when capacity equals demand. Thus the problem of choosing between long-run and short-run marginal cost as a basis of pricing only arises when the wisdom of hindsight shows past investment decisions to have been wrong.

The theory of peak pricing has now been cleared up. Indeed this has happened more than once! Although we were unaware of it at the time, the new French marginalist school was getting into its stride. Since then, through conferences and translations, contact has been established even though it is less extensive than it should be. Economists still tend to judge electricity pricing in France and Britain by what Boiteux wrote in 1947 and what Houthakker wrote in 1951!

An intellectual innovation of the last twenty years has been the introduction of second-best theory. No doubt we would have accepted the basic proposition (that since everything depends upon everything else what should be done here depends upon what is being done there). But it took Lipsey-Lancaster to make us feel really gloomy about it. The gloom is now lifting; mainly for four reasons, which I list in decreasing order of methodological rectitude. The first is the recognition that the pricing system can still transmit useful messages even if some of its components are behaving non-optimally, so that only the direct effects of a non—optimality upon price or a marginal cost require the latter to differ from the former. In other words, piecemeal analyses of second-best situations are respectable. Second, there is the argument that the rule 'price not less than marginal cost', though only a necessary condition, is still valid in a second-best world except only where some important complement is sold at much more than its marginal cost. Third, there is the belief of the people who actually fix prices (and cannot postpone doing so while academics confer) that it is no use telling them to take account of things that neither they nor anyone else can quantify. Finally, we have the point that one second-best solution breeds another - an old argument with the other kind of tariffs, those on imports - so that they should be avoided and price set equal to marginal cost right now.

Twenty years ago, while gloom about second-best had barely started, the alleged impossibility of saying anything without making complicated value judgements about income distribution was casting its shadow. The shadow seems to have gone, but in this case I am unsure whether it has really done so or is only being ignored. Perhaps the answer is just that we like making value judgements and so do not fret about making them.

While marginal cost pricing interested the academics, including those then in the Cabinet Office, it was foreign both to Whitehall and to public enterprises. In Whitehall there has been a very great change, culminating in the recent report of the Select Committee on Nationalised Industries with its firm advocacy of marginal cost pricing and its criticisms of the primacy of financial targets. The nationalised industries too are beginning to get the message and the electricity industry at least has got used to economists. In some cases they have been urged in a marginal cost direction by the Prices and Incomes Board where we clearly said that we approved of marginal cost pricing.

These developments have brought two intellectual problems to the fore: the measurement of marginal cost and the detailed choice of pricing structure. Both of these only arose once attention centred on the application of the principles to particular industries and both are proving far more difficult and interesting than we used to think.

Having tried to set out recent developments in the marginal cost concept in a paper for the *Economic Journal*, I will not describe them here. But it is worth noting that the interesting problems were all assumed away in postulating given long-run cost curves which embodied an enterprise's knowledge of optimal production solutions. Where inter-connected systems are involved, as they often are, marginal costs should emerge as the by-product of overall optimisation in investment planning. Unless this has already been done with the aid of an explicit system model, anyone wishing to estimate marginal cost must construct such a model and thus involve himself in system planning. Fortunately mathematical programming has not merely proved a valuable tool for this; it has also provided the economist and the engineer with a common language. This turns out to be essential, since no economist could hope to sort out the complexities of, say, the railway system except as a member of an inter-disciplinary team.

The reason why the detailed choice of pricing structure is more interesting and complex than we used to imagine is basically that an ideal tariff would be impossibly complicated. A complete account of the cost structure of, say, the gas industry would involve hundreds of deriv-atives. There are therefore hundreds of conceivable alternative simple tariffs which would logically provide equally approximate simplified representations of the cost structure. Those of them which are practic-able will differ in their costs and in their effects thus setting an inter-esting problem of choice. One simple example of this arises where costs are found to be separable and additive functions of time and distance but where, for technical reasons, charges have to be related to time *or* distance. In principle the answer is to be found by maximising the sum of consumer and producer surplus net of the cost of charging. This requires knowledge about demand structure as much as about cost structures, which is unfortunate since even when data are available, which they often are not, econometrists can rarely construct reliable estimates of the relevant demand elasticities. The choice of tariff there-fore involves an element of judgement.

I suggested above that the problem of financing a deficit arises in relation to accounting costs. This does not mean abandoning Professor Coase's argument in favour of multi-part pricing as a means of covering total escapable costs while yet retaining equality between marginal price and marginal cost. This argument is more generally accepted than it was; we are now more used to looking at total conditions as well as marginal conditions. The point is simply that we should have distin-guished the two issues and recognised the significance of Professor Lewis's distinction between accounting costs and escapable costs in this context.

Many other topics were discussed in Lionel Robbins' seminar. I have mentioned only some of them in order to recall and thank him for the benevolent stimulus which he gave us all.

Public Utility Pricing:
The Case of North Sea Gas

Maurice Peston

Surely much more probable than the decentralised semi-atomistic production units, guided solely by prices and costs ... is the organisation of industries in giant corporations, exhibiting in an even heightened degree the rigidities of monopoly capitalism and little of its tendency, occasionally to yield to outside pressure ... You may say that one should not worry overmuch about nice adjustments of prices and marginal costs. I should not dissent from this view — though it is sometimes expressed in very unexpected quarters. The important thing is not that at every moment we should be in an exact state of ideal distribution of resources, but that in a broad way there should be no obstacles causing gross divergences and that our organisation should be such as to afford the maximum scope for continual progress by way of cost reduction and innovation. Lionel Robbins *The Economic Problem in Peace and War* pp. 78-79.

With the discovery of North Sea Gas it happens that some of the existing plant owned by the Gas Industry is rendered obsolete. By this is meant that it is cheaper for the industry to incur the extra capital cost of replacing this plant by new plant rather than carrying on running it. Now, it can also happen that this replacement of existing plant can occur before it has been written off in an accounting sense. Since the criterion for replacement is that the discounted present value of costs is less with the new plant than with the old, revenues less costs will be greater when replacement takes place than before. If existing prices and outputs are maintained, this means that the unwritten off part of the old assets can still be met and a higher profit still earned. If, however, prices and outputs are changed it is possible that profits do not increase, and there is no extra fund to write off the obsolete plant with.

This can be seen easily as follows. Let K_1 be the initial capital cost per unit and R_1 be the initial running cost per unit. Average cost per unit will be $C_1 = K_1 + R_1$ (We arrive at R_1 by considering the total capital stock required to produce a given rate of output, and converting it to an annual charge, given a rate of interest and a fixed life for the machine). Assume we are dealing with a constant average cost (equal to marginal cost, of course). In perfectly competitive conditions price, P_1, will equal C_1.

Let some technological change occur so that the average cost per unit of output becomes $C_2 = K_2 + R_2$. (We again assume constant average costs.) Assume that

$$C_2 < R_1$$
i.e. $$0 < R_1 - R_2 - K_2.$$

In this case it will pay to replace the old asset with the new. Also, since $P_1 = C_1 = R_1 + K_1$,

$$P_1 > C_2$$
$$P_1 - C_2 = K_1 + R_1 - K_2 - R_2$$
$$\therefore \quad P_1 - C_2 - K_1 > 0,$$

i.e. the extra profit earned having met the costs of the new technology is at least enough to meet the capital charge on the old equipment.

But we have assumed that the industry is perfectly competitive. Suppose the technological breakthrough is available to any firm in the economy. Price will now settle down to a new level equal to the new marginal cost. There will be no surplus to meet the capital charges on the old assets. Suppose the technological breakthrough is available only to the existing firms. If they act independently, it will pay each one to cut price and expand; then again the new equilibrium will again be at the new level of marginal cost. It is only if the firms collude and are able to restrict entry that they are able to recover the unwritten off part of the old capital equipment. We have the seeming paradox, therefore, that technological advance may be to the detriment of existing firms even though they are the firms that carry out the innovation and find it profitable to do so according to the usual decision criterion.

It is apparent that the marginal cost pricing rule will achieve the same result in a nationalised industry which for this purpose may be interpreted as behaving like a perfectly competitive industry. (Strictly speaking, this is to put the matter the wrong way round.) It is the marginal cost pricing rule which is paramount and derived from the desire to maximise welfare. (The market forms or industrial behaviour which achieve this end are then derived one further stage on. so to speak.) In other words, a nationalised industry may discover that the opportunity costs of new plant are less than those of existing plant, but yet when it sets output by putting price equal to marginal cost it does not receive a sufficient revenue to meet the capital charges on the old plant.

Let us now turn aside and consider how the Ministry of Power and the Gas Council interpret this problem of obsolescence. Ample material is contained in the Second Report from the Select Committee on Nationalised Industries, *Exploitation of North Sea Gas*. (H/C. 372. 1967-68). The following quotations are of interest:

> Part of the price for a rapidly changing technology is a legacy of plant which has not been fully amortised. This liability, which will vary according to the rapidity of absorption of natural gas, will be spread over a period of years; a rough estimate of the total amount is £300 million. p. 28.

Gas Council Memorandum

> ... in working out long-run marginal costs there would be no place for obsolescence; it would not be a cost that one would take into account at all; one would work out the cost in a different way, without taking into account any obsolescence of plant which was not concerned with the supply of gas we are talking about. I think I ought to have said that we regard obsolescence as something that has to be provided for in one way or another, unless of course the money is written out at no charge to us. I am not suggesting that that is likely to happen. But if it does not happen, we would provide for obsolescence out of our general revenues or surplus which we will be expected to earn out of our trading. p. 162

Gas Council Oral Evidence

Mr Mikardo   Suppose the Gas Council had not had a monopoly. Other people could have bought North Sea gas and distributed it; they could have started new companies for the purpose. They would not have been saddled with the cost of obsolete gas equipment. They would have been able to sell it at a price which took no account of writing off the cost of obsolete gas equipment. They could have put the Gas Council out of existence, could they not?

Ministry of Power witness   Yes.

Mr Mikardo   Why should the monopoly position of the Gas Council and the fact that they apparently did not do sufficient to anticipate the technical revolution put the gas consumer on a worse footing in respect of the prices he has to pay for North Sea gas than would be the case in a competitive situation?

Ministry of
Power witness

I think the answer to that is that a great deal of the investment of the gas industry – most of it in fact – has been financed either from its own earnings but more particularly from Exchequer borrowing. The question arises whether an industry with excellent prospects, as this is, should be entitled to a write-off of capital at the public expense. This is the way in which the industry is organised; it is not in the private sector.

Mr Mikardo

It is not open to it to create and set up separate companies to distribute North Sea gas; this has to be handled by the Gas Council, which has access to public capital. p. 176.

From an economic point of view the premature scrapping of plant does not give rise to any cost; although the cost has not been fully written off in the accounts the plant has, in fact, already been paid for. To delay the introduction of natural gas merely in order to utilise existing plant, however efficient, would not make economic sense. So far from producing any benefit such a policy would in fact cause a loss the measure of which would be the extra cost of production over the total cost of a similar quality of natural gas; or, put another way, the savings which are foregone as a result of the delay. p. 201.

Gas Council Memorandum

It is not unreasonable to say on the basis of this evidence that a certain amount of confusion reigns. In particular, both the Ministry of Power and the Gas Council seem to have some idea of the economic arguments, but do not like their financial consequences. As a result they appear to be trying to hold two contradicting positions simultaneously.

To return to the analysis it is easy to show that the difficulty under discussion can arise even in circumstances of increasing marginal and average costs.

In figure 1 ATC_O is the initial average total cost curve and A_O is the average running cost curve. The initial equilibrium is at an output of X_O with price P_O. The new average total cost curve is ATC_1. At an output X_O this lies below A_O, the average running cost. This means that the existing assets can be replaced and a greater profit earned. If, however, the existing assets are replaced, the new price would be P_1 at which the new marginal cost curve M_1 intersects the demand curve. The new

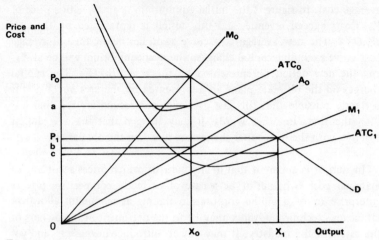

Figure 1

output will be X_1. The profit, having met all capital charges in the new situation, is represented by the area $P_1 cOX_1$. The capital charges on the obsolete assets are represented by the area $abOX_O$. It is entirely possible that the latter is larger than the former.

It is indeed worth noting that it is also possible that the reverse situation comes about in conditions of diminishing marginal and

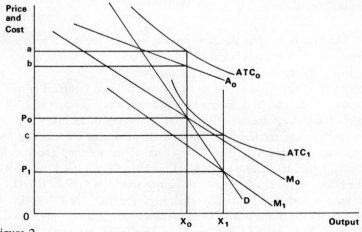

Figure 2

365

average cost. In figure 2 the initial equilibrium is at X_O with a price of P_O. Costs exceed revenue, and this deficit is represented by the area aP_OOX_O. The new average cost curve again lies below the old average cost curve excluding capital charges. The new equilibrium will be at X_1, and the new deficit is represented by the area CP_1OX_1. The capital charges on the obsolete plant are represented by the area $abOX_O$. It is perfectly possible that this last area plus the second are together less than the first. In other words, it may happen that the new deficit together with the old capital charges are less than the old deficit.

In sum, it is apparent that in any industry which prices according to marginal cost (whether it be a case of perfectly competitive private enterprise or of a public corporation trading at maximum allocative efficiency) technical advance may be to the detriment of the owners of the assets of the industry. It may pay to introduce new assets, and yet on grounds of allocative efficiency a level of output and a price may be set which fails to meet the capital charges on existing assets. In the case of perfect competition, it is the competition which leads to this end. In the case of the public corporation it is the application of the decision criteria recommended to them which has the same effect.

Having got to this point it may be thought best to leave the matter as it stands. It is tempting, however, to go further and look for an explanation or interpretation of the analysis which puts it into a perspective which makes it appear less of a puzzle. There are three possibilities worth pursuing.

The first is to view the new process which leads to the premature replacement of existing plant as equivalent to the emergence of a new industry. In the case of natural gas compared with gas produced from coal and oil this appears not at all unreasonable on technical grounds. In the case of a perfectly competitive industry a new product which is a perfect substitute for an existing one by reason of its lower costs of production has rendered the method of producing the existing one obsolete. The result is that the owners of the existing assets make capital losses. In the case of the Gas Council, although it is a monopoly, the effect of the marginal cost pricing role would be to make it act as if it were a perfectly competitive industry. The fact, therefore, that it owns both the obsolete assets and the new assets, and controls both the declining industry and the emerging one is an incidental without economic significance. The puzzle only arises because attention is paid to the form of the industry, i.e. that it is a monopoly. The point of the marginal cost pricing rule, however, is to take no notice of this monopoly which may exist for economic reasons connected with returns to scale and the optimisation of large systems or for political reasons, but not in order to earn monopoly profits.

This leads on to the second point which is that there is an income distribution effect involved. The consequence of the innovation of natural gas is a benefit to consumers of natural gas. At the same time there will be a loss to tax-payers in general. This loss is not directly connected with the original investment in real capital which is a bygone. It is that the interest and repayment of the original capital has still to take place, and must come from the general tax-payer if not from the consumer. Alternatively, if the original investment were to be interpreted as tax financed the excess of returns over costs would be available to finance future investment or other public expenditure (directly or indirectly), thus again relieving the taxpayer of a burden. Now, it seems to me that this argument does not carry a great deal of weight. In the first place, it is surely not unreasonable to argue that the general taxpayer as owner of a nationalised industry must be ready to bear capital losses as they occur. This, after all, is one of the implications of ownership. Secondly, if he wishes to exert his monopoly power to avoid such capital losses, why exert it only in such situations and not all of the time? It is possible to redistribute income away from the consumer of any nationalised industry towards the general taxpayer by using the monopoly power of that industry. It may be that the nationalised industries are especially suitable as tax raising devices and should be used for that purpose, but there is no rationale for introducing such considerations simply to deal with the financial consequences of a particular technological advance. (While I am on this point it may be that on second best grounds the nationalised industries should be used for revenue purposes both as an alternative to other forms of taxation and to take account of sub-optimalities elsewhere in the economy. It would then follow that the optimum allocative role would be to place price above marginal cost while still relating it to marginal cost. Such a pricing policy would not affect the argument of this paper.)

The third point is to note that the whole of the preceding discussion has ignored uncertainty, but must, nonetheless, have made some implicit assumptions about uncertainty. In a world of complete certainty the technological change which has been analysed would have been anticipated and account taken of it in earlier investment decisions. The emergence of a new technology at time *t* would have influenced the investment decision at time *t-θ*, and capital charges and prices would have been modified accordingly. There would then have been no unwritten off assets and no special financial problem at the time of the innovation. It must be, therefore, that the technological change was not anticipated. If this were the case it follows that some allowance for risk and uncertainty ought to have been made in the original investment decision. It could indeed well be that some of the surplus earned by the gas industry in earlier years although not used to write off these assets in an accounting sense is properly attributable to them for risk and uncertainty. (Equally, in a perfectly or quasi-perfectly competitive industry with risk and uncertainty price will include some return to the owners of firms and capital as the bearers of risk and uncertainty.) In addition, it is no longer apparent why the consumers of a particular industry should bear the whole of this particular cost solely because in the nature of things the future is known only imperfectly. This is a matter of swings and roundabouts. If obsolescence or any other untoward event occurs very early in the lives of particular capital assets, consumers will contribute very little to their costs, but if they occur very late, consumers will pay much more than their costs, assuming, of course, that proper allowance is made for risk.

My conclusion, therefore, is that the phenomenon under consideration is merely a curiosum, and certainly does not provide grounds for abandoning the rule of marginal cost pricing assuming that that (suitably modified for other reasons) is the correct pricing rule for nationalised industries. The worries of the Gas Council and of the Ministry of Power arise from a misunderstanding of the economics of the matter, and of a misplaced emphasis on financial criteria. It may well be that they do not care for allocative efficiency, anyway, but if that is so, they would do well to provide a consistent alternative policy rather than proceed against allocative efficiency on various occasions when they dislike its financial consequences.

Price Theory and Petrol Prices

Harry Townsend

Twenty years ago Lord Robbins resumed the main Economic Principles course at LSE. We sat at his feet, impressed by his erudition and devotion to economics, wondering whether what he had to say was of any use whatever. This is a belated apology for such undergraduate scepticism.

There was no difficulty in recognising the purpose of monetary theory, national income theory or the theory of international trade. Great issues of state hung upon the forces we analysed. The trouble lay with the core of economic theory, with price theory, that elegant logical structure carefully constructed by generations of scholars.

The assertion that Marshall's notions of elasticity were a great contribution to knowledge, that they pervaded the analysis of almost any economic problem sounded splendid enough. Yet did the responsiveness of quantity demanded to price matter very much?

One could see that if Commodity A were produced alone for a cost of £7 and Commodity B produced alone for £6, but that they could be produced together for £10, A and B would be produced together. One could further see that the difference made by not producing B of the combination would be £3, and the cost saving of not producing A would be £4, so that £3 of the total cost could be attributed to B and £4 to A. There would remain a joint cost of £3 that could not be allocated to either commodity separately. This knowledge gave one a feeling of superiority over the more conventional type of accountant who persisted in allocating the unallocable, but did it have further use?

We seemed to be getting nearer to the world in which we thought we lived when we were introduced to oligopoly, perhaps because here it seemed anything might happen. It was easy to see that competition could easily get out of hand if only a small number of rivals was

369

involved. Decisions would be interdependent with the wisest thing one competitor could do depending upon what he thought his rival would do, who in turn would decide on the basis of what he thought the first competitor would do in the light of the first competitor's expectations of what he would do, and so on in an infinite regress. There would be search for strategies to which rivals could not react with identical countermoves: competition might be in quality of product, methods of production or ingenuity of advertising. Price competition might be avoided because one price cut could be matched by another in a downward spiral. Alternatively rigid prices might be explained by each competitor thinking in terms of a kinked demand curve. If each expected price-cuts to be matched and thus to be associated with only pro-rata increases of shares in total market sales, whilst price increases were not copied so that rivals could gain increased market shares, there would be a kink in individual demand curves at the going price, a discontinuity in marginal receipts curves at the same price, and the possibility of changes in costs which resulted in no changes in prices or outputs.

In this paper we use the concepts of price and income elasticity of demand, joint costs and oligopolistic competition in an explanation of two features of petrol distribution, the retail price of petrol and the prices of filling stations in the property market. These prices are of special interest because of the system of exclusive dealing in petrol retailing, the 'solus system'.

The solus system and pricing problems
Petrol is usually distributed through outlets which sell only one brand of petrol. 80 per cent of retail outlets belong to independent property-owners, owner-dealers or multiple garages. The dealers operating these outlets almost all restrict their sales to one brand in return for an exclusive dealing rebate and often for additional financial assistance from oil companies such as loans on favourable terms. The remaining 20 per cent of outlets are owned by oil companies and operated by tenants: the leases restrict the tenants to the landlord's brand of petrol. There are about 37,000 petrol stations in the UK, 30,500 independently owned and operated as solus stations, 5500 owned by oil companies, and 1500 multi-brand outlets.

Solus trading began in Britain in 1951 when petrol brands were re-introduced in place of the war-time pool petrol. Esso began tying stations and the other oil companies quickly followed suit. At first there were simply gentlemen's agreements of a year's duration arranging exclusive supplies in return for an additional rebate of ½d. per gallon and small loans to repaint filling stations. As the oil companies vied with one another for outlets, formal contracts were drawn up offering larger and larger rebates and loans in order to attach dealers to particular suppliers for periods of increasing length. It is doubtful whether the courts would now enforce exclusive contracts of more than three years' duration; but as the solus system was built up oil companies made contracts of up to twenty years. They also bought filling stations outright. Before 1951 they had not owned any retail outlets.

In 1960, the supply of petrol to retailers was referred to the Monopolies Commission for investigation. It would not be surprising if the Monopolies Commission asked oil companies a question something like 'does solus trading result in the public paying a higher price for petrol than they would otherwise have to pay?' They may also have asked 'does competition to acquire company-owned sites result in inflation of site values?'

How does one answer such questions? A layman would possibly reply that of course solus trading must lead to motorists paying higher prices for petrol: oil companies would not make such arrangements if there were not something in it for themselves rather than their customers. He would also probably reply that oil companies would bid up the price of filling-station sites. If Shell-Mex and BP compete against Joe Bloggs, what else could happen? A tyro-economist might answer that exclusive dealing restricts entry to a market and restricted entry leads to higher prices. He might argue that oil companies are oligopolists and if they bid against one another for sites this may easily generate an inflation of property values. These answers may seem fair. They have one thing in common: they have been made without any appeal to the facts. Theory has not guided factual analysis, it has replaced it. Let us see what happens when we attempt to use price theory to sort out the facts.

Does solus trading result in a higher price for petrol?
We may begin by examining the demand for petrol, market structures

371

and costs of supply. This leads to an examination of competition at the wholesale and retail levels.

Market demand Petrol is sold branded, in three main qualities described by different superlatives by different companies, and according to a British Standards classification which allows petrols with different performance characteristics to be sold as falling within the same class. There are some real and fancied differences between brands of petrol of about 90 octane (two-star, standard petrol), 97-99 octane (four-star, premium petrol) and 100-plus octane (five-star, super petrol); but competition in quality ensures that petrols in each class will be close substitutes for one another.[1] The Consumers' Association reached the conclusion after testing different brands that they had 'found little difference between different brands of petrol, all brands performed their function well'.[2] Petrols of a given grade are therefore sufficiently alike to permit enquiry about the nature of the total market demand for petrol as well as the demands facing individual wholesalers or retailers.

The main feature of the demand for petrol as a whole is that it is price inelastic. Estimates of the price elasticity range from 0·1 to 0·5: a guesstimate for Britain would be 0·2. The main reason for the low elasticity is the absence of direct substitutes for petrol. There is no other fuel available to the motorist and so, if petrol prices rise, his only adjustments can be to substitute something else for motoring or pay up for the petrol. A second reason is that petrol is not bought on its own but together with the other outlays on motoring. Petrol accounts for about 60 per cent of the running cost of a car. A 10 per cent increase in the price of petrol would therefore represent a 6 per cent increase in running costs. In the long-run it is possible to buy smaller cars which give more miles per gallon; but then we have to consider the total cost of a car and not just its running cost. Petrol accounts for about 25 per

1.   The octane number most commonly quoted, and used above, is the research octane number. Research octane numbers are obtained by comparing petrols, in a single cylinder laboratory engine, with a reference fuel whose properties are known. The comparison may be made in a four-cylinder motor car engine running on the road. This gives a road octane number which is always lower than the research octane number but which differs in relationship to the research octane number with different petrols. There is also a distribution octane number.

2.   *Which?* January, 1964, p.11.

cent of the total annual cost of a car, and thus a 10 per cent increase in the price of petrol would represent a 2·5 per cent increase in the total cost of motoring.

Demand appears even more price inelastic from the point of view of petrol suppliers. An oil company sells premium petrol to retailers for about 1s 3½d per gallon net. The retailer sells it for 6s 3d, but 4s 4d of this is tax. If an oil company should reduce its price by 25 per cent (i.e. by 4d per gallon) this would make possible a reduction in the post-tax retail price of 5 per cent. Taking the market elasticity of demand as 0·2, the quantity demanded would increase by 1 per cent. A 25 per cent change in price for the oil company is associated with a 1 per cent change in the quantity demanded. The elasticity of demand for the oil company is not 0·2 but 0·04.

The unresponsiveness of demand to price changes means that wholesale suppliers will be reluctant to engage in price competition as this would be at each other's expense. There is little possibility of expanding the total market by lowering prices. Securing retail outlets by long-term exclusive contracts or outright purchase of petrol stations will appear especially attractive as this allows an oil company to achieve its sales target without increasing the amount of competition in the retail market. There is the further point that the inelasticity of demand would make possible monopoly profits if it could be exploited.

A second feature of the demand for petrol is that it is income elastic. Demand has grown over the post-war years by about 7 per cent per year whilst real incomes have increased by just over 2 per cent per year, which suggests an income elasticity of more than 3·0. The growth in demand for petrol has meant that the British market has been an attractive one to enter. Mobil, Total and Gulf are among the more notable companies who have responded to the attraction.

The growing ownership of new and second-hand cars mediates between increasing incomes and increasing demand for petrol. Low price elasticity means that annual consumption may be predicted with considerable accuracy by multiplying the number of cars by the average number of miles run each year. This second quantity, 7000 miles per year, is one which motorists, perhaps understandably, exaggerate when asked to report their mileage. Just as they underestimate their consumption of alcohol and tobacco, they overestimate their mileage. The average reported is 9000 miles per year.

Retail demand and market structure   Demand has a special appearance to the individual retailer. We cannot divide the total demand by 37,000 in order to get a representative local picture. The total market is made up of thousands of small market areas where quantities sold are almost entirely independent of sales in contiguous areas. Local market areas consist of clusters of dealers in direct competition with one another. An increase in the market share of one dealer would be at the expense of a small number of neighbours. The boundaries of market areas might be defined as lying between pairs of dealers experiencing low cross-elasticity of demand, or low conjectural price flexibility. They are drawn in more matter-of-fact ways by oil companies. Oil companies in planning marketing strategies divide the country into such areas and seek a national position by successful penetration in each local area.

Local markets are sometimes obvious, e.g. a group of filling stations on a main road at the edge of a town, but often their geography is more complicated, depending upon the habitual routes of motorists living in a neighbourhood or the convenient routes for through motorists. A railway line, river or main road may place petrol stations separated by only small distances in different markets. A dual carriageway or thick traffic flow may place stations on opposite sides of a road in different markets. Filling stations on each corner of a crossroad may even be in only limited competition with one another. Traffic approaching a simple crossroad may turn left, go straight ahead, or turn right. A motorist turning left has the choice of only one station; a motorist going ahead might choose the station before or beyond the junction but will find it more convenient to rejoin the traffic if he makes the second choice; a motorist turning right will be in the outside lane, away from the first station he passes, and so can only conveniently call at the station at the right-hand egress from the junction.

Within local market areas the operator of a filling station may well consider that he faces a kinked demand curve. If he should reduce his prices his neighbours would be forced to follow, and they would each gain few additional sales because of the low price elasticity of demand in the total market. If he should raise his prices the other dealers would be unlikely to follow since they could gain sales at his expense. The demand for petrol at a particular station is likely to depend upon the traffic flow, the density of the local motoring population, the convenience of its location, the popularity of its brand of petrol, the amount and quality of service offered, the appearance of the station. and the credit facilities offered.

Supply When we turn to the costs of supplying filling stations with petrol we run into immediate difficulties. Oil companies supply petrol along with a wide range of other products, from chemical feed-stocks to fuel oil. Refinery flexibility makes possible estimates of costs of adding to the output of particular products, but in the end there remain joint costs which cannot be attributed to any one product in isolation. The problem of determining the cost of petrol to an oil company is made even more difficult because such companies do not simply refine and market products. They also explore for, produce, and transport crude oil. The accounting cost of refining is therefore affected by the transfer price at which the crude oil is brought into the refinery. This transfer price is influenced by the incidence of taxation in different countries and on different stages of production, and by the exigencies of concession negotiations in oil-bearing countries. There is no means of knowing what petrol costs to supply, and so no means of knowing what the profit is on supplying petrol alone.

In connection with the question we face of the effects of solus trading on petrol prices we may make a little more progress. If we do not know the total cost of supplying petrol we may still enquire whether solus trading is likely to increase or decrease the unknown quantity. Oil companies were asked by the Monopolies Commission to estimate cost savings which they thought attributable to solus trading. The methods of making the estimates differed from company to company, but they all arrived at cost savings of the order of 1d per gallon.[3] These estimates suffer from the limitation which is common to all attempts to quantify the effects of features of industrial structure. The effects can only be discovered by comparing a known situation with a conjectural one. In this instance, if petrol retailers should continue to buy only one brand of petrol in the absence of solus contracts there would be no cost saving attributable to exclusive

3.   The Monopolies Commission, *Petrol: A Report on the Supply of Petrol to Retailers in the United Kingdom*, HMSO, 1965, p. 91.

dealing. The estimates were made on the basis that the alternatives to solus trading would be situations with varying amounts of multibrand trading, and so they show cost savings resulting from having a single wholesaler instead of a number supplying a retail outlet.

The major saving lies in delivery costs. Suppose that four filling stations take fortnightly deliveries of 4000 gallons, first in 4000 gallon drops from single oil companies, and secondly in four 1000 gallon drops from four different oil companies. In the first case four road tankers would journey straight between the depot and a filling station, setting out full and returning empty. In the second case the tankers would have to journey round, calling at all four stations, before disposing of their loads. The tankers would make longer journeys because of the cross-hauling, and they would take much more time because they would have to manoeuvre on to four stations, make and break four linkages with storage tanks, and carry out four invoicing procedures. In addition to savings on physical distribution there are further economies in stock-holding when fewer brands are retailed, in wholesaling when orders have to be filled rather than solicited, and in clerical work. It may therefore be that solus trading reduces the costs of distribution. Oil companies have sought economies in distribution throughout the period of solus trading. What has happened to prices?

Wholesale prices   The prices which motorists pay for petrol have risen continuously since 1945. However, one needs no economics to explain this. The excise duty on petrol has been increased again and again. The prices which call for explanation are the prices before tax. Here experience has been unusual.

Wholesale prices have fallen not simply relative to other commodities but also in absolute terms. The net price received by oil companies for standard petrol fell by 10 per cent between 1953 and 1969, and the net price of premium petrol fell by 13 per cent. Super petrol, introduced in 1957, fell by 19 per cent in the following twelve years. Prices in general rose by 60 per cent from 1953 to 1969. Moreover the size of the price reductions is concealed by the monetary terms as petrol improved in quality. Between 1953 and 1969 standard petrol was raised in octane number from 75 to 91, and premium petrol was raised from 90 to 97-99 octane.

In addition to selling their petrol more cheaply, oil companies have offered financial assistance to dealers on favourable terms which represent in effect a concealed price reduction. The Monopolies Commission mention that a twenty-five-year loan of £1·2 million at 2 per cent was extended, in 1964, by an oil company to a multiple retailer in return for representation at twenty-three outlets. Taking 6½ per cent, a low figure, for the commercial rate of interest, the annual loss of interest to the oil company would be £54,000. If the twenty-three stations were exceptionally good ones offering average annual throughputs of 300,000 gallons each, this would be equivalent to a price reduction of 2d per gallon; on more likely throughputs the equivalent price reduction would be correspondingly higher. This loan is an extreme example, but it emphasises that price rebates of the order of 1¾d per gallon for exclusive representation are only part of the story of price competition at the wholesale stage.

The solus system has certainly not prevented price competition between oil companies. It has provided the institutional framework for such competition. We cannot, of course, prove that competition would not have been fiercer in the absence of solus distribution. There were a large number of forces making for price reductions over the 1950s and 1960s. Crude oil production expanded rapidly in the Middle East and North Africa, Russian oil re-entered world markets, oil has been diverted from the US market by quota restrictions, tanker freight-rates have fallen, and refinery balance has been constantly threatened by the rapid inroads made by fuel oil into coal's traditional markets. Oil companies have been seeking markets for a swelling volume of petrol.

Retail prices Despite the falling wholesale prices, retail prices, excluding tax, of standard and premium petrol have remained steady. They have fallen relative to prices in general, but the lower wholesale prices have resulted in larger retail margins and not lower absolute retail prices. If solus trading has kept prices up to the motorist the explanation would have to be found mainly in the retail trade. Here there are a large number of small local oligopolistic markets displaying price rigidity. There have been instances of price competition but they have usually been associated with the sale of little known brands or with sales through new or isolated outlets. Gift stamps have been used more widely as a means of offering price reductions as within each market area the franchise of the stamp companies prevents rivals being able to retaliate with identical stamps should one of their number offer

377

stamps.

Muted price competition is what one would expect in oligopolistic markets, especially if the demand envisaged by dealers may be represented, as we have argued, by kinked demand curves. There is no reason to suppose that the competitive behaviour of retailers would change if they were supplied on other than solus terms. Their behaviour is explained by the market structure in which they sell rather than by the contractual terms on which they purchase.

The influence of market structure is most clearly seen in the exceptional and extreme cases of the motorway service areas. The Ministry of Transport requires that these be multibrand stations but they are operated by single retailers who enjoy geographical monopolies. They have no rivals for fifteen or twenty miles. The operators of service areas enjoy the lowest wholesale prices of any petrol retailers in the country, and they sell at the highest prices. They are multibrand but they are monopolists, and any other behaviour would be unexpected.

Large retail margins enjoyed on the motorways do not make service areas especially profitable to operate. The rents of motorway filling stations are also amongst the highest in the country. This brings us to our second question.

Does competition for company-owned sites inflate site values?

If we are correct in attributing price behaviour in retailing to the structure of retail markets it follows as a corollary that purchase of filling stations by oil companies, which does not change that structure, will not affect property values. An oil company may seek custom by offering price rebates and loans on favourable terms, or by purchasing outlets to be operated by its tenants. If it is attempting to maximise profits it should pursue the various methods to the point where net receipts per gallon are equal. In this case, the price which an independent dealer could offer for a filling station should equal the offer price of an oil company. The retail price of petrol is determined by the market structure so the offer price of an independent dealer for a site depends on the net wholesale price he would have to pay for petrol.

The fact that oil companies do attempt to maximise profits is

378

suggested by the fact that they employ discounted cash flow techniques to evaluate investments in petrol stations. It is further substantiated by calculations that show that the cost per gallon of petrol in terms of rebates to independent dealers equals the cost of smaller rebates plus rent concessions offered to company tenants. There is no advantage in supplying one type of customer rather than the other.

This situation is reflected in the course of property values. Property values in petrol retailing have risen over the years. This is to be expected as sales have increased and retail margins have widened. However, the prices of filling stations have not risen more rapidly than those of other properties. For example, in SE England house prices and prices of filling stations have increased in step with one another and to much the same extent.

It may therefore be seen that with property prices and petrol prices things have not been as the layman would expect. Economic theory helps one to understand more of the working of the economy even though this often seems unlikely in undergraduate days.

The Dynamics of Urban Problems and its Policy Implications[1]

W.J. Baumol

Sisyphus, King of Corinth, was repaid by the gods for his wickedness in life by a punishment that has fascinated observers from Homer to Camus. In the lower world he was forced to roll a large rock uphill; as soon as it neared the top the rock always rolled back down again.

Martin Nolan, 'A Belated Effort to Save our Cities'. The Reporter, Dec. 28 1967, Vol. 37 No. 11, p.16.

1 POLICY IMPLICATIONS OF A CUMULATIVE PROCESS

Among students of the subject it has for some time been recognised that a number of cumulative processes serve to compound the problems of the city; perhaps these dynamic relationships constitute the critical component of those difficulties.[2] For example, it is well known that urban deterioration and the exodus of the middle classes feed upon one another – the more rapid the migration to the suburbs the more quickly does the process of decay in the central city proceed, and vice-versa, each of those processes serving to stimulate and speed up the other. What has not generally been understood, however, is the policy implication of such a dynamic process. In fields such as engineering, which have long dealt with relationships of this variety, it is well known

1.   I would like to thank the Ford Foundation and the Brookings Institution whose sponsorship of our project 'The Self-Sustaining City' facilitated greatly the completion of this paper. But above all I want to indicate my gratitude to the editors of this volume for another opportunity to express my deep admiration and affection for Lord Robbins, to whom I owe so much as a teacher and a friend. The paper, as a piece of theoretical reasoning applied to an economic issue of the utmost urgency, follows, I believe, the spirit of his teaching as much as anything I have written. Furthermore, it brings me back to the area of economic dynamics, a field in which Lord Robbins first aroused my interest more than twenty years ago.

2.   See, e.g., Vernon, Raymond *The Myth and Reality of Our Urban Problems*, Cambridge, MIT-Harvard Joint Center for Urban Studies, 1962.

that malfunction in the system must often be treated by means which have no simple intuitive explanation, and that measures which seem appropriate in terms of common sense sometimes are shown by rigorous analysis to aggravate the problem, or, at best, to treat only its symptoms.

Precisely these complications arise out of the cumulative process which affects the cities. The intricacy of the relationships means that policy approaches, which seem on the basis of informed judgement to promise to come to grips with the problem, may or may not in fact turn out to do so. One simply cannot be sure, without a far more careful analysis, whether the measures that have been tried or proposed will in fact help the community toward a long-run improvement in its circumstances. It may even turn out that most of these policies are incapable of producing any significant long-run effects or that some of them can be absolutely harmful.

To illustrate the point, consider the cumulative problem of public transportation schedules – fewer passengers lead to a reduction in the frequency of departure, which in turn drives away still more passengers and so leads to a still poorer level of train service etc., etc. The most obvious policy measure in such a situation is a subsidy to the transportation authority to permit it to run more trains than it would otherwise find feasible financially. Suppose it is permitted to run ten trains a day more than it would otherwise have operated, and that in the absence of the subsidy the average number of trains run per day would have exhibited the following time pattern:

As a matter of fact, such cumulative processes and their consequences for the prosperity of individual localities have been recognised much earlier. For example, one finds them considered in writings on the local rate reforms in Great Britain in 1928 and 1929. Thus, in her discussion of these changes Lady Hicks writes, 'This disparity between the financial resources of districts has the disadvantage that since rates can be interlocally shifted, it tends to be cumulative . . . . Rates may be shifted by residential removal or by industrial removal . . . . This tends, moreover, to be concentrated on the better-paid workers, who can afford to move elsewhere and who are the most useful ratepayers. Those who remain are too often changed from an asset to a liability. In the meantime the high rates, or the fear of them, act as a deterrent to other entrepreneurs . . . This is an important aspect of the depressed-area problem.' Hicks, Ursula *The Finance of British Government, 1920-1936,* 1938, pp. 158-9. See also Plummer, Alfred 'The Reform of Local Taxation in Great Britain', *The Quarterly Journal of Economics,* Vol. XLIII, August 1929. I am grateful to my colleague Professor Lewis for pointing this discussion out to me.

year	1967	1968	1969	1970	1971
No. of trains	30	25	22	20	19 etc.

It can be shown that in the absence of a change in the underlying dynamics, the addition of the ten trains, say, in 1970 may well lead to the following time path

year	1967	1968	1969	1970	1971	1972	1973	1974
No. of trains	30	25	22	30	25	22	20	19 etc.

That is, the additional trains have served to postpone by three years the process of deterioration in train service, but they have not come to grips with the underlying problem nor have they improved the ultimate state of extremely poor service toward which the system is headed.

A physical analogy should suggest the nature of the problem. Consider a ball rolling down a child's slide in a playground, in which the bottom of the slide has been blocked off so that the ball will not fall to the ground. If one wishes to raise the height of the point at which the ball will utlimately come to rest it does no good to stop the ball in mid-passage and push it a few feet back up the slide. For while that will temporarily raise the position of the ball it does not affect the underlying dynamics of the arrangements. To achieve the true objective of this game — the raising of the final location of the ball — one must find ways to increase the level of the slide itself, and no amount of adjustment of the position of the ball can have that effect. The analogy to the train case should be clear — the addition of a few trains to a deteriorating schedule is like an upward push on the ball which moves it temporarily back up the slide. What is not so clear is the analogue of the low point on the slide and the means that can be used to raise it, in the case of the train schedule, or in the case of progressive urban deterioration.

To get at these parameters we must have recourse to a bit of mathematics, characterising the deterioration process in terms of an elementary mathematical model. Before turning to this model it should be emphasised that it is so oversimplified that its conclusions cannot pretend to offer any direct guidance to policy. Rather its policy implication is largely negative — it is intended to show that even in so simple a dynamic situation the formulation of appropriate policy measures is extremely difficult, and plausibility considerations constitute an extremely unreliable guide.

Turning now to our model, let us this time deal for variety of illustration with the dynamic process characterising the inter-relationship between per-capita income of urban residents, Y_t, *and* the state of deterioration of the city, D_t, however measured. Here we have a double relationship.

First, there is the fact that increased deterioration drives out wealthier residents and so lowers per-capita income, so that if the relationship is linear we have

$$Y_t = r - s D_t \qquad s > 0, \tag{1}$$

i.e., the greater the level of deterioration in period t the lower will be the per-capita income of the persons willing to remain in the city.

Second, we have the relationship in the reverse direction: a reduction in current income leads to further deterioration soon after the current emigration of wealthier inhabitants, so that in a simple linear case

$$D_t = u - v Y_{t-1} \qquad v > 0, \tag{2}$$

i.e. a reduction in yesterday's per-capita income (income in period $t-1$) leads to a higher level of deterioration today (period t).

Substituting from the second equation into the first we eliminate the variable D_t from the relationships and obtain the following first-order difference equation in the variable Y_t alone:

$$Y_t = r - su + sv Y_{t-1}. \tag{3}$$

This equation obviously determines completely the characteristics of the dynamic process — the future history of per-capita income in our city. To show this we represent this equation graphically in the standard difference equation diagram. Since it is a linear equation its graph will be a straight line, call it the time relationship line, RR' in Figure 1.

The time path of income is then found by following the path $ABCDF...$ which, in the diagram, moves steadily toward the equilibrium

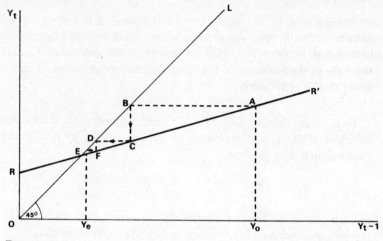

Figure 1

point, *E*, the point where the time relationship line *RR'* crosses the 45° line.

Now it will be noted that a supplement to per-capita income (or for that matter some slum clearance) which serves to offset to some extent the process of deterioration is, in effect, a backward move along the time path, say, from *F* back to *A*. It is like the uphill push on the ball on the slide in our earlier example, and it need have no long-run effect on the time path *because it has not changed the position of the time relationship line RR' or that of the equilibrium point E.*

To see what is necessary to change the equilibrium point we must return to our basic equation (3). We note that at the equilibrium point, since it is on the 45° line, we must have $Y_t = Y_{t-1}$ so that we may call this equilibrium income, Y_e and write simply $Y_e = Y_{t-1}$. Thus from our equation (3)

$$Y_e = r - su + sv\, Y_e$$

or solving for Y_e

$$Y_e = (r - su)/(1 - sv).$$

Thus the co-ordinates of the equilibrium point depend entirely on the

384

magnitudes of the four parameters, s, v, r, and u, and are entirely unaffected by D_t and Y_t, the magnitudes of our variables at any particular dates. The implication is clear — if we wish to do something about Y_e, the equilibrium level toward which the city's per-capita income is heading, an outlay on slum clearance or a direct income subsidy will not help. Instead, one must try to change the magnitudes of one or more of the parameters, whose interpretation can be inferred from the two initial equations (1) and (2), which may be described as follows:

s = The change in per-capita income resulting from a unit increase in deterioration, i.e. it is the rate of response of income to a change in urban living conditions,

v = The rate of increase in deterioration resulting from a one dollar decline in per-capita income,

r = The level of per-capita income that would be obtained if the city were totally unblighted,

u = The maximal rate of deterioration (with zero per-capita income).

Of course, since this oversimple model is hardly realistic, its policy implications should be treated with strong reservations. Yet even this model is sufficient to bring out the basic point that the magnitudes of the preceding parameters are not directly related to D_t and Y_t themselves. That is, if one does something to decrease blight or raise per-capita income, by itself this may have no effect on the long-run (low level) equilibrium point toward which the city is headed[3] In addition, and perhaps more important, it should be observed that s, v, u, and r are parameters whose magnitudes may not easily be subject to

---

3. While the effects of such once-and-for-all change will certainly be transitory in our present model, the practical implications of this result do require qualification. An influence that is transitory may nevertheless produce substantial consequences that are felt for a considerable period of time. A measure whose influence is marked for several decades is not permanent in its effects; yet for practical purposes this may not matter. In formal terms, the full solution to our basic equation (3) is

$$Y_t = (Y_0 - Y_e)\,(sv)^t + Y_e$$

where Y_0 may be taken to be the current level of income and Y_t is the corresponding figure t years in the future. If a once-and-for-all outlay increases Y by $\triangle Y$, then t years in the future demand will still be increased by $Y\triangle(sv)^t$, an increase which will be negligible only if t is very large or if s and v are very small.

change. Certainly the haphazard pouring of money into a metropolitan area may have little effect on their values.[4] Thus, while this simple model cannot pretend to offer any specific basis for policy proposals, it does show that improvement of the long-run prospects of an urban community may require a set of approaches far more subtle and more carefully planned than had previously been imagined.

2 IMPLICATION OF NONLINEARITY

The argument to this point has assumed that the relationships are linear. Of course, there is no reason why this should be so in fact. There may here be operating, for example, some sort of diminishing returns whereby at a low level of per-capita income a relatively small increase in income attracts back to the city a substantial number of middle class families, but after some point one runs into the hard core of suburbanites so that there is a decline in the migration response to further income rises. In such a case the slope of the RR' curve decreases as one moves to the right. It might also be that at very low levels of per-capita income the response rate (slope of RR') is very small because some minimum level of average per-capita income is required before any substantial number of suburbanites are even willing to consider a return to the city. These remarks are, of course, not intended to imply that the empirical relationships do assume such shapes; the discussion is only intended to suggest how nonlinearities might arise, and to indicate the relationship between the slope of the RR' curve and the underlying economic facts.

In any event, under the conditions postulated, the RR' curve would assume the general shape depicted in Figure 2, though its relation to the 45° line need not be of the variety shown.

Now, in the situation illustrated in the graph there is a radical change from the linear case in the policy implications of the dynamic model. The position of the initial point, Y_O is no longer irrelevant to the location of the equilibrium position, and a once-and-for-all subsidy to

4 Here, however, we must distinguish a permanent subsidy from a once-and-for-all governmental investment (or one which is intended to last for a very limited number of years). A permanent subsidy which is designed to keep deterioration below what it would otherwise have been must produce a fall in the intercept of the equation (2), i.e., it must produce a decline in u.

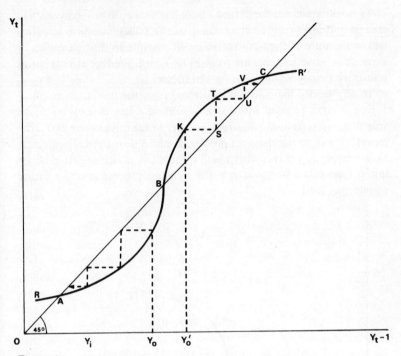

Figure 2

income (or a once-and-for-all programme of urban renewal), *provided it is of sufficient magnitude,* is capable of reversing the process.

This is very easily shown. It will be observed that in Figure 2 *RR'* has three points of intersection with the 45° line. However only two of these, *A* and *C*, are stable equilibria. From any starting point such as Y_O which lies between *B* and *A* the direction of movement will be downward toward lower equilibrium point *A*. There is no formal difference between this segment of the diagram and the relationships depicted in Figure 1

However, if a once-and-for-all income subsidy succeeds in pushing income beyond what we may consider the turning point *B*, say to point Y'_o the situation changes completely. Now per-capita income growth begins to take care of itself and the time path, *KSTUV*, moves steadily upward toward point *C*. It will approach *C* asymptotically and, in the absence of exogenous shocks, will continue to rise forever.

In such circumstances, then, slum clearance, urban renewal and income subsidies may be the most effective policy measures but they will work only if they are sufficient in magnitude. For example, an increase in per-capita income from Y_i to Y_O will produce effects just as transitory as they would be in the linear case.

In any event, the conclusions derived from the nonlinear model of Figure 2 must be used with extreme caution. First, it is by no means true that *any* type of nonlinearity provides to the initial value of Y_O the means to reverse the dynamic process. Figure 3 shows several nonlinear time relationship curves with which no amount of manipulation of the initial income levels can reverse the dynamic process toward a higher equilibrium level.

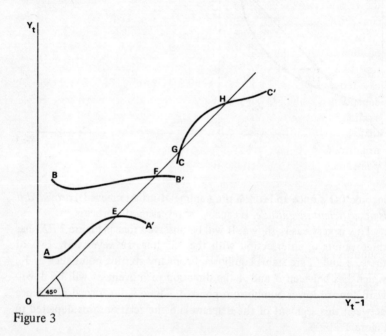

Figure 3

Since where the curves AA' and BB cross the $45°$ line their slopes are positive but less than unity, points E and F on these respective curves are stable equilibrium points whose qualitative implications are precisely the same as those of equilibrium point E in the linear case represented in Figure 1. And the multiple intersection point case represented by CC' involves an unstable intersection point G which cannot serve to raise income above that corresponding to the stable equilibrium point, H. Note also that AA' is very similar in shape to RR' in Figure 2 — thus, it is only the special position of RR' relative to the $45°$ line that accounts in the Figure 2 case for the power of a once-and-for-all change in the value of the variable to reverse the direction of movement. It follows that evidence of nonlinearity in the relevant relationships is not an adequate basis on which to justify the conventional approaches to urban problems. Only in the presence of the right sort of nonlinearity in the right position does an increase of expenditure on urban renewal offer any hope of a reversal in the dynamic process. It would clearly require very powerful evidence on whose basis we would undertake a careful estimation of the shapes of the relevant functions before one could conclude with any degree of conviction that the relevant nonlinearities were of the requisite variety.

In any event, even if the conventional means are capable of producing the desired results they may be far from the least expensive way to go about it. It must always be remembered that the nonlinear case requires a critical minimum expenditure to produce a change in the dependent variable sufficient to reverse the cumulative process. Without explicit investigation one cannot legitimately rule out the possibility that a shift in the time relationship curve, i.e. a change in the magnitude of its parameters capable of raising the relevant equilibrium point, may not provide similar results at a lower cost.

3 TOWARD SOMEWHAT MORE COMPLEX MODELS

It is easy to indicate directions in which our basic model can readily be expanded. For example, one can take cognisance of the role of the suburbs in the population movements. Suppose for the sake of simplicity that the total middle class population in some metropolitan area is fixed at level M and is divided between its urban residents M_{ut} and its suburban inhabitants M_{st}, so that

$$M_{st} + M_{ut} = M. \tag{4}$$

Suppose, moreover, that as in (1) the state of deterioration varies inversely (and linearly) with the number of urban inhabitants that belong to the middle class:

$$D_t = a_o - a_1 M_{ut}. \tag{5}$$

However, the suburbs after some point tend to become crowded so that some measure of crowding, C_t, varies directly with the number of suburban residents:

$$C_t = b_o + b_1 M_{st}. \tag{6}$$

Finally, suppose the number of middle class urban residents in the next period varies inversely with the current level of urban deterioration and directly with the current level of suburban crowding

$$M_{ut+1} = c_o - C_1 D_t + c_2 C_t. \tag{7}$$

We have by direct substitution of (5) and (6) into (7)

$$M_{ut+1} = (c_o - c_1 a_o + c_2 b_o) + c_1 a_1 M_{ut} + c_2 b_1 M_{st}$$

so that since $\quad M_{st} = M - M_{ut}$

$$M_{ut+1} = (c_o - c_1 a_o + c_2 b_o + c_2 b_1 M) + (c_1 a_1 - c_2 b_1) M_{ut} \tag{8}$$

which is a linear different equation of the same form as (3),

$$M_{ut+1} = k_o + k_1 M_{ut}.$$

The analysis can be complicated further, to include a lower income population which divides itself between the city and some rural area.[5] Here we might take P_{rt} and P_{ut} to represent the number of persons in this group in the two areas. We may postulate, for example, that this group expands at an autonomously determined growth rate so that

$$P_{rt} + P_{ut} = P + kr^t. \tag{9}$$

In addition, in such a model instead of (5) one might have an urban deterioration function which varies inversely with M_{ut} and directly with P_{ut} so that

$$D_t = a_o - a_1 M_{ut} + a_2 P_{ut}. \tag{10}$$

Finally, in this model the number of poor in the city in period $t + 1$

390

may, for example, be taken to vary directly with the number of rural poor in period t and inversely with the number of urban poor in period t, i.e

$$P_{ut+1} = w_o - w_1 P_{ut} + w_2 P_{rt}. \tag{11}$$

Our model is now composed of equations (4), (6), (7), (9), (10) and (11) which can be collapsed into a two variable difference equation system consisting of the following two linear equations:

$$M_{ut+1} = (c_{\dot o} - c_1 a_o + c_2 b_o + c_2 b_1 M) + (c_1 a_1 - c_2 b_1) M_{ut} - c_1 a_2 P_{ut}$$

$$P_{ut+1} = (w_o + w_2 P) - (w_1 - w_2) P_{ut} + w_2 k r^t. \tag{12}$$

It should be obvious that the model can easily be complicated further and that elements such as taxes, transportation, crowding and a variety of other relevant phenomena can easily be built into it. Our basic objective, however, is not to exhibit a number of increasingly complex models for their own sake. What is important is their policy implication.

It is well known that qualitatively there is absolutely no difference between the solution to a more involved linear system such as (12) and the rudimentary systems depicted in Figures 1 and 2. It follows that the addition of complexity is unlikely to change the basic policy conclusions of our analysis.[5]

4 CONCLUDING COMMENTS

Our analysis has been intended primarily as a means to convey a number of warnings:

1) That in a cumulative deterioration process such as that which characterises our cities, we can have no confidence without detailed

5.   This suggests strongly the analogy between such formal models of the urban dynamic process and the mathematical models of ecology which depict the relationships of various biological species and the dynamic process resulting from their competition for available food supplies, etc. For an early and fascinating study in this area see Volterra, Vito, *Leçons sur la théorie mathématique de la lutte pour la vie,* 1931.

knowledge of the relevant functional relations that *any* long term effects can be achieved by the most obvious policy measures such as urban renewal projects, *no matter how large their scale.*

2) Even in cases where such programmes can effect a long-run improvement in the basic situation, they must still be sufficiently large in scale or their effects are still likely to prove entirely transitory.

3) Even where such programmes are capable of producing the desired results there is no *a priori* reason to presume that these direct approaches are the cheapest or most effective way to go about the matter.

This discussion also shows dramatically how a rather abstract analysis based on only limited empirical information can provide results relevant to pressing matters of policy by pointing out booby traps that are hardly obvious to the unaided investigator.

But while the basic model does serve the purpose for which it is intended, the questioning of facile policy proposals and apparently obvious approaches to difficult social issues, it does not quite so easily provide a set of reasonable alternatives. On its face the model is a vast oversimplification. one on which one would hesitate to base important decisions.

Perhaps even more important, it may not grapple with the right problem. As Arrow has pointed out so forcefully, in the area under discussion it is all too easy to pursue plausible objectives which in fact have little to do with the really important issues.[6] It does not help the urban poor if the middle classes are brought back to the city by a process that simply drives the impoverished further back into their ghettos. Nor is it clear that preservation of the cities is an appropriate objective if this can be achieved only at the expense of its inhabitants.

Obviously much more must be done before we can begin to provide

6.   See Arrow, Kenneth J. 'Economic Criteria for Urban Renewal', (mimeographed), RAND Workshop on Urban Problems, Paper No. 14.

a model that captures these and the other economic problems. But even if our models are not yet ready to offer usable answers we have seen that they can be employed to expose the weakness in allegedly practical measures whose plausibility only serves to render them more dangerous.

Index

ability; tests of, 256; *see also* effort
Accepting Houses Committee, 357
Ackley, H.G., 22, 36n
Adelman, M.A., 311, 312n
Agassi, J., 33n
Alchian, A.A. 296n
Aldcroft, D.H., 194n, 197n, 201n, 205n
Alford, R.F.G., 324-55
Alhadeff, D.A., 295n
Ali, M.A., 331n
Allen, R.D.G., 12
Andic, S., 92
Archibald, G.C., 3n, 224-45
Arkwright, R., 192
Armstrong, Lord, 193
Arndt, H.-J., 94n
Arrow, K.J., 392n
Asch, P., 307
Ashworth, W., 205n
Attwood, T., 169
Aukrust, O., 199-200, 202n, 205n

Bach, G.L., 6n
Bagehot, W., 103, 106, 113
Bagiotti, T., 312n
Bailey, M.J., 6n, 93n
Bain, J.S., 300, 301, 306, 308, 313n
balance of payments, 92, 96, 199, 203, 351; deficit, 179, 181, 224; disequilibrium, 184; equilibrium, 92, 96, 170n, 171n; and price policy, 243
Ball, J., 331n
bank advances, 173-4, 180-1, 183, 339, 342-6 *passim*; Government guidance

on, 349-55; restriction of, 181; *see also* controls, direct
Bank Charter Act (1844), 168, 182n
bank liquidity (liquid asset ratio), 218-22, 347
bank note issue, 169-71, 173, 175, 179-81, 183
Bank of England, 169-73 *passim*, 175-81 *passim*, 183-4, 216, 217, 223, 342, 348-9
Bank Rate, changes in, 345, 347
Bank Rate policy, 216, 217
bank reserves, 170-1; *see also* reserves
banking, 215-23, 324-55; clearing banks, 342, 344-8 *passim*; foreign banks in London, 342; prices of outputs, 294-5; Scottish banks, 174n, 342, 346, 347, 348; *see also* controls, direct; discount houses; special deposits
Banking School, the, 168, 178n
banks, country, 169-70, 173, 175-6, 184n
bargaining power, 69-70, 73-6 *passim*, 81; and equality of opportunity, 255n
Barkai, H., 160
Barry, B., 247n, 249n, 250n, 251n, 253, 255n
Barton, J., 100
Bauer, P.T., 296n
Baumol, W.J., 43n, 238n, 380-93
Becker, G.S., 43n, 122, 139, 145
Beckerman, W., 198n, 202n, 205n
Beecham, A., 191
Bell, I.L., 194

160-7 ; three-way, 164; *see also*
desert
distributional principle in educational
policy, 257
distributive justice, 246, 251-6 *passim*
distributive principles, 249
dominance of characteristics, 58-61
Dougherty, C.R.S., 120n
Dow, J.C.R., 91n, 328n, 331n, 336n,
344n, 354
Drake, P., 331n
Dunning, J.H., 201n

Economic Man, 99-117; altruism of,
108-9; denunciations of, 100-3;
egoism of, 108-9; function of,
114-17; objectives of, 111-13
economic policy; Dutch (Theil/
Tinbergen) model of, 82-3; linear
decision rule model of, 83; theory
of, 88, 90, 97
economies of scale, 320
Edgeworth, F.Y., 63, 64-5, 72, 81,
108, 112
Edgeworth, R.L., 189
education; as capital-goods-producing
industry, 259; content of, 274,
276; differential, 257; duration of,
274-5; efficiency in, 257-87; equality
of opportunity in, 247-9, 252,
256-87; for industry, 187, 192;
intensity of, 274, 275-9; private
demand for, 133-47; psychic
benefits of, 138-41; scientific and
technical, 188-94
educational expenditure, 257-87;
changes resulting from voucher
scheme, 273-82; justification of
public, 271-2; optimal amount of,
268-71, 273; various aspects
distinguished, 274-7; *see also* rate
of return
educational finance, source of;
family as, 258-9, 262, 264-71,
283-4; loans to students as, 263,
281; possible results of change
from state to family as, 270; state
as, 248, 262-3, 271-87; vouchers as,

258, 264, 271-87
educational growth, models of, 140,
142-6
educational investment, 'neighbourhood effects' of, 262-3, 282
educational planning, 118-47;
fluctuations in, 141-2
educational policy, 263; *see also*
distributional principle
educational reform, 247
Edwards, F.R., 295n
Einhorn, H.A., 312n
Eis, C., 315n
effort and ability, 252-4, 255n
elasticity of substitution, 162, 163-4
endowments, factor; *see* distribution
Engel's Law, 50
engineering, 219, 380; civil, 191
Enke, S., 77n
equilibrium, 72, 79, 272; of balance
of payments, 92, 96, 170n, 171n;
of competition, 63-5 *passim*;
defined, 67-8; of income theory
models, 3, 4, 5-8, 11, 29-30;
Keynsian short-run macro-, 154;
local, 76; of manpower needs,
123; price, 65-6, 298; static, 77
Eucken, W., 251n
European Economic Community, 188
European Free Trade Area, 210
Evely, R. 315n
exchange rate, 172
expenditure; capital, 351-4; defined,
26-7; government, 157, 159;
unintended, 9
expenditure damping, 224
expenditure flows, 26-32
expenditure policy, 224-5, 231-4,
237
expenditure switching, 224
exports, British, 209; commodity
composition of, 207, 208;
destination of, 207, 209; fall in
level of, 196, 198; slow rate of
growth of, 199, 202, 210

fairness in educational provision,
256-8

397

398

399

Lever Brothers, 191
Levinson, H.M., 306
Lewis, A., 359
Lewis, H.G., 296n
Lewis, J., 191
Lewis, W.A., 72n, 195n, 196
lexicographical ordering, 58, 60n
Lindahl, E., 35, 36
Lipsey, R.G., 3-42, 84n, 86n, 357
Lipsey's disaggregation hypothesis, 226
Lipton, T.J., 191
liquid asset ratio; see banking liquidity
Little, I.M.D., 315n
Lockyer, N., 192n
London Discount Market Association, 342
Lunar Society, The, 189
Lutz, F.A., 36, 39
Lyons, J., 191

MacAvoy, P.W., 297
McCracken, H., 153n
McGee, J.S., 291n
MacKay, D.I., 226n
Machlup, F., 66n, 99-117
Mack, R.P., 310n
macroeconomic theory, textbooks on, 3, 4, 18, 40
Maitland, J., Earl of Lauderdale, 153-9
Maizels, A., 196n
Malthus, T., 108, 153, 159; see also Ricardo-Malthus exchange
management, qualities of, 191-5, 201-9
Mandeville, J.de, 153
Mann, H.M., 300, 302n, 308
manpower; forecasting, 118-32; need, 136-8; see also overmanning
Mansfield, E., 318n, 320, 321n
manufacturing industry, 196-7, 199, 201, 294, 299-303, 308
marginal cost, 63, 70-81 passim, 361-4 passim
marginal cost pricing, 69, 72n, 77-9 passim, 356-60, 362, 366-8
marginal product, 122, 130, 163, 251; see also labour
marginal productivity, 251-2
marginal rates of return, 122; on

expansionist, 216
monetary system; Keynes' model of, 217-19; models of, 325; reform of,
marginalists, 50, 54, 357
Marglin, S.A., 120n, 137n
market; automobile, 48; financial, 216, 217, 222; general theory of, 65; labour, 120, 131, 135, 226; micro-economic theory of, 66; petrol, 374-5, 377-8
market control, 292, 299
market forms, analysis of, 66, 75
market imperfection, 229
marketing techniques, 197
Marshall, A., 35, 50, 190-1, 291, 292n, 369; teachings on monetary system, 217
maximisation, 104, 108, 112, 113, 117; see also welfare
Mayer, J.P., 190n
Mead, W.J., 296, 297n
Meade, J.E., 257, 269n
Menger, K., 50, 51
merit; and distributive principles, 249; Hayek's use of the term, 250-1
methodology of economics, 91, 113
migration; see labour
Mill, J.S., 35, 100-1, 103-7 passim, 111, 112, 113, 158n
Miller, R.A., 300n, 301, 302, 306
Mints, L., 168n
Mishan, E., 3n, 5
mobility, social, 248-9, 254
models, econometric, 325; input-output, 231-2; two-factor, 162; see also central banking theory; consumer; disequilibrium; economic policy; educational growth; equilibrium; fiscal policy; monetary system; national income theory; period lag; price theory
modernisation of industry, 189, 191, 195, 203, 204, 361-8; hindered by lack of competitiveness, 195-6; British resistance to, 189, 195-8
monetary conditions, control of, 215-17
monetary policy, 95-6, 169, 215-23, 324, 350; contractionist, 216;

282